Japan's Hidden Face

Japan's Hidden Face

A Call for Radical Change in Japanese Society & Commerce

by
Toshihiko Abe

with Jeanne Rejaunier

BainBridgeBooks
Philadelphia

First published in June 1998 by BainBridgeBooks,
an imprint of Trans-Atlantic Publications Inc.

Website address: www.transatlanticpub.com

ISBN: 1-891696-05-X

Printed in the United States of America.

SUBJECTS:
Japan
Politics
Commerce
History
Autobiography

Library of Congress Catalog Card #98-70339

ACKNOWLEDGMENT

I am particularly thankful to Bonita K. Nelson, my literary agent, for her dedication. Without her firm determination and unceasing efforts this book would never have come to life. I am also very thankful to John J. McDonald, my lifetime American friend, who took the initiative to find her for me. My special thanks go to Jeanne Rejaunier for her invaluable assistance with the manuscript.

CONTENTS

Part Two: Japan's Cultural Background

Part Three: Post-War Politics and Economics

PREFACE

A volume I found by chance on the shelf of a bookstore in London changed my life completely. Had I not read author Tomeo Yagiri's works on Japanese history, I would still be faithfully serving a Japanese electronics manufacturer, as the sole purpose of my life then was to make this company number one in the world. However, Tomeo Yagiri's lucid analysis of Japanese history was based on ample experience and research, and his surprising conclusions overwhelmed me on first reading. Once the blinders were removed from my eyes, I was liberated from countless myths which I, like millions of other Japanese, had been brainwashed into accepting as gospel. These myths are based on feudalistic ideas, in particular on an ideology designed in Japan's so-called "Meiji Era" (1868-1912), manufactured to support Japan's emperor institution. I refer to this set of myths as "Meiji ideology," which will be explained in succeeding chapters of this book.

Tomeo Yagiri's thinking enabled me to evaluate more objectively, to become more open-minded and rational. Aspects of Japanese society appeared entirely different when viewed with new perception. Many things that once seemed natural became doubtful or questionable. The deeper I deliberated, the stronger I perceived the sense of incongruity in alleged Japanese culture and the ways of the Japanese people. Gradually, I came to form new opinions. A sense of obligation pressed me to spend three years writing this book, in order to help reach understanding between Japan and the West.

Japan is known as a democratic state belonging to "the free world." True? The answer is legally yes, but mentally no. To us Japanese, democracy is not our nation's supreme value; rather, our emperor institution, which is built on a feudal concept, is more important. Unfortunately, the two values are opposed and intrinsically incompatible. Yet in our Constitution, we are unconcerned about this incongruous marriage; Japan's Meiji ideology, from which the symbolic authority of the emperor was derived, has been modified with idealistic pacifism to suit our current age of peace.

It is ironic that the undemocratic social order contained in the emperor institution became the main driving force to cause unprecedented success uniting our people to work hard for the recovery of a devastated Japan. But it should not be overlooked that two exactly opposite values have ripped the Japanese mind, all too often causing impotence.

During the U.S. occupation, General Douglas MacArthur made our decisions. Later, Japan followed the U.S. government's cold war policy faithfully. Only when the interests of Japan and the U.S. collided as the result of Japan's growth as an economic giant have we faced a new situation in which we have been forced to make our own decisions. Our impotence is shown in U.S.-Japan trade negotiations. In *honne* (practice), we do not wish to make any compromise that may spoil the main idea of Japan, Inc.

Japan may be organized as a democratic system, but it is managed by people believing in feudalistic ideas and values deeply rooted in the Meiji ideology, which is clearly against the values of democracy and freedom. Japanese people know that *okami* (emperor, rulers such as shoguns, feudal lords, governments, and employers) will protect the ignorant from domestic and foreign evils with integrity and benevolence. Our regulations exist for that purpose. Why must we have to lift these regulations, exposing our nation to free competition from the outside? Business is a reward for loyalty. Why should we buy components from manufacturers not submitting to us? This is a dilemma Japanese people face.

On the one hand, we know we cannot afford to demolish our *tatemae* (principle). Free trade with free nations has brought Japan tremendous benefits. A realistic analysis of the economic and military relationship with the U.S. tells us we should remain friends of the U.S. and other free nations. So we reluctantly make a minimal compromise, not because of our understanding of the problem but because of *gaiatsu* (pressure from outside). Our attitude is incomprehensible to Western peoples and helps encourage negative feelings toward Japan. Having learned lessons from past actions, the U.S. government is putting greater *gaiatsu* on Japan to squeeze out bigger concessions. At present, objective criteria for specific market sectors are controversial issues. However, thus far, this method has not led either nation to a happy settlement.

Japanese impotence toward responsibility becomes more pronounced when we are required to participate in international military operations, such as the United Nations peacekeeping operations in Cambodia. If we endorsed only the values of democracy, we would be willing to assume responsibility in such activities without hesitation; few reasons could make us unwilling to defend common values. In the spirit of the Treaty of Security between the U.S. and Japan, American soldiers are prepared to stake their lives to defend Japan from possible attack. If we Japanese believe in this treaty, why do we refuse to shed our blood to save other nations sharing the same values?

Why? Because of a compromise made between Japanese government leaders and General MacArthur right after the war. This compromise resulted from the desire of Japan's leaders to save the Emperor, the center of the nation, and for the General to insure a successful U.S. occupation. The fangs and claws of Japanese militarism had to be extracted before the marriage of two exactly opposite values could result.

In Article 9 of our Constitution, Japan becomes the first and only nation in the world to have pledged renunciation of war. The bloody morals and precepts of our Meiji ideology, which obliged everyone to die for the emperor, were discarded, replaced with idealistic pacifism. Yet emphasis on the integrity and benevolence of the emperor as "big father" of the nation, as well as the myth of Japan as a mono-racial nation led by an emperor with an unbroken line from the infinite past were upheld, in order to rebuild the authority of the Emperor during the Cold War. Feudal values such as submission and loyalty to rulers, servility and hard work by employees, are well preserved in current society, with the emperor at the top. A new Japan was founded with a democratic face but with feudalistic guts.

The result is that Japan is not yet fully democratized. Furthermore, a servile mentality has been ingrained in the Japanese people throughout a thousand years of slavery, ever since domination by the T'ang Chinese in the 7th century, a fact that has been hidden from the people. In place of the truth, a standard history was designed by Japan's 19th century Meiji government, largely for the purpose of integrating all races in the Japanese archipelago under the emperor and establishing a modern nation. The truth—misery of a slavery instituted by foreign conquerors—has been covered up, kept a national secret. Glorification of the imperial household and establishment of the Emperor from an unbroken line were substituted for truth. To justify its falsified history the government burned ancient Korean books and destroyed old records that did not agree with its "imperialistic historical view." As a result, the Japanese nation was brainwashed to obey the *okami* under all circumstances and at any cost.

The Japanese image of the emperor is that of a selfless man with the welfare of the nation at heart. Appointed by such an emperor, a shogun shares the emperor's virtues, as samurai TV dramas broadcast each week in Japan attest. The Japanese prime minister today is regarded similarly. Democracy, for the Japanese, is not an absolute need. More important is that everyone should endeavor to become like the emperor. If ministers, government officials and Japanese Diet (Parliament) members share the emperor's virtues, then politics and policies will be fine. Benevolent *okami* will graciously look out for individual rights and the welfare of our nation. What everyone must do is work hard, be loyal and honest. Unless the Japanese servile mentality and belief in a fictitious history are removed, Japan cannot be a true democratic nation.

Regrettably, the Japanese have neglected to reflect on the nation's role in World War II. Annexing Korea and Formosa, conquering Manchuria, invading mainland China, attacking Pearl Harbor, Japan went into allout war with the allied forces of the West. The tragedy of the war, in which nearly twenty million soldiers and civilians were killed by the Japanese military force in China and South East Asia, eventually ended after the dropping of two atomic bombs on Hiroshima and Nagasaki. Who is responsible for this unprecedented disaster? The Emperor? A military clique? The national system? Or the Meiji ideology? These things have never been clarified, and no national leaders have ever been convicted of war crimes by the Japanese.

My father was a naval officer who died in action. I often wondered, throughout my life, did my father die for nothing, the result of his nation's wrong purpose? I would hope my children and grandchildren should never die as my father did, pawns of a nation misled by false ideology.

This book will introduce three different histories: (1) the imperialistic, historic view of Japan's Meiji government, based on Meiji ideology; (2) the current government's authorized standard history; and (3) Tomeo Yagiri's version of history.* Comparison of these three will indicate how Japan's true history from ancient times was falsified, and

---

*Some of the writings of Tomeo Yagiri, a novelist and historian, do not represent the mainstream of academic thought. For other perspectives of Japanese history, see *Shinto & the State, 1868–1988* by Helen Hardacre (Princeton University Press, 1989) and *New Directions in the Study of Meiji Japan*, edited by Helen Hardacre & Adam L. Kern (Brill Academic Publishers, 1997.)

for what purpose it was inculcated on the people when the Meiji state was established.

Comparison of the two standard histories indicates both are essentially the same. Yagiri's is totally different but the most convincing, and well aligned with human nature. To illustrate, I include views that reveal facts of Japanese traditions and culture such as samurai, bushido, harakiri, kendo, kabuki, caste, religion, arts, etc. The reader will see why the Japanese believe in primitive fictions. In fact, the Japanese even discriminate against Westerners for lacking a similar history, which invites isolation. This book may be useful for Western readers in finding answers to oft-asked questions, such as "Why do Japanese look inscrutable?", "Why do Japanese have no principles?" and "Why do Westerners misunderstand the Japanese?"

Yagiri claims Japan is a multi-racial nation, and that Japan's evolution is exactly the same as that of other nations in the world. For instance, Yagiri's history is very similar to the British: several races met in the Japanese archipelago around the time Jesus Christ was born in the West; these races fought each other; those races with higher civilization and better weapons won. The great T'ang Chinese and Korean Paekche conquered the indigenous aboriginal races of the Japanese archipelago, (known as Ya, Yottsu and Zoshiki), and established a dynasty to govern Japan in the 7th century. Those who refused to submit to the conquerors were sent into camps in secluded mountainous areas. Later some of them were used in ensuing civil wars as expendable "human shields". Lucky "human shield" survivors became samurai and daimyo (feudal lords). Some settled in villages and towns, but were confined to reserves, and engaged in lower occupations under close control. Power shifts, conflict, betrayal, exploitation by rulers, and slave rebellions were standard fare throughout the course of history.

One great difference between Japanese history and that of Western nations is that no democratic thoughts were ever born in Japan. Power changed from one hand to another but each time a new power group went through the formalities of being appointed by the emperor when replacing a former power, the simplest and most economical way to legitimize new power. The imperial household, descendants of (Chinese and Korean) T'ang/Paekche blood, set up the legal codes of Japan in the 8th century. Although they had lost military power earlier, they were able to maintain the position of masters of the nation with the concept that no other bloodline could rule Japan as emperor. The lives of slaves never changed; from generation to generation slaves had to endure the destiny of a subhuman life. A few managed to attain positions in the ruling machine through money or by marriage.

As soon as these entered the establishment, they glorified their family with false lineages and looked down on their previous associates in the same way as the ruling blood looked down on them. Thus, a vertical society in which "man is made under man" was endlessly perpetuated, continuing to the Meiji Reform, and on till the end of World War II.

The greatest crisis of the Meiji ideology came at Japan's defeat in 1945, when the compromise that saved Hirohito allowed the ideology to survive. This has been rehashed to suit the *tatemae* of democratic Japan, when a new standard history was edited to restore the authority of the emperor, which continued through the cold war. Some descendants of the aboriginal races, people known as *burakumin*, still suffer severe discrimination in Japan, yet no one knows exactly the reason—that Meiji ideology still keeps the Japanese in a state of mass hypnotic trance. Yagiri teaches that history is not exceptional. Unless we fight hard for human rights, we may again find ourselves in the same slavish life our ancestors experienced.

If the Japanese had been aware of Yagiri's view, I am sure we would have appreciated the values of democracy much more fervently. We would not have agreed to allow two exactly opposite values, democracy and the emperor, even in the form of a symbol, in our Constitution.

My father was a man imbued with the Meiji ideology. His death in World War II, going down with his ship, was not instant death by a bullet in combat; a great deal of time passed until he actually drowned—his death was a kind of suicide. I thought if I kept searching for the reasons my father chose to die, I could examine the values of Meiji ideology one by one, and also clarify how it brought our nation to the catastrophe of World War II. I wanted to know if my father died for a worthy cause; unfortunately, I arrived at the conclusion he died for a wrong cause.

I was 14 years old when the war ended, a student at a cadet army school who had been brought up with Meiji ideology and ultra nationalism. After experiencing the difficulties of my country's defeat, I was later employed by Casio, the Japanese electronics firm that produced electronic calculators. My job was to sell these calculators in overseas markets. I was one of the "human shields" in the war to make Casio number one in the world. We made it. Thus I consider myself eligible to testify on the evolution of Japanese society as an insider. Though I am a businessman now, I am a soldier in my essence.

Toshihiko Abe
Tokyo 1990-1997

Part One

ORIGINS

Chapter One

Shinano

On the morning of November 29, 1944, the Japanese Empire rested her last hope for an organized counterattack against American forces in her secret supership, Shinano. The Shinano was to be the world's largest carrier with 72,000 displacement tons. Shinano embodied the ultimate weapon which would reverse the tide of inevitable defeat and provide the leverage needed to negotiate peace with America. But Japan's ultimate weapon could not join what was left of the shattered imperial fleet without final adjustments; she was being sent to Kure naval base to finish her final rigging. Time was everything as Shinano set forth from Yokosuka. The Pacific was rough and the wind relentless that morning when the great Japanese carrier headed west towards Kure's sheltered waters. Shinano's maiden voyage suddenly halted at 3:15 a.m. when four torpedoes from the American submarine, Archer-Fish, blew open her hull.

I will try to reproduce the situation before and after the sinking of Shinano, based on *The Life of Shinano*, by Jo Toyoda (published by Shuueisha, 1980), as well as *Shinano! The Sinking Of Japan's Secret Supership*, by Captain Joseph F. Enright, USN, with James W. Ryan (St. Martin's Press, 1987), and its Japanese translation (K.K. Kojinsha, 1990).

Shinano was supposed to carry *shinyo*, suicide speedboats made of plywood. They were 6 meters long, and travelling at full speed of 23 knots, they could plunge into enemy ships with 300 kg. of powder stored in their heads. Shinano also carried about 20 *ohka*, a single-seated rocket 6 meters long, with one to two tons of powder. Bombers usually carried these nasty weapons. Over an enemy ship, a mother plane would release the *ohka* from where it hung under its belly and would drop it straight down like a bomb. Rocketed at a speed of 930 kph, the *ohka* was a manned bomb rather than just a plane. Once released, the pilot could either direct the *ohka* to its target or fall into the sea, both with the same result, the pilot's certain death. The Japanese Navy designed this horrible suicide weapon in desperation in an attempt to defeat the American fleet.

Imperial headquarters planned to rescue Japanese soldiers of the 35th Army from extermination on Leyte Island in the Philippines by sending these suicide planes to Kure. The Ohka and Shinyo were supposed to be transported to a port in Kyushu in southern Japan, then on to Leyte, from where a barrage of suicide attacks was going to be made on the American fleet in Leyte Gulf.

After four years of effort and sacrifice to complete this enormous warship, Shinano, a mere four torpedoes sank her along with 791 crewmen, 100 civilian workers and the horrible weapons aboard. When the hopes of the Japanese Navy sank to the bottom of the sea, the declining fortune of the Japanese Empire was clear.

For eight desperate hours, Shinano's crew struggled to save her, 65 miles southeast of Shiono Misaki at the tip of Honshu's southern peninsula. Shinano dipped her stern deep into vicious waves that were crashing against her bow raised high against an angry gray sky. That image remains in my mind 50 years later. But when my mind's eye zooms in for a close-up on her vertical bow, I see a tiny spot clinging to it. Closer inspection shows it is the Shinano's captain, Toshio Abe, my father.

His fate inevitable, Captain Abe listened to the gush of cold waves coming up the deck. At 10:55 a.m., his life ended, together with his new ship that had been commissioned by His Majesty Emperor Hirohito only ten days before, when the Shinano suddenly groaned and shivered, plunging to the 400 meter depths with her captain, her short life ended on her maiden voyage. I ask myself now: what were my father's thoughts in that last moment of his life?

Captain Joseph F. Enright of the U.S. Navy submarine Archer-Fish, who sank Shinano, testified that he could never have caught her if she had been able to flee at her maximum speed of 27 knots with her full 150,000 HP. Archer-Fish's maximum speed was only 19 knots. With only eight of twelve boilers in operation, the Shinano's maximum speed was cut down to no more than 20 knots. She was a slow moving target. Her destiny was etched in time.

Shinano was still far from being "ready" for war duty. Her interior was a mess, with wires, tools and parts scattered everywhere. 300 civilian technicians of Yokosuka Naval Shipyard were busily working in total chaos so as not to waste time while she was en route to Kure.

Shinano had many basic tests pending—a test for pumping water to prevent listing; a test to maintain balance under torpedo attack; a compartment airtight test to isolate flooding—all these were essential to ensure safety and survival when attacked by the enemy. When a warship is hit by either gun or torpedo, a large hole will be made in the hull and sea water will come into the ship. To prevent a ship from sinking, it is divided into a number of sections, and each one is made watertight, so that even if one section fills with water the others will be safe. If the ship is hit on the port side, she will list to the left, but the other side will be safe.

J. Toyoda, author of *The Life of Shinano*, described the ship's delivery on November 19, 1944 at Yokosuka Shipyard. Crew member Commander Mikami saw that Captain Abe's hands were shaky at the ceremony when the Yokosuka Shipyard commander handed him the certificate of delivery. My father was not shaking from tension or worry, but rather from stifled anger. He was given an incomplete, defective ship with no time for testing or training, and he was to be held responsible for the life of a couple thousand crew members. Yet he could not refuse to accept Shinano, or he would be removed from command and tried by courtmartial. The crest of the imperial chrysanthemum fixed at the ship's bow forbade Capt. Abe from protest; he had been taught from the time he joined the Imperial Navy to faithfully perform his duty under any circumstance without exception.

To make matters worse, Shinano was a huge maze herself. Crews gathered from other ships to man her did not know how to get from one place to another, and were often confused and disoriented. For a captain setting out for battle, a lot could go wrong. In peacetime, a captain would have two years to train his crew. It remained a question if the watertight door would function properly, and if pumping water could stabilize the ship's balance. Headquarters ignored all these technical problems because of the war situation. The order had been given; Shinano would have to go out immediately.

Shinano's timing and navigational course had been decided the night before. Three destroyers of the 17th unit would escort her to Kure. But Captain Abe knew he could not depend on them. Their crews were exhausted. In the battle off Leyte, they had defended a group of battleships from persistent attacks by the U.S. air force and destroyers. Although wounded, they had been given permission to escort the high speed battleships Nagato and Kongo to Yokosuka. On November 21, Kongo and its flagship destroyer were sunk in an attack by an American submarine, the Sea Lion. The crew had arrived just three days before Shinano's commission. With no rest following their desperate struggle, they were expected to protect Shinano en route to

Kure. They had few supplies and the maintenance of vital equipment such as sonar, was insufficient. One destroyer was short a boiler. After the disaster they had just experienced, the captains of these destroyers wanted to make a daylight voyage along Japan's coast to better insure safety against American submarine attack.

"Captain Abe," one captain appealed, "when you were captain of Ohyodo in the battle of the Marianas last June, you saw the 34,000 ton aircraft carrier, Taiho, go down from a single torpedo. We thought Taiho unsinkable, but an interior gas explosion sank her. You saw the same with the veteran carrier Shokaku. From your flagship of the combined fleet with its up-to-date radio equipment and superior design, you were as helpless then as you are now to prevent a submarine attack. There is no escape from a torpedo even with air cover. Our three destroyers were engaged to escort and rescue survivors. Experience has taught us that carriers are most vulnerable to submarine attack. We feel that three destroyers cannot assure the safety of a huge ship cruising in the open sea at night. Please reconsider and agree to a daytime cruise along the coast."

Captain Abe was convinced that an attack on Shinano would come from the air, because an American B-29 had flown over Yokosuka on November 11 with enough time to take photographs—the U.S. Navy reconnaissance mission had exposed Shinano's test run. The image of devastating destruction to a huge carrier by air attack was burned in my father's memory from the battle of Midway, where he was commander of the 10th Destroyer Unit and the ship Hiryu. On June 6, 1942 at sunrise, America attacked by air. The Hiryu was the last carrier still unhurt out of four. The flames from her destruction blended with the brilliant sunrise so that there was no visible horizon. There was no way to save her. Everything was engulfed in red when my father carried out the order of Rear Admiral Tamon Yamaguchi to sink her with his own torpedoes. He had a premonition that the same fate might await him this time. His calculations told him that the Shinano could withstand several torpedo attacks from submarines, but if she were attacked by air, coordinated attack from a dozen torpedoes could sink her. When he received word that no protection by Japanese air cover would be available during his voyage to the Kure base, Captain Abe decided to leave port that evening.

My father played the percentages. He thought there was less risk at night; it was the wrong decision. The American submarine Archer-Fish was waiting for the Shinano outside Tokyo Bay. Captain Enright of the Archer-Fish captured Shinano's image on radar at 8:48 p.m., just after she came out of the bay, and began his chase immediately, looking for the best opportunity to attack. At 3:17 a.m. November 29, four out of six torpedoes struck Shinano.

As requested by a friend of my father's at the Navy Ministry, a three page memo was written by Lieutenant J.G. Sawamoto, Officer of the Deck, informing my mother how my father died in action; written in an informal manner, in pencil on Navy letter paper, given to my mother confidentially, it is the oldest record available, and reads:

"At about 3:25 a.m. on 29 November 1944, `S,'" (he could not write Shinano's full name) "was attacked by enemy submarine in open sea south of Honshu. Four torpedoes hit her in the starboard side, causing her to list quickly 13 degrees to the right. The captain ordered the pumping of water right away in the necessary places. He also instructed watertight measures and made an investigation of all damages incurred. By pumping, the list was improved to 9 degrees, but soon worsened, increasing gradually from 11 to 13 degrees. The captain busily dealt with the situation, taking proper measures, such as filling water into the port side magazine, dumping the left anchor, shifting heavy materials, and pumping water. At 5:30 a.m., dawn rose. As the captain was engaged with various aspects of the operation, he encouraged the crew, Sunrise is coming. A little more effort from us could save her.'

"About 9:00 a.m., pushed by strong northeast wind and huge waves, Shinano came to a halt. The captain decided to tow her by destroyer and ordered the preparation. He continued to encourage the crew, saying that only a few more hours of efforts would save her. At 9:30 a.m., he gathered all civilian workers onto the deck and gave them a farewell address.

"`You see the situation of this carrier before your own eyes,' he said. 'But she is not going to sink. We are going to save her. However, you are not the crew of this ship. So you will not share the destiny with her. All of you will be moved to destroyers. The damages incurred by the ships of the Imperial Navy from American submarines are tremendous. You have seen an example here today. I hope you will do your best to improve anti-submarine arms to destroy our enemies. Do your best to defeat our enemies for the country. Good-bye.'

"Then the captain decided to transport the portrait of the Emperor and instructed three of us to guard it (one was myself). However, the boat that was to carry it was overturned by waves and we could not carry out his order. The captain urged all crew members to work harder and take all measures possible. But at 10:50 a.m., powerful waves reached the level of the boiler room's intake holes and the list to starboard became as bad as 30 degrees. The captain ordered all hands on deck. He went down to the bridge and stood at port side for a moment. He looked reluctant to give up the ship just yet. Apparently, he reconsidered in order to save the lives of his crew, so they might live to fight again and to destroy our enemies. He finally ordered every able body to leave the ship. The captain was seen walking towards the bow. But what happened to him after that is not exactly known. Someone thought they saw him in the sea, but was not sure.

"Knowing the captain's personality from his daily attitude, his words and his deeds, I believe he wanted to sink with her. But in spite of his will, he was thrown out into the sea by her capsizing and then sucked into the swirl made by her sinking.

"P.S. The portrait of the Emperor was picked up safely by a destroyer.

"Written by Lieutenant J.G. Sawamoto."

It is apparent even in the dying days of the Japanese Empire, the safety of the Emperor's portrait was most important. Not mentioned in Lieutenant Sawamoto's memo is the account of his own instructions to Radioman Petty Officer Yamagishi to take the Emperor's portrait tied firmly around his waist when he jumped into the water. Yamagishi swam as fast as possible so as not to be sucked back into the swirl of the sinking ship and meet certain death. As he was floating out to sea holding a piece of wood, a destroyer came to his rescue. He was picked up and brought on deck. Resting briefly, he started to feel pain from a laceration on his jaw. The cut required three stitches, which the medic applied without anesthesia. Yamagishi could not help crying in pain. The medic told him to be thankful he could feel it. At least he was alive. Then, Yamagishi turned white. In his confusion, he let go of the portrait. The loss was reported to the captain of the destroyer, who communicated to other destroyers to watch for the box containing the Emperor's portrait. Luckily the portrait was found by one of the destroyers and picked up safely.

Yamagishi and other crewmen rescued from the Shinano were confined to barracks on Mitsukojima Island for a month, where Imperial headquarters kept them isolated to keep word of Shinano's fate from leaking to the enemy. To Yamagishi, these were disgraceful days spent like a criminal. He felt great sympathy for the dead crewmen, and in his heart, for the Shinano herself. Yamagishi vowed then that he would build a monument to his fellow seamen and lost ship. After the war, he became a Buddhist priest, and almost single-handedly over the next two decades, built the monument to honor his shipmates with their names inscribed on stone. He organized the *Shinano Kai*, an annual meeting of "the survivors and the bereaved", beginning in 1963, and became its chairman for the next 30 years. It was a difficult task for Yamagishi because of his low rank. He was not an officer in the Imperial Navy and could not rally general support. Post- war hardship left the Japanese devastated, yet Yamagishi stuck to his goal.

Yamagishi was a great man. He personally brought photographs to my mother of the first Shinano Kai memorial services at Kure in 1963, as my mother could not afford to travel there.

Nine months after the Shinano sinking, America crushed Japan's fighting spirit with two atomic bombs dropped on Hiroshima and Nagasaki. My father was 48 years old when he went down with Shinano. Over half a century has flown by since his passing; the world had gone through many changes. Japan's economic development from the ruins of war to one of the most important nations in the world makes her success unprecedented among defeated nations in history.

Yet Japan's complacency with her economic achievement in recent decades clouds her perspective. Japan must address mounting frictions and tensions with the United States and other Western powers resulting from her tremendous growth. I believe that the best way to confront our current problems is to trace their roots by looking at the past. At the same time, this can also help understand why my father chose to die. Was his reason blind loyalty to the emperor? Bushido, the way of the warrior? Anger and protest over absurd command in a foolish war? Or mere sorrow and despair over defeat? Most importantly: did my father die for a worthy cause?

The reader may think these personal questions have nothing to do with frictions between Japan and the West, but I believe that all values we call "the Japanese tradition" were condensed in my father's mind at the moment of his death. By tracing these values back to their roots in Japanese history, we can understand what truths and falsehoods founded in Japanese tradition have brought us to conflict with the West, both past and present.

Therefore, a quest for answers to problems in today's Japan simultaneously becomes a requiem for my father.

Chapter Two

Kamakura

Kamakura is located at the mouth of the Miura Peninsula south of Tokyo. Surrounded by majestic hills, it faces sunny Sagami Bay, which opens to the Pacific Ocean. An hour commute to Tokyo by train, Kamakura is a famous resort town known for its vistas of mountains and sea with warm weather all year round. Its trendy beaches attract millions of tired Japanese from the stressful pace of Tokyo.

Before World War II, Kamakura was pollution-free with an abundance of flora and fauna. Rich rice paddies spread out from hills free of chemical contamination, lavish with wild Japanese parsley. Peaceful and calm, Kamakura was famous for its historical remains that go back 800 years. Among its most famous sightseeing attractions are the shrine of Tsurugaoka Hachiman Gu and a great bronze statue of Buddha, 37 1/4 feet high, called Daibutsu. In 1185 A.D., Yoritomo Minamoto established the city's first samurai government, called Kamakura Bakufu. The history of Kamakura is especially intriguing to me, because of its personal relation to my family's history. Near Kamakura on the other side of the Miura Peninsula facing Tokyo Bay was the city of Yokosuka, the largest Japanese naval base during World War II, and currently the largest U.S. Navy base in the Far East. Yokosuka was a sharp contrast to the sleepy, peaceful town of Kamakura, which many naval officers enjoyed for its relaxed atmosphere. During my childhood, Kamakura was inhabited by artists, scholars, lung diseased patients, and retired elderly Japanese, all for the same reason, for its serenity.

I was brought up at a time of ultra-nationalism and militarism. In 1931, the year I was born, the Manchurian Incident broke out, and caused Japan to drop out of The League of Nations in 1933. This was a fatal step for Japan, thrusting her into a mire of ensuing wars. In 1937, war with China started. Born into a family of samurai tradition, I was educated to become a warrior. At age 5, I started to practice kendo, martial art of the sword. When I was in the 5th grade at primary school in Kamakura, the Japanese Navy initiated their surprise attack on Pearl Harbor, December 7, 1941.

After primary school, I was sent up to Tokyo to attend Seijo middle school to prepare for the examination for the Cadet School of the Imperial Army. Competition was fierce, with the odds of acceptance only 50 to 1. Everyone wanted to become a soldier at that time. I threw all my youthful energy into my studies and fortunately passed the examination. It was the happiest and proudest day of my life when I received my notice of admission on February 11, 1944. I was innocent, with a burning desire to fight for my country as a soldier. As a child, I saw no difference in the navy or the army. My mother's grandfather was a major general of the Japanese army while my father's elder brother was in the navy. Only after the war did I come to know there was serious conflict between the two. I decided to go to the Cadet School because I could qualify at 13, while I would have had to wait until 15 to qualify for the Naval Academy. I had no doubts about the value of loyalty, and was truly willing to die for the Emperor and my country.

I have easily recalled that great day in my life each year for the past 50 years, because the date of my admission coincided with Japan's National Foundation Day. According to the mythical imperial view of our history, that date in 660 B.C. marked the beginning of the Great Empire of Japan. This holiday was abolished after World War II, but with controversy over the history of the mythical age, was reinstated in recent years. (The controversy will be analyzed in Chapter Four).

In April 1944, I entered Cadet School and became a little soldier. That August, my father was appointed chief of the Shinano's rigging committee and lived at home in Kamakura during my brief summer leave. I shared a week with him. It was a rarity that all three of us were together. My father spent the whole time on the water. Before I knew it, the week was up, and I had to return to school. On August 28, 1944, during a blackout, my father saw me off at Ofuna Station. In darkness, on the platform as we waited silently for my train, my father said nothing. When my train arrived, I saluted my father with respect for a superior officer. He responded in kind. I boarded and departed without exchanging any words or thoughts with my father. It was the last time I would see him. In my youth, I lacked insight to read anything imminent on my father's decisive face. And since he could not tell me anything about his new assignment on the Shinano, it is only in retrospect that I understand he was already determined to die.

My father was born in 1896, the eighth son of Katsumi Abe, a public prosecutor and lawyer. My family belonged to the *Shizoku*, samurai class, and my father was brought up to be a warrior. He graduated from the Naval Academy and was appointed an officer in 1918. He spent most of his service on destroyers as a veteran torpedo officer. He was a daring fighter with no fear of death. His naval career was marked by action in Asian wars in the period leading up to World War II.

As commander of the 8th Destroyer Fleet, the battle of Bali was my father's most remarkable victory. On February 19, 1942, he led two Japanese destroyers, with only two more destroyers for reinforcements, against two Dutch cruisers and seven destroyers in a nighttime confrontation on the sea of Selat Lombok, east of Bali. My father was honored for this successful action the next year, and made a public address to veterans and civilians regarding the victory. The occasion of this speech was the 38th anniversary of the battle of the Sea of Japan, commemorating the Imperial Navy's decisive victory over Russia's Baltic fleet in 1905. The following text is from his speech that day:

"The dog fight in darkness against this superior enemy started when a sister Japanese destroyer ahead of my flagship discovered two enemy cruisers about 5000 meters ahead, in the narrow Strait of Selat Lombok, only five miles wide. The enemy immediately shot up flares. My sister destroyer switched on her searchlight.

"Simultaneously, both sides opened fire in a violent exchange. The enemy took the worst blow, which caused a great fire aboard. But at the same time, the enemy's fire hit our sister destroyer's searchlight, and several Japanese sailors were blown off her deck, leaving remnants of flesh and blood littered over the flaming deck. The damaged destroyer returned fire without benefit of light. Unable to bear up against our attack, the enemy destroyer turned away and laid down smoke screens. Quickly, we chased after the remaining enemy cruiser, which was also attempting to lay down smoke screens.

"Suddenly, an enemy destroyer appeared 800 meters ahead and the captain ordered a quick left turn. At 600 meters, the ship sent a volley of gunfire into the enemy and she sank instantly. My flagship found two enemy destroyers moving southward just after I saw the huge fire of the first enemy cruiser. I immediately opened fire at the two destroyers from a distance of 4,000 meters. They turned northward, trying to escape. My fellow Japanese destroyer, which had just sunk the enemy, joined me to form a fleet in continued battle. Regrettably, the enemy destroyers succeeded in out-running us, and escaped.

"Soon, we found two other enemy destroyers at a distance of 7,000 meters. We immediately opened fire. Our first volley hit the first enemy, causing a fire aboard ship. Then we concentrated our fire on the second enemy destroyer. Apparently, several of our volleys hit her magazine with a great explosion that tore her to pieces in the blinking of an eye. We returned fire to the first enemy, still afloat but aflame, and quickly sank her. Shortly afterwards, we detected a black spot on the sea ahead. Our spotlight zoomed in on a small boat with a white flag—the survivors of the destroyer we had just sunk. My flagship accommodated them. They were one Dutch ensign and nine seamen. They told us their flagship was the Deloiter; another cruiser was named the Java, and they were escorted by three destroyers.

"Momentarily, our watch spotted an enemy cruiser 8,000 meters to the north. I gave the order to speed up to catch her. As we neared the enemy, we found one Java-type cruiser and two destroyers, each with four funnels. We closed in on the enemy with our lights on and fired several torpedoes. We heard a great explosion, but could not visually confirm a hit. Then I lost sight of the enemy in the shadows of Bali Island.

"We continued our search northward and confronted an enemy cruiser turning back toward us. As we prepared to attack, she turned parallel to us and opened fire. A closer look showed two more enemy destroyers following closely behind her. Both sides exchanged the full force of fire power. Enemy gunfire hit my flagship, but our fire was more accurate. I saw a gaping hole spread as we continued battle. I was about to launch my torpedoes against her with a coup de grâce when enemy fire hit us, cutting our electric power, disabling our ability to fire torpedoes. Fortunately, my sister destroyer was able to launch her torpedoes. I heard the explosion, but again, could not visually confirm the enemy's sinking. The battle ceased for a while in darkness.

"Soon, more gunfire broke out to the north, so we rushed in that direction, and encountered two Japanese destroyers that had been escorting our sea convoy. Having completed that mission, they received word of our battle, and were coming to our aid, when they encountered two enemy destroyers. In an exchange of gunfire, they sank one and damaged another. Soon after, they met with an enemy cruiser and inflicted heavy damage to her before she fled northward. On February 20, 1942, the battle of Bali ended at 3:30 a.m.

"Though a mini-battle, it was a total victory for Japan. I had to tow one of our destroyers because damages kept her from navigating herself. As I was towing her, seven American B-17 bombers attacked us with a barrage that cut our tow lines and blew several of our crew into the sea. At a speed of 5 knots, under American bombing attacks en route, we finally succeeded in towing her back to base.

"I knew why I was given this small victory. I owe thanks to the Emperor's infinite power and to my men's invincible fighting spirit which made them demonstrate the utmost of their ability, cultivated by long and hard discipline."

My father's warrior nature is well-painted in his speech. He was a staunch veteran officer accustomed to fighting at the front of every battle. He continued his fight till the final moments of his death with his ship. He had no mercy for the enemy and was proud to carry out his job. That side of my father's personality was unapparent to me until recently, when I read the many vivid accounts of Captain Toshio Abe as a man who fought desperately for his country.

The profile of my father that I saw on the rare occasions he was on leave during my childhood was completely different. There was another face beneath my father's stern warrior mask. I remember him as a kind, warm-hearted, and affectionate person. Above all, he loved my mother, and I never saw them quarreling.

In February, 1943, my father's appointment as head teacher of the Torpedo School in Taura, Yokosuka, allowed him to stay home for over a year before his assignment as captain of the heavy cruiser Ohyodo in May, 1944. Like any sailor, my father enjoyed walking over the hillside on solid ground, the soil beneath his feet. He used to pick up ginkgo nuts from the ground and bring them home, removing the pulp, because my mother, had an allergic reaction to the pulp. It comforted me to see how my father seemed to love his intermittent times at home with us.

Each morning he commuted to Yokosuka, preceded by a ceremonial ritual with my mother. He would leave through our front gate and walk to the main street, then turn around at the corner to wave back to my mother who was watching from the gate. White gloves in hand, he would wave, then turn and go. There was no exception to this exchange until that fateful morning when he left to take command of the Shinano.

My mother felt a foreboding that morning when my father handed her the photo of herself he always carried with him. It was worn and faded, showing my mother wearing a kimono, smiling, her hair combed in an old-fashioned style. My mother understood: my father was showing determination to die for his country. My mother said she foresaw his death that day. It was the last time she would see him alive. He went out the front gate with his white gloves in hand, but did not turn around to wave farewell. He kept on going, resigned to his fate. December of that same year, a naval officer came to our door with the same white gloves in his hand to express his deepest sympathy and condolences, and to tell us of my father's death in battle.

What impressed me most about my father was the gentle, compassionate side of his nature, hidden behind his military facade. My older brother died from an illness at age three when I was a year old. My father concentrated his love on me as the only child. His love was too overflowing to be fully concealed behind his formal sternness. His heart was full of love that extended beyond his immediate family. For this, I respected my father, and I have a greater appreciation for his tenderness than for any of his accomplishments as a warrior.

Before my family moved into our house in Kamakura, we lived in a larger house further eastward in Joumyouji, which was owned by my father's elder brother, Hiroaki, who also fought in World War II as a naval officer. My father's mother was over 80 years old and sickly. She lived with us, so my mother could take care of her with the help of a nurse and a maid. My father treated our servants as if they were family. He gave them regular holidays and limited their work time till 9:00 p.m., after which, except in an emergency, their time was their own. The servants' rooms were furnished the same as the family's. My father would never eat unless he was sure there was enough of the same food for his servants.

One of our amenities was the Japanese way of bathing, called *ofuro*. A round-shaped bathtub made of cast iron was filled with cold water, wood burned at its base to warm the water. A wooden slab covered the iron bottom to prevent our feet from burning as we stepped into the tub. This style of bathing was called *goemon buro*. Warming one's body with an abundance of warm water was, and still is, a most important pleasure to the Japanese.

After World War II, Western hotels had a difficult time accommodating Japanese tourists with their need for a much greater amount of hot water than the average Westerner. As a result, Japanese tourists complained when a hotel ran out of hot water. Today, with so many Japanese tourists, hotels worldwide have increased their hot water capacity. The hot bath is essential to Japanese relaxation. Actual washing was done outside the tub with a pail of hot water, so that the hot water in the tub had to be replenished constantly. To continuously enjoy the relaxation of the hot bath, someone else had to attend the wood fire beneath the tub. In winter, it was a particular nuisance, since the fire door was outside the room.

Generally, servants had to manage without an ample hot water supply. Since they were last to bathe in the household, the water supply decreased, got colder and progressively dirtier from previous bathers. My father cared about his servants and my mother shared the communal task of preparing the baths with the servants. He never spared the cost of wood, so that his servants would have the same hot bath that he and his family enjoyed. Though it might seem trivial by today's standards, the Japanese tradition of the feudal system distinguished sharply between classes 50 years ago. My parents' treatment of their servants was extraordinary for the time. I loved my father's warmth and his idea of equality practiced in our home.

On a hill behind our house in Kamakura is the tomb of shogun Minamoto no Yoritomo. As a child, I would often climb the steep old stone steps leading to the tiny shrine and tomb and play there with my friends. I remember the day I came home from cadet school in Nagoya to attend my father's funeral. There were frequent air raids by the U.S. Air Force in the winter of 1945. My mother and I sought shelter with our neighbors in the tomb. In the morning, I would run up to the shrine to read aloud the Rescript of the Emperor Meiji for soldiers and sailors, and do kendo exercises, using a Japanese sword to cut off tree branches.

In 1180 A.D., Yoritomo rose up against the Heike, a powerful family in the imperial court at the time. Yoritomo responded to a secret appeal from one of the princes who was angry about the Heikes' exceeding the emperor's authority. Yoritomo was from the Minamoto family, whose ancestors were said to have built the big shrine of Tsurugaoka Hachiman Gu in 1063 A.D. Yoritomo married Masako, a daughter of the Hojo family, to form a military alliance to defeat the Heike. In 1185 A.D., he destroyed the Heike's power in a decisive battle and established the Kamakura Bakufu (samurai government). In 1192 A.D., the imperial court appointed Yoritomo Sei-i-Tai Shogun (great general to subjugate barbarians), and he became the practical ruler of Japan and the country's first hereditary shogun.

After Yoritomo's death, his wife Masako took power with the support of her father, Tokimasa Hojo. In 1221 A.D., she led the biggest revolution against the imperial court since the 8th century. Defeating the imperial army, her troops occupied the capital, Kyoto. She exiled all imperial families and nobles hostile to Hojo and confiscated their fiefs. She founded a strong intelligence office in Kyoto to watch the court's every move. The emperor system remained, but she deprived the court of political power. It was an important change, the first time in Japan's history that the center of power shifted to the east. Power was not returned to the court until the fall of Tokugawa Bakufu in Edo (now called Tokyo) in 1867. My hometown of Kamakura prospered for about 150 years as the political and military center of Japan.

Underlying this brief introduction to Kamakura's history, I discovered astounding secrets which may well have undermined the present structure of Japanese society. I also uncovered a strange tie between people related to my own family, a tie that is intricately woven within the greater scope of world history, an intriguing story which this narrative promises to unfold.

Chapter Three

Loyalty At Any Cost

Why did my father dedicate his life to the navy? What made him believe that dying for the Emperor in battle was a worthy cause? Upon his death, did he cry out, "Banzai," (the Japanese battle cry meaning "May his Imperial Majesty reign eternally")? To find answers, I must unravel threads that created the fabric of dedication and loyalty, woven into the intricate pattern of my father's upbringing and education in early 20th century Japan.

The precepts of modern Japan were a legacy of the so-called Meiji Era (1868-1912) which began with the successful coup d'etat by anti-Tokugawa court nobles and daimyos (lords) on December 9, 1867. Reorganization of the government followed when the "great order to restore the power of the emperor" was issued to the fifteenth shogun, Yoshinobu Tokugawa. The order required Tokugawa to resign and relinquish his power and fief to the imperial court.

When the old Bakufu vassals of the samurai government turned against the emperor, the Boshin civil war ensued. Though the conflict continued into May of 1868, the imperial government's victory was clear from the start. After 265 years of shogunate rule, from the first Tokugawa shogun Ieyasu to Yoshinobu, the civil war fully restored power to the emperor.

Emperor Meiji (Mutsuhito) promulgated the Five Articles Charter Oath, his pledge to the gods in carrying out his government policies. The next year all daimyos (feudalistic lords) returned their fiefs and people to the emperor. To ease this transition, former daimyos were initially appointed governors of their former fiefs, which became national prefectures that answered to the imperial court.

Long before this era, Japan had been divided into hundreds of hans, the Japanese word for fiefs or provinces, that were each governed by a daimyo. The shogun and his Bakufu (samurai government) had the power to rule the daimyos. The shogun could appoint the daimyo governor, giving him full power to rule the people, and change or confiscate his fiefs. Within the daimyo's han, his power was nearly absolute, being restricted only when in conflict with the overriding powers of the Bakufu shogunate officials in a way that might be construed as a conspiracy towards insurrection.

In 1863 there were 268 daimyo families. With the initial organization of the Meiji government's prefecture system, there were 305 divisions, which by 1888 had been reorganized into 46 prefectures. (*A Study of Japanese History*, by Kazuo Kasahara; Yamakawa Shuppan Sha, 1990). Before the Meiji era, there had been no sense of a central government that could be called a Japanese nation. Iyeyasu and Hidetada united Japan under a military power in 1603. Cannons imported from Holland were used to destroy Osaka castle. Iyemitsu, the third shogun, prohibited trade with Spain and Portugal and gave exclusive rights to the Dutch, accommodating them at Deshima, an artificial island connected to Nagasaki by a bridge. Japan was completely closed. The Tokugawas monopolized importation of saltpeter, the main material for gunpowder, which was not produced in Japan at all, a policy that made it impossible for the daimyos to attempt rebellion against the Tokugawa shogunate, and enabled the Tokugawas to maintain power and peace for 264 years.

After Commodore Matthew Perry opened Japan, some of the *hans*, such as Satsuma and Chosu, developed methods of importing saltpeter from Western countries. They could obtain fresh high quality saltpeter, whereas Tokugawa Bakufu troops had damp, old powder. This made Kangun (an imperial army newly organized with soliders of Satsuma, Choshu and other *hans*, plus Yottsu and Ya guerrillas driven out under the reign of the Tokugawas) strong enough to beat Bakufu troops in less than ten years. Furthermore, rifles disposed of by the U.S. government following the civil war were sold to Choshu and Satsuma by international brokers and greatly strengthened the ranks.

During the rule of Tokugawas, the population of Japan increased drastically, while production stayed flat, with inflation the result, and Bakufu and *hans* suffering financial difficulties. As a result of frugal policies, the samurai lost its practical power to rule. Meanwhile nouveau-riche merchants became influential and supported the new powers against the Tokugawas.

The Tokugawas' religion changed from Kami, the religion of the Yottsu race, to Buddhism. During the rule of Iyemitsu (1622-1651), the third shogun and fifth shogun Tsunayoshi (1680-1709), non-Buddhists (Yottsu, Ya and Zoshiki) were oppressed, causing anti-Tokugawa feeling. The Satsumas and Choshus won these people over to their side, promising to make Shinto (*jin* of Yottsu, and *gi* of Ya) the national religion. When the Meiji government was formed, the religion of the imperial family was changed from Buddhism to Shinto, in order to make the emperor a living god and father of the nation, thus integrating all races and religions. For this reason, after the Meiji Restoration, Buddhist temples and statues were destroyed and the Ministry of Jin-gi formed (only to be dissolved at a later date, as the Buddhist powers contributed big money to a political slush fund of the Meiji government).

The government of the first Meiji emperor was first to gain enough power to govern all prefectures in a sovereign nation. Most important, the Meiji Emperor's strength allowed him to organize a central educational system that recognized him as the supreme ruler of Japan based on the Meiji ideology and view of history. Prior to this change, when a man from Satsuma Han referred to "my country," he meant the country of Satsuma rather than Japan. In 1867 at the Paris Exposition, Satsuma participated separately from the central government of Tokugawa Bakufu. This presented doubts among other world leaders whether the Bakufu had the power to govern Japan as a nation.

The Meiji Restoration, with its epoch-making revolution, quelled any exterior doubts about who was in control of the Japanese people. Domestically the new system was vulnerable at its outset to various internal oppositions. When the imperial government took a census in 1872, they learned the population was much larger than the combined figures which had formerly been registered with the Bakufu in the caste of samurais, farmers, craftsmen and merchants. It was known that there were "outcasts"—descendants of the aboriginal Japanese races: Yottsu nomads, Ya agricultural and fishing people, Zoshiki, the oldest inhabitants, and Sanka people, a combination of Yottsu and Ya who lived hidden in towns and the mountains; but the new census showed that there were millions more of these people than previously estimated. This entire group was looked down upon as subhuman but allowed a kind of autonomy. For example, the leader of the Yottsu lived in Edo (Tokyo) and Yottsu people used to pay him a poll tax until the new Meiji central taxation system, when the government forced the Yottsu to follow new guidelines, taxing them in cash based on the value of the mountains and forests they lived in. Fearful of rebellion, the government hunted down Sanka hostile toward central authority, which made them even more rebellious.

In 1873, a draft law was enforced, whereby subject to physical examination and limited exemptions, all healthy men 20 years old were inducted into military service for three years. Farmers' second and third sons were the primary targets, resulting in loss of family labor, which became a great burden to the farmers. The draft meant that loyalty to the country demanded payment not merely with money but with one's heart and body. In the West it was interpreted as the "blood tax". Ignorant farmers believed their blood would actually be drawn to pay the tax. The Land Tax Reformation Act enforced by the government the same year caused more frustration among farmers who rose up, causing social unrest to spread throughout the nation.

With the dissolution of the hans, proud samurai found themselves suddenly unemployed. Their salaries had been paid with rice which exchanged for money by rice brokers. In 1876, the imperial government dismissed the samurai with severance pay in the form of government bonds. When the government prohibited the samurai from carrying swords that same year, a series of revolts broke out in Kumamoto, Fukuoka and Yamaguchi. The Meiji were most seriously threatened in 1877 when ex-Satsuma samurais under Takamori Saigo revolted in the Seinan War (Satsuma Rebellion). It took the full force of the Meiji to suppress the revolt and maintain the central government of the new Japanese nation.

The new taxation system caused riots among farmers and outcasts alike. In 1876 the people's protests against the land tax compelled the government to reduce it from 3% to 2.5%. The samurai remained a social class long after that, but lost the privileges they had enjoyed for centuries.

In the following decade, Western thought became another headache to the Meiji government. For the first time, human rights were seriously questioned, even among the ex-samurai class. French thought became popular, influencing an anti-government movement with individual-oriented philosophies like Rousseauism, which gave credence to the natural human right of freedom at birth. Exposure to Western thought made people resent the arbitrary network of Meiji control. The object of the protest was to protect individuals' rights against the despotic government by forming a people's parliament.

In 1881 the Liberal Party was formed and other political parties soon emerged from the embittered masses. Numerous anti-government incidents erupted between 1882-1886, so that the government deemed the idea of people's rights dangerous to the security of the new Japanese nation. Though the Meiji government came down hard to control the people, it compromised politically by instituting an imperial parliament under the constitution granted by Emperor Meiji in 1889.

The Meiji government was in haste to establish its authority to rule the people and strengthen national power, in order to safeguard Japan's independence against possible aggression by the Western nations. Some Japanese, enlightened by Western rationalist ideas such as liberalism, socialism and communism, began questioning feudalistic ideas of the Tokugawa rule; however, they were quickly suppressed by the government as dangerous rebels against *okami*. Although the Japanese legal system was modernized, nevertheless, feudalistic ideas based on a vertical society were preserved, and the people were kept in as slavish a state as before. The first Meiji general election of the House of Representatives was held in 1890. After two decades, domestic politics proved the Meiji system to be firmly established.

Dominated by worldwide imperialism, the international situation surrounding 19th century Japan was particularly dangerous. The great world powers looked for any opportunity to take over weaker struggling nations. Russia was pushing down from the north. The Opium War in 1839 between Great Britain and China broke down the walls of that vast land. Japan's leaders saw the dangers of colonization by the world powers. A powerful central government was the key to self-preservation against invasion. Only an independent nation could develop into a modern country to oppose such threats.

Making the emperor the head of state and legal sovereign was not enough to unify the divided Japanese people. They needed a spiritual leader, someone to worship above all other gods, including Buddha. At this time, the emperor was made a living god, someone to teach the people by setting precepts and moral standards to live by. The emperor's role was the same as God in Western civilization but personified in a living emperor. In this way, the varied philosophies of the Japanese people were unified to one social ideology manifested in the government and military leader, the emperor, whose myths and unbroken lineage was most respectfully taught in schools. The emperor was proclaimed an inviolable living divinity, loyalty to whom was the supreme value and duty of the Japanese people.

Once Japan's domestic political system was in place, the government focused the people's attention on threats from the outside world. The centripetal force of loyalty to the emperor drove Japan toward economic modernization and militaristic nationalization. Since feudal times when the people went part and parcel with the land under the daimyos, it was the nobles' policy to keep people ignorant and dependent, in order to control them. A knowledge of history and politics could open the door to questions and make the people unmanageable. Ideas of freedom and human rights could overthrow despotism, so the precepts of gentle obedience to power and loyalty to the emperor became the foundation of the new national concept.

To perpetuate the buildup of a strong national military force loyal to the emperor and protective of the new imperial system, Emperor Meiji issued the Rescript to the Soldiers and Sailors in 1882. The emperor was the direct supreme commander of the armed forces. This proclamation set forth the foundation of Japan's imperial army and navy, which lasted until the conclusion of World War II. The Rescript begins with the words: "In our country the Emperor has always been at the head of the armed forces through the ages..." and continues, "My subjects may take charges of various aspects of military affairs, but I will not entrust matters of fundamental principle to anyone. I keep these to myself because I hold supreme power..."

The first article states: "The duty of servicemen is to serve the Emperor and country most loyally. You must think that the weight of your life is as light as the feather of a bird while the weight of justice is as heavy as a mountain. You must be determined to give your life to the Emperor without doubt or hesitation in the cause of the nation..."

Loyalty to the Emperor was synonymous with patriotism. To foster military spirit, the Rescript was read every morning until all members of the armed forces memorized it. This is the Rescript which I read every morning as a student of the cadet school. Behind the school there was a small hill. I would run up to the top and shout out these words as loud as I could. I also practiced pronouncing commands. Then I ran down the hill back to the school. I injured my knee from this exercise, and to this day, it aches when I play golf on cold winter mornings, serving as a reminder of 50 years ago. My father experienced the same indoctrination in the navy. For soldiers and sailors to pledge their loyalty to the emperor was essential to the preservation of the Japanese nation and its sovereign. The emperor personified those national values which needed military protection.

The public school system was instituted as early as 1872 and the Education Act was enforced in 1879. With the Education Rescript in 1890, the central government set the morals and precepts upon which Japanese education would be founded. It particularly stressed loyalty to the emperor and the nation, which was in accord with Confucian family doctrine. Soon students nationwide were imbued with the Meiji ideology that Japan was the country of the gods, guided by a divine and benevolent emperor who was like the father of a single family. It was considered a privilege to be born in such a country and to have the opportunity to express loyalty by dying for the emperor. This attitude gave the Japanese a growing sense of superiority.

The Meiji ideology of loyalty at any cost enabled Japan to rise rapidly from an undeveloped country to a modern nation and military power capable of winning an unexpected and spectacular victory over the Chinese Empire (1894-95), in which Japan gained the island of Taiwan. At the same time the Japanese government was able to persuade the U.S. and European powers to end unfair treaties, and thus to become the first Asian nation to break the chain of Western control.

The Russo-Japanese War (1904-05) gave Japan the south of Sakhalin and concessions in China. In 1910, Japan annexed Korea. These early military victories allowed Japan to maintain her sovereignty and independence. But with this success came an imperialistic attitude of aggression in a continued series of wars. After World War I, Japan took German holdings in the Pacific, and sent troops to Siberia in a cooperative effort with the U.S., U.K. and France to rescue Czechoslovakian troops. She took Manchuria in 1931 and withdrew from the League of Nations 1933. Japan declared war on China in 1937 and attacked Pearl Harbor in 1941, which led to her ultimate demise in 1945.

Millions of soldiers sacrificed their lives to the emperor with utmost loyalty, as requested in the Rescripts. The Russo-Japanese War, in particular, marked the first conflict between Japan and a great white nation from Western civilization. One of the largest nations in the world, Czarist Russia stretched from eastern Europe to the Sea of Japan. Russia extended her interests to the Far East by expanding her already vast land mass into Manchuria and Korea. Although Japan had defeated China ten years before, she was still a small, relatively poor nation. If Japan had lost to Russia, she would surely have been colonized. Japan staked her fate against Russia and won, but paid a tremendous price.

One of the most famous battles of the Russo-Japanese conflict was the Japanese Army's all-out attack against the Russian fortress at the port of Lueshun on August 19, 1904. In four and a half months, Japan suffered 57,780 deaths, until Lueshun was finally captured. Every route to the fortress was littered with Japanese casualties, but reinforcements charged repeatedly, stepping over bodies of their own dead against relentless Russian machine guns. Each Japanese soldier faithfully adhered to the pledge of the Rescript with no consideration for personal safety. The weight of these soldiers' lives was literally "as light as the feather of a bird" with their unyielding suicide attacks. It seemed that the Meiji ideology and education were effecting great success for the young Japanese nation. Unyielding loyalty backed by early success was leading Japan blindly into the unforeseen disaster of World War II.

Under this new system, individual rights were ignored, not just for the military, but even for civilians who followed the ethic: "Give up all your personal interests and faithfully serve the emperor and nation with all your heart and soul." The Japanese people believed that the whole of Japan could be saved by each selfless act of an individual who laid down his life. They believed that selfless acts brought favor from the gods to accomplish what might otherwise seem impossible. Toward the end of World War II, this belief reached the extreme, when it was interpreted conversely as failure, meaning someone had not done his selfless best. Logic and reason were abandoned. Any officer who hesitated in battle, waiting for reinforcements, was considered lacking in fighting spirit, selfish and disloyal, even if he were outnumbered ten to one. This occurred in 1942 at Guadalcanal, when 1,000 Japanese of the Itsuki corps charged the American position held by 10,000 marines. The Japanese hurled themselves at the enemy with the traditional Imperial Army belief that spirit could offset material disadvantage. The result at Guadalcanal was disaster as the Japanese sacrificed themselves in droves.

Hiroyuki Agawa reveals in his biography *Isoroku Yamamoto* (Kabushiki Kaisha Shinchosha, 1973), that in the fall of 1941 in Tokyo, Prime Minister Fumimaro Konoye asked Admiral Yamamoto, commander of the Imperial Navy's combined fleet, "Admiral, if Japan fails to reach an agreement with the United States by negotiation, we may have to go to war. Do you have confidence in our navy to defeat the Americans?"

Yamamoto replied, "I am sure we can do fine against the Americans for a year, perhaps a year and a half. But I have no confidence in an extended war against the Americans. I suggest you make every effort to avoid war with the United States." An admirer of Yamamoto for his judgment and leadership, Admiral Shigeyoshi Inoue criticized his naval commander after the war for his lack of firmness with the prime minister. With no appreciation or understanding of naval warfare, the indecisive Prime Minister interpreted Admiral Yamamoto's reply as a positive one. Yamamoto did not foresee that Prime Minister Konoye would find a vague hope in his answer and believe that Japan could win a quick victory in the first year and a half of battle against America. Yamamoto's ambiguous answer may have given Japan's leaders false hope. Had Yamamoto made a firm statement to the effect, "No, we can never win in the long run," it probably would have resulted in his forced resignation. Yet it would have been better for Japan not to have taken that fatal risk of putting loyalty before reality.

Admiral Yamamoto is best known for his sneak attack on Pearl Harbor on December 7, 1941. But America has painted a false picture of the man as a dirty fighter and fanatic. The timing of Japan's declaration of war, after the bombing of Pearl Harbor, left America virtually defenseless, but this timing was the fault of the Japanese embassy in Washington D.C. A series of administrative blunders and red tape, coupled with a lax Sunday mood, set the pace for a delay in contacting U.S. Secretary of State Cordell Hull with the declaration of war. Admiral Yamamoto had no knowledge of this blunder that announced Japan's war intentions after Pearl Harbor had been under attack for almost an hour. The result of this error was the spark that inflamed the Americans to respond in outrage over the surprise attack, and the hatred and vengeance by Americans against the Japanese for that incident is a stigma which remains with us today.

Ironically, Admiral Yamamoto was one of the few Japanese military leaders who had been exposed to the West. He was a worldly man, and as a naval attache spent enough years in the United States to have realized their naval superiority over Japan. Yamamoto had attended London disarmament talks where, on several occasions, he negotiated with the U.S. and Great Britain to reduce the number of warships. Based on his knowledge of the West, having established friendships in the U.S. and U.K., Yamamoto was in a position as an exceptional naval officer to make reasonable judgments on international affairs that might have averted war. Witty and charismatic, he was trusted in both naval and political circles. He was opposed to an alliance with fascist Germany and Italy. As vice minister of the imperial navy, he risked his life by hazarding such an outspoken opinion against the tide that was pulling Japan towards war.

Admiral Yamamoto commanded a combined fleet of over 40,000 seamen, for which he had budgeted a tremendous amount of money. Even if it were within the realm of Yamamoto's conscience to face the grim reality that his proud naval force, despite early victories, would be crushed by a greater American navy, it was the Emperor's decision to go to war; this forbade Yamamoto to speak out against the order. Junpei Gomikawa writes in his book *Gozenkaigi*, (Kabushikikaisha Bungei Shunjuu, 1978): "At the last *gozenkaigi* on December 1, 1941, Prime Minister Tojo concluded the meeting with the resolution to go to war...Emperor Hirohito left the conference without saying a word, as usual...He played constitutional monarch. All 16 attendants (ministers plus army and navy chiefs and vice chiefs of staff and the President of the Privy Council) signed the resolution. Then both chiefs of staff...reported to Hirohito to obtain his approval for the military campaign...Next day they reported to him again, asking for his decision on the day to open war. The date was decided to be December 8, 1941 (Japan time). Imperial headquarters issued the "great order" in the name of Hirohito to Admiral Yamamoto, Supreme Commander of the Combined Fleet." Based on this, we can believe it was the Emperor's order to attack.

The military spirit cultivated in the Rescripts and backed by the central education system set loyalty as the supreme value above any other considerations, even possible annihilation of the Japanese people. Admiral Yamamoto, like my father, had been indoctrinated by Meiji ideology to believe that loyalty to the Emperor would bring aid from the gods, so that unyielding, self-sacrificing loyalty would miraculously reverse odds and crush the more powerful enemy forces. When Yamamoto put time restraints of a year and a half to effectively stand up to America at sea, it was the last resistance of his logic that dared to weigh the facts against his loyalty. Loyalty won out over reason and Yamamoto accepted the emperor's order to fight with inferior forces, just as my father accepted a ship full of holes unfit for battle. Both men believed they made the only honorable choice.

Emperor Hirohito did not customarily reject valid decisions made by his cabinet officers. Though loyalty was to the Emperor's official decision, it was actually the prime minister's judgment to go to war. The vertical line of loyalty was a chain of command that toppled, like a row of dominos, and plunged Japan blindly into a war that the Japanese people accepted as the Emperor's supreme judgment.

One of the arguments supporting Japan's decision to start the war against the United States was the problem of her petroleum stocks. The encircling net of ABCD Nations (America, Britain, China, Dutch) imposed economic sanctions which blocked Japan from obtaining petroleum supplies. If this condition continued for months, Japan would lose her power to fight, and would be forced to allow the United States to dictate terms. Though it was a gamble, it was better for Japan to start the war immediately while she still had enough petroleum. With the help of the gods, Japan followed her impulse of a preemptive strike.

Secretary of State Hull's note to the Japanese ministry in 1941 was interpreted as an ultimatum to make Japan retreat to her position prior to the Manchurian Incident in 1931. Just such a request had made Japan withdraw from the League of Nations in 1933. From the Western point of view, Hull must have reasoned that Japan clearly saw she stood no chance of victory over the U.S.; consequently, a Japanese concession was expected. Anything else, from the Western view, would be suicide. If Japanese leaders gave in to U.S. pressure contrary to the emperor's will, it would be considered the ultimate disloyalty. Better to try harder to satisfy the emperor's great mind. If it took war to accomplish this, why not? If it was a gamble, it was merely one of loyalty versus odds, which in Japanese minds would always be in their favor.

In the Meiji era (1868-1912), the emperor's ministers were all survivors of revolutionary battles which had put him back in power. They were realists who could lead both emperor and nation to right decisions, while simultaneously imbuing the notion of loyalty in the people. When these men died, only the spiritual idea of loyalty remained as a tool to bond the people and the emperor. As a supreme value of the nation, loyalty produced ultra-nationalism, which inhibited reasonable judgment and irresponsibly started the war.

The Japanese should acknowledge responsibility for the disaster incurred from their decision to go to war. The Tokyo tribunal was held by the allies to judge war criminals, but thus far the Japanese have not officially held themselves accountable to one another. If blind loyalty founded in the Meiji ideology forced the people to follow the Emperor towards a wrongful purpose, all value of loyalty was lost in self-deception. To insure against a recurrence of the nightmare of ultra-nationalism, the Japanese must clarify what was wrong in the Meiji ideology, that leaders used it as a means to suppress opposition for their own selfish ends.

Chapter Four

The Meiji Ideology

The Meiji ideology was developed to integrate peoples belonging to fiefs which under the feudal system had been owned and ruled by daimyos, to form a new Japanese nation under the central control of the emperor. The most important concept under the Meiji was that since the beginning of recorded time, the entire nation had been a single family guided by a divine, father-like emperor. Why did the Japanese require such an ideology? First, let us examine the question from the aspect of international politics.

In the beginning of the 19th century, Russians, British, Dutch and Americans sailed to the Far East one after the other, but Japan remained closed to foreigners under the Tokugawa Shogunate. Commodore Matthew C. Perry, U.S.N., came to Japan with his black ship fleet to deliver the sovereign a letter from U.S. President Millard Fillmore. Perry was received, succeeded in opening Japan to U.S. ships on March 3, 1854, and negotiated a peace treaty of amity between Japan and the United States. It was the dawn of the Meiji Reformation and modern Japan.

Among the most powerful daimyos, Satsuma at the southern end of Kyushu, and Choshu at the western end of Honshu, were smuggling modern arms and supplies from the Western countries. Their alliance could probably have defeated the troops of Tokugawa Bakufu, but they lacked the power and authority to unite the whole of Japan and govern the people. The Western countries were attuned to the general unrest and chaos in Japan and waited eagerly for a chance to colonize a divided people. Satsuma and Choshu realized they needed someone with supreme authority above them and saw the emperor as the best choice to fill that role. It was Satsuma and Choshu who jointly used their united power to institute the modern Japanese emperor system of Meiji.

To understand the Meiji ideology and the emperor system, it is essential to understand the position of the Meiji Emperor. He was the sovereign who granted to the people in February 1889 the Meiji Constitution, which defines his role in these articles:

Article 1:
> The Emperor of the imperial line, unbroken for ages eternal, rules the Great Empire of Japan.

Article 3:
> The Emperor is divine and inviolable.

Article 4:
> The Emperor is the head and sovereign of state and exercises his power in accordance with the provisions of this constitution.

Article 11:
> The Emperor commands the Imperial Army and Navy.

The constitution was modeled after Prussia's 1850 model, with German legal advisors helping draft it. (Prussia's monarch had the greatest power in Europe). The Japanese emperor was clearly defined as sovereign, the people his subjects. The people's basic human rights were secured, but limited. The emperor had the power to appoint or dismiss ministers and government officers, to declare war, to conclude peace treaties and international agreements. The emperor's power was collectively called "supreme power." As supreme commander of the army and navy, the emperor personified the nation. It was the supreme duty of soldiers and sailors, as it was with my father, to pledge their lives in loyalty to the emperor.

In addition to the army and navy, the emperor commanded the Prime Minister and Cabinet, the Privy Council, the Board of Audit, the Court of Administration Litigation, the General Staff Office, the Chief of Naval operations, the Divisional Commanders of the Army, the Fleet Commanders of the Navy, the Courts, the Imperial Household, the Governor-General of Korea, the Governor-General of Taiwan, and others. The Imperial Parliament had two houses, the House of Representatives and the House of Peers, but the Emperor had all the power.

Absolutism of the emperor was the basic concept of the Meiji Constitution. However, having all power in his hands was the same as having no power, because it was impossible for the emperor to personally control so many organs of government. Consequently, he became accustomed to entrusting power to ministers and parliament. Conversely, ministers and parliament were held responsible for counseling the emperor correctly. Veteran politicians of Satsuma and Choshu under this new system of constitutional monarchy could freely exercise power in the name of the emperor. During the course of the lives of these well-experienced founders of the Meiji ideology, the national system worked because the founders exercised realistic, pragmatic judgment. But when these original leaders died, power descended to elite leaders of the younger generation of the Showa era, who had less experience and whose reason was poisoned by spiritualism and ultra-nationalism. They failed to control the national system and led Japan to the catastrophe of World War II.

To insure support of the Meiji ideology, the government invented Japan's history to suit its needs. It was no coincidence that the Emperor Meiji granted the constitution on February 11 to coincide with the date of the imaginary accession of the first Japanese emperor, Jinmu, in 660 B.C. This supposedly occurred in Yamato, the ancient capital of Japan, according to the description of the *Nihon Shoki* (*Chronicles of Japan*, another name being *Nihongi*). February 11 of the solar calendar was converted from January 1 of the lunar calendar, with which the *Nihon Shoki* was written. By making the day a national holiday, the government authorized the myths of the *Nihon Shoki*.

One of the oldest history books, *Nihon Shoki, The Chronicles of Japan*, was compiled in 720 A.D. It contained myths of the age of gods, ancestors of the imperial family. It described the origin of Japan with the creation of the Japanese islands from the sea by two gods, Izanagi and Izanami, who lived in heaven. Izanagi and Izanami made Takamagahara, the plain of High Heaven, where the Sun Goddess Amaterasu Ohmikami was born. Amaterasu Ohmikami sent her grandson, Ninigi-no-Mikoto, down to the summit of a mountain in Kyushu with three treasures to symbolize his authority to found a country. Ninigi established this country in northern Kyushu. After two generations, his grandson Jinmu conquered the Yamato area, where he was enthroned as emperor, and where his descendants ruled continuously for 2,500 years through the Meiji era. From Izanagi and Izanami in the infinite past to the 20th Century, Japan and the Japanese race was believed to have emerged thus.

These myths were written by the government in a tone as if every Japanese had personally participated in the scenes of the stories. As we read of Ninigi-no-Mikoto's descent to the summit of Mt. Takachiho, we saw ourselves following him. In the telling of Jinmu's conquest of the east, each of us felt as if he had joined in the adventure, as together we had all conquered Japan's enemies. The Japanese asked no logical questions about these great, supposedly historical victories. What happened to the defeated enemies? Were they all killed to the last man?

The book said the imperial forces defeated evil barbarians wherever and whenever they rose up. Nothing more was asked; nothing further was said. Did some enemies retreat from the Japanese islands, or were some enslaved in Japan? If so, who and where were their descendants? How many were there? But these were sacred legends of the gods about the ancestors of the imperial family, and no one was allowed to pose such foolish questions.

This historic view developed to support the Meiji emperor system was called the "imperialistic view." The following is a summary of its special features:

1: The Imperial family of one lineage has continued since the beginning of the country's history.
2: The beginning of the country was so long ago that it is difficult to separate the age of the gods from that of men.
3: The Emperor has always been the head of the divine country of Japan, which is a great single family of one race.
4: The unification of the Japanese islands was made peacefully, except for a few unavoidable wars. The Emperors' reigns were always benevolent, attentive to the people's welfare.
5: Japan was never defeated by any attack from outside enemies; she has always maintained her independence.
6: The Imperial court was always a cultural leader; Buddhism was propagated under their patronage; they introduced Chinese thought and culture to help the people's spiritual lives.
7: Because of his god-like high virtue and integrity, the Emperor has always been venerated and worshipped by the people, even during the period when he temporarily lost political power to the samurai government.
8: It is a blessing and a privilege to be born in the land of the gods. Therefore, all Japanese should selflessly devote themselves to work for the Emperor and the nation in response to this privilege given. Above all, to die for the emperor is the supreme value.

Another important concept in the Meiji ideology was *kami,* a primitive belief of Japan's aborigines in the immortality of the soul, which originally meant "soul of the dead". Everyone became a *kami* after death. It was believed that the soul of a man killed on false charges would cause disasters. Great fires, typhoons, earthquakes, epidemics and plagues were all considered deeds of an angry *kami*. Out of fear, people enshrined *kami* and worshipped it to calm it.

When Western thought and religion were introduced to Japan during the Meiji era, "God", or "the god" in English, was translated to *kami* in Japanese, causing serious confusion, because the emperor was called *Arahito Gami* or *Akitsu Kami*, which was interpreted by the Western concept of "God," and understood as the "living god". Westerners and the average Japanese were misled to believe the emperor was the God of Western religion. Actually *kami* simply meant "the soul of the living emperor in which the souls of his ancestors of the imperial lineage were embodied since the beginning." In various court ceremonies the emperor stood to one side to pray to the gods, certainly not on the side to be prayed to by the people as god. The picture of Japan that the imperialistic point of view painted was of a nation of a great single family. The emperor, as the father, worshipped the souls of his ancestors and followed their precepts, while the ancestors kept the same relationship of emperor to people, i.e., father to children. It is important to note that the relationship between father and children could never be broken by any means and that a vertical society was permanently established under the emperor system.

In Western religion everyone was equal under God; it made no difference if you were a king or a beggar. God established the order in heaven, which had nothing to do with temporal order. If a saintly Christian died, his soul would be received by God in heaven, placed in a position by the hand of God, but it always remained the soul of a man and was never worshipped as a god. In the Meiji era, however, if a man served his emperor and country extraordinarily he was enshrined as a god. For example, General Nogi, famous for the capture of the Lueshun fortress in the Russo-Japanese War, was enshrined in Nogi Jinja as *kami*. And Admiral Togo, who commanded the combined fleet to defeat the Russian Baltic fleet in the battle of the Sea of Japan, was enshrined in Togo Jinja. *Jin* or *shin* has the same meaning as *kami*. Both of these great military leaders are still worshipped by some Japanese today in Tokyo.

In the imperialistic view, when the emperor died, he joined his ancestors' souls as *kami* when his subjects died they became subject *kami*; the relationship of emperor and subject would not change in death. At the Yasukuni Shrine, souls of soldiers and sailors who died for their emperors were enshrined and worshipped as *kami*. The shrine was Shinto, the religion which unified the ancient and primitive religions of the Japanese aborigines (Ya, Yottsu, Zoshiki). During wars, Shinto was nationally sponsored, giving religious grounds to fanatic ultra-nationalism. As the present Japanese constitution stipulates the separation of religion and state, the Yasukuni Shrine and Shinto are no longer sponsored by the state, but several years ago Prime Minister Yasuhiro Nakasone worshipped at the Yasukuni Shrine in official capacity, causing controversy among politicians and scholars. After that, no other prime minister has worshipped officially, although the concept of *kami* was never clarified.

In his book *A Study of the Emperor Showa*, Shichihei Yamamoto wrote it is generally understood by Japanese that the Emperor denied his divinity in the Rescript of 1946, at the request of the American occupation forces.

However, a notice by the Ministry of Education in 1937 clarifies that: "The Emperor is *Akitsu Mikami*, who reigns over our country in compliance with the wishes of the soul of the Imperial ancestors he has inherited. The terms *Akitsu Mikami* or *Arahito Gami* are completely different from the meaning of God as the absolute being or the Almighty...(the terms mean that) the souls of the emperor's ancestors and the soul of the living emperor come together as one, making (the emperor) a limitless venerable man, (and) original generator of the development and growth of the people and the land." The rhetoric employed in this statement gives much respect to the emperor, while clearly stating that he is a man.

Still there was confusion among the average Japanese because some actually worshipped the emperor as a god, while some felt he was a man who was immeasurably close to god. Everyone agreed that he was supreme above all. Anyone who disagreed was not Japanese. The idea that Japan was the land of the gods and was ruled by the emperor as a great father of a single family since the beginning of time made the people proud of their nation's integrity and undefeated history.

I have coined the phrase "Meiji ideology," though there is no established scholarly theory under that name; this ideology, however, has been implanted in the people's minds through the educational system and social guidance. This was good in its purpose to integrate the Japanese people, allowing the government to direct the people's attention to the international crisis. The government pushed policies for enhancing wealth and military strength, and succeeded in making Japan strong economically and militarily.

In 1922, when the Washington agreement was signed, limiting naval forces among the United States, Great Britain, and Japan in a 5:5:3 ratio, Japan already had the third largest navy in the world. To imbue the people with fighting spirit, Bushido was taken up from the foundations of old moral precepts peculiar to the Japanese. Samurai were glorified as warriors with fighting spirit, willing to fight for their lord without fear of death. This was regarded as a supreme value, like that of loyalty to the emperor. It was, in a sense, national brainwashing, to make the people believe a set of values and willing to die for military commands. The racial superiority complex of the Japanese grew out of their military prowess. Once respected and admired by the Japanese for a thousand years, the Chinese were suddenly looked down upon after their defeat in the Sino-Japanese War. By World War II, Japan's racial prejudice against fellow Asians extended to include Western people as well. Japan's success in military ventures, backed by the illusion of national values based on a fictitious history, became a powerful drug that made the people drunk with loyalty to the emperor and the nation. Though these Meiji precepts were essential to establish an independent Japanese nation between 1894 and 1904, they succeeded in leading Japan toward international isolationism and the ultimate catastrophe of World War II.

In retrospect, one must wonder why the Meiji ideology gave the emperor such a supreme position in making him head of state and spiritual leader of the people. If you think no one questioned these precepts, let us reflect on two incidents of men who did.

Dr. Tatsukichi Minobe (1873-1948), professor in the law department at Tokyo Imperial University, lectured on the constitution, and developed a theory that the main constituent of sovereignty was the state, not the emperor. The emperor, as head of state, was the supreme organ of the state, executing supreme power in accordance with the provisions of the constitution. In Minobe's theory the legislative authority of parliament was equal to the emperor's. In principle, parliament was independent, not subject to the emperor's orders. In 1935 Minobe's theory was criticized by a member of the House of Peers who had served in the military. Military authorities protested en masse, insisting that the main constituent of sovereignty was the emperor alone. Minobe was forced to resign and his books were banned.

According to Shichihei Yamamoto, Emperor Hirohito agreed with Minobe's theory, by strictly observing the provisions of the constitution. Emperor Showa (another name for Hirohito) always respected the plans and decisions submitted by his government, never exercised his supreme power over parliament, and only twice, admittedly exceeded his position as constitutional monarch. On February 26, 1936, an incident broke out called "the 2.26 incident," named for the month and day when the Imperial army rebelled. The last time Emperor Showa exercised supreme power was in the decision to surrender, ending World War II.

Constitutional monarchy was developed to restrict the absolute power of a monarch. It was obvious that a king was merely a man who was apt to abuse his power, particularly in spending and taxation. Since the emperor under Meiji ideology was both absolute ruler and spiritual leader, it was impossible for parliament to exercise independence when its own members could not resist the need to bend humbly to the emperor's great mind. Though parliament was within its rights to reject an emergency request to increase the military budget, their reason conflicted with the precept of loyalty, especially at the height of fanatical nationalism in the 1940s. This was clearly a self-defeating fault of the Meiji ideology.

In another incident of conflict with the Meiji ideology, Dr. Soukichi Tsuda, professor of history at Waseda University, denounced the stories of the *Nihon Shoki*, (*Chronicles* edited in 720 A.D.) and *Kojiki*, (*Record of Ancient Matters*, compiled in 712 A.D.). Tsuda studied Japanese history based on positivism and concluded that these myths about the imperial lineage were complete fictions manufactured to explain the derivation of imperial rule. Tsuda's position was that the Japanese should accept their history as mythical, but based on real people's lives and feelings. Since ancient times, the emperor had not been "a god", but a symbolic embodiment of everything good in Japanese culture.

Ultra-nationalists accused Tsuda of treason. A prosecutor charged him and his publisher with violation of public law. A trial opened against him in 1941 and his book was banned. But surprisingly, after World War II his view was widely supported, and was established in the academy of history.

If the true history of Japan had been known by the Japanese people at the height of fanatical nationalism, they might have understood why and how they had been so manipulated. Had my father understood this in 1944, his outlook and willingness to die for a perceived cause might have been quite different.

Chapter Five

Japan's Altered History

In our examination of the Meiji ideology, we found it was created to set up the emperor in a supreme position with absolute power. Under this system, by assuming a role much like a god, the emperor became head of state and the source of a centripetal force used to guide the Japanese people in their spiritual life. Loyalty was the bond connecting the people directly to the emperor. The Constitution was created as the foundation of this order and Japanese history was altered to fulfill that purpose.

Experience and common sense has shown that when a powerful group stresses a particular notion, the opposite is probably the case. If Meiji claimed the idea that Japan was "a single family country", she was not. If Meiji insisted there was only one lineage of monarchs called *Tenno* (emperor) supported by the imperial court, there most likely had been several other independent monarchs with their own courts. If it were stressed that the emperor's lineage originated in the infinite past, it was most likely to be more recent history. If it were emphasized that the emperor had unified Japan peacefully by governing with benevolence, the assertion was probably not true.

Though I suspected this for some time, I did not have a concrete idea about Japan's true history until I was stationed in London in 1975. I was seeking the identity of the Japanese because my daily contacts with the English culture put it at the forefront of my mind. Then one day in a Japanese bookstore in London, I found the book written by Tomeo Yagiri which completely changed my view of life. Yagiri's ideas were shocking, unique and totally different from what I was taught in school, yet the arguments were convincing.

Perhaps the most important aspect of Japan's true history is her multiracial origin, in which a minority 4% of the population enslaved the others by conquest. This same ruling minority is presently about 10% of Japan's population; yet the Japanese people have no knowledge of this fact.

According to Yagiri's view, the earliest inhabitants on the ancient Japanese islands were races who came from the south: Malaysia, Vietnam, southern China, India, etc. They drifted on the Kuroshio, known commonly as the "Black Stream" or "Japanese Current." This strong surface current flows from Luzon in the Philippines to the south and southeast coast of Japan, where it brings a warming effect. A great migration to Japan began as early as 20,000 years ago, and another wave occurred 5,000 years ago. One race that came from India was pygmy-like. There were simultaneous migrations from the north across the Bering Currents, with people landing on the coast facing the Sea of Japan. Although comprised of many different races, these aborigines of the Jomon period (12,000-300/200 B.C.) were collectively called Zoshiki.

Between 200 and 100 B.C. an ancient Persian race drifted on the Black Streams and landed on various Pacific coast beaches, a migration initiated by the conquest of Alexander the Great, King of Macedonia, in 334 B.C. Formerly, these immigrants to Japan had lived in parts of Ancient Persia and followed the beliefs of Zoroaster, which required good deeds by men against an evil spirit. They built the shrine in Gion and may have been the same people called Sumerians (from Sumer, or ancient Mesopotamia). When Greek troops invaded Achaemenes in Persia, they enslaved these people and sent them to frontiers to develop Greek colonies reaching as far as Malaysia. These Persian slaves were to be sent to Vietnam and to Yunnan in southern China, but many fled by drifting on rafts on the Black Current to Japan. The names of the places they landed could be easily identified because they started with the letter "A:" Akashi, Awaji, Awa, etc., (from *aqua*, water).

The migration of these people was not systematic: small groups landed at random, forming autonomous groups which developed into a loose confederation of villages. They were a higher civilization than the indigenous Zoshiki, and taught the Zoshiki how to grow rice and other grains, how to fish and use salt. Bell-shaped bronze vessels of the Yayoi period were probably part of their culture; their swords were made from shells and they brought family crests from their motherland. Most Japanese crests originated from Persia and Babylonia (Iran and Iraq). These people's religion, Zoroastrianism, was called *Gi* in Japan. In Kyoto their shrine was "Gion." The shrines of Gi, called *Gu* or *Miya* were painted red, their ethnic color. The Tsurugaoka Hachiman

Gu, mentioned in Chapter Two, was their shrine in Kamakura. When they died their bodies were cremated.

This ancient sea race from Persia was contemptuously called Ya or Hachi by the Chinese when the Chinese T'ang conquered Japan in the 7th Century A.D. According to Yagiri, these Persians were sent to the Bahan area of Malaysia as slaves of Alexander's troops and were thus called Bahan. The Greek pronunciation is Yabahn, which became corrupted into the word Japan in English and German, Japon in French. I searched the name Bahan on the current map of Malaysia, but found only the Pahang River.

Around the 7th Century A.D., the Sassanian Dynasty in Persia fell during the Mohammedan era, causing non-Moslems to flee, some as far as Japan. The last people to migrate to Japan from that area came in 1132 A.D. and were known as Heike or Pei. In the broader sense, they were the same as Ya people, but the new Heike people were handsome and mixed with Western blood from the crusades. The Heike came ashore at Kumanoura on the Kii Peninsula, were promoted to court nobles, and became related to the imperial family. They peaked with supreme power in the 1160's. According to Yagiri, descendants of the Ya, (who were enslaved by the T'ang Chinese in the 8th Century), surprisingly make up 45% of Japan's current population, and are the largest race in the country.

The Bering Current from the north cuts across the Sea of Japan and hits the Noto Peninsula of Honshu, where it splits in two directions, one toward Izumo, one of the oldest settlements in Japan, the other toward the Akita/Iwate area. The people from the north who landed on the beaches of the Sea of Japan were nomads, a Mongoloid race from the Primosky areas of Russia and from the Korean Peninsula. They brought a tiny horse with them, the first horse on the Japanese islands. These people were the same race as the Yuan in China, pronounced Gen in Japan. They were referred to as Gen Ji or Minamoto ("original people") and were contemptuously called Yottsu (four) by the T'ang Chinese rulers of the 8th Century, who referred to the four limbs of the horses they brought. The Chinese were Buddhist vegetarians who despised this meat-eating race. Their migration came about 100 B.C. In 94 B.C., Emperor Sujin was supposedly the first emperor from that nomadic race to accede the throne. The nomadic people of Koguryo and Silla in Korea were of the same origin as the Yottsu.

These nomads made contact with the Ya and Zoshiki people as they penetrated inland. Skirmishes took place, but the newcomers were stronger, because they had horses and copper weapons. In the 70's A.D. a peace treaty was marked by the marriage of the Emperor Keiko, grandson of Sujin, to the princess of the Ya people. It was a good alliance because the Ya produced crops while the Yottsu were good horse soldiers who hunted game.

Sometimes the ties between races were unusual. This same alliance between the northern and southern races was revived a thousand years later. The tomb mentioned in Chapter Two, that of Yoritomo Minamoto, located behind my house in Kamakura, belongs to the head of this Yottsu nomadic race. Minamoto's marriage to Masako from the Hojo family of the Ya race was also a good union, because the Hojo family had plenty of gold to finance war, while the Minamoto family (Gen Ji) were good soldiers to fight it. As already indicated, Minamoto defeated the Heike and established the Bakufu government in Kamakura, and when Yoritomo died, his wife, Masako, sent her Hojo troops to Kyoto to defeat the imperial army in 1221. She exiled the imperial families and confiscated their land in revenge against the Fujiwara family (Japanese name of T'ang China conquerors) and the imperial court who had enslaved her Ya race in the 8th Century A.D. According to Yagiri's theory of the Japanese surname, my family belonged to the Ya race. It was the heritage of this race that made my father join the navy. It was an enlightening revelation for me to discover my family's strange historical tie to Japan's true history.

The beliefs of the nomadic Yottsu were called Hakusan Shinko (White Mountain Belief), and the people worshipped mountains. The Yottsu shrine was made of plain wood, and their ethnic color was white. They buried their dead. This same nomadic people from Koguryo and Silla came down the Korean Peninsula and colonized the Japanese islands between the 2nd and 4th centuries A.D. The descendants of these people make up between 22 and 23% of Japan's population today.

The Kudara (Paekche) people in Korea inhabited a small country originally named Shinkan and were of a different race from the people of Silla and Koguryo. Kudara expanded in 360 A.D., and by 362, occupied all of South Korea except Silla. They established their dynasty in Nara, and by the beginning of the 7th Century A.D., dominated the major western areas of Japan. With iron swords they conquered and enslaved the Yottsu, Ya and Zoshiki people, using the Ya and Zoshiki to produce food and the Yottsu as slave soldiers. They established a central government with local offices and organized their own political system.

In 663 A.D., the Kudara dynasty in Japan sent 27,000 slave soldier troops back to their motherland in Korea to protect that country from invasion by the allied forces of the T'ang Chinese and Silla. They were defeated in the battle of Hakusuki no E and were captured by the T'ang Chinese. The Kudara dynasty collapsed with that defeat. Though the Kudara people were enslaved at first by the T'ang Chinese, their success in putting down internal rebellions for the T'ang eventually brought them freedom and acceptance into the court of nobles. The Emperor Kammu of Kudara blood took power in 781 A.D. and continued the lineage for at least five generations. Their religion was Buddhism and their ethnic color was yellow.

With their iron weapons, the T'ang Chinese, the highest civilization in Asia, were unrivaled in war. According to Yagiri, the T'ang occupied Japan in 664 A.D. and enslaved all previous inhabitants. A T'ang man was probably enthroned in the beginning, but later maintained power firmly behind the emperor as the Fujiwara family. Together with the Kudara, the Fujiwara were the masters of Japan for a long time. The T'ang comprised 5% of the population. Combined with another 5% of Kudara blood, Japan was ruled by 10% of the population. This ruling race was called Tou or Fuji-wara. They were Buddhists and their ethnic color was black.

At the beginning of the 10th Century A.D., a tribe called Khitan founded the Liao dynasty in north China, following the fall of T'ang. They sailed across the Sea of Japan on the Bering Current, and landed in Japan. The T'ang nobles of the court hated the enemy Khitan who had ruined them in China. Only a few young, good-looking girls of the Khitan were accommodated at Court, while the rest were enslaved or killed. Some of these people from Khitan fled into the mountains and joined with the Sanka, a mixture of Ya and Yottsu people, who, refusing to surrender to the Kudara or T'ang, hid in the mountains. The enslaved people from Khitan were sent to undeveloped lands in the east and were later driven further north.

In an effort to rescue their enslaved countrymen, the Liao dynasty sent troops to Japan. Though successful at first, they were forced to give up due to domestic strife. These incidents were recorded in the government history as *Jouhei-Tengyo no Ran* (rebellions in the eastern area, 935-939 A.D. and in the western area in 939-941 A.D.). The invasion of the Khitan in 1019 A.D. was recorded as *Toui no Nyuko*.

The Tenjin beliefs were peculiar to the Khitan. The Khitan (also sometimes called Kitsu), were highly intelligent, survived under severe circumstances, and accounted for about 20% of Japan's population. Other races arrived in Japan, such as the people in Sakai near Osaka, who were believed to be from the Philippines. Possible links to a Jewish migration to Japan also exist.

The four major races which accounted for 98% of Japan's population and played a major role in her history were: Gen, Pei, Tou and Kitsu. Under the feudal system when there were more than 300 hans, Japan was like 300 separate countries. Under the rule of each daimyo, however, the people within a han were seldom of one race. The racial components within each han varied, but most often the ruling race was in the minority within each han.

Normally, the concept of a nation is a land with one currency. Traditionally, Japan had two currencies, gold in the east and silver in the west. But the west was the country of the imperial court, while the east was considered to be the country of barbarians.

Although the government kept the Japanese people unaware of their true multi-ethnic history, there were efforts by some to find the truth, but attempts were always obstructed by the government. A Mr. Kozo Abe wrote a book titled *History of Slaves in Japan*, published at the beginning of the Showa era (Emperor Hirohito 1926-1989), which clarified the slavery system in Japan. The author was arrested by the police and died in prison.

In his bibliography, Kozo Abe listed some 700 books on the subject. When Tomeo Yagiri tried to obtain these books for his own research, he was surprised to find they were unavailable; vast volumes of data on the evolution of Japanese culture had been confiscated by the government and destroyed.

This same kind of government pressure exists today. In the past decade or more, Yagiri has been boycotted by the Japanese media, for what reason remaining a mystery. Yagiri was forced to start his own publishing company to continue his work, since the Japanese government's policy was to hide the truth, maintaining its power by making the people believe the fiction they created.

In the northern district of Japan, there is a famous festival called *Nebuta*. Floats with the faces of the samurai are brought into the streets for the celebration. Part of this ritual is when crowds stomp their feet, dramatizing the time when the imperial court troops killed rebellious Japanese who refused to become slaves. The rebels were thrown into a deep hole, while slaves were forced to stomp the ground solidly so that none of the dead souls of the rebels would come back from *Ne no Kuni* (country of the dead). Today, 90% of the people participating in this ceremony are probably descendants of the rebels rather than of the Chinese and Korean soldiers who put down the rebellion for the imperial court. The name *Nebuta* means "to put the cover on the country of death." With the strong Japanese belief in the souls of their ancestors, how ironic and sad that these descendants unknowingly mock the sacrifice of their ancestors at this festival.

The Sanka people, remember, were those of mixed Ya and Yottsu blood who fled into the mountains between the 6th and 8th centuries A.D. when the Chinese and Koreans ruled Japan. Khitan people later joined with the Sanka when they were oppressed by the T'ang invaders. The Sanka kept their pure blood, maintaining refuge in the mountains for a thousand years. The Sanka kept to themselves with strict precepts, so much so that in the 19th century Meiji census, the government was surprised to learn there were so many Sanka among the population. The Meiji government feared retribution from the Sanka because the imperial court was made up of the Chinese and Korean descendants of T'ang and Kudara who had driven the Sankas' ancestors into the mountains in the first place. The Sanka had preserved their culture and were well aware of Japan's true history, but they kept a low profile, living quietly for fear of being massacred. For an excuse to hunt them down and kill them, the Meiji government labelled them criminals; still many survived. The Sanka struggle was not unlike that of the native North American Indians, though their true history is unknown to the Japanese public.

The brief history described in this chapter, showing higher civilizations conquering weaker races and enslaving them, portrays the natural course of mankind, with the fall of various races ensuing because of being in the wrong place at the wrong time. The need to expand, the curiosity to explore, or the fear of enslavement or extermination drove people to new lands where encounters with other races brought conflict. Westerners reading this account will have no problem accepting the plausibility of its truth. Japanese people, however, hold firm to their myths, and would even be angry with the view that the imperial family's blood is Chinese or Korean. A multi-racial view was most inconvenient for the Japanese establishment who wanted to invade Korea and China in the late 1800s and early 1900s, and the Meiji ideology has carried over to today's Japanese scholars. Many disagree with facts, even when documented by archaeological specimens. What excuse does the Japanese government have today for continuing to capture the minds of its people with such a false history?

Although the Japanese have no history of resistance to human rights, the miserable story of our enslavement will tell of its importance. If the true history of Japan were revealed, the Japanese would no longer be the people of the gods, but simply human beings. A nation's values must emanate from individual attitudes, and it is essential that every individual have the chance to discover the truth for himself.

Chapter Six

Origin of the Japanese Motherland

Japanese history established by government scholars is taught in high schools throughout Japan. According to this source, primeval man lived on the land we know as Japan in the Old Stone Age as far back as hundreds of thousands of years. Jomon man is considered to be the direct ancestor of today's Japanese population. The Jomon Age (12,000 B.C. to the 3rd/2nd century B.C.) was symbolized by Jomon ware, straw rope-patterned pottery. The Proto-Japanese theory states that the current Japanese race is made up of a blood mixed from a variety of neighboring countries.

Japanese is classified among the Altai languages, which includes Turkish and Mongolian, but it also contains elements of Austronesian. The standard reference book suggests that the Japanese language originates from Dravidian. During the Yayoi Age (3rd/2nd century B.C.-3rd century A.D.), paddy rice farming started, bronze and iron instruments appeared, Yayoi style earthenware was produced, clothes were fabricated, small countries with local administrations were founded, and a hierarchy was born.

The first mention of ancient Japan is found in a geographic book of Han China, which states that a land of Wa existed far across the sea south of Lo-lang, Korea. Among the 100 odd countries comprising the land of Wa, some regularly paid tribute to the Han Dynasty at the beginning of the 1st century. A book of the later Han Dynasty in China (30-219 A.D.) states that the King of Wa no Na, one of the Wa countries, sent an envoy to China's capital, Luoyang, in 57 A.D. to pay tribute. In return, Emperor Kuang-wu-ti presented the envoy with a gold seal of kingship. In 1784, by chance, a peasant discovered this seal in his field in the Fukuoka Prefect of Kyushu and submitted his discovery to the Shogunate government, Tokugawa Bakufu in Edo, (now Tokyo). Ancient writings mention that in 107 A.D., King Suisho of Wa presented 160 slaves to Emperor An of China.

Gishi Wajin Den, contained in a volume of eastern barbarian histories recorded by China's Wei Kingdom, is the most famous report about ancient Japan's Wa people. Wei was one of China's Three Kingdoms: Wei, Shu and Wu (220-265 A.D.). According to the present Japanese high school text, Queen Himiko governed Yamatai and twenty-eight other countries of Wa. She lived in a palace, while her younger brother administered the country as regent. Other government officials were delegated authority to prosecute, tax and control the other countries. Society was marked by class strata with the queen at the top and slaves at the bottom. There were market places. The people wore no shoes. They ate cooked rice heaped on a food stand, and the art of tattooing was prevalent.

From 239 A.D., the queen often paid tribute to Wei via Lo-lang, Korea, in return for her title as pro-Wei Queen of Wa, and the articles that authorized her reign. These writings described how to get to the land of Wa from Lo-lang, Korea, but the directions are incomplete, opening the doors to a variety of theories about the precise location of Wa today. After hundreds of books have been written on this subject, the location still remains a mystery. Two major theories have evolved, one claiming Wa was in Kyushu, and the other in Yamato, the Kinki area of mainland Japan.

The location of the Wa Dynasty is important to determine when the Yamato Dynasty unified the major regions of Japan. If unification occurred in Kyushu, it didn't happen in the 3rd century. If it occurred in Yamato, it was well underway by the beginning of the 3rd century. By the middle of the 4th century, it is certain to have happened. It is generally admitted that the imperial court of the Yamato Dynasty was firmly established, and controlled territories from Kyushu to the Chubu area of Honshu with its central government. The king of the Yamato Dynasty was called *Ookimi* (Great King), then *Sumera Mikoto* or *Tenno* (emperor), showing the country's progress toward integration. In the 5th century, hereditary reign was strengthened with further progress of integration. The following traditions contained in *Kojiki* and *Nihon Shoki* reflect its process: the conquest of the east by Emperor Jimmu; the subjugation of *Kumaso* (barbarians in Kyushu) and Ezo (barbarians in the northeast of Honshu) by Prince Takeru Yamato; the dispatch of four regional generals at the time of the Emperor Sujin: the conquest of the three *Kan* (ancient Korean countries), Mahan, Chinhan and Pyonghan, by Queen Jingu.

The current Japanese government maintains that only one imperial dynasty existed then and now. By that standard, any reference to the

Wa Dynasty is synonymous with the Yamato Dynasty, and the timing of this Yamato unification depends merely on the place that it happened. This narrow viewpoint loses ground, as will be seen in later chapters, with historical documentation of at least two dynasties, one in Yamato and one in Kyushu.

Historian Yasuko Kobayashi writes in her book *Who Was Prince Shotoku*? that the honorific posthumous title of Tenno was first given in Japan to the Emperor Temmu (673-686 A.D.) following the historical fact that T'ang China's Emperor Kaotsung had used the title in 674 for the first time. Note that the Emperor Temmu's reign corresponds to the period shortly after the T'ang Chinese occupation of Japan in 664, according to Yagiri's view.

The son of Emperor Keiko of the nomad race referred to in Chapter Five, Prince Takeru Yamato took his army on an expedition to subjugate barbarians throughout Japan. After many successful missions, the prince was poisoned traveling homeward. According to a popular myth, after his death, his soul transformed into a swan and flew back to his home. Though this beautiful and tragic tale is loved by the Japanese, harsh reality, according to Yagiri, indicates that all Emperor Keiko's sons were killed by the Chinese, who gradually penetrated Japan and built strongholds in the Okayama area of Honshu during the 1st and 2nd centuries. This Chinese dynasty was called the *Nakatsu Kuni* or *Kibi* Dynasty. The Chinese were able to eventually subdue and enslave Emperor Keiko's people, a conquest made easier by the use of iron weapons supplied by the Chinese motherland.

Since there were no Japanese forces available for an invasion of Korea, the tale of *San Kan Seibatsu* (*Conquest of the Three Korean Nations*) must be fictitious. Actually, the three Kan (*Korean Nations*) migrated to Japan, established colonies and eventually subjugated the Yottsu and Ya peoples. This view seriously differs from the official Meiji ideology, which follows the nationalistic Meiji position that a powerful central government was developed by a purely Japanese Yamato Dynasty in Nara. In fact, the Japanese archipelago was a frontier for Chinese and Korean expansion.

What was the political evolution in Korea, the nearest foreign country to Japan, and what was its association with ancient Japan? During the 4th century, political integration was in progress. The Koguryo people, who came from the southern part of Manchuria, rid Lo-lang of Chinese rule in 313, and ruled northern Korea. Mahan expanded to Paekche in the southwest, Chinhan developed Silla in the southeast, and Pyonhan became Kaya (Kara or Mimana in Japanese) between Paekche and Silla, by the middle of the 4th century. They fought each other to hold hegemony in the Korean peninsula.

To resist the pressure of Koguryo, Paekche had diplomatic relations with Wa. The inscription on the blade of a special sword with seven branches preserved in the Isonokami Shrine (Yamato area) reads that the sword made in 394 was the present from the king of Paekche to the king of Wa.

At the end of the 4th century, Wa troops invaded Korea and fought with Koguryo. The inscription on the stone tablet dedicated to King Kwanggaet'o of Koguryo in 414 at T'ung-gu says: "In 391, Wa crossed the sea and defeated Paekche and Silla, making them subjects." The inscription tells of King Kwanggaet'o's violent wars with Wa thereafter and his eventual victory in 404. Some ancient accounts differ from the latest studies, particularly those of Korean residents in Japan and North Korean scholars. For example, one view claims that to justify Japan's aggression prior to World War II, the military altered certain letters of inscription. An alternate interpretation of the inscription claims that Wa was not the Yamato Dynasty in Japan, but a branch of Korea occupying Japan.

According to the Meiji ideology, beyond a shadow of doubt, the Wa troops appearing in the inscription dedicated to King Kwanggaet'o are the expeditionary forces of the Yamato Dynasty. This interpretation remains unchanged to this day. Though Soukichi Tsuda's view denying the truth of the imperial myths of *Nihon Shoki* and *Koji Ki* has become popular, the inscription dedicated to King Kwanggaet'o is still considered the best evidence to prove, apart from myth, that the Yamato Dynasty was the unifying central power over Kyushu and the major regions on Honshu. The text reference introduces divergent views but suggests that by the middle of the 4th century, an independent country was formed of a single Japanese race governed by the Yamato Dynasty. This implies that Yamato is the origin of the current imperial household, and has been the only sovereign in Japan since the age of Wa. This has become accepted belief, despite the uncertainty of the location of the Wa country in the 3rd century. In postwar Japan, denial of the myths has actually worked to enhance the Meiji ideology.

A few historians are challenging the above view. Takehiko Furuta in his book *Reviving Himika, When Japan Was Initiated* (Shinshindo Shuppan Kabushiki Kaisha 1988), claims the Wa troops were of the Kyushu dynasty, apart from the Yamato dynasty, and that several different dynasties existed in various locations. Furuta also claims the Wa had a branch in Kaya. His theories may well undermine current historical views, and so far, they have been ignored by the Japanese academia.

Tomeo Yagiri believes that Korean power was dominant in Japan from the death of Prince Takeru Yamato, son of the Emperor Keiko, to the Chinese invasion in the 7th century. The Korean peoples of Paekche, Silla and Koguryo colonized Japan and enslaved the Yottsu and Ya aborigines. It is difficult to conceive how any Japanese force of that period could have expelled these Korean invaders, unless the Wa of Kyushu used their alliance with the Chinese court to receive military aid, which could have included iron weapons proven to be available among the Chinese powers occupying certain areas of the Kyushu and Okayama areas of Honshu. It seems the only logical explanation for Wa's early defeat of the three Kans, as inscribed on these historical tablets. Kaya may well have been a country over a southern area of the Korean peninsula and the northern area of the Kyushu of Japan, with the Japanese side called Wa. In this case, the Korean side should have been the suzeraine. Paekche soon took the lead in the competition for hegemony and should have been able to maintain its control of Wa. It seems certain that the soldiers of Wa who fought in Korea were all enslaved Japanese aborigines.

Between 413 and 502 A.D., articles about Wa appeared twelve times in Chinese history books of the Tsin, Song, Nan-Tsi, and Nan-Liang Dynasties, stating that five hereditary kings of Wa paid tribute thirteen times to the Chinese court. Though there are some historians who disagree, most Japanese scholars have compared the names of Japanese kings in Chinese records (San, Chin, Sei, Ko and Bu) to Japanese records, and assert those names correspond to Emperors Oujin (or Nintoku), Nintoku (or Richu or Hanzei), Ingyo, Anko and Yuryaku. The purpose of Wa's tributes to the Chinese court was to obtain title to resist Koguryo's invasion, to authorize Wa's power to govern domestically, and to aggressively digest advanced cultures of the continent. In the letter King Bu submitted to Chinese Emperor Shun-ti (477-478), he boasted that he and his ancestors conquered many countries to build a big country. Despite some exaggeration, progress in the unification of the Yamato Dynasty is indicated.

Furuta in his *New History of Ancient Japan* (Kabushiki Kaisha Shinsendo 1991), insists that the five kings were of the Wa dynasty in Kyushu, not of Yamato. Japanese academic scholars stick to their theory, despite the fact that when they compare the names recorded in *Nihon Shoki* and *Koji Ki*, which record history from the Yamato perspective, the names don't match up.

Was the purpose of paying tribute to the Chinese court to obtain a title? It is doubtful a mere title would have been enough to keep Koguryo from invading the south. The procurement of iron weapons from the Chinese was probably Wa's predominant motive to pay these tributes.

During the 5th and 6th centuries, China and Korea introduced new technologies to material civilization, but on the spiritual level, they brought with them Chinese characters for communication, and Confucianism and Buddhism as religious practices. The new technology and culture brought by Chinese and Korean immigrants stimulated the development of politics, the economy, and the overall civilization of Japan. For example, the immigrants brought the technology needed to build huge tombs for emperors and nobles, which preserved artifacts such as saddles, stirrups, armor, gold and silver jewelry, tools, agricultural implements and iron weapons, which serve to trace this history.

These immigrations from the continent to Japan took place in three waves, mainly from Korea:

1. 5th century—ruin of the Lo-lang Commandery and the invasion of Wa troops.
2. Latter half of the 5th century to the beginning of the 6th Century —mainly Paekche, because of strong pressure from Koguryo and Silla.
3. Latter half of the 7th century—ruin of Paekche and Koguryo.

In ancient Japan, voluntary immigrants adoring the virtues of the emperor were called "naturalized citizens," while the current term *toraijin* (immigrants) includes political refugees and protected immigrants with specific skills; also the term *toraijin* is dedicated with nuances that mean more than simply "immigrants." The context is that there was the Japanese race which, though made up of many races, became one race over 5,000 years. This Japanese race accepted Koreans as immigrants including those who "adored the emperor." These immigrants contributed much to Japan's progress by bringing advanced technology, which included the manufacturing of earthenware and iron, weaving, civil engineering, silk worm raising, irrigation, etc.

At the time *Nihon Shoki* was written in 720 A.D. following the Chinese domination, editors could afford to take a high posture towards the Koreans, particularly the Paekche, who were second only to the Chinese masters when the *Nihon Shoki* was written. Before then, Koreans masters dominated Japan. The Koreans were more than just "immigrants," but the Japanese will never admit it.

A divergent theory among Japanese scholars is mentioned in the supplementary history reference book used in Japanese high schools: it theorizes that in the 4th century, a nomadic race of the current imperial household, probably from the dynasty of the 15th Emperor Oujin, came from the north of China to northern Kyushu, to make the first foundation of Japan. In the 5th century, a second foundation was made in the Kinki area (current term which includes the Yamato area). Popular after World War II, this theory is considered a branch of the immigration theory from China and Korea, and ample archaeological artifacts from the 5th century support it.

The use of Chinese characters in Japan was believed to have been initiated by 5th century immigrants. The sovereign letter of the King of Wa sent to the Chinese emperor in 478 was written in Chinese characters. At the beginning of the 6th century, Korean scholars such as Achiki introduced Confucianism to Japan, and also in the 6th century, Paekche King Song-myong-wang presented Emperor Kimmei with a statue of Buddha and a sacred book.

Current teachings would have us believe that this gracious gift provided a smooth acceptance of Buddhist teachings in Japan. On the contrary, there was much resistance and dispute from court nobles who believed in Persian or nomadic gods. The Yottsu were considered subhumans by the Paekche, because unlike the vegetarian Buddhists, they ate meat. The Paekche applied much pressure to heathens, but resistance to Buddhism made the ruling Chinese and Paekche develop a special sect to include them by distinguishing between the sacred "light" in the east and the sacred "land" in the west. Many historical conflicts arose out of this discrimination, which lasted until the Meiji Restoration in 1868.

During the 5th and 6th centuries in Japan, to govern the people, two institutions were initiated. *Shi-Sei* stood for the rank and order of the ruling class above all others, while *Be no Tami* defined class distinctions among people according to occupation. *Shi* means *Uji*, families with *Uji Gami*, their own gods. The *Uji* made up most of the household nobility of the imperial court of the Yamato Dynasty, most of whom were probably Paekche.

The head of these *Uji* families was given a *Kabane*, in accordance with rank. In Chinese-style pronunciation, *Kabane* is referred to as *Sei*. The highest ranking ministers' *Kabane* were *Oo-omi* or *Oo-Muraji*. *Be no Tami*, on the other hand, means a group of people classified by occupation. The groups of different occupations belonged to an *Uji*. The people of a Be are all engaged in the same occupation. The *Nuhi* are at the bottom, slaves forced to do physical labor.

If the *Uji* are studied more carefully, it will be discovered that all of this group were Korean, mainly Paekche. Also, a more precise study of *Be no Tami* will reveal the enslavement of the Yottsu and Ya, and document the contention that Japan is a multi-racial state.

The Koguryo moved southward again in the latter half of the 5th century. Accordingly, Paekche and Silla pressed Kaya harder, jeopardizing Japan's interests. In 512, Japan was forced to cede four states of Kaya in the Korean peninsula to Paekche. Japan prepared 60,000 troops to send to Kaya to protect her interests, but could not, because her attention was divided by a two-year rebellion in Kyushu which weakened her. In 532, Silla invaded the eastern states of Kaya. Japan formed an alliance with Paekche, but could not resist against the strength of Silla, which eventually took over Kaya in 562.

Appointed regent by Empress Suiko in 593, Prince Shotoku made remarkable achievements in politics. He set twelve ranks for government officials, enacted the first constitution, adopted a calendar, edited history books (which were unfortunately burned in 645), promoted Buddhism, and established diplomatic relations with Sui China. Prince Shotoku was one of Japan's most influential rulers. His concept of Wa, order and harmony (not to be confused with Wa country mentioned through this chapter), is proclaimed in the constitution and still influences modern Japan today.

Right after Prince Shotoku's death came the reform of Taika in 645. In a coup d'etat, the Soga family was ruined when their family head and arbitrator, Iruka Soga, was assassinated by Prince Naka no Ooe and his accomplice Kamatari Nakatomi. A new government was formed under Emperor Kotoku. Among the new policies and measures was the promulgation of the Rescript Reform, consisting of four articles which set fundamental political policies. First, the emperor and his government took control of all land; second, the government was centralized under one system; third, census registers were formed; fourth, a new taxation system was fixed. The reform restored the emperor's power and unified Japan as a nation.

The Taika reform was the example used for the Meiji Reformation, in which the purpose of the coup d'etat was twofold: to restore the emperor's power to rule the people directly by overthrowing Soga's despotic politics, and to establish the emperor institution strongly enough to integrate the people domestically and internationally by the emperor's deification. As Yagiri and Furuta claim, there should have been several independent dynasties of different races in various regions. Most had been unified by the Yamato dynasty of the Paekche by the middle of the 7th century, yet even after subjugation by force, there should have been strong resistance among the people. On the Korean peninsula, Silla allied with T'ang China to resist invasion by the Paekche-Kogu*ryo* alliance. Since the Soga family came from Silla, the coup d'etat can be construed as an international plot whereby pro-Paekche forces overturned Japan's pro-Silla government. There is the opinion that the history of the Reform was no more than another fiction of the *Nihon Shoki*, a myth to convince the people of an admirable history (Yagiri, *Study of The 'Ama' Dynasty in Ancient Japan*). Despite lack of confirmation, official government history gives the impression to readers of current textbooks that its analysis and conclusion is decisive.

Chapter Seven

Scholarly vs Political View of History

Dr. Hitoshi Takeuchi, professor emeritus of Tokyo University and internationally renowned geophysicist, wrote about the origin of the Japanese in his book *The Japanese Came From The Continent of Mu*. Takeuchi thinks there were three major migratory waves of evolution on the Asian continent, and that newer migrants of a higher civilization pushed older inhabitants to the north and south.

The first wave took place about 20,000 years ago, when two races, one from the north and another from the south, landed in Japan. Old mongoloids of an Indian/Manchurian type race with "B" blood types (according to the six types grouped worldwide by Ottenberg in 1825) came down narrow land bridges that connected the Russian Primorsky area with mainland Honshu. At that time, the glacial period, the water level was some 100 meters lower than today's. Consequently, the Mamiya (Tatar) and Soya Straits were closed by narrow land bridges, a fact which is supported by archaeological evidence. At about the same time, other old mongoloids of the Pacific/American type race drifted on the Kuroshio (Black) Current and landed on the Pacific coast. They had "O" type blood.

The old mongoloids were pushed north and southward by the new mongoloid race. The "B type blood mongoloids are identified today as the Ainu in Hokkaido, and those with "O" type blood are now identified as Okinawaians.

The second wave of big migrations took place about 5,000 years ago. Earlier, the old mongoloid race with "B" type blood had moved from the west to Manchuria, the northeastern area of China. At that time, two races were living in mainland China. One was the Pacific/

American race with "O" type blood, and another was the Konan (Hunan—Chinese areas south of the Yanagzi River) race with "A" type blood. The old mongoloids with "B" type blood, the Han people, went down the mainland and mixed with the Pacific/American type race, and as a result, a semi-new mongoloid of the South Asian/African type race with "O" type blood was first born.

The semi-new mongoloids went down the mainland of China and spread over most of the areas of the Pacific and Indian oceans, arriving at the southwestern coast of Japan as early as 10,000 years ago. Later, they finally became the new mongoloids of the South Asian/African type, and were the migrants of the second wave that took place about 5,000 years ago.

The Konan type race, pressed down by the new people from the north, moved east and west. Those who moved west became the minority race who lived in southern China, Burma, Tibet and Nepal. The people who moved east reached as far as northern Kyushu via South Korea. They were the new mongoloids. All the races mentioned above are collectively called Jomon people. In Japan the Jomon period is approximately defined as follows:

Pre-Jomon period:	4,000 - 3,000 B.C.
Early-Jomon period:	10,000 - 4,000 "
Middle-Jomon period:	3,000 - 2,000 "
Latter-Jomon period:	2,000 - 1,000 "
Last-Jomon period:	1,000 - 1,300 "
Yayoi period:	1,300 B.C. - 300 A.D.

"Jomon" means straw rope pattern of earthenware. The oldest earthenware is considered to have been produced in west Asia in 8,000 B.C., but actually the oldest Jomon earthenware dates back past 10,000 B.C.; recently older ware of 12,000 B.C. was found in the southern Kanto area, making Jomon earthenware the oldest in the world.

The migratory third wave was of Konan people with "A" type blood, who landed at the northern Kyushu area around the time of the birth of Jesus. These people brought to Japan the Yayoi culture, featuring metal products and rice paddy farming. The invasion of Konan people drove the Indian/Manchurian type mongoloids with "B" type blood as well as the South/Asian/African type mongoloids with "O" type blood to northern and southern Japan.

Takeuchi examines current local distribution of blood types in Japan, noting that "A" type blood is found most frequently in western Japan, such as in the northeastern half of Kyushu Island; in Shikoku Island (except Kagawa Prefecture); in Shimane Prefecture (formerly

Izumo-no-kuni) of mainland Honshu, and with less frequency the farther one goes east. "B" type is found most frequently in the northeastern area, but decreases as one goes west. The distribution of "O" type blood lacks the clear delineation marked by "A" and "B" types, but is generally found in Pacific coastal areas such as Chiba, Iwate and Aomori Prefectures.

In his book, Takeuchi submits proof to corroborate his thesis—language, myth, tradition, distribution of particular virus antibodies, genes and fingerprints. His scientific views do not deny Yagiri's theory. If migrations of various races happened as Takeuchi describes, then ancient Persians who made their way to Japan via southern China, Vietnam, Burma, or Malaysia on the Black Current between 200-100 B.C., could have become absorbed with the people with "O" type blood, and thus become unidentifiable. Similarly, the Yottsu people who migrated (with horses) from the Primorsky areas of Russia around 100 B.C. may be unidentifiable from other people with "B" type blood who migrated earlier.

These migrations from across the southern seas to the Pacific coasts, and across the Sea of Japan to the northern coast, continued randomly, with an occasional large wave, such as the Heike people who came to Japan on the Kii Peninsula in 1132. Yagiri says that in the late 15th century a certain priest, head of a temple, noted in his diary the presence of a camp at Sanjo Horikawa near Kyoto, where foreigners from the Middle East, India and Southeast Asia were temporarily accommodated, to remain until they learned the language and customs of their new homeland, when they were assigned to other temples or camps. Those who did not become priests were given the surname Taira, a known surname of the new Heike family. From the diary it is now known that Taira was the surname given to all foreigners from the southeast except those who became priests. The diary also tells us that migrants continued arriving from the southwest to the end of the 15th century, and that monsoon winds and ocean currents aided massive traffic between Japan and these areas.

Furuta, the historian we met in Chapter 6, is quoted by Takeuchi, regarding his views on the foundations of ancient Japan. Historian, high school teacher and bestselling author, Furuta was born in 1926. Since 1970, he has dedicated his life to the history of ancient Japan, stressing scientific method, reading old documents exactly as they are written without fixed ideas or arbitrary changes to the original text.

Furuta has done much to clarify the story of ancient Japan. However, his work has never been duly appreciated by governmental academy scholars, who tend to disregard him, probably because Furuta asserts that there were several different dynasties in ancient Japan in addition to the one which became the ancestor of the current imperial household, a theory in opposition to the governmental position of one dynasty existing throughout Japan's history having its origins in a single race.

Furuta's views are well expressed in his study of Izumo Fudoki in a book called *Revival of Himuka*. Izumo is the eastern half of the present-day Shimane Prefecture, where type "A" blood people are found most frequently, according to Takeuchi. (Himuka is Furuta's way of pronouncing the name of the Queen of Wa, which is generally pronounced Himiko); Fudoki were reports submitted to the emperor by all provinces regarding traditions, customs, geographies, productions, etc., in the year 713.

The *Izumo Fudoki* is written in Chinese classical style and begins with descriptions of geography. "The country lies generally with its head in the east and tail in the southwest, from the east toward the south. North of the palace is the sea. 139 ri and 109 ho to the east. (Ri and ho are units of measuring distance). 183 ri and 173 ho from south to north."

The above describes the location of Izumo quite exactly, taking the Kizuki palace as its center. Kizuki is the name of the palace where Ooanamochi no Mikoto, the main star of this story, resided. Furuta has considered Ooanamochi no Mikoto the sovereign of Izumo and the palace his royal court. This means that there was a previous dynasty before the one that requested the reports of provinces at the beginning of the 8th century.

This line of thought is intolerable to old nationalists as well as current pro-government scholars. Azumamaro Kada (1668 - 1736), a Shinto priest and classical scholar, was one of the first to declare that the imperial court was one only, located in Yamato. To suit this position, he deliberately altered *Izumo Fudoki* text to read, "The country lies generally with its head in the east and tail in the southwest. There are mountains in the east and the south. The west and the north face the sea. 139 ri and 109 ho from the east to the west..." Kada changed the word "palace" to "mountains" and made other significant changes as well, resulting in a geographical contradiction. There is no doubt that the older copy is the valid one; however, despite glaring errors, Kada's version remains the accepted one. Arbitrary changes in original texts to suit the view claiming there was only one dynasty in Yamato were made many times. The above is only one example. Therefore, one must be very careful when reading books on ancient history to know whether one is reading the true original or a falsely changed version.

Takeuchi summarizes Furuta's view of the Wa. Yamaichi Koku (Yamaichi is same as Wa, Koku means country) was the leader of a federation of 30 odd Wa countries which existed in south Korea and the northern Kyushu over the Korean and Tsushima Straits. During the 3rd century, the Wa raised rice and produced silk using silkworms. Men had tatoos on their faces and bodies; their clothes were a single cloth with a hole in the middle through which the head protruded. These descriptions indicate the Wa customs and culture were similar to those of South East Asia, which included the Hunan people. The record says the Wa are the same people as those of Hainan Island off China. In any case, they remind us of the Joumon people with "A" type blood. It is also interesting that some Wa countries existed in south Korea, as people there also have "A" type blood.

Archaeological evidence supports the above view. Recently, rice paddies of the Joumon age were discovered in northern Kyushu, corroborating descriptions of Wei records. In 1989, the remains of Yoshi-no-gari were discovered, not in Yamaichi Koku, where Queen Himuka resided, but in one of the Wa countries. The site contained inner and outer moats, the outer one surrounding the entire hill, stretching 2.5 kms. At least two 10 meters tall watchtowers were discovered in a space that spreads over 25 hectares and closely resembles descriptions of Wei records. Silk products and bronze arms, such as swords and pikes mentioned in Wei records, were also discovered in northern Kyushu areas.

Furuta believes Ama Kuni (the country of the Ama dynasty, the motherland mentioned in *Nihon Shoki* and *Koji Ki*), was on the islands of Iki and Tsushima, in the middle of the Tsushima Strait between Kyushu and South Korea. Amaterasu Oomikami, goddess of the sun and queen of Amakuni, took over Izumo-no-Kuni, once the suzerain of Amakuni, and ordered her grandson Ninigi no Mikoto to take northern Kyushu. Evolution took place during the early Yayoi period (300-100 B.C.). The original version of *Koji Ki* was edited in the middle of the Yayoi period (100 B.C.-100 A.D.) in Chikushi. Himuka was of the latter Yayoi period (100- 300 A.D.). But her enthronement as Queen of the Wa federation must have relevance to the story of the Queen Amaterasu, a Wa dynasty that lasted until its defeat in 663. The five kings of Wa appearing in the Song history book must be the kings of this Wa dynasty in Kyushu. It is inexplicable that no description of Mt. Fuji appears in *Koji Ki*, unless it was originally edited in the Kyushu area.

Furuta thinks Jimmu's conquest of the east, stated in the *Koji Ki*, is an historical fact, not myth. Jimmu was head of the local clan of the Wa dynasty in Kyushu. Seeing no hope for his people's future in Kyushu, Jimmu and his elder brother organized troops and started eastward. Crossing the Kanmon Straits, they proceeded along the cost to Seto Nai Kai (the inland sea between Kyushu island, the mainland Honshu and Shikoku island) up to Kibi country (now the Okayama area), where they stayed eight years, before taking the long way through the Naruto Straits south of Awaji island. They encountered no problem until landing in enemy territory at Kawachi (now Osaka), where Jimmu's elder brother was wounded and died. Jimmu gave up his plan to get to Yamato directly and took his people south, down along the Kii Peninsula to Kumano Ura, then north along the Kumano River. Invading through the Yamato basin, they killed priests and desecrated shrines and bell-shaped vessels.

According to Wei records, a federation of Ya or Yawata countries were in conflict with Wa countries; the Seto Nai Kai area was where the Ya powers, symbolized by bronze bell-shaped vessels, and Wa powers, symbolized by bronze sword and pike were mixed together. Jimmu's troops could go through without much trouble, with the help of those pro-Wa countries, and by avoiding Ya countries. (Kibi, where they stayed eight years, was a pro-Wa country of Chinese migrants who founded the Kibi dynasty).

Jimmu was enthroned in Yamato, where he founded a dynasty that was, however, confined to the Yamato area for the next nine generations, because enemy powers surrounding Yamato were strong. This explains why the history of this age is not mentioned in *Nihon Shoki* and *Koji Ki*. In the Yamato area many bronze bell-shaped vessels and their molds from the early and middle Yayoi period were discovered in abundance, but none was discovered from the latter Yayoi period (100-300 A.D.), corresponding to the period of the nine gener- ations. This archaeological evidence checks with the above historical evolution.

It is quite probable that the Ya and Yottsu made an alliance to resist the invasion of Wa troops. It is also clear from the imperial edict of Amaterasu Oomikami given to her grandson Ninigi. She said, "Ashihara-no Mizuho no Kuni is the land of my descendants to rule. Get down there and take it." Ashihara and Mizuho were two countries, the former a swamp field of reeds where nomads lived, the latter a Ya country with plenty of rice. Both were eventually defeated by the Wa or Yamato dynasty. Later the Paekche from Korea came to control the Kyushu and Wa in Yamato and established their own Yamato dynasty, enslaving all other races. Every piece comes together like a jigsaw puzzle.

The above historical evolution of the Wa dynasty in Kyushu and Jimmu's enthronement in Yamato clearly indicate the existence of other dynasties and other races, in other areas of Japan at that time. Nevertheless, the Academy of History keeps silent about Furuta's work; governmental scholars never admit the multiracial concept or the possibility of more than one dynasty of Japanese emperors. They will admit to a mix of races with foreign migrants, but only in so far as these other races were a minority gradually absorbed into the Japanese culture. The Japanese became a single race in the period of two thousand years by sharing a common language, customs and culture, through which the current imperial household was always at the center as the only imperial court.

Why must the government uphold this position? The answer is simple. Because it is only the link that binds the emperor with the Japanese people as their symbolic sovereign. No historical view which spoils the accepted government position will be adopted, even if it is true. In Japan political views have priority over truth.

The *Nihon Shoki*, consisting of 30 volumes, was originally edited in May, 720 by the Fujiwara family, the T'ang Chinese occupying Japan.* As a great revolt broke out in northern Japan about 60 years later, the Fujiwara enthroned the son of Niigasa Takano, a Paekche, as the emperor Kammu, and the Fujiwara took refuge in the Okayama area, after instructing Kammu to subjugate the rebels. Free to write their own history, the emperor Kammu and his Paekche nobles burned all the old history books, including the *Nihon Shoki*, which they rewrote to glorify the Paekche. The rebellion was subjugated by General Tamuramaro Sakanoue, when the ringleader Aterui surrendered in 802.

The Fujiwara family came back to the imperial court again as peace was restored, burned the Paekche version of the *Nihon Shoki* when the Emperor Saga began his reign, and hired scholars to write a third version of *Nihon Shoki* in 833. However, this is not the current version, as a fourth version was written by the new Heike family, claiming that they were the founders of Japan. When the Heike were defeated by the Genji, a *Nihon Shoki* copy was obtained by Kagetoki Kajiwara and submitted to Masako Hojo, the wife of Yoritomo Minamoto, who had a fifth version of the *Nihon Shoki* rewritten in favor of her Ya race, after she defeated the imperial household. This version was burned when the Genko (invasion of the Gen) took place in the late 13th century.

According to Yagiri, the Hojo family treated the Genji with cruelty, destroying their major clans and driving the survivors into mountain camps. The Hojo were Ya, and the Genji Yottsu, related ethnically and racially to the Yuan (Mongol) dynasty of China. Yagiri believes one of the main motivations of the Yuan invasion of Japan was to rescue the surviving Genji. At any rate, the Hojo destroyed the fifth version of the *Nihon Shoki* out of fear it would be used against them.

This evolution of the *Nihon Shoki* is an example of history being written and rewritten by the victor in a battle for power. At the begin-

*Other historians claim that the Fujiwara's heritage should not be considered "Chinese" in that their migration to the Japanese archipelago took place over several centuries.

ning of the Showa era, (1926), the *Nihon Shoki*, which was supposed to have been destroyed completely, suddenly emerged, re-edited by Katsumi Kuroita, an imperialistic historian, and became one of the bestsellers during the decades of ultra-nationalism. Currently Kuroita's version is believed to be authentic and any other histories which do not conform with this *Nihon Shoki* have been altered to fit. Governmental scholars have authorized this new *Nihon Shoki*. Where did Kuroita find it?

He states in the preface of his first edition of the book that he used the work of Kenrin Matsushita, which was published by wood block printing in 1673, as the original text. He also considered Nobutomo Ban's work a useful reference. Later, prior to the publication of a second edition, Kuroita obtained *Ruiju Kokushi, (Collection of Histories)* edited in 1738 by Yoshimune Tokugawa, the 8th shogun, as a further reference. Kuroita's final version, published in 1934, based on the writings of Emperor Gosai-in (1655-1662), is the version used today.

Kenrin Matsushita's book was probably a reproduction of the third version salvaged from court nobles. Gosai-in's works are important, considered authentic and are available.

Tsunamune Date, a powerful daimyo family in the Sendai area, was a relative of Gosai-in on his mother's side. Once, when the financial situation of the imperial court was tight, the emperor sent a court noble to Tsunamune, asking for help, a fact that was detected by Toshikata Yagiu, the FBI of the Tokugawas, and reported to the Bakufu as a conspiracy to overturn the Tokugawa reign. As a result, Tsunamune was ordered to retire and Emperor Gosai-in was forced to abdicate from the throne at age twenty-seven in 1663, and confined to a small shack by the Tokugawa Bakufu for the rest of his life, until he died at age forty-nine. When Tsunayoshi Tokugawa took power as the 5th shogun, he believed himself qualified to become emperor because of his Korean blood, his mother having been born on Cheju Island. Tsunayoshi had everybody call his Chiyoda castle the imperial court and the officials of his Bakufu court nobles. Envoys of the imperial court at Kyoto even had to resign ranks temporarily when visiting the court in Edo.

During twenty-three years of confinement, Gosai-in collected every fragment of the third version of the *Nihon Shoki* and wrote down fifty volumes of history as a protest against Tsunayoshi's claim that he was the emperor. This is what we read now, not the version originally edited in 720.

The oldest history book, *Koji Ki*, is said to have been compiled in 712; however, the preface contains many quotations from the *Nihon Shoki*, which was supposed to have been compiled in 720. Another mystery is that none of the copies were kept in the official library of the imperial household. The clue to solving this question, in Takeuchi's opinion, is that the original was compiled in Kyushu by the Wa dynasty. As the Paekche power had come to control Wa at a later time, *Koji Ki* was left by the court as the history of the *Sen*. Later, Norinaga Motoori (1730-1801) glorified the starving *Sen* prisoners confined in mountain camps and published his commentary on the *Koji Ki* which we read currently.

Past rulers always tried to justify their power by altering history. In our pursuit of truth, we must be careful not to be misled. It is time to find out Japan's true history by thoroughly examining local histories one by one, then judging the material with reason. It is painstaking work, but there is no alternative; the Japanese must learn that the power of government should derive solely from the people.

Let us now summarize differences between the imperialistic view of the Meiji ideology and current texts used in Japanese schools.

Current texts have replaced the Meiji ideology's naive point of view that Japan's imperial family had an "infinite" past, with references to the Wa country in Chinese chronicles of the 1st century. The emperor's divinity and the myths of the land of the gods is now denied; immigrations to Japan from Korea and China are now admitted. Though some myths are considered fiction, many Japanese, in their gut, chose to endear them as truth.

Current texts introduce the Proto-Japanese theory that the Jomon people were the direct ancestors of today's Japanese, asserting that the Jomon were the original ancient race which, despite mixed blood over centuries of immigration, has remained the same initial people governed by one imperial bloodline to the present. A close analytical look reveals that today's text books have preserved the basic Meiji political intent to integrate the nation, but replaced its former militarism with pacifism. This fixed ideology of who the Japanese are and what Japan is has been authorized by the Japanese government throughout its history. We will see this in the next chapter as we compare Yagiri's view with the government's authorized history with regard to the 7th century Chinese invasion.

Chapter Eight

Foundation of the Imperial Institution

Early in the 7th Century, the Sui dynasty in China fell and the T'ang dynasty took power (618). The Chinese passion to regain domination over Korea continued from Sui to T'ang, but the first invasion by the T'ang against the Koguryo in 645 failed. In the meantime, the Koguryo formed an alliance with the Paekche against the Silla. To cope with that situation, the Silla allied with the T'ang. With open hostilities, the united troops of T'ang and Silla defeated the Paekche in 660. Surviving Paekche retainers asked the Wa to help restore them. In response to Paekche's plea for aid in 661, Empress Saimei sent her troops to a military base in northern Kyushu, but she became ill and died there. Crown Prince Naka-no-Ooe took over troop command and sent 32,000 soldiers to Korea to help the Paekche against the T'ang-Silla forces. In August 663, they fought the fatal Battle of Hakusuki-no-e, and were defeated. The Paekche king defected to Koguryo, but T'ang and Silla forces kept militant momentum, crushing Koguryo in 668.

The evolution of Japan's history around the defeat in Korea is described in the *Chronicle of Japanese History,* edited by the Academy of History (Kabushiki Kaisha Iwanami Shoten, 1987). Its contents, based on the *Nihon Shoki*, are summarized:

661: In March, the Empress Saimei arrived at Chikushi (Fukuoka) of Kyushu. She died in July, and Crown Prince Naka-no-Ooe took over the power as regent without accession to the throne (he did not accede until 668, when he became Emperor Tenchi).

663: 27,000 troops commanded by Gen. Kamitsuke-no-Wakako were sent to Korea in March. In August, Japan-Paekche forces were defeated by T'ang-Silla forces at Hakusuki-no-e. In September, the Japanese troops returned with Paekche refugees.

664: In May, Gen. Guo Wu Zong, envoy of the T'ang, came to Chikushi and submitted a letter with gifts for the emperor, but was not allowed to enter the capital. In December, he was sent back. In preparation for possible attack by T'ang-Silla forces, the government reinforced national defense that year by establishing military bases, dug moats and prepared to light signal fires on the islands of Tsushima, Iki and Chikushi.

665: In August, three castles were built in Chikushi. Another T'ang envoy, Liu came to Chikushi in September. Envoys to T'ang were appointed.

668: Crown Prince Naka-no-Ooe ascended to the throne in January as Emperor Tenchi. Silla paid tribute in September.

669: In October, Nakatomi-no-Kamatari died and was given the special court rank of Dai-Shokukan (Great Noble). Appointed minister, he and his descendants were allowed to use the family name of Fujiwara. It was said that T'ang envoy General Guo was coming to Japan with 2000 men.

671: In January, T'ang envoys, Li and others, submitted a letter to the emperor. In November, news was brought from Tsushima to the Chikushi local government that T'ang envoy Gen. Guo and 2,000 men would soon arrive in Japan. In December, Emperor Tenchi died.

672: In June, a coup d'etat, *Jinshin-no-Ran*, erupted. Prince Ooama won the civil war.

673: The prince ascended to the throne in February, becoming Emperor Temmu.

In Korea, the alliance between the T'ang and the Silla had been broken soon after the fall of Koguryo, the Silla having driven off the T'ang forces and unified the entire Korean peninsula in 676. The Hakusuki-no-e defeat should be an important event in Japanese history, however, it was not mentioned in the government history of the Meiji era because it would have spoiled the glorious history of the Empire of Japan. The question is whether the account is historical fact or not.

In the above narrative, it was claimed that Gen. Guo, bearing gifts for the emperor, was not allowed to enter the capital, and returned home. Yagiri's view is clear; he claims the *Nihon Shoki* descriptions are false. No one has asked the question: what reason could there be for the winner of the war to present gifts to the defeated enemy's emperor, then return home without concluding the war with him at his court in the capital? It is still fresh in our memory that the Emperor Hirohito visited General Douglas MacArthur at his headquarters right after the surrender of Japan.

From the Meiji viewpoint, it was intolerable for the government to admit the defeat of Hakusuki-no-e, to say nothing of the Chinese intrusion into Japan. Anything that would spoil the Eternal Imperial Lineage or suggest the defeat of the Land of the Gods was strictly prohibited, particularly during the period of militarist domination for the four decades leading up to 1945. But half a century has passed since World War II, and Japan is now supposed to be a democratic country. Why is there no discussion in the current Japanese academy? I believe the Japanese prefer the past of glorified invincibility rather than looking squarely at the truth.

Yagiri claims Gen. Guo landed at Chikushi with his troops and marched to the capital to occupy the Court at Yamato. *The Chronicle* says that the 27,000 troops sent to Korea returned to Japan in September of 663. Is that feasible? No. Common sense tells us it simply isn't possible. What happened to Japanese soldiers in Manchuria, for example, when World War II ended? They were taken to Siberia by the Russians for several years of forced labor. In the 7th century, it was even more difficult than today to come back across the Korean Straits. The surviving Japanese slave-soldiers surrendered and became slaves of the T'ang. It didn't matter to the slave-soldier whether the Paekche or the T'ang were their masters. Shrewd Chinese generals relished the conquest of Japan. Gen. Guo used Paekche officers from Japan as guides for his occupation. To prove loyalty to their new Chinese masters, Paekche officers helped invade Japan. Since Japan had sent all its men out as soldiers, its land was left empty and defenseless. For Gen. Guo, Japan's occupation was a simple matter. Yagiri estimates that after the initial 2,000 T'ang soldiers, (accompanied by 10,000-20,000 in supply units, plus civilians) came to Japan, another 2,000 plus 10,000-20,000 followed as reinforcements.

The theory of this Chinese occupation is based on numbers, particularly a T'ang invasion of 2,000 men. If Japan had tens of thousands of troops in reserve, the T'ang would have sent a greater number of troops to conquer her. On the other hand, if they sought a friendly relationship between the two countries, 2,000 troops was too many to send on a peaceful mission. If the T'ang knew there was no huge reserve of Japanese troops to resist attack, 2,000 men were adequate for protection and to deal with any situation that might arise. The T'ang should have realized after the first invasion they could take the whole country, then send for reinforcements.

The story about the building of castles and moats in Kyushu is contradictory. These were to be military bases of the Chinese occupying forces landing at the northern coast of Kyushu, and were to accommodate the troops initially and to protect them against possible attack by pro-Paekche Japanese guerrillas.

It is interesting to note that right after this war, everything in Japan changed to T'ang style—the political system, court ranks and hierarchy, even hairstyles, clothing, and written characters. (We see a repetition of this in 20th century Japan, right after the U.S. occupation). The Tse-t'ien characters of Wu Tse-t'ien, the only empress in Chinese history, were adapted as official, though none of the inhabitants could read them except government officials and Buddhist priests of Paekche nationality. *Nihon Shoki* and *Koji Ki* are written with Tse-t'ien characters and Chinese grammar. Since the 7th and 8th centuries, China and Chinese became authoritative, respectable and noble in Japan, which lasted for a thousand years. Only Chinese or Korean ancestry qualified one for sovereignty.

Would common sense allow the recording of one's national history in a foreign language? Once again, we are reminded of similarities in the U.S. occupation of Japan, when, in order to ingratiate himself with his new American masters, a Japanese scholar proposed Japan use Roman characters.

Unfortunately, the above evidence is merely circumstantial. But Yagiri does present direct proof of Japan's Chinese occupation. In one of his books, he displays a "rubbing" copy of the report which he believes Gen. Guo submitted to the Empress of T'ang China, which reads:

"On May 19th in 664 (I) gained control (of the court) with my forces and confiscated all weapons and rolls of cloth. Use of Tse-t'ien characters here was enforced. Compulsory delivery of large stones to build castles was officially announced. Gen. Guo, Commander of Expeditionary Forces and Chosandayu (rank in the T'ang court) begged to report.

"—Ru dingzu."

(Gen. Guo's Signature)

(From the cover of *The Supplement to Yagiri View—Japan's Trial*, published by Kabushikikaisha Nihon Shell Shuppan, 1983). ("Rubbing copy" refers to the method of printing, using an inscribed copper plate applied with Chinese ink, rubbed with paper pages to print the Tse-t'ien book).

The above rubbed copy of the Tse-t'ien book was used by the Chinese to brainwash Japanese prisoners of the Sino-Japanese War in the

1930's and 1940's. In particular, the communist resistance army at Yan'an camp in Baljun, China, used this method. The last characters are believed to be Gen. Guo's signature. Their meaning is: "Your humble subject to support you like the legs of tripod kettle." From this signature, Yagiri reasons that Kamatari Fujiwara (or Nakatomi-no-Kamatari before) could be Gen. Guo's other name in Japan because in Chinese characters, Kamatari means legs of a kettle. This coincidence makes Yagiri reason further that Gen. Guo might have purposely let his other name die in the book of *Nihon Shoki* when he enthroned himself as Emperor Tenchi (or Temmu).

The articles of the *Nihon Shoki* were missing for about four months after the defeat in Hakusuki-no-e; pages were cut out, so that it is impossible to know what happened during those months in Japan. The *Nihon Shoki* was completely rewritten by Emperor Kammu, who restored the position of emperor from the Silla lineage back to the Paekche about 120 years later. During the course of history, the *Nihon Shoki* was revised several times by whomever was in power at the time, so that its story is not very reliable.

However, the *Nihon Shoki* article of the year 669 presents another clue that hints at a different situation. It says: "This year, the great T'ang has sent Gen. Guo and 2,000 odd men to (us)." Although "us" is omitted in the original text, there is no other interpretation than that the troops were sent to the writer of the *Nihon Shoki*, i.e. the imperial court. There would be no reason for the T'ang to send Gen. Guo's forces to the Wa dynasty government, whom the T'ang and Silla had just destroyed, as their common enemy. It would make sense only if interpreted that "our" supreme headquarters in T'ang China sent "us" (a branch in Japan) reinforcements. This would mean that the imperial court had become the branch of T'ang China, indicating a clear change of power; but Yagiri points out that Japanese scholars overlook this, perhaps purposely, to suit their Meiji concepts.

The reference book referred to in chapter six summarizes what influence this defeat had on Japanese history in its "conclusion of the defeat":

1. Japan, (the Wa or Yamato Dynasty), abandoning all interests in Korea, was compelled to retreat from the Korean Peninsula.
2. The government put more emphasis on domestic politics to fix the political system.
3. Many Paekche and Koguryo refugees immigrated to Japan.

This is a primary example of how the Japanese view an historical "fact." The coup d'etat in 672 mentioned in the Chronicle was obviously caused by the Chinese shift of power from Paekche to Silla ancestry, if that part of the story is reliable. The Emperor Tenchi, or whomever was on the throne, was merely nominal, and all practical power was held by the Chinese.

The question still remains which Wa dynasty sent 27,000 troops to Paekche. Was it the Kyushu dynasty or the Yamato dynasty? The *Nihon Shoki* definitely suggests it was the Yamato. Yet we cannot eliminate the possibility that another Wa dynasty in northern Kyushu sent troops to the Paekche, one more geographically accessible and closer by blood to the Paekche. It is possible that Gen. Guo crushed this Wa dynasty in Kyushu before he proceeded to conquer another Wa dynasty in Yamato. Guo used a preliminary maneuver as Nakatomi-no-Kamatari in an elaborate gesture over an extended period. In any case, we can be convinced that a Chinese occupation was the foundation of Japan and her emperor institution.

When T'ang forces occupied Japan, the masters of the country changed from Paekche to T'ang. According to Yagiri, in an announcement to the entire country, the T'ang made it clear they were *ryo* (nobles) and everyone else was *sen* (humble slaves). *Sen* included the Ya, Yottsu, Zoshiki, Silla, Koguryo, Kaya, and even the ex-masters, the Paekche. All *sen* were systematically enslaved nationwide by the T'ang take-over. The enforcement of this system in 702 was called *Taiho Ritsu Ryo*, which breaks down into penal codes of *Ritsu* and administrative and civil laws of the *ryo*. Yagiri estimates that 96% of the population was enslaved by Chinese power, with the Ya people made slaves for farming, fishing and salt making, and the Yottsu slave soldiers. All women were taken by the Chinese and accommodated in facilities called *Kaito*, (open door) for their masters' sexual entertainment. Male slaves were separated from women and forbidden to have children, except for those chosen as bosses. The descendants of these slaves, therefore, were of mixed blood, whom Chinese masters did not recognize as legitimate. Thus, the Japanese masses are currently called *Shomin* (illegitimate people).

According to the reference book, *Taiho Ritsu Ryo*, defined as the laws to support the centralized political system initiated by Prince Osakabe and Fubito Fujiwara, was later supplemented by the enforcement of *Yoro Ritsu Ryo*, drafted by Fubito Fujiwara. The imperial household, nobles, government officials, farmers with citizenship, *Shinabe* and *Zakko* comprised the *ryo* rank, with those up to the government officials being the ruling classes.

All others were *sen*, of which there were five kinds: guards of imperial and lords' tombs; men holding governmental odd jobs; men doing odd jobs for nobles; government-owned slaves and privately-owned slaves. (From *Comprehensive New Japanese History*).

The first three categories were allowed to live in their own homes, while the latter two were subject to sale. The first, second and fourth categories were owned by the government and could receive paddy field allocations. All lands were owned by the government, and any duly registered were entitled to allocations irrespective of *ryo* or *sen*. The third and fifth categories were privately owned and entitled to only 1/3 of the land allocated to *ryo*. Slaves over 66 years old were upgraded to positions as odd job men and those over 76 were upgraded to *ryo*.

This view currently taught to Japanese students admits the existence of slavery in ancient Japanese history, but portrays a picture much less harsh than Yagiri's. The idea of rule, either by the same race or by foreigners, makes the things look quite different. While the reference book carries no sympathy to the Meiji ideology, its fixed idea of Japan's independence and single race makes people blind to the facts.

In reality, the T'ang masters acted harshly and cruelly toward slaves in order to crush their backbone, racial identity, values and pride. Slaves were forced to show absolute obedience and loyalty to the master under all circumstances. As a warning to others, anyone who disobeyed or was disloyal was killed instantly. Those captured by T'ang forces were classified and separated into groups. Those who were good as peasants were admitted to the *Tera Nin-betsu* (Buddhist temple register). Some were made policemen, executioners or tomb guards.

At this time, Buddhism was made the national religion, and served to control the peasant slave. Each temple was equipped with a bell to alert the guards in an emergency when local resistance attacked the temple. Nomads were made imperial mausoleum keepers, horse raisers, policemen, executioners, and slave warriors. Most were obliged to take dangerous occupations since they had no particular skills.

Those considered useless, or who were unwilling to obey, were segregated in camps in secluded mountainous areas, isolated by rivers over which bridges were forbidden to be built. These ancient barbarian camps were called *sansho*, *bessho*, or *kegai*, names which remain in various places on the map of Japan even now. The true meaning of the names Sansho and Bessho are unclear and are often mistaken as places where women deliver babies. The meaning of Kegai is "out of the world," where subhumans are confined.

If detainees came out of these camps, they were killed instantly. There was little food in the mountains and *kai* (shell fish) in the rivers was valuable. Shell mounds marked the last remains of these people, many whom were left to die of starvation. The Japanese expression *no kai mo naku* derives from this historical tragedy, and means "at the end of all resources available." *Kai* was the last food for them.

The places where the prisoners were separated into groups according to their fates were called *oi-wake*, and remain scattered in various territories of Japan today. Numerous tragedies of separations between husbands and wives, mothers and children, are overlooked in Japanese government history, with only the sorrowful tune of the *shakuhachi* (Japanese flute) left as a subtle reminder. But for those who have no knowledge of this sorrowful past, the *shakuhachi* lament seems to be just another melancholic melody.

Those who survived the mountain camps were hunted down later in the 10th and 11th centuries and made "human shields" in battle. They started as the lowest class of samurai, but lucky ones succeeded in becoming daimyo (feudalistic lords) in the middle ages.

Of course, some people refused to surrender to the T'ang forces and fled into deeper mountain areas with their families. Sometimes the Yottsu and Ya joined forces to help each other. They were collectively identified as Sanka. Later in the 10th century, the Khitan people, who were also oppressed by the government, joined the Sanka in the mountains, where they roamed for a thousand years, hidden from the villagers until the Meiji era. When the Meiji government's census revealed the Sanka's vast numbers, this original Japanese people was believed to be dangerous to the central government; they were branded criminals, oppressed, killed or deported to wherever they could be accepted. Instead of being appreciated by the central government for the endurance of their race, they were simply discarded.

Many Sanka never gave up their fighting spirit against the Chinese foreign invaders, despite their isolation within the mountains, and northern Japan saw several sizeable rebellions in resistance against foreign rulers. The last and biggest uprising began in 789, and came in three waves over the next fourteen years, until 803, when the people of Silla and Koguryoe ancestry united, forming an alliance with the combined forces of the Ya and Yottsu against the central government troops. To counter this uprising, the Fujiwara establishment of T'ang ancestry took refuge in the west at Okayama, which had been a traditional Chinese colony since the 2nd and 3rd centuries. It was once called the Kibi dynasty or Naka Tsu Kuni, meaning the country of China. This Fujiwara establishment had denounced the emperor of Silla ancestry and made Kammu its emperor in 781. Kammu was promised by the Fujiwara establishment: "If you succeed in stopping this rebellion, the status of your Paekche people will be upgraded from *sen* (humble slaves) to *ryo* (court nobles).

There is a story about a general who was punished for his ignominious defeat by the rebels. In 789, at the peak of their resistance, the rebels pushed the government troops back to the Fuji River in the Shizuoka Prefect. In April of 802, the rebel chief, Aterui, surrendered and was killed. The rebellion was suppressed the following year, but it took until the middle of the 9th century for the imperial court to completely pacify the northern areas of Japan. From the perspective of the rebels, Aterui was a great hero of the Japanese aborigines. His spirit of resistance against foreign invaders should have been embraced as a national virtue, to be remembered forever by the Japanese. But the position taken on Aterui's leadership in that rebellion is the same in today's textbook as it was with the Yamato imperial court of the time, namely, "brutal boss by barbarians who rebelled against the imperial court." Any rebellion against the emperor is intolerable.

The result of the conflict was the Paekche people being freed by the Fujiwara establishment, while all others were made slaves, outcasts or forced to retreat to the mountains. Yagiri estimates that the addition of Paekche to the court and Chinese immigration made the *ryo* class 10% of Japan's total population, a ratio that remains constant in today's society, which means, surprisingly, that 90% of today's Japanese have descended from slaves.

The Nara Dynasty, which began with the Emperor Kammu, was the second dynasty of the Paekche. It is believed that old documents and books edited by the Fujiwara establishment were collected and burned by Emperor Kammu's order. The *Nihon Shoki* and *Koji Ki* were no exception; Emperor Kammu had his scholars rewrite the *Nihon Shoki* from a Paekche viewpoint. When the Fujiwara establishment returned to power, they rewrote *Nihon Shoki* yet again from their T'ang view.

The Fujiwara establishment did not enthrone its own emperor, preferring to remain apart, with the real power in their distant hands controlling the Paekche emperors. Many Fujiwara women, however, became empresses by marriage to the Paekche. The Fujiwara placed their own powerful army of T'ang soldiers at Tabuhou, near the capital, to protect the imperial court. The emperor institution began in this way in the beginning of the 8th century. The Ritsu *Ryo* codes, based on T'ang codes, ruled Japan until the Meiji era in 1868.

I have introduced an historic view which is completely different from the Japanese government-made history known to the people. History, to Japanese today, is merely something to memorize in order to pass university examinations and thus ensure a promising future. Therefore, the authorized government-made history with its "correct answers" has absolute power over students, because anyone who writes different answers will be refused into the system.*

---

*For additional information on the history of the emperor institution, see Joan Piggott's thorough analysis, *The Emergence of Japanese Kingship* (Stanford University Press, 1997).

Chapter Nine

The Emperor Institution

The prewar education which formed my imperialistic viewpoint of Japanese history was crushed by the new insights I derived from the writings of Yagiri. Perhaps it is my personal link with the Ya race that allowed me to absorb Yagiri's astonishing revelation of Japan's true history into my heart like water into sand.

Westerners may not fully appreciate the radical thought that Yagiri professes to Japanese, who have lived so long with the fixed idea of their pure race. To most other cultures, the history Yagiri relates is normal: it is human nature for a nation to evolve from warring races, foreign invasions, slavery, exploitation and the eventual mixing of races over centuries, with a higher civilization conquering a lesser civilization—this is the pattern of history worldwide. It makes perfect sense that Chinese, Koreans northern nomads, ancient Persians and others from the south met on the Japanese Islands and struggled for power, nor is it surprising that the Chinese and Koreans, with their advanced weapons and technology, would be dominant. The modern Japan which led other Asian countries a step ahead in weapons and technologies after the Meiji did the same things.

Had the Japanese been taught to accept this true history, their cultural conflicts with Americans and other Westerners might have been diminished. Because they have set themselves apart with a false history of their racial evolution, they have made other nations leery of them as an incomprehensible race. Japanese differences in politics, business and social behavior would have been more readily accepted had the Japanese not manifested this mystique about their pure imperial lineage from the land of the gods.

It is common worldwide that people in power will try to justify their reign to maintain it. The *Nihon Shoki* was certainly not written as a textbook to teach schoolchildren about the 8th century; rather, it was to authorize power to the conquerors' descendants. Whenever you read a history book written by a dynasty, you must keep in mind that the facts may have been altered to serve its own means.

I sense two strong inner forces in Japanese society: first is the tendency to stifle any insight or imaginative concepts of Japanese history, especially if they conflict with acceptance of the emperor institution. The history described in the standard reference book for high school students may actually be below the standards which the current establishment wants to keep. The vertical structure of Japanese society itself is a deterrent to any new radical view that might overturn the power. Government university professors are conservative in proposing any opinion that might challenge their predecessors, because it will not benefit them in any way.

There is a more direct force. For example, Yagiri, (who died several years ago), was boycotted by all publishers over the past fifteen years, even though his books were selling well in the market. Even when he was contracted to write a magazine article, the contract would later be canceled without explanation. To continue his fight, he established his own publishing company, a fact which was hard for me to believe at first, because I was convinced that Japan honored freedom of speech and thought.

Recently, I have realized that the cost of exercising this right in Japan is prohibitively high. When the mayor of Nagasaki laid the responsibility of World War II on Emperor Hirohito, he was shot in the back by a right wing hoodlum, and was lucky to survive. Anyone whose opinion is deemed detrimental to the current emperor institution will be boycotted, demoted, or fired from their job. I am no exception. I write this book out of my love for Japan and for the values of democracy. I am fully aware of the risk, but for me, truth is the most important value to be fought for.

Contradictions in the accepted version of Japanese history are not difficult to find. What happened to the Ezo people, for example? They were said to be a barbarian race who lived in northern Japan, who were subjugated by the imperial troops in the 9th century, according to the *Nihon Shoki*. What race were they? If they were naturalized, why is there no official ancestry of them listed? The Ezo are much like the Native American (Indians). These great rebels once defeated 53,000 imperial troops. They could not have simply vanished without a trace, so where are their descendants? A thorough study of the Ezo alone should provide enough evidence of the fiction of Japanese history and its claim to always having been a single race united in peace.

By piecing together local histories of different races like the Ezo, the true history of Japan will come to the surface. The patchwork will form a truthful pattern that reflects the facts. These studies, unlike the *Nihon Shoki*, which was written to provide political justification for a ruling dynasty, will reflect the broader truth that the whole nation can embrace with both humility and pride.

The second strong inner force working in Japanese society is one which encourages a new emperor institution above the current political system. It is not an exaggeration to say that the Japanese media is mobilized to this cause. Much publicity and news coverage is given to the Emperor and Empress, as well as to the royal families, especially when the emperor receives foreign dignitaries in ceremonies as Japan's head of state. There is an ongoing campaign to place the emperor above the people. Even the image of samurai on TV and in novels paints the picture of loyalty to the lord in support of the emperor institution. TV commercials are tainted with the Japanese touch. Those values considered unique to Japanese culture are, no doubt, the foundation of the emperor institution.

Perhaps one of the most sophisticated views is that of the late Shichihei Yamamoto, (referred to in Chapter Four). Yamamoto wrote a number of valuable books in which he thoroughly discussed Japanese culture based on wide observation, extensive knowledge, and logical reasoning. His broad scope even includes an understanding of Judaism, so foreign to the Far Eastern tradition.

In his book *A Study of Emperor Showa* (Hirohito), (Shoden Sha, Tokyo, February 1989), Yamamoto refers to Soukichi Tsuda, the great scholar who denounced both the stories of Ki Ki (*Nihon Shoki* and *Koji Ki)*, mentioned in Chapter Four. Tsuda was charged and prosecuted for the "insult and denial of the emperor's divinity." Yamamoto says the records of Tsuda's trial are the best material to study, because he gave complete lectures to his prosecutors in court. In prewar society, he was seen as questioning the unquestionable, and thus he angered the political right wing. Tsuda maintained his views consistently in the postwar period as well. Shortly after the surrender of Japan, radical left wing scholars with a materialistic view regarded Tsuda's writings as an outdated, undeserving defense of the emperor institution. It is ironic that Tsuda's views have become more popular as society has become more conservative. His is currently the most generally accepted theory of Japanese history. Yamamoto agrees with his views.

Tsuda's opinion can be summed up as follows: The stories of various affairs of Ki Ki from the first Emperor Jimmu to the 14th Chuai, are mere fictions. However, such fiction could not have been born of itself from nothing; a philosophy lies behind these stories, and the lives of the people serve as a background for the philosophy. This underlying philosophy is "historical fact" itself. Studying the philosophy and background neither desecrates nor denies the emperor's divinity, but rather is a reasonable approach.

One example concerns a famous episode of the Emperor Nintoku, who, one day from a hilltop, observed his people, saw no smoke coming from their chimneys, realized they had no food to cook, so by special consideration exempted them from taxation.

Every Japanese educated before the war knows this story of the emperor's benevolence from his primary textbooks. Tsuda proved that this story derived from Chinese origins. His obvious argument is that the story is fiction, yet the philosophy behind it, illustrated in the people's lives, is "historical fact." Tsuda extends this logic to the idea of "an unbroken imperial bloodline for ages eternal." Likewise, this may be fiction, but the idea behind it is "historical fact." Tsuda questions the origin of this concept of a pure imperial lineage when Chinese influence was prevalent, since the Chinese themselves embraced no such idea. In fact, the Chinese accepted the fallibility of their emperors, who, if found lacking in virtue, were overthrown by revolution and replaced by someone more suitable, by heavenly decree ("Mandate from Heaven" concept).

The ancient histories of most countries contain war epics and sagas which the people pass down through generations. The lack of such stories in Japanese recorded history lends credence to the belief that ancient Japan was unified peacefully by the imperial household. On that premise, the assumption is that everyone was happy under benevolent emperors, and that harmony and peace instilled the wish among the people that this virtuous imperial bloodline should continue unbroken forever.

Regarding the unique ideology of *Arahito Gami* (or *Kami*), that the emperor is a living god, Tsuda states in a 1950 essay: "The word 'symbol' first appeared in the new constitution of 1946 as the legal term for the Emperor. But in my opinion, he had actually been a symbol ever since...I don't know who chose this word, but it is very good...I suggested the same meaning in one of my books thirty years ago...There are controversies about the constitution...which may not be perfect, but (one is) impressed by the definition of the imperial household as the symbol of the state and integration of the people."

In *A Study Of Emperor Showa*, (Shodensha, Tokyo, 1989), Yamamoto summarizes Tsuda's five accounts of why and how the Japanese emperor is completely different from the Chinese emperor:

1. The Japanese imperial household did not come from outside Japan or conquer the Japanese race to attain power and the monarchy. Instead, they rose within the same race and caused the people

to willingly submit to the imperial household gradually and peacefully.
2. There were no wars with different races. Local disputes left no decisive influence on the political system.
3. In ancient Japan, there were no conspicuous political achievements by the emperor. These were unnecessary, since the people were content, and the emperor left the political decisions to his ministers.
4. The emperor had a religious mission and authority.
5. The imperial household led the cultural revolution which introduced Chinese culture and Buddhism to the people, and this in turn generated reverence and amiable feelings toward the imperial household. The imperial household remained the center of the people even during the period of the samurai government, which took political and military powers away from the court in the Kamakura age.

On January 1, 1946 in the Rescript of the Foundation of New Japan, (known as the Declaration of Man), Emperor Hirohito said, "...I am always with you, the nation. I have the same interest as you and want to share your pleasure and sorrow. The bond that connects me with you, the nation, has always been one of mutual trust and respect. It has been neither mere myths, traditions, nor the imaginary concept of the emperor as a living god that makes the Japanese superior to other races and destines us to rule the world..."

He says, in short, "I'm not a god, but a man. Japan, my country, is not the land of the gods. But I'm your emperor because of our long history of trust and respect. It has nothing to do with myths or the concept of the living god." Like the ideology painted by Yamamoto and Tsuda, this historical view must be an absolute condition to justify the emperor institution: this is the frame of Japanese history set forth by the government and why two strong inner forces are working.

The reader may wonder why the Japanese wanted to keep the emperor institution. We needed a strong centripetal force to integrate the nation and concentrate on economic recovery. After her surrender in 1945, Japan was in serious danger of disintegration and her leaders realized that a strong central government unified by the emperor institution was the only way to direct the defeated nation to economic growth. It was important for the U.S. government, too, to make the occupation of Japan successful, and it became even more important later in the fight against the common enemy, communism.

It is difficult to refute the argument that the fictional stories of the *Nihon Shoki* reflect the history of the people and their thoughts at the time they were created. Let us ask for what purpose was the *Nihon Shoki* written, and when? It was not edited to simply teach history in 8th century schools, but rather to justify the emperor's reign with stories of his benevolence. Since there were no printing presses, bookstores, or xerox machines in the 8th century, the book was hand written for the small elite of the imperial family and its court who had access to books and could read Chinese characters. Then how can one accept the view that the *Nihon Shoki* reflected the thought and lives of the people of the times when the elite recorded this fiction from the narrow perspective of their ivory tower? We must wholeheartedly reject Tsuda's view and deem it pure nonsense. How could the viewpoint of slaves be reflected in written histories when 96% of the people could not read the Chinese language, in an elite society that had no regard for them?

Here, Yamamoto is in sharp contrast with Yagiri. Yamamoto claims the emperor rose within the same race to unify Japan peacefully, while Yagiri insists Japan was originally the land of the Ya, Yottsu, and Zoshiki, who were conquered by the Paekche and other Koreans by the 6th century. During the 7th and 8th centuries, T'ang Chinese invaded and occupied Japan by violence. As a small minority race in control, the T'ang used all means to justify their rule; true history was downplayed to emphasize peaceful unification by the T'ang Chinese and justify their reign; thus, the Ki Ki sources alone are unreliable in proving a peaceful evolution of power.

Yamamoto says the imperial household were leaders in cultural progress and propagated Buddhism, but Yagiri insists it was the vanguard of Chinese invasion. Today in the ancient capital of Nara, we are privileged to worship the great image of Buddha made from 500 tons of copper, 438 kilograms of gold and 2.5 tons of mercury, which required a total of 2.5 million man-days over 10 years to build. Rumors suggest that Nara's streets were littered with dead slaves in the process of constructing it. In ancient times, religion was absolute; no one easily surrendered his beliefs to another. Only by force did the Chinese make others worship Buddha. The Japanese did exactly the same thing to the Koreans and Chinese in the 20th century, when imperial forces occupied these countries; the Japanese built Shinto shrines and forced the people to worship the souls of the ancestors of the imperial household as gods.

8th century T'ang Chinese kept a firm hand, manipulating the emperor of Korean ancestry like a puppet, which made the imperial court readily assign all military and political power to the Bakufu (samurai government) at a later time.

Allowing a constitutional monarchy, the maximum compromise the U.S. and Far Eastern Commission made after the war, posed a conflict in ideologies: American initiative for democracy, versus the Japanese government's resistance to change; it has also created confusion in understanding the current constitution.

The Japanese nation needs to cling to Tsuda's and reject Yagiri's view or risk economic collapse: this is the thinking of the Japanese who rule behind the scenes today; as long as an ideology propagates economic growth, the symbolic emperor institution merits justification.

But now Japan is required to contribute more than money to maintain its standing in international affairs. Japanese troops were sent to Cambodia as part of a United Nations peacekeeping operation (PKO). This presented a serious situation to the Japanese people: values such as democracy, freedom, equality and individuality remain foreign to most Japanese. Though they may understand them theoretically, they feel no urgency to defend them with their lives, especially on foreign soil. How to encourage the Japanese to share Western values as worth fighting for?

Unfortunately, the easiest way is also the most dangerous: strengthening the new emperor institution by tightening the old vertical structure of society with the emperor at the top will increase the centripetal force to drive the nation in whatever direction the government wants to lead the people. The right wing would get on the bandwagon to support this move and put down any opposition. There lies the danger, perhaps setting the stage for history to repeat itself in the worst way.

A much better way would be to promote the people's awareness of Japan's true history, to incorporate democratic values in a firm foundation that can never be eroded. How nice to be free! How good not to be discriminated against! How important individual independence is to maintain democracy! We can learn all these values from our own ancestors' miserable lives as slaves. Then, for the first time, each of us will be determined to never lose them, even at the cost of our lives. Correct historical knowledge of one's own past enables an individual to make judgments which, through the democratic process, leads the whole nation to better moral judgments.

The better choice is clear. There are no true values in a fabricated history. The glorification of a monarch to form a vertical society is dangerous in the long run. We don't want to repeat the disaster of 50 years ago. Our children, grandchildren, and all future Japanese generations must face the negative lesson of that terrible time in our history, as it must accept our history of slavery if they are to build sound values that can never crumble.

Part Two

JAPAN'S CULTURAL BACKGROUND

Chapter Ten

The Samurai Myth

What is your image of the samurai? Typically, it may be some of the following: a daring warrior unafraid of death: master of martial arts, particularly of kendo (sword), karate, judo, hara-kiri (ritual suicide by disembowelment); a man of loyalty, honor, self-control and pride; shogun, daimyo (feudal lord) and ninja. The Japanese might add the image of a respectable man of his word; justice, integrity, courtesy and scholarship.

Currently, Japanese TV broadcasts several *Jidai Geki* (samurai plays) in its weekly schedule. The stories are simple and clear. The shogun or his retainer samurai in high position disguises himself as a *ronin* (lordless samurai) or *chonin* (townspeople in the Edo era), and lives among the common folk to learn about the life of the masses. He detects conspiracies and crimes of rich merchants and high-ranking officials of the Tokugawa Bakufu (shogun's government) against the reigning leader. He punishes these bad guys by death with his sword, usually swiftly and without trial. The good samurai is always a master of kendo and can easily defeat a dozen villains with a quick flurry of the sword. There are hundreds of samurai fictions in bookstores, all similar to TV portrayals.

The more serious image of the samurai has been portrayed in books dating back to the turn of the century, such as *Bushido, the Soul of Japan*, written in 1900 by Dr. Inazo Nitobe, translated by his English wife, and published by G.P. Putnam's Sons in 1905. A later version was published in 1969 by Charles E. Tuttle Co., Inc., from which are taken the following references applauding the samurai and bushido, the Japanese feudal equivalent to chivalry:

"Chivalry is a flower no less indigenous to the soil of Japan than its emblem, the cherry blossom; nor is it a dried-up specimen of an antique virtue preserved in the herbarium of our history," Nitobe says, regarding bushido as an ethical system. He tells us proudly, "Samurai grew to be the *beau ideal* of the whole race. And so sang the populace, 'as among flowers the cherry blossom is queen, so among men the samurai is lord.' Barred from commercial pursuits, the military class itself did not aid commerce; but there was no channel of human activity, no avenue of thought which did not receive in some measure directly or indirectly the work of knighthood." He goes on: "The precepts of knighthood began at first as the glory of the elite, became in time an aspiration and inspiration to the nation at large; and though the populace could not attain the moral height of those loftier souls, yet Yamato Damashii, the soul of Japan, ultimately came to express the Volksgeist of the island realm."

Hagakure may be little known to the Western world, however, it was famous in Japan and well-advertised by military authorities during World War II, because of its claim of fanatic loyalty to the samurai to die willingly for the lord. James Clavell's best seller *Shogun* was later made into a TV mini-series to popular acclaim. That coupled with typical movies dubbed in English have made the samurai warrior a stereotype to the modern world. Whether this image represents the truth is another story, as is reflected in the view of Yagiri.

The Japanese sword is said to be the soul of the samurai. It is beautiful and sharp, and the samurai, master of the art of kendo, could draw it as quick as lighting and cut off a dozen enemies' heads in the blinking of an eye. But a samurai sword is single-edged, sharp on one side only. It's dull back side, called *mine*, is thick and heavy, making it unbalanced. The sharp edge is 30 cm long from top to bottom. It is not double-edged like European swords, which could be effectively wielded offensively. Even other ancient Japanese swords, from the *tumuli* of kings and nobles, were double-edged like European weapons. Why was the samurai sword, with its single edge, unique?

The origin of the samurai is different from the European knights of the Middle Ages. Nitobe is misguided in his comparison of chivalric European knights with the precepts of bushido in Japan. Chinese and Paekche descendants, who made up the Japanese imperial household and noble court, kept their philosophy: "Good iron never makes a nail, and the son of a good family never makes a soldier."

This ancient tradition believed in the philosophy of fighting one evil with another. Thus, they fought off barbarians threatening their realm with their own well-trained barbarians, slave-soldiers called samurai. Japanese nobles never took part in battle except in myths, such as the conquests of Jimmu or the adventure of Takeru Yamato. The dirty work of killing was left to prisoners of subjugated barbarians, the ancestors of the samurai. They were also sometimes called *bushi*, a term corrupted from the 8th century Chinese word *buxin*, a contemptuous word meaning untrustworthy. Therefore, the mercenary soldiers of the mythical age who soon vanished from history cannot be considered ancestors of the samurai.

The officers leading those slave soldiers were loyal, most probably as in the poem: "I am starting on my honorable trip to be a human shield for the Emperor. From today forward, I'll stop caring about my personal things anymore." But the soldiers were prisoners hunted out of their camps. They were mainly Yottsu, some Ya, and possibly some Zoshiki who did not totally surrender to the T'ang Chinese and Paekche rulers. They maintained resistance to Chinese culture and remained rebellious. Nitobe praises the spirit Yamato Damashii, the soul of Japan, but his was not the slave soldier's point of view.

According to the government history, *sakimori* (defenseman) is considered to be the origin of the samurai. The term appears in *Man-yo-shu*, a compilation of old poems written about 770 A.D. *Sakimori* were soldiers drafted by the Japanese government and sent to strategic fortresses in northern Kyushu to defend Japan against foreign invasion. But according to the rescript of October 806 included in the record of the Supreme Council of the Emperor, it seems basically different. It says: "Let the prisoners of barbarians be stationed in strategic positions. Their presence will be good in an emergency. Move 640 of them currently in Oomi no Kuni (the province of Oomi—currently Shiga Prefecture) to military headquarters in northern Kyushu, and make them Sakimori. Their treatment should not be same as the common people (meaning that it should be worse). Control them not to have any ambition (of revolt)."

When in 1019 the invasion of the Khitan people took place, as mentioned in Chapter 5, the Fujiwara family was taken aback. They mobilized all swordsmiths throughout the country, who hastened to produce as many swords as possible. To save time and cost, single-edged swords were quickly produced in large volume and given to the slave soldiers human shields, who would fend off enemies' flying arrows with two swords, one in each hand. The single-edged sword was a defensive weapon safe for those in power to furnish to their slave soldiers. That is why samurai swords are single-edged. The swords were a great accomplishment by the swordsmiths and considered works of art, with their beautiful design and finish worthy of being called "the soul of the samurai." Though we are proud of this tradition, it does not change the facts of their origin.

In 1051, Yoritoki Abe, slave head in northern Japan, revolted. The army that had been organized to stop the Khitan invasion was sent instead to suppress the slave revolt in accordance with the philosophy, "Fight one evil with another." Yoriyoshi Minamoto was appointed general of the government troops. The surname Minamoto shows this man was from a family of the original race of Yottsu. He was the head of the enslaved nomadic Aborigines. After the subjugation of the revolt of Abe, some slave soldiers were employed by the emperor as guards of the imperial palace, and were thankful to the emperor for this favor. They are considered to be the origin of the samurai.*

As mentioned in Chapters 2 and 5, Yoritomo Minamoto of the Yottsu first established his government in Kamakura (the Kamakura Bakufu) in 1192. When Yoritomo died, the Hojo family of the Ya people gained political power in what Japanese historians call the Hojo Regency. The Hojo ruled for about 140 years when they were overthrown by the Ashikaga family in 1333.

From 1336 to 1392 two dynasties ruled Japan, one called the Northern Dynasty (supported by Ashikaga) and the other the Southern Dynasty, supported by the Yottsu, ancestors of the samurai. The Southern Dynasty was eventually defeated by the Ashikaga, who made an alliance with Ming China, and the ancestors of the samurai who supported the Southern Dynasty were forced back to their camps in the forests and mountains.

In 1467, Ounin-no-Ran broke out, a great civil war between the daimyos (feudal lords), Hosokawa against Yamana. Hosokawa gathered 160,000 troops from twenty-four provinces and took a position east of Kyoto. Yamana occupied a position west of Kyoto with 90,000 troops recruited from twenty provinces. The war lasted until 1477. The Ounin-no-Ran was the beginning of the civil war age that involved the entire Japanese nation until 1600. To meet the need for soldiers, Yottsu descendants were brought from their camps and employed by various daimyos as Ashigaru, the lowest class of samurai. The Ashigaru became the human shields of the civil war age.

Lucky survivors in the Ashigaru ranks collected armor and weapons of the dead, piece by piece, from the battlefields. These were refitted for use by the surviving Ashigaru, who were upgraded to Musha (a fully qualified samurai). They were called Zunpou Musha (self-made samurai). These self-made samurai took court nobles' fiefs by force, and the most successful of them became daimyos. They were later ranked within the nobility under the Meiji Restoration in 1868 and re-

---

*For a detailed account of the Samurai tradition in Japan, see Eiko Ikegami's *The Taming the Samurai* (Harvard University Press, 1997).

mained nobles until the end of World War II (1945), when all noble classes were abolished.

The civil war age ended officially when the 2nd Tokugawa Shogun, Hidetada, took power. In 1615 the famous Osaka Castle, headquarters of the Toyotomi, was destroyed and the last opposition to Tokugawa rule fell.

In this war between Tokugawa and Toyotomi, the Shogun Hidetada had the size of one of the Ashigaru's swords shortened because two swords of great size were too heavy and would significantly exhaust one's physical power. The role of the Ashigaru as human shields had become outdated due to the development of guns, but since that period the samurai have carried two swords of different sizes in their waistbands, one long and the other short.

During the civil war period the main weapons of the samurai were always spears and bows. The spear was considered to be so powerful that a samurai with spear a could match ten men with swords. The samurai sword never played a main role in war, since it was broken or bent easily when it hit armor or any hard object. Its major applications were not so brilliant, i.e. to command a corps, cut off an enemy's head after he had been killed with a spear, or to deflect a spearhead in a sudden attack. In an old book, it was recommended to have many retainers carry spare swords because they would break easily when a samurai had to use them in battle. This explains the origin of the samurai's need for the services of retainers. It also suggests that all official swords carried by retainers belonged to the lord, that the retainers were just keeping spare swords at hand for him.

In any case, the true history of the samurai sword shows little practical value as an effective weapon; but in samurai myths, kendo was considered the highest value, not only as a fine martial art, but also as a means to seek the samurai way of life and its precepts. Did samurai actually kill each other with these swords? Or would a samurai kill an impolite civilian at his own discretion without punitive consequence?

Unfortunately, this false image of the samurai was created by popular movies, TV shows, and other fictions. The origin of kendo might date back as far as the 14th century, when the Ashikaga Shogun took kendo lessons in self defense for the purpose of deflecting spear heads. A daimyo family called Yagiu taught kendo to Tokugawa Shoguns successfully. However, teaching kendo to a shogun was a superficial excuse, and the substance of the Yagiu family was something like the CIA. All daimyos were obliged to employ Yagiu's pupils. They were supposed to spy on daimyos to see that they were not plotting against Tokugawa. By the reign of the 8th Shogun Yoshimune in 1716, Yagiu Dojo (training halls) had already disappeared.

After the unification of Japan, under their control, the Tokugawa set up a code of behavior for the daimyos in 1615. It was revised many times, but in principle, provided political and moral precepts, maintenance of peace and order, and protocols and ritual ceremonies. It is ironic that the first article encouraged daimyos to improve in the military arts. However, the Tokugawa were in no mood to promote the martial art of kendo or any other form of military training, for fear that such training might create forces capable of overthrowing their rule.

The Bakufu closed the country, monopolizing importation of saltpeter from the West. Saltpeter was the main component of gunpowder and was not produced domestically. This move made all guns and rifles of the daimyos powerless. This deterrent to rebellion by the daimyos was as strong and as effective as a nuclear bomb today. In the initial period of their reign, the Bakufu found any excuse to destroy dangerous daimyos. A serious violation of code, particularly in military affairs, was enough for the Bakufu to use its overwhelming power to destroy a daimyo. In the first fifty years of the Tokugawa Shogunate, the number of Daimyo houses was reduced from 213 to 198.

At first, it was an unwritten law that a samurai should not draw his sword without permission of the lord; later, it was included in the code for daimyos. Remember, official swords carried by samurai were all property of the lord. This prohibition was considered an effective means to maintain peace. Punishment for violation was severe. The samurai was ordered to commit hara-kiri or seppuku (committing suicide by ritual cutting his abdomen), and his family was executed.

Under the circumstances, there were no masters of kendo nor battles with swords among samurai until the 19th century. It could never have happened that a samurai would have beheaded a civilian in the street with a flash of his sword for merely being impolite, first, because of the punishment he would face; second, for his lack of skill to do so. The Japanese are familiar with Koudan stories of great masters winning competitive kendo meets. In fact, no such competition ever took place. Instead, one of the samurais of Mito Han, (feudal clan of Mito, at present Ibaragi Prefecture in Kanto), Touko Fujita, wrote: "The first training hall of kendo was opened in 1828 and lessons were put on view for the samurai. It caused much controversy among the samurai and most of them sneered or abused it because it might hurt the bodies the samurai inherited from their parents and surrendered to the lord."

If movies and TV shows were made in accordance with the realities described above, samurai stories would lose the most attractive scenes at the climax, where the hero samurai of justice punishes the villains with his sword. Imagine how an American western without a gunfight would spoil the film's popularity. Japanese fiction would suffer similarly. So many Japanese are involved in the vast samurai commercialism that it would be an economic disadvantage to sacrifice the manu- factured samurai image for the truth. Truth is sacrificed, yielding to commercialism to sell cheap satisfaction.

Then how has the martial art of the sword been passed down? Simply by saying that sheriffs and their deputies used it as weapons when arresting criminals. There were only three training halls in the city of Edo, i.e. at the northern and southern metropolitan governments, and at prison. In local districts, training halls existed only at Sekisho (feudal immigration stations at the borders of daimyo territories, or the direct domains of the shogun where a passport had to be presented by travelers) and at administrators' offices in the shogun's direct domains controlled by government authorities, off limits to the general public.

At the beginning of the 19th century, when the international situation became progressively strained, daimyos feared foreign invasion, but had no effective means of defending themselves because they lacked gunpowder. To defend their rule, the Bakufu kept a strict policy monopolizing the import of saltpeter. A daimyo's only chance to procure the material was smuggling. A revolt against the Tokugawas could be successful only if the rebels could get a large supply of high grade saltpeter. (When the Satsuma and Choshu daimyos did get the saltpeter they successfully overthrew the Shogunate.) In preparation for the day when they would rise up against the Tokugawas, some daimyos strengthened their military power in secret and developed sword corps for close combat by training young men in the art of kendo.

Even the Bakufu could not go against the current of the times, and had to comply by opening kendo schools throughout Japan. This created a demand for teachers and a numbers of great kendo masters were born. They were all from very low classes, many from Ashigaru, the lowest class of the regular samurai. For example, Shusaku Chiba was from the family of a horse doctor; Yakuro Saito and Saizo Hijikata were both apprentices of a trading house in Edo. Many young men, dreaming of becoming samurai, took lessons for high fees, and as a result, many schools competed in the cities. To glorify and to attach authority to these schools, mythical origins and fictious stories of great champions were created and passed on to the pupils.

At the same time, development of new methods of paper production caused the cost of paper to fall sharply, and book publishing boomed. Among the writers born at the time of the boom, Nobutomo Ban was a great samurai writer who wrote more than 300 books in his lifetime. He created well-known characters of the great masters of kendo, such as Musashi Miyamoto and Bokuden Tsukahara, names familiar to most Japanese even now. Since he was a samurai himself, Ban's creations were received by readers with confidence that anything he wrote was true, and helped spread the glorified image of the samurai.

The notion to respect the Japanese sword as the divine soul of the samaurai was developed around this time. It injected a morality into kendo and made it an essential part of bushido. In the fight with swords, you must disregard your life and death to keep freedom of movement. If you feel the terror of death, it will stiffen your nerve and make you defensively clumsy. The result is obvious—you lose your life. To keep a calmness of mind, discipline of the soul is most important, so religions like Zen became a part of kendo. The daring, fearless image of the samurai was thus evolved.

The image of the samaurai created in the 19th century was one so daring that a samurai did not spare his own life. But true history showed samurai served as slave soldiers whose personal wills were not a factor; sacrifice was a requirement of their lowly status. During the civil war age in the 16th century, they developed a unique mutual life-saving system as professionals.

Hara-kiri is another aspect of the samurai that needs clarifying. It is debatable whether one can really commit suicide by cutting one's abdomen. Is it the samurai way to express his protest, or his apology? Was this ritual actually carried out by the samurai? These questions will be answered later. Let us now investigate the true story of the ninja.

The image of the ninja created by popular movies and TV is something like this: they were feudal secret agents or commandoes of unrivaled physical strength and special athletic skills; they acquired magical powers to conceal themselves by special training and were skilled in disguise, masters of kendo and a variety of weapons.

In Iga-no-kuni (a feudal province in the mountainous area of present-day Mie Prefecture) were homes of the ninja families of Iga and Koga. As Kaige ("outside the borderland where human beings live"), still remains, it is certain that this was one of the old camps where resisting aborigines were confined as prisoners by the Chinese and Korean powers in the 8th century. During the civil war years these ninja families were not strong, suffering more defeats than victories. Both families were later employed by Ieyasu, the first shogun of the Tokugawa family, but their rank was very low and they were treated poorly.

Books still exist detailing secrets of ninjutsu, the art of the ninja, the art of concealment and espionage) written by the leaders of both families. The contents are quite absurd. Koga's secret book is merely a copy of old Korean and Chinese military books that describe the magic of a legendary hermit with miraculous powers who could disappear in a flash or dazzle people by mass hypnosis. Iga's book is more practical, instructing how to disguise oneself, steal, and use special weapons, tools and skills such as knife-throwing, or how to cheat the enemy. According to a joint study of K. Adachi, H. Ozaki and N. Yamada published by Sanichi Shobo, titled *Ninpou* (same as ninjutsu), these books were written to justify their authors' salaries as ninja; the books established ninja ancestry and exaggerated the art unrealistically. The ninja's usefulness was diminished by the continuance of peace under the reign of Tokugawa.

There is one thing worthy of note, in Iga's third volume, describing the use of firearms and explosives. Iga explains that the use of explosives had its origins in ninjutsu. It seems that the handling of dangerous explosives was given to the descendants of the 8th century aboriginal prisoners, whose lives were of little significance, and therefore expendable. Japanese fireworks displays in the skies of summer nights are so exciting and beautiful, but the fireworks are so dangerous, even now, that a few pyrotechnicians lose their lives by accident every year. This was the reasons they were so important during the civil war period, when spears and bows were replaced by guns and explosives. However, when the Tokugawa Bakufu prohibited import of saltpeter, monopolizing it by closing the country, daimyos lost the means to rebel against the Bakufu, and peace continued up to the end of the Edo era. Unfortunately, it made the ninja useless, and ninjutsu disappeared, leaving just two books of "secrets."

As mentioned, the ninja were the descendants of the prisoners in the 8th century who were confined to camps in the mountainous areas, outside the world where most "human beings" lived. If these people went beyond their borders, they were killed mercilessly. The origin of ninjutsu must have developed as a means of concealment to avoid being killed. The letter *nin* means "endurance," and *ninjutsu* is, after all, a means to endure one's destiny in the subhuman existence of slavery.

The true samurai history is not glorious but vainglorious. One can learn many things from it. For example, the samurais' indomitable spirit pushed them from their role as human shields up to the position of daimyo or even shogun. In this respect, they resemble leaders like the originators of Sony, Honda, and so on, who rose up from the devastation of the war and achieved Japan's miraculous economic recovery. However, the samurai myths served as a basic philosophy that resulted in death for young Japanese in wars.

Fabrication and glorification of history that denies humanity can only lead to inevitable tragedy.

Chapter Eleven

Obligation

The battle of Midway was the biggest aero-naval clash ever in the history of naval battles. The immense sea battle to control the Pacific was fought by the main fleet of the Japanese Imperial Navy, using four front line aircraft carriers, against the U.S. Navy, with three aircraft carriers. Midway was a necessary operation for the Imperial Navy, which had previously succeeded in destroying many American battleships in its surprise attack on Pearl Harbor. Isoroku Yamamoto, Supreme Commander of the Combined Fleet, wanted to destroy remaining American offensive aircraft carrier strength at the core in order to assure Japan's control of the Pacific. According to the book *Midway*, by ex-naval officers Mitsuo Fuchida and Masatake Okumiya, the Imperial Navy mobilized unprecedented forces, committing 350 warships, 1,000 airplanes and 100,000 men to win this operation.

Although many books by U.S. and Japanese authors have been written in detail about Midway, a few points about the battle can be touched upon from different angles. The Japanese strategy was viable and our commitment to the battle sound. However, not all our tactics were fully implemented. As a result, the loss of all four of our aircraft carriers turned the operation into a blunder from which the Imperial Navy could not recover, thus we were unable to initiate further offensive against the U.S. Navy until the close of the war.

Yamamoto's idea was clear: to destroy American carriers that maintained a striking force against the Japanese fleet. First, Japan would need to catch the American carriers at a certain point in the vast expanse of the Pacific Ocean. Yamamoto thought that if the Japanese attacked an American air base on Midway Island, the U.S. fleet would come to defend it; thus attacking Midway was a means to lure the American aircraft carriers while the ultimate objective was to destroy them. The commander of the First Carrier Striking Force, Vice Admiral Chuichi Nagumo, was supposed to maintain that specific objective. But the initial easy victory in Pearl Harbor made Nagumo and his staff arrogant enough to believe the American fleet would lack the fighting spirit to make air assaults against the Japanese fleet, and Japan did not plan adequately for this contingency, a contradiction which caused the Japanese Navy to lose its most powerful striking force.

This operation, built on the sound premise that the Americans would come out to defend Midway, was wrong from the start. Nagumo should have spent more effort on reconnaissance. When he received a first hand report from the commander right after the air-raid on Midway recommending a second strike, he should not have given the order to change anti-fleet torpedoes to anti-land bombs. Shortly thereafter, when a report was issued that the Americans were closing in, Nagumo had to reverse orders, and the crews hurried to fit torpedoes again. A moment known as "the fatal five minutes" arrived at 7:24 am, when the first Japanese bomber took off from a carrier. Had the American counterattack been delayed by five minutes, all Japanese bombers could have been airborne, and might have been able to avoid fatal damage due to explosion of their own torpedoes. But American dive bombers swooped down from the clouds and sank three carriers with the first blow.

The Hiryu was the last carrier sunk in the battle of Midway. While the three other carriers were disabled by fire from the first American attack on the morning of June 5, 1942, the Hiryu was unhurt, alone in her furious counterattack against the U.S. fleet. American bombing eventually sank her that afternoon; but the fierce fighting spirit of Rear Admiral Tamon Yamaguchi, Commander of Carrier Division 2, exemplified the noble death of the samurai tradition fulfilling Bushido (the unwritten code of laws governing the lives and conduct of samurai). What my father saw here could have strongly influenced his behavior when his ship, the Shinano, was sunk.

At 7:42 a.m. on June 5, 1942, three American dive bombers assaulted the Akagi, flag carrier of Nagumo's Striking Forces. Two aerial bombs dropped by American dive bombers went through her deck and exploded where the Japanese bombers, explosives, torpedoes, and fuels were lodged, causing instantaneous fire and explosion in a chain that was impossible to avoid. Nagumo and his staff were on the bridge, unable to continue commanding the battle, since the ship was already disabled. They decided to move to the cruiser Nagara. Captain Awoki, skipper of the Akagi, remained, determined to die with his ship; however, he was eventually saved, in sharp contrast to Yamaguchi's death, which will be discussed later.

Yamaguchi immediately took command of air fighting, ordering eighteen dive bombers to attack the American carriers. They took off at 7:40 a.m., under cover of six zero fighters. American fighters intercepted and shot down ten bombers. The remaining eight bombers assaulted the American vessel Yorktown, hitting her with three bombs, and causing her to halt. However, she soon recovered and a few hours later started cruising on her own power at a speed of 20 knots per hour.

Meanwhile, Yamaguchi got a report from reconnaissance identifying the three American carriers, Yorktown, Hornet and Enterprise. He decided to use all his remaining power to launch a strike against them. Finding only ten able torpedo planes and six fighters, he sent all of them out. They were the last Japanese warplanes to attack American carriers. They pounced on Yorktown again and hit her with three torpedoes. Yorktown again stopped. Only five torpedo planes and three fighters returned to the Hiryu.

The Hiryu lost most of her warplanes after she attacked Midway once and the American fleet twice. Only six fighters, five dive bombers and four torpedo planes were left by 1:30 p.m. The crew had been fighting since early morning and was exhausted. Yamaguchi, ever alert and seeing enemy planes approach, exhorted his men to avoid danger, primarily to the ship. He was still imbued with fighting spirit after being attacked by 115 American bombers, and having made a narrow escape from 60 torpedoes and 70 bombs since early morning.

Yamaguchi believed an assault by only 15 planes in daylight would not be successful, thus he decided to attack at twilight. He let his men have a late lunch just before 2:00 p.m. Day would end; the time of the last attack was drawing near. As a high speed reconnaissance plane was about to take off at 2:30 p.m., an urgent lookout reported the approach of 13 American dive bombers. At the lookout's cry, Captain Tomeo Kaku, skipper of the Hiryu, started to turn right, but too late. The Hiryu escaped the first three bombs, but the next three successfully hit her deck adjacent to the bridge, blowing off the front elevator and hanging it over the bridge. The bridge was in tact, but it was impossible to see ahead. Soon fire and explosions broke out, and black smoke soared up to the sky. The ship came to a halt and started to list gradually. The ship was disabled and her captain could not contact the engine room.

Assuming risks, my father, as commander of Destroyer Division 10, skillfully pulled his flagship destroyer Kazagumo alongside the Hiryu to help the crews extinguish the fires and provide food and drinks.

The Hiryu was dead and hopeless. Yamaguchi notified Nagumo he was going to let his men leave the carrier, and called his surviving 800 crew topside. He announced, "I am responsible for the loss of the Hiryu and the Soryu (sister carrier) and I will see her die with my own eyes. All of you, leave now, and continue to fulfill your duty." Yamaguchi's staff was determined to die with the ship, but the captain's orders changed their decision. The captain exchanged farewell cups of water with his crew and they moved to the destroyer Kazagumo. Commander Ito, senior staff officer, asked if Yamaguchi had any last message to convey. The captain bluntly replied, "Nothing. Hand this to my family," and gave Ito his black deck cap. In return, the captain received a length of cloth to tie him to the bridge so that he would not fail to go down with his ship. Captain Kaku also offered to share the fate of his ship.

At that time, Captain Abe, my father, went to the Hiryu in an effort to try to persuade the commander and skipper to refrain from dying with their ship. However, their resolve was too strong. They ordered my father to sink the Hiryu with his destroyers' torpedoes. Then both men stepped up to the bridge with their usual gentle look, as they waved farewell to the crews aboard the destroyers.

Near sunrise on June 6, Captain Abe gave the signal to the Hiryu that she would be sunk by torpedoes, then ordered each of his destroyers to launch the attack. Soon a series of deafening explosions were heard, and the Hiryu's huge body was believed to have plunged beneath the surface of the sea soon after. At about 2:20 a.m., Captain Abe's report arrived at Yamato, the flagship of Admiral Yamamoto. However, a reconnaissance plane found the Hiryu and reported she was still afloat at 4:00 a.m. with several of the crew still on her deck. Nagumo sent the destroyer Tanikaze to the location to search, to no avail. It was learned after the war that she did not sink until 5:20 a.m., and that 416 crewmen died with her commander and skipper.

Who knows the fate of warriors in battle! Some sailors were locked in the engine room; efforts to save them had been in vain. But a miracle took place. Torpedoes of friendly destroyers made large holes in the hull, and the men were able to escape to the deck. These were the survivors the plane reported. Later they were rescued by American sailors, while floating at sea.

Fuchida and Okumiya state in their book that Tamon Yamaguchi was one of the most outstanding officers of the Imperial Navy, a man who successfully held all the Navy's important posts; he attended Princeton University and served as a naval attache to the Japanese Embassy in Washington D.C. His character was similar to Admiral Yamamoto's, whose successor he was considered to be. Yamaguchi was a man of few words, who made his opinions succinctly clear when necessary. His best quality as a naval officer was his ability to deal with difficult situations calmly with the full exertion of his power, relying on his bravery and inherent physical strength. He made no mistakes in judgment. His subordinates accepted his decision to die with his ship without a second thought because he lived in the tradition of the samurai precept: "Death of a samurai is the same as being born." He chose to inspire others rather than serve again among the living. Such decisions may be considered an unhappiness brought about by the national character of Japan that led many to die in this manner in wars.

It is a tradition of the British Navy that the skipper is married to his ship and must share her fate. Perhaps it was a good tradition for the British Empire, but some will find it hard to understand why a captain must die with his ship. When a major battle is fought, damage cannot be helped. Why should it be the responsibility of a commander that his ship is struck by shells, bombs and torpedoes in the course of battle, unless he committed some gross tactical blunder? Yamaguchi's case involved force majeure. After his ship was bombed, he did his best to save her.

For what else would he be held responsible? Or did he assume the responsibility of defeat? Certainly it is the duty of a military man to win. Which is better, to take the responsibility of defeat by committing suicide, or to live and continue fighting till victory? It is much harder to continue fighting, because every time an officer fights, he has to go through the same ordeal. Isn't death an escape from duty? The officer may be able to fulfill Bushido personally this way, but isn't it irresponsible to the navy and the nation?

One can disagree with the way Fuchida and Okumiya profile Yamaguchi. He is dehumanized and idolized to suit the samurai model, fulfilling Bushido by suicide. Yamaguchi has been made into a legendary national hero. In admiration of him, innocent youngsters would be willing to impose on themselves impossible training and precepts. As they endeavor to live up to the Bushido legends, they become more dehumanized. Eventually, Bushido became the unwritten laws to govern samurai as well as soldiers and sailors. Yamaguchi was a victim of Bushido in this very same way. Such glorification was given to my father as well.

It took nearly three hours for Hiryu to sink after she was hit by friendly torpedoes. What did Admiral Yamaguchi and Skipper Kaku think and say to each other during their own death vigil? It is relatively easy to commit suicide impulsively in anger and protest, but how about bearing a slow, voluntary death? It is clear they did not wish others to follow their example. In fact, Captain Awoki of the Akagi, who survived the battle, went on to live quite a different way of life.

His ship, the Akagi, was sunk by friendly torpedoes. Her sister carriers, Kaga and Soryu, also were hit. Direct damage from American bombs was not so great, but fuel, bombs and torpedoes from carrier-based warplanes created a succession of explosions that caused instantaneous fire, which damaged communications equipment on the bridge. Nagumo and his staff could not resume command of the fleet again, so they moved the flag to the cruiser Nagara at about 8:30 a.m. Captain Awoki tried to extinguish the fire, but explosions continued, communication with the engine room was cut off, and nothing could save the ship from sinking. Awoki ordered the emperor's portrait be secured first, then all able bodies to leave at 6:00 p.m. Surviving crew were accommodated on escorting destroyers.

Awoki waited on the Akagi on the anchor deck at the ship's bow, tying his body to a prop with a rope. He instructed one of the crew to telegram Nagumo from the destroyer, asking for approval to sink Akagi. The cable was intercepted by headquarters on the flagship Yamato, which replied directly to "wait."

The Akagi did not sink for some time. Finally, Yamamoto decided to sink her and instructed Nagumo, who ordered Captain Ariga to sink her around midnight, which was done at 1:55 a.m. the next morning. Awoki accepted solicitations of his staff and was transferred to the destroyer. Thus, he survived the battle, though it probably was not his choice, since all the other skippers died in action.

Afterwards, Captain Awoki's staff were sorry they had saved him because his life became miserable with the belief that he should have gone down with his ship. Because he did not perform as Bushido indicated, he was immediately placed in the reserves. He was called up again, but demoted to the commanding position of a local air base.

He suffered from this dishonor until he died. Though his active duty had been performed loyally, his failure to perform Bushido made others shun him. He was never judged by courtmartial, but rather by the unwritten laws of Bushido which govern the life of a samurai. Commander Tanpo, chief of engine rooms, who came to the bridge to report, was blocked by a fire from returning to his duty, and was also thus judged, and his life ruined by Bushido as well.

Another man pressed hard by Bushido was Vice Admiral Nagumo, Commander of the first carrier strike force. As Yamaguchi was more widely praised than he, Nagumo felt the cold eyes of his colleagues more strongly, which continued until he died in Saipan later.

According to Hiroshi Kamei's *Records of Midway Battle*, Rear Admiral Ryunosuke Kusaka, Chief of Staff, tells the following: he was lying in a hospital room of the cruiser Nagara for medical treatment of burns and sprains incurred in battle, when Commander Tamotsu Ooishi,

Chief Staff Officer, suddenly came into his room with his face drawn in tension. In a stiff manner, Ooishi said, "Sir, on behalf of the staff I would like to request you to advise Commander Nagumo to commit suicide, taking the responsibility of defeat. All of us are determined to follow his death by committing suicide right after."

Kusaka became angry and said, "Do you think everything is over if you commit hara-kiri (suicide by cutting one's own abdomen; *seppuku* has the same meaning). You fellows are too easygoing. You get on cloud nine when things are going well, but when you're struck with bad luck, you talk about hara-kiri." Kusaka ended abruptly by exclaiming, "You fool!"

The admiral went to see the staff and said, "It is obvious that responsibility of defeat lies with us and deserves death. But I don't think it is right to persist to one's own course of action while our nation is in a crisis. It will be hard for us to face our nation alive after such a blunder, but I can't agree to commit suicide simply to escape from responsibility of defeat. I believe to stand up from defeat and return a blow to our enemy is the only way to fulfill our duty."

No one said anything. The admiral thanked them and added, "I will tell my opinion to the commander, too." He went to see Nagumo, who appeared much smaller than he ever had looked before. Nagumo looked at Kusaka and smiled, but his eyes were unsmiling. By insight, the admiral realized Nagumo was determined to die, and told him his opinion. At the end, Nagumo said, "I understand." But Nagumo's wish was fulfilled on July 6, 1944, when he committed suicide in an underground defense position of the Japanese Army just before the allout Banzai charge in Saipan.

The arrogance and self-righteousness of the Japanese are evident. Why did the Japanese so readily believe they could prevail in battle? Backed by help from the great power of the gods, the Japanese military was determined to win. If a leader lost a battle, it was only due to his own fault, and he should take the responsibility, according to Bushido. Preliminary reconnaissance was of little consequence. "Cut the enemy down with a flash of the Japanese sword with belief in victory, and victory surely will be yours."

Bushido, an unwritten code of laws governing the life and conduct of the samurai, most probably obliged not only my father but a great many young military hopefuls to choose death in war.

Chapter Twelve

Bushido, Hagakure and Hara-kiri

Bushido is popularly believed to be an old tradition of Japan. However, only in the Meiji era was it widely practiced among the masses. *Naniwa-bushi*, a recital of ballads of loyalty and human feeling to *samisen* accompaniment, played by Tochuken Kumoemon to imbue bushido with the story of the forty-seven samurais who avenged their lord's death, was sponsored by the Meiji military and right wing political faction, and was a great hit in 1899. Today's concept of bushido is diffused by *Naniwa-bushi's* most moving passage in the famous phrase: "As among flowers the cherry blossom is queen, so among men the samurai is lord," quoted in Inazo Nitobe's book, *Bushido*, mentioned in Chapter 10. The ballads were part of a national effort to encourage fighting spirit in preparation of the coming war with Russia. Five years later, the Russo-Japanese War broke out, and the Russian positions were buried in big piles of hundreds of thousands of bodies of Japanese soldiers who had hurled themselves at Russian machine guns under the obligation of bushido, as described in Chapter 3.

Bushido grew more bloodthirsty at the end of the Tokugawa era, when in 1863, a special corps called Shinsen-gumi was organized by the Bakufu to recruit men from the non-samurai classes. Isami Kondo, a well-known commander, was the son of a farmer adopted by a samurai family, and Saizo Hijikata, right hand of Kondo, was an apprentice of the Matsuzakaya Kimono Store. These two were unaware of the old rules and customs of the samurai established during the civil war age (1467-1600), when samurai did not die easily. Members of the Shinsen-gumi were new and unscathed; there was nothing to make them one united body to fight anti-Tokugawa forces; the Shinsen-gumi needed something to create iron unity, and instituted formal rules to control the members under the glorified name of bushido. Rules were dictated so strictly that any violation was punished by the sentence of death by hara-kiri.

In 1616, a year after the first Tokugawas Shogun Ieyasu died, his instructions were published as precepts. He stressed keeping the peace, instructing all samurais to "bag the bows and cap the spearheads," forbidding private fights among samurais, taking steps to prohibit a samurai from drawing his sword by reason that all swords listed on the samurai register were the property of the lord. Some samurai were actually sentenced to death for being prepared to draw a sword in the palace of the Shogun. (To draw a samurai sword, you must release the blade from the lock contained in the sheath with a push of your left thumb. This motion is regarded as "preparing to draw your sword"). Therefore, samurai could not fight with swords until the end of the Tokugawa era, when the martial art of kendo attracted the attention of the Bakufu and Hans as a necessary means to resist foreign invasion, allowing the Bakufu to loosen its control on martial arts.

Fearful that the Bakufu would interpret them as a conspiracy against the Tokugawas, daimyos never authorized martial arts. Kendo was passed down to the police and vigilante corps among non-samurai classes. Regular samurai never learned kendo; on the contrary, they despised it as the image of a human shield given to the lowest semi-samurai rank of *ashigaru*. The samurai's main weapons were bows and spears. Bushido consisted of precepts, teaching the samurai how to live, and contrary to popular misconception, did not require expertise in kendo. Thus a great many masters of kendo were born from non-regular samurai classes in the 19th century. Shinsen-gumi, newly organized as a special corps under direct command of the Bakufu, stormed the old capital of Kyoto with terrors of assassinations and killing, maintaining iron unity with the so-called bushido they had invented.

Hara-kiri was directly coupled with bushido and considered an honorable death specially given to samurai. In his book *Bushido*, Nitobe explains hara-kiri: "In our minds this mode of death is associated with instances of the noblest deeds and of the most touching pathos...Death involving a question of honor was accepted in Bushido as the key to the solution of many complex problems, so that to an ambitious samurai, a natural departure from life seemed a rather tame affair and a consummation not devoutly to be wished for." He adds further: "Now my readers will understand that *seppuku* (hara-kiri) was not a mere suicidal process by which warriors could expiate their crimes, apologize for errors, escape from disgrace, redeem their friends, or prove their sincerity. When enforced as a legal punishment, it was practiced with due ceremony. It was a refinement of self-destruction, and none could perform it without the utmost coldness of temper and composure of demeanor, and for these reasons it was particularly benefitting to the profession of bushi (samurai)."

However, the reality of hara-kiri seems completely different. Yagiri writes of a personal experience: "I was in Fengtian (now Shenyang) in Manchuria, in the summer of 1945. As the Red Army marched into the city with a long queue of heavy tanks on...August 18, a big riot of Manchurians broke out downtown near Fengtian station, and the Japanese took refuge in a primary school. Four officers of the Japanese army among the refugees said they were going to commit *seppuku*. The oldest one drew his sword, and wrapped the middle of the blade with a towel to hold it. After making a polite bow to a shrine, he stabbed his abdomen with the sword, shouting, but the blade point bounced back when it hit his thick fat, merely leaving a small trace on his skin. Momentarily, a little blood came out and stained. He muttered in pain and lost willpower to carry further with hara-kiri.

"Another man standing by remarked that the officer's strength was not enough to stick the blade deep enough into his abdomen, so he must put the point at the right place while standing upright and fall forward, pushing the blade into the abdomen hard with the weight of his body. He did so, causing splashes of about three bowls of blood. The officer was down unconscious with his eyes open. Someone remarked that when he regained consciousness, he would be in great pain until he died gradually from the loss of blood, but if he were treated by a doctor right away, he would be fine. So I went out to find a doctor. When I came back with him, three officers were gone, including the officer who first tried to stab himself in the manner of seppuku but failed. Another officer who had successfully stabbed himself and became unconscious was treated by the doctor. Four days later, he was gone, too, with a bandage wrapped around his abdomen.

A comment by Hondo, Precinct Chief of the Akasaka Police Station, about the suicide of General Nogi and his wife by hara-kiri, in order to follow the Emperor Meiji to his grave, appeared in the *Kokumin Shinbun (The Nation's News)* dated September 15, 1912. Hondo said, "I am afraid wrong information is being circulated among people as to the death of the Nogis by hara-kiri at 8:00 p.m. on the 13th, and I would like to relate the real facts of the case. I have seen many suicides by now; however, this is the first time I have seen such a samurai-like death, and I believe it is exemplary. In an eight mat room on the second floor, General Nogi seated himself squarely (the Japanese way of sitting down on a tatami mat with his knees and toes touching the mat and his body resting on his heels) with his wife on his left side. He wore only a shirt.

"He stuck his sword first through the left side of his abdomen, drawing it horizontally to his right, then up at the end, cutting the abdomen about 24 cm, fulfilling the laws of hara-kiri in a fine manner. Then he put the point of his sword at his throat, keeping it upright on the tatami mat with his hands, and pushed his body down forcefully so that the sword would pierce through his throat. The point of the sword actually came out the nape of his neck 18 cm. General Nogi was dead with his face down. His wife, dressed formally in a kimono, first cut her throat with a dagger, then put the point to her heart, holding the shaft at a pillow, and pushed her body down to the floor so the point would penetrate her heart. The point went through her rib and nearly came out of her back. Her clothes remained neat and orderly. In a sea of blood, it was a respectful and solemn death."

Hondo's commentary is so detailed, almost as if he had been present while the Nogis committed hara-kiri. However, if it were truly like that, why were there rumors of murder among the people while the newspapers issued this report? And why was it necessary for the police chief to announce his commentary the next morning in denial of public opinion? The reason was simple. The couple groaned and writhed in pain. It would have taken a long time for them to die. The door to the room was shut tight, but unusual sounds could be heard by maids, which led to the rumors.

Most probably, the article on Nogis' hara-kiri is the first and last commentary by the authorities ever found in the newspapers from which we can induce the exemplary manners of hara-kiri, as follows:

1. Stick sword into abdomen.
2. Cut abdomen to right, 24 cm horizontally with sword.
3. Turn sword upwards to finish.
4. Pull sword out of abdomen.
5. Put sword point to throat, changing grip.
6. Keep sword upright on the floor.
7. Push head down hard.

According to forensic medicine clinical data, in 80 out of 83 cases, one lost consciousness as soon as a foreign material penetrated the body, at step one. Nogi would have to be a superman to have remained conscious through all seven steps. Would you be willing to test this theory on yourself?

In spite of a slow death, it is said in Koudan stories that every Japanese samurai could patiently endure terrible pain to die of hara-kiri in composure, as if he were going back to a place where he originally belonged. One reads many exaggerated stories, such as those of Tametomo Minamoto, who, according to a book entitled *Hogen Monogatari*, committed hara-kiri leaning back on a post to cut off his own head. Yoshisada Nitta, one of the typical great samurai of old Japan, cut his own head off with his sword in his left hand, buried it himself in the ground, and covered the place with his dead body, according to descriptions of Taiheiki.

These are just foolish exaggerations; however, these stories entertain the Japanese masses, apparently satisfying us by letting us believe our ancestors could accomplish things which no other nation could; despite unrealistic attributes, the stories maintain popular appeal.

What value do we see in enduring such terrible pain while dying calmly and quietly? What you believe makes a great deal of difference. Do you believe the Nogis could methodically commit hara-kiri in the way Hondo described? Or do you think it is unrealistic to believe anyone could do such a thing because it is beyond human limitations? The Japanese have traditionally accepted the former view, believing that Japan's unparalleled history of bushido gives great value to the practice of hara-kiri. Western thought, however, takes the latter view, that since no other nations claim a history which can parallel Japan's claim, it must be fiction and the practice of hara-kiri is beyond human limitation to endure. Therefore, it is inhuman to impose such impossible obligations under the code of bushido. Why do the Japanese give so much value to painful death? Why do they lie to themselves by accepting the impossible as possible?

The prouder the Japanese become of their uniqueness, the more they appear inhuman and incomprehensible to foreigners. The legend of the imperial household is a major example, and unfortunately, has caused unnecessary misunderstanding and racial discrimination. The typical foreign stereotype of the Japanese is "arrogant", "liars", "cruel" and "sneaky" (as a result of the Pearl Harbor attack), prejudice attributable to this basic difference in thinking.

Yagiri is the exceptional Japanese, with critical power to read the truth behind the official announcement of an *okami* like Hondo. Anyone as sophisticated as Yagiri will see that hara-kiri is not a proper means of suicide because of the pain and slowness in reaching death. If death solves all problems, e.g., expiates crimes, apologizes for errors, escapes disgrace, redeems friends or proves sincerity, why not choose a quick and easy death? Why a slow and painful one?

The reason is clear. Because it was the Chinese masters' cruel punishment to impose a slow and painful death on their Ya slaves in ancient times. As a warning to other slaves, punishment had to be cruel, painful and slow. The Ya race's pride, dying with composure, caused them to resist the ruler's attempt to show victims writhing in agony as warnings to others; painful endurance was the Ya's only protest against outrageous punishment.

The pen name Tomeo Yagiri has relevance to the above. Yagiri means to cut Ya and Tomeo means the man to stop it, i.e., the man to stop the outrageous killing of Ya people. As proof that hara-kiri was a punishment for aborigines, it was never applied to Kuge, court nobles.

The system of *kaishaku* (up to the Tsunayoshi era, *kaishaku* meant a go-between for marriage) was initiated to reduce the pain of punishment. Kaishaku was assigned to cut off the head of the samurai performing hara-kiri, as he cut into his abdomen with his sword. Later the practice was formalized, whereby the beheading took place with the motion to commit hara-kiri. Nitobe quotes in his book *Bushido* a hara-kiri episode by a samurai named Zenzaburo Taki, from *Tales of Old Japan*, written by Mitford, who claimed to have been one of the eyewitnesses himself.

For the charge of firing on foreigners living in Kobe, Taki performed hara-kiri in front of seven Japanese and seven foreign witnesses. The honorable role of *kaishaku* was given to Zenzaburo's skillful pupil of swordsmanship, who successfully cut Zenzaburo's head off with the first try. Even so, a cruel and ghastly scene resulted.

The Meiji military imbued bushido in the people with the *naniwabushi* play. Ex-Choshu Han samurai monopolized the military hierarchy and hara-kiri was the tradition of that Han. The administration of the Han had Seigyoku Nakamura, Han's Confucian, make a digest of the Han's precepts, originally edited in 1767, and printed in 1855 as a text for education. At the beginning of this text, a letter from Takamoto Mouri, son of the lord Motonari Mouri, founder of the Choshu Han in the 16th century, is exhibited under the title *Hara-kiri*. The letter says that no samurais of Choshu Han would refuse to perform hara-kiri if so ordered by the lord. Young students were requested to follow loyal predecessors' examples of dedication to the Han; all Choshu samurais had to be prepared to commit hara-kiri at any time.

It is no coincidence that General Nogi elected the ritual of hara-kiri to follow his master, Emperor Meiji, to the grave. He was from Choshu. There is little doubt that Nogi's belief in hara-kiri, fostered by education in his early years, made him go through all the pain and agony of that slow death. Surprisingly, the hara-kiri education initiated by Choshu Han and taken over by the Meiji military later, was based on misinterpretation. The original word used in the letter was *harase-wo-kiru*, not hara-kiri.

Harase-wo-kiru could certainly be confused with hara-kiri. It was a local dialect in the area where Motonari and Takamoto were brought up, and meant to work one's fingers to the bone, or to serve faithfully without being two-faced. The area was forcibly conceded to other daimyo by Ieyasu Tokugawa in 1600, and Confucian scholars 255 years later did not know the original meaning of the word anymore.

In Choshu the precept of hara-kiri encouraged fighting spirit. Hara-kiri is a painful death. It is much easier to plunge into combat with the enemy and find a way to avoid danger. Once you start committing hara-kiri, there is no way to escape from death. However, if you fight hard in battle, there will be an opportunity to survive. Surviving battle rather than dying was a precept; however, it was changed to admiration of death by further glorification and misinterpretation.

On checking the record of official harakiris by samurai criminals, we find only twenty executed it with the help of *kaishaku* under the jurisdiction of the Bakufu between 1703 and 1867, including a big case in which ten died in 1858. All of these were conducted in official, closed facilities. Nevertheless, harikiri ceremonies were known to the people in detail through descriptions in various books. One, for instance, stated: "Two tatami mats covered with red carpet are placed on white sand. The convicted samurai appears, dressed in a white kimono and light blue *kamishimo* (a formal jacket with hemp-cloth wings to put on a kimono) and sits down. Momentarily, he receives a stand of the kind used in temple offerings, on which lies an unsheathed short sword 9 1/2 inches long, the middle of the blade being wrapped in white paper, in order that the sword can be held without hurting the samurai's hand. The samurai picks up the sword, and puts the stand behind him. Then, slowly and with dignity, he takes off the hemp-cloth wings and opens his kimono..."

This is nothing but a copy of a harikiri scene from a Kabuki play. Tragedy played by popular actors in colorful scenes made hara-kiri famous among the populace, and helped spread a glorified image of this honorable suicide ceremony privileged only to samurai. However, as we have seen, it was not actually suicide. One may be able to commit suicide in protest, in despair or to escape pain, at will. If death were the purpose, the quick, easy way would be chosen. But this was the execution of a death sentence to give the victim more pain and terror, though later somewhat eased by the introduction of a *kaishaku*. One will not accept losing one's ego by compulsion, even if it were by execution of a sentence duly imposed by legal trial. Hara-kiri was in some cases nearly a lynching to take away life under an equivocal moral code of bushido, which is more cruel.

The terror of bushido, that one would suffer pain and agony worse than death in the event one violated it, often impelled the Japanese to make banzai charges in World War II battles. A book entitled *Hagakure* played an important role in this. In Nabeshima Han in Hizen (now

Saga Prefecture), *Bushido*, from Tsunetomo Tashiro's notes on what Tsuramoto Yamamoto said in a retreat, was edited into a book of eleven volumes. Yamamoto's words were spread nationwide in the 1940's to imbue fighting spirit in Japanese soldiers; above all, "The way of the samurai is found in death," was often used for military propaganda and made Hagakure very famous.

The following is Yamamoto's profile, in accordance with descriptions by Miyoshi Ookuma in his book *A Modern Translation of Hagakure* (Shin Jinbutsu Ooraisha), and *The Book of the Samurai—Hagakure*, by William Scott Wilson (Kodansha International, 1979).

Yamamoto was born in Saga in 1659, the last son of Shigesumi Yamamoto, a samurai of the Nabeshima Han, and died in 1719. In infancy, he was nearly sold by his father to a salt vendor, but one of his relatives important to the Yamamotos objected, took him and raised him in his own family. He was employed as a page to Mitsushige Nabeshima by the time he was nine, and later apprenticed to the official in charge of writing and books, with the hope of further promotion. He was soon dismissed, however, and rehired at the lowest rank. His state of mind is written in *Hagakure*.

"Supreme loyalty in the service of the samurai is to advise and help the lord govern his country right. If I remain in a low rank I cannot do so. I thought a young man would not be able to assume the position of *karo* (minister in charge of administration and civil service of a Han); since Yamamoto was engaged in a literary job it was the right target, because it was the highest as retainer, and I was determined to become a *karo* by age fifty. And I decided to work like hell."

Like young employees of business corporations today, Yamamoto worked hard to obtain an executive position. "Since I was young, it was my single-minded desire to do my best." In the end, he was presented a set of futon (Japanese style bedding) from his lord as a token of appreciation for long service.

After his lord Mitsushige died, Yamamoto lost hope of success and retired to a hermitage where he wrote *Hagakure*. "The Way of the Samurai is found in death," he said. "...If by setting one's heart right every morning and evening, one is able to live as though his body were already dead, he gains freedom in the Way. His whole life will be without blame, and he will succeed in his calling."

When he said that the Way the samurai should live was found in death, he meant that death was the worst thing that could happen to anyone, and therefore, if he were prepared to face it, nothing else could be feared in life. Most Japanese interpret this as: if you find bushido to "die", you will gain freedom in fighting martial arts, because the Japanese word originally used in the book is *budo*. *Budo* normally means martial arts today. However, *budo* formerly meant the way of the samurai to live, the same as bushido, and therefore, the English translation, "he gains freedom in the Way (of samurai life)" is quite right. Furthermore, the phrase, "he will succeed in his calling" makes sense.

Yamamoto never participated in battle; he was not a master of any martial art; he thought highly of himself and did everything he could for Mitsushige. When he wrote, "If it were ancient times, I would have performed hara-kiri to accompany my lord in death, sitting on the futon and wearing the quilt with sleeves that Mitsushige gave me. I was so thankful to him." What was actually on his mind? I feel this is a paradoxical expression of his anger.

Hagakure is essentially a book of anger. However, the Japanese military leaders took the phrase "the Way of the samurai is found in death" only and used it manipulatively in World War II to drive young men to their deaths. Yamamoto added, "When it comes to either/or, there is only the quick choice of death..." This was literary emphasis to be prepared for death; however, many interpreted it literally, my father perhaps among them. Did any of our leaders take responsibility for this after the war? Nobody did.

Hagakure means "hidden by leaves," a word to be given to the coward who hides himself under leaves in battle. *Hagakure* is here respectfully presented to those who drove so many soldiers to their unnecessary deaths in World War II.

Chapter Thirteen

Injected Morality

Whether you are good at a martial art or not so good depends upon your reflexes. Whether you will be able to kill your enemy in close combat or you will be killed ultimately depends on your luck. You have won this time but you never know what will happen next time. If you are injured you have a big risk of losing your life, since injury may cause festering or tetanus. A samurai's fight in battle was really a big gamble on his life at poor odds. If possible, one would have preferred to avoid being either a samurai or ashigaru (lowest rank below samurai), which involved high risks. I believe when the Chinese said, "The son of a good family never makes a soldier" they meant it; so they gave the job to the humblest, who had no choice but to take the job to survive. As stated earlier, samurai took the role of human shields in the battles of ancient Japan.

The medical situation in feudalistic Japan is quite different from that which has been depicted in modern samurai fictions and TV. Contrary to popular belief, there were few medical practioners in Edo. Ryojun Matsumoto, an ex-family doctor for the shogun and first surgeon general of the Meiji army, wrote in his memoirs: "There were only a few doctors with private practices within the city of Edo." If Edo, one of the largest cities in the world with a population of millions, had only a few private doctors, you can imagine what it was like in local areas. As a substitute, people went to faith healers who burned marijuana, the smoke from which made the patient feel better for a while. During the Meiji civil wars Matsumoto served as an army surgeon and taught doctors in northeastern areas how to treat external injuries. It is hard to believe there was an effective way of treating external injuries in the 15th-16th centuries.

Samurai would have needed several lives if they really fought hard at all times. The Buddhist concept of seven rebirths was imbued popularly to make the samurai feel a bit easier about death. However, it was an absolute necessity that the samurai's family would be maintained by his descendants. Fees for an annual memorial service would be paid regularly so that the samurai could be reborn in the right place. It was traditional to believe in the continuity of family. Samurai would fight at the risk of annihilation when the fate of a clan hinged on battle, but under normal circumstances they observed their own rules to avoid the risk of losing life.

It was said a samurai would cry his name in a loud voice before he charged the enemy, to show his commander he was actively involved in battle, so that his reward would be greater at the battle's end. At the same time, this served as a means to avoid unnecessary fights with samurai of the same clan, possibly employed by the enemy. By crying his name and the place he came from, the samurai's identity would easily be known. If the enemy samurai belonged to the same clan, they would never fight each other, since there were standing rules that same clan should not fight each other.

It was important to take a good look at the enemy before challenging him. If he was tired or wounded he was good game to fight since it would be easy to win at much less risk. When your enemy looked tough, you and he would lower spears, cry out your names as loud as possible, then part without fighting.

When you were tired or wounded and felt you had no chance to win, then you would shout, "*Tanma*! (wait a moment!) and you could negotiate with your enemy a "life money" called *otoshimae* (money to be paid before the head is cut off). The money you had in your pocket was going to be his anyway after he cut your head off, therefore, to settle the matter you would be required to offer a substantial amount of additional money to be paid on credit. If the amount was agreed to by the enemy, you wrote a promissory note and put your handprint on it instead of your signature. You would be released upon handing it to your enemy together with your cash. This is the reason why a promissory note is called *tegata* (handprint). Perhaps you have seen a samurai carrying a white paper in his breast pocket. It was not for wiping his sword after he killed, but for writing a promissory note. For a samurai it was very important to carry the paper and cash, since they could save his life in the last minutes of battle. Later, during the age of peace, the custom became a mere formality.

Tegata was the tradition of professional samurais to survive in a severe occupation. Their system depended solely upon credit. They had to keep promises, otherwise the *tegata* system would have failed. A proverb was born on this account, "A samurai never breaks his word."

Until orthodox neo-Confucianism was introduced by the Tokugawas at the beginning of the 17th century, the samurai's motivation was only to be rewarded. Of course there were clan precepts to govern the samurai's life, and samurai normally served only the lord of their own clan through an unwritten contract. The lord paid a salary, and in return the samurai served him to the extent of the payment. Samurai were free to change lords if they were dissatisfied with the rewards. For instance, Saizo Kani, one of the greatest masters of spearsmanship, changed his lord nine times in his life. Samurai and lord was a rather dry and unemotional relationship. When a castle was about to be taken by the enemy and the owner became insolvent, the lord was requested to fulfill his last obligation under the contract to save the lives of his retained samurais with his life. The samurai cut the lord's head off and submitted it to the enemy.

Samurai in the civil war age lived life freely, with tremendous energy. The situation was fluid. Every daimyo had a chance of success in building power, according to his skills. The clarity of a contract between a professional soldier and his lord based on money seems better than the arbitrary rules of a shogun who governed through a system of feudalistic morality and cruel, hypocritical Buddhism in the Edo period.

As the Tokugawas gained control over large areas of Japan, daimyos lost their potential for further expansion. In addition, the Tokugawas threatened the daimyos' very existence by the Bakufu's demand for total surrender to shogunate rule. As we have already seen, the Tokugawas held the monopoly in the saltpeter trader; as a result, the daimyos were unable to defy the Bakufu.

It was at this time that the Bakufu forced neo-Confucianism on the Japanese. This was intended to set up an orderly society by establishing relationships of shogun to daimyo, daimyo to samurai, samurai to commoners, masters to employees, teachers to pupils, fathers to sons and so on. This firmly established the shogun as the real ruler of Japan. Loyalty and faithful service to shogun as lord and master was emphasized. To establish a hierarchy of power was the objective, and at the top of the hierarchy was the Tokugawa Shogun.

At first it was convenient to have the imperial household to legitimatize the power of the Tokugawas, but later many problems were created because of recurring plots hatched within the household against the Bakufu. There was no room for two monarchs in one country. Political demands completely changed the concept of bushido, from the end of the Tokugawas' reign into the Meiji era, when the concept evolved through the injection of severer morals and more militaristic ideals.

During the civil war age the population of Japan was about 10 million, but it doubled towards the end of the 17th century due to the continuing peace. There was little chance to show feats of arms in battle and the fiefs of daimyos were fixed. Production of rice did not increase proportionately, and while the level of the Hans' income remained unchanged, severe inflation took place, causing serious financial problems. Thus frugality became one of the major virtues of samurai in bushido, as it was considered the only efficient way to cope with economic problems. Nitobe states in his *Bushido*, "Money and the love of it being thus diligently ignored, bushido itself could long remain free from a thousand and one evils of which money is the root. This is sufficient reason for the fact that our public men have long been free from corruption..." Quite the contrary, love of money governs everybody in Japan, noble *tatemae* (principles) notwithstanding. The daimyos' entire concerns were focused on the economy. How to finance the Han? How to pay retainers' salaries? The samurais' most important objective was to get a post in the government of the Han or the Bakufu because good allowances were paid, in addition to the family salary, which was fixed. Then as now, money was the most important issue, just as it is in most periods of history.

Nitobe sighed for grief in his book, "...but alas! How fast plutocracy is making its way in our time and generation." However, in Japan money was almighty all the time. At the entrance hall to homes of important people, a *shikidai* (wooden floor) was usually provided. Anybody who wished ask a favor of the owner was required to make a thud with a bag of money. Hearing the sound, a secretary would come out, to ask what the caller wanted. The request was compared with the amount of money offered; if insufficient, the secretary shook his head; then the visitor put more money down. This was called *iro wo tsukeru*, and the expression is still used in business in Japan today. Without advance payment, a wish would not be conveyed to the master by his secretary. As a *tatemae* (principle) of bushido, the samurai was supposed to be a man of integrity. However, at any level *honne* (true mind) was always the love of money.

Nitobe mistakenly thought, when he wrote *Bushido*, that ethics in politics existed in the past, because samurai observed bushido and ignored the love of money. Yet Nitobe saw that corruption in his own time was not unusual. Again, this is the normal pattern of Japanese thinking: "The past was always good, while the present is no good." No doubt the teaching of a glorified history has made the Japanese think this way.

"*Okami* (ruler) is always right" is another idea which influenced people for a thousand years and justified building a vertical society in which a godlike man rules other men. This also influenced the Meiji ideology of "we, the single Japanese race, lived gently, innocently and peacefully on isolated islands under the benevolent reign of a god-like emperor; the longer one goes back in history, the purer the morals and ethics of the people." This kind of history may teach people to pay reverence to past rulers; however, it will not supply any lessons. One cannot fully appreciate laws unless one knows the history of violence that was used to rule the people; one cannot find effective ways to prevent politics from being polluted with money unless one recognizes the history of plutocracy. If the *okami* is as good as was supposed in the past, then we don't need a democratic system; the *okami* is still good today; the ministers and politicians around the emperor are the ones doing wrong. Therefore, if they are removed and replaced by good and honest people everything will be all right again.

Knowledge of the abuse of power and the people's resistance throughout history made the value of democracy and human rights supreme in the West, whereas glorification of our history has failed to give the Japanese any instruction. The Japanese are educated in school about why democracy is important to us and to try to understand it. But has each of us made due effort to know precisely what democracy is? We have not fully recognized it, since we don't know exactly what happened to our forefathers. Our history does not instruct us how to protect ourselves politically. We expect the *okami* will save us all like in the good old days.

This upside down way of thinking is making today's Japanese impotent in politics. However, despite misconduct on the part of leaders, the current political system is much more representative of the Japanese people than any that existed in the past. In fact, the more we look back to the past, the worse the morals and ethics of people seem to be. If current politicians still love money, their predecessors loved it more.

Samurai had little chance to use their arms in battle as Ieyasu, first shogun of the Tokugawas, instructed "to bag the bows and sheathe the spears." Even when severe inflation made a samurai's life difficult, there was no increase in salary. At the end of Edo era, when the financial situation of the Hans became extremely tight, 1/3 to 1/2 of retainers' salaries were requisitioned by the Han. Given the poor economic situation, frugality came to be considered an important part of bushido; to be frugal was the same as loyalty to the lord. A simple life and plain clothes were emphasized as the ethic of bushido. Any act causing financial burden on the lord was considered disloyal.

For example, it was undesirable to receive any reward from a lord, even a fan. There was urgent material reason to force samurai to be indifferent to money in the name of bushido in spite of Nitobe's admiration. When the Tokugawas gained power, they were merciless in destroying their enemies and often used minor misconduct to confiscate the fiefs of a daimyo. There were many *ronins* (lordless samurai) in the country and their life was indeed miserable. Daimyos in financial difficulties dismissed retainers to save personnel expenses. The way of the samurai became tense and conservative. It was more important to execute tasks faithfully than to stake one's life for an ambition. Most important, for the sake of the samurai's family, was a secure salary.

In the mid 19th century, toward the end of the Tokugawa reign, the art of kendo as a means of fighting Western invaders became the focus of attention. As previously noted, the art of kendo was handed down by Bakufu police and farmer-vigilantes. As the Bakufu's control loosened, many kendo schools were founded and advertised their various superiorities. Fictions and exaggerations were created in effort to gain fame. In order to fit kendo into the vertical society system, the idea of do was introduced. Do is used as in *bushi-do* or *ken-do*, and is normally understood as a way, like the way of the samurai or the way of the swordsman.

Do means a road on which a man will have to keep walking until he finishes his life. *Do* injected morals into martial arts. Training improves swordsmanship to a certain extent, but quick reflexes will count in the final analysis. In sword fighting, it is said one cannot win if one fears death; fear will stiffen the muscles and prevent quick, free motion. If one attains a philosophical view in accepting one's death, motion will be free, and with luck, one can be invincible. In short, *do* adds a spiritual value, an uncertain element to physical strength, which is visible. By this measure, elderly teachers can be a match for younger, stronger contenders.

Can one really get rid of the terror of death by spiritual training? This question is difficult to answer. Remarks by soldier Junpei Gomikawa in his book *Nomonhan* give a possible reply. "I (Gomikawa) asked a silly question, `Do you still perceive terror after you have become a veteran by attacking a Soviet tank with a Molotov cocktail?' He stared at me with scornful eyes, 'I've never ever seen any soldier who had got used to dying.'"

The way of ranking a person in *do* is somewhat vague and often leaves room for controversy. In a society where everyone is equal, ability alone, as measured by rules, will qualify a person for a championship and athletic honors. However, in a vertical society, evaluation of one's spiritual perfection is added to the quotient of determining a champion. It opens the way to put well trained but elderly swordsman who are unable to match younger men in terms of mobility into positions higher than younger men, due to a "higher perfection" in their way of life.

Of course there is no chance today of fighting with real swords. Therefore, there is no way to find out how spiritual perfection offsets the disadvantage of slower mobility.

Sumo wrestling is a different kendo. A *sumo yokozuna* must always win his match in front of an audience. Today men are closely matched in terms of physical strength and it is difficult to find a man who always wins. The sport is a gamble, as in kendo. If one sumo wrestler keeps winning, we begin to suspect rigging.

The Japanese sword became the soul of the samurai. In other words, morals were injected into the martial art of kendo, thus the current view of bushido was generally completed in the Meiji era at the same time the nations of the world were entering the age of modern warfare.

Following the code of bushido led many young soldiers to die unnecessarily in World War II, when seeking bushido in death, they participated in suicide charges against heavily armed American positions with swords and bayonets.

Under the strong pressure of bushido, my father had no way to escape from death. It is most cruel to expect a person to commit suicide by hara-kiri, sinking with a ship, or in a suicide attack, under a vague concept like bushido. If my father had made any mistakes in his command, the right punishment would have been to courtmartial him and determine an appropriate penalty. Many Japanese leaders committed mistakes more egregious than my father; they were neither tried nor forced to commit suicide, although they directed others to do so.

Chapter Fourteen

Loyalty and Bushido, A Fatal Combination

In 1931, the Japanese Kanto (Kwantung) Army was stationed in northeastern China. It behaved like an independent army and seized Manchuria. Manchuria was renamed Manchukuo and set up as a satellite or puppet of Japan. In 1937, the army caused the Marco Polo Bridge incident by firing at Chinese troops, which led the Army to fullscale undeclared war with Nationalist China, commanded by Chiang Kai-shek. In July 1938, the army also clashed with Soviet-Mongolian troops at Changku-feng, near the junction of the Manchurian, Korean and Siberian borders. They were defeated by a Russian army well equipped with modern weapons. Fighting lasted two weeks, the Kanto Army suffering heavy casualties, until a truce was reached.

In May, 1939, the first large scale modern battle before World War II broke out around Nomonhan near the border between the Soviet Union and Manchukuo. The strategic and tactical thought peculiar to the Japanese General Staff and the code of bushido that dominated are well documented in records of this conflict. Perversion of the old samurai code had become abnormal and bloodthirsty.

According to Junpei Gomikawa in his book *Nomonhan*, the land around the Nomonhan area is desert and steppe where two rivers merge. Japan claimed the border between the two countries was the western river, while the Soviet Union claimed it was the eastern river. The honor of both nations was at stake and caused a vast amount of blood to be shed. The battle took place along the Halhin Gol River in Sumber, the easternmost province of Mongolia. The Soviet Union was not in war against Japan at that time, however, alarmed when Japan established the puppet state of Manchukuo and in anticipation of further aggression, the Soviets dispatched troops to Mongolia to reinforce the 80,000 strong Mongolian army.

When the Kanto Army attacked in May, 1939, Russians and Mongolians were ready to fight back. On August 20, the Russo-Mongolian troops launched a fierce preemptive strike with tanks, bombers and ground troops in a fight lasting until mid-September. Mongolians claim they caused 61,000 casualties to the Japanese army, while Russians and Mongolians sustained only 10,000 and just over 1,000 respectively. These figures might be exaggerated, but whatever the death toll, it was a significant defeat for the Japanese. Most historians agree this defeat made Japanese generals change strategy by avoiding further war with Russia and instead focus attention on southeast Asia and the Pacific islands.

During this time, Japanese propagandists—citing the legend that Genghis Khan came from Japan across the sea—claimed that the Mongolian people originated in Japan, which was to say that Mongolians and Japanese had reunited after having been separated a long time. The Mongolians did not buy this sales pitch. There are numerous war memorials along the riverbanks, socialist masterpieces, built to honor Russian and Mongolian soldiers who died there. The monuments were officially dedicated in 1984. The largest is the 50 meter high Hamar Davaa. Ironically, most tourists visiting this remote part of Mongolia are Japanese. There is a small museum in Tsagaannuur, the provincial capital, offering explanations (in Mongolian) about the battles.

Though the Mongolians did not buy into Japanese propaganda, Japanese and Mongolians are certainly related. But Japan is not the homeland of Mongolians; quite the contrary: Mongolia is the motherland of *Yottsu* nomads. Yagiri indicated that *genko* in 1274 and 1281 were Chinese Yuan efforts to save the Yottsu nomads who were being oppressed by the Hojo (*Ya* people). (*Gen* is the Yuan, Mongolian dynasty in China—*Genko* means Yuan invasion).

Let us return to the Nomonhan Incident. After several minor skirmishes near the border, full-scale warfare broke out when a corps of 1000 Japanese infantry attacked Russian positions on the eastern shore of Halhin Gol. The plan was simple, following conventional tactics of the Japanese army. The main force was to hit the enemy from the front while a detached force was to move around the enemy's rear. This combined attack was supposed to completely destroy enemy forces, but instead was the opening of a great tragedy. No attention was paid to reconnaissance or intelligence; the enemy's dispositions and military strength were no matter. Enough that commanders should rely on the destructive power of the Japanese infantry, deriving from the code of bushido.

The detached force of 220 infantry started its flanking move at night on May 27, 1939, and went over sand hills without contacting the enemy. They advanced two kilometers to a point where Halhin Gol met the second river at about 5:30 a.m. There they saw the powerful Russian-Mongolian corps, armed with tanks, positioned on heights in the northeast. On the plateau to the west of Halhin Gol, Japanese soldiers saw many tanks and heavy artillery amassed. The commander realized they had moved too quickly and were now isolated deep in enemies. They tried to contact the main force by radio but failed. The commander ordered his men to dig themselves in and wait for the main force to start attacking.

When the attack began, they met heavy resistance and stopped. At the same time a combined force of Russo-Mongolians attacked the small detached force with tanks, infantry and artillery, continuing throughout May 28 and into May 29. By mid-afternoon of the 29th, 115 out of 220 men had died and most of the rest were wounded. With such heavy losses and with no chance of reinforcement, a Western army would have surrendered. However, in the imperial army of Japan, surrender was not an option under any circumstance. Shortly after 6 p.m., the remaining soldiers staged a banzai charge against the Russian tanks and all were killed. The battle was over. They were annihilated. Quietness and darkness descended over the blood-soaked battlefield.

The commander asked for reinforcements at least seven times. His requests were never answered. The main force was compelled to pull back to Hailar base on May 31. The first stage was over. One wonders why the commander of the main force did not send an order to the beleaguered detachment to pull out. Without that order, there was no choice but to fight till death.

At the end of May, 1939, General Staff in Tokyo asked the Kanto (Kwantung) army in Manchuria if they needed reinforcements to fight the Russians. The reply was negative; the Kanto army was confident they could deal with the enemy. The main Russian base was in far away Nomonhan; all supplies had to come in by rail; it was thought the Russians would not be able to mobilize large forces for aggressive action. The cost of this mistake in estimating the enemy's potential was very high.

The morning of June 19, the commander of the Kanto army received an emergency telegram from the commander of the 23rd Division front. Russian-Mongolian forces had defeated the Manchukuo with powerful tanks. In addition, the Russian air force had bombed Japanese bases. Kanto army staff opinion was split. Strong action was proposed by Major Tsuji, who suggested crushing the enemy at an early stage with a strong offensive. Otherwise, Tsuji insisted the Russians would think the Japanese forces weak and expand aggressive action to other areas along the border.

A more timid approach was suggested by other staff members, to reinforce front line positions for defense. No attack. As usual, the strong opinion won. Junpei Gomikawa raises an interesting question: "Why did Tsuji think it possible to crush the enemy in a short time? And why did other staff members agree with him? It was clear from the battle at Changku-feng the previous year that Russian forces should never be underestimated. As a matter of fact, the Japanese 75th Regiment incurred casualties up to 51% of its manpower and the 76th regiment 31% in two weeks of fighting. In the Nomonhan-Khalka battle, the Japanese suffered significant casualties to the main force in addition to annihilation of the detached force."

Tsuji had no grounds for making his suggestion. He did not accept the facts of the Changku-feng battle or early stages of the Nomonhan battle and looked down on the Russian-Mongolian forces' fighting spirit and armaments. (In his memoirs, Tsuji wrote: "None of us could imagine the Mongolian troops had so many tanks"). Because of his misjudgment, Japanese soldiers had to fight against tanks with cider bottles filled with gasoline, which when hurled caused a fire ("Molotov cocktails"). This primitive method was effective at first, though at great risk to the soldiers. After the Russians changed their engines to diesel, the method was no longer effective. Many soldiers' lives were wasted.

Lieutenant Colonel Hattori, Tsuji's direct superior, supported Tsuji. An offensive campaign was going to be launched. (These two names would appear in the battle of Guadalcanal three years later). Tsuji's disposition was to use the 23rd division plus reinforcements, the maximum power the Kanto army could mobilize without reducing its deployment against the Russo-Mongolian forces along the rest of the border.

Forces to be used were: 13 battalions of infantry; 112 artillery; 118 airplanes; 400 vehicles; 70 tanks. Tsuji estimated the Russian-Mongolian forces: 9 battalions of infantry; 150 tanks; 120 artillery; 150 airplanes; 1000 vehicles. His estimate was far too optimistic; however, underestimating the enemy was commonplace in the Japanese army. Kanto army soldiers departed the base with confidence of victory based on false perceptions.

The plan was to get the 23rd Division to cross the Halhin Gol, advance to the south along the river, assault the enemy on the west bank, then attack another enemy on the east bank from the rear. Meanwhile a detached force reinforced by two tank regiments was to attack the enemy on the east bank from the front: thus the enemy was to be exterminated totally. By 5:30 a.m. on July 3, using a bridge built by military engineers, the 23rd Division main force crossed the river. As they advanced south they were met by enemy tank corps. A fierce battle broke out. At first the Japanese soldiers destroyed several tanks. However, the Russians had many more tanks, and by mid-afternoon, held-back Japanese had dug themselves in and set up a defense line in the trenches. Ammunition was running out and anti-tank guns were destroyed. Japanese soldiers jumped at tanks with Molotov cocktails and anti-tank grenades. Loss of life was heavy.

The divisional commander ordered his men to retreat via the same route they had came in the morning, as there was only the one bridge available for crossing the river. The confused and arduous retreat lasted until 5:00 a.m. the next morning, during which the division incurred heavy casualties.

The attack of the detached force also failed in its mission. Half the Japanese tanks were destroyed. The remaining soldiers made a successful night attack on the Russian-Mongolian position and captured it. However, when morning came the Russians launched a fierce artillery bombardment and the Japanese were forced to retreat to their original position. A stalemate came as quiet descended on the battlefield.

Kanto army analysis of the battle placed the blame for failure on weak artillery support. A decision was made to reinforce the 23rd Division with 38 heavy guns. A new battle plan was drawn. Japanese artillery would be used to destroy Russian artillery on the west bank, then the infantry would assault enemy positions. On the morning of July 23, all Japanese guns opened fire. The barrage seemed to have silenced the Russian guns. But as the infantry made its advance, hidden Russian artillery began returning a heavy barrage. Despite firing almost 12,000 shells, the Japanese attack failed. The 23rd Division requested the Kanto army supply them with additional ammunition.

Kanto army headquarters ordered the 23rd Division to set up defensive positions, and at the same time sent reinforcements to replace casualties. All rapid-firing cannons in Manchukuo were quickly collected and sent to the 23rd. The Japanese committed a double error: first using forces piecemeal rather than in allout attack; second lacking intelligence and underestimating the enemy. Reviewing the battles of Nomonhan, one cannot but feel the staff was irresponsible and that their strategy and tactics left much to be desired. The Japanese made no effort to reconnoiter the enemy's position and strength. Tactics were developed based on optimistic, subjective assumptions. Many Japanese soldiers died due to staff incompetence. The voice of duty and bushido forced those who opposed the plan to keep silent.

The Japanese did not have the courage to say no to an impractical plan. Japan was a poor country then and it was impossible to respond to the request for arms, even if requests were reasonable. However, loyalty to the emperor and the code of bushido were absolute. *Yamato damashi-i* (Japanese spirit) is almighty. Inferiority in arms and numbers are no matter. Charge the enemy with Japanese swords. The gods would help us.

The Japanese military advocated the "invincible imperial army" in the war against China. But when facing a stronger enemy, defeat was no matter, casualties were nothing: what was important was to die for the emperor, to perform the code of bushido. The imperial army placed the highest importance on spiritualism and banzai charges; they were not eager to stress tactics and strategy. Too much knowledge might result in impossible conditions: though ordered to fight by the emperor, the emperor's order could not be executed, resulting in intolerable disloyalty.

Fearing military power was not enough to hold the Russian attack, the Kanto army supreme commander suggested reinforcement of the 7th Division. Tsuji and other staff objected, insisting the 7th Division should be reserved for potential Russian attack in other areas. A compromise was made with worse results. The commander was in a position to assume full responsibility in this battle; if he lost he would have to commit hara-kiri (though he did not do so).

The process of reaching a decision by compromise is often taken by the Japanese because it saves the faces of both parties; but such decisions should be made on concrete grounds, in this case, a correct appraisal of Russian military power.

The Kanto army staff's appraisal that Russian supply bases were too far away to support Russian-Mongolian forces in the Nomonhan area was misjudgment. A good 650 kilometer road was built from the railway terminal to the Halhin Gol, from where vast amounts of supplies and manpower were transported to the battlefield. By August 20, the Russian force had 18,000 tons of shells; 4 infantry divisions; 6500 tons of aerial bombs; 3 tank brigades; 15,000 tons of air and truck fuel; 3 armored brigades; 4000 tons of food; 2225 machine guns; 7500 tons of other fuel; 216 cannons; 286 anti-tank guns. In reserve, they had five infantry divisions and four tank brigades. The Russian-Mongolian force was far superior to the Japanese in manpower and supply. The Russians had 1 1/2 times the Japanese troops. In supplies:

Tanks	Russian	450	Japanese	0
Airplanes	"	581	"	113
Machine guns	"	2225	"	1283
Cannons	"	216	"	135
Anti-tank guns	"	286	"	142

At dawn on August 20, one day before the announcement of the Nazi-Soviet Non-Aggression Pact, the Russians launched an allout attack on Japanese positions. Despite overwhelming odds, Japanese forces held on until the end of August, when all Japanese positions were overrun. The rate of casualties was extremely high, 76%—12,230 out of 15,975. The Kanto army wanted to strike back and asked for reinforcements. However, imperial headquarters issued orders to stop all military action and a ceasefire agreement was concluded on September 16.

The war was over, but the misfortune of the Japanese soldier continued. 88 prisoners of war were returned to Japan on September 27 and 116 on April 27, 1940. There should have been many more, perhaps 3000-4000. The fate of those soldiers is unknown. They were captured wounded, many of them unconscious. But since it was terrible shame to be captured by the enemy according to bushido, many might have elected to remain in Soviet Russia. Those who returned were not received as heroes of war. Officers were put on trial by courtmartial and given pistols to commit suicide. Japanese military law made no provision to punish soldiers taken as prisoners of war after they had fought bravely. How could anyone punish soldiers who had fought tanks with their bare hands? However, the code of bushido, born of misconception, was ruthless. It dictated that Japanese soldiers should die before being captured under all circumstances. The fate of many Japanese junior officers and their men was determined by this ethic. Thousands were killed in desperate suicide charges. Many committed suicide in final moments of defeat. Suicides continued after the war to avoid the disgrace of capture.

Lt. Colonel Ioki committed suicide on September 16, after being held responsible for retreat from his position without approval of his superior. His corps had been left isolated deep in enemy terrain and his communications with headquarters had been cut. He was left with a decision whether to fight through to the end or pull out to fight another day. He chose to pull out and saved the lives of as many of his men as possible. Heroically, he was able to return to Japanese lines; unfortunately he was forced to commit suicide by his superiors under the narrow ethics of bushido.

Yagiri has a unique view of this. He claims it is the slave mentality that made the military prohibit soldiers from surrendering to the enemy. For a slave, change of master had little meaning. He would serve a new master just as faithfully as the old. This was so when the T'ang Chinese ruled Japan in the 7th century. It was also true when Japanese soldiers were captured by the Russians during the Russo-Japanese War of 1904-05. Japanese soldiers were instructed that they had no obligations other than telling their names and birthdays when captured by the enemy, but they often volunteered information about Japanese military forces, including deployment of forces, layout of positions and types of arms, in full cooperation with their "new masters". Due to this, the Japanese army changed its standing order: everyone was ordered to fight to death or commit suicide to avoid capture.

Highranking commanders and staff officers sitting at headquarters were not punished so severely. Some were ordered to retire, put on reserve duty or transferred to other departments. None was ordered to commit hara-kiri, although they forced others to do so. This unequal justice was another remarkable feature of the Japanese army. General staff learned little from defeat. However, the Nomonhan incident may give us insight into the Japanese army crimes, their massacre of civilians and ill treatment of prisoners of war and people of occupied lands. One finds many similar situations in the battles of World War II.

Despite defeat, Tsuji and Hattori were never questioned about responsibility but transferred to important positions in the General Staff Office in Tokyo, where they guided World War II from imperial headquarters.

A concept peculiar to the Japanese army derives from a creed that the Japanese military is invincible with *tenyuu* (god's help), which will be given if each selflessly dedicates his life to the emperor; the gracious emperor will forgive and honor them if they fight to death; through bushido, their souls will be enshrined in the Yasukuni Shrine, where they will be worshipped as gods eternally.

Officers were thoroughly indoctrinated in bushido from childhood. But no matter how many died in an operation, the staff was never held responsible for casualties, no matter how great. This situation is similar to that of the subhuman slave warriors in ancient Japan, where nobles were never questioned about slaves' deaths. Japanese soldiers were also considered subhuman. The treatment of American soldiers on Bataan and British in Singapore can be explained with the same notion.

Westerners who visited Japan before World War II found Japanese people kind, polite and fair. These Japanese suddenly changed to devils in the war years, killing millions of enemies, including civilian women and children. Why? The answer is simple. Discriminatory vertical society is a society built on slavery. A vertical society has its precepts and images. A general must act like a general; everything must conform to appropriate precepts and images to be glorified, or if not conforming, be concealed. Not knowing the truth, the Japanese people are unable to admit that our fathers, brothers or children committed evil acts during the war.

Chapter Fifteen

Human Shields

Shiko-no-Mitate is understood in military circles as an imperial "shield of men." Before World War II it was a supreme honor to be drafted into the armed forces to serve as one. I was educated to this idea in cadet school. The character for *shiko* in Chinese stands for "ugly." Yagiri wondered why the emperor's human shield should use this character; one would expect a glorifying character to be selected to express an honorable action. Yagiri solves the riddle: when the Paekche (Koreans) founded their dynasty in Nara before the 7th century, they assigned to Yottsu slaves the service of raising horses, a profession which they called *shiko* (*shi*=to raise; ko=door, house of the horse raiser). Later the Yottsu became human shields for the imperial household.

How were the *Shiko-no-Mitate* used in World War II, particularly in the battle of Guadalcanal? The following analysis is based on *Guadalcanal*, by Junpei Gomikawa, (K.K. Bungei Shunju, 1980).

On August 7, 1942, the U.S. 1st Marine Division landed on Guadalcanal, supported by a powerful naval task force, including three aircraft carriers. The objective of the operation was to prevent the Japanese from completing a large naval air base on the island. Japanese strategy was based on cutting links between the U.S. and Australia, for which purpose imperial headquarters was planning an assault on Port Moresby in New Guinea, and occupation of Fiji, Samoa, and New Caledonia.

Japan's major naval base in the South Pacific was located on Truk Island; they had also built a major advanced air base at Rabaul in the New Britain Islands. These two bases presented serious threats to Port Moresby and to the important Allied base at Darwin in Australia. As allied planes had made repeated attacks on Truk and Rabaul from Port Moresby, from the Japanese point of view Port Moresby had to be neutralized; Guadalcanal was to be the advanced point for the neutralization.

To the Allies, control of Guadalcanal was equally important. Control would deny the Japanese a strategic base and at the same time the airfield on the island would give the U.S. an advanced base for further attacks on Truk and Rabaul. The two warring forces collided on these islands in the South Pacific, where bloody battles would be fought for seven months.

Japanese naval air force patrol missed sighting the large American fleet of 82 ships approaching Guadalcanal. Poor weather conditions were given as the official cause of failure. Japanese patrols often missed the enemy while American patrols never seemed to miss Japanese fleet movements, even in bad weather. In short, the Japanese did not put much importance on patrols. The number of patrol places involved were few and the area allotted to each pilot too large. To a Japanese naval pilot, patrol was not a duty to be preferred or to die for. If he had to die he wished to die in a more glorious manner, such as diving against an American carrier. The significant defeat of the Imperial Navy at Midway was caused in great part by lack of intelligence and negligent patrols. Yet the Japanese Navy did not change its tactics.

The concept of Japan's strategy to close the link between the U.S. and Australia was grand but not feasible. Distance between Rabaul and Guadalcanal was 560 sea miles, with no relay bases in between. Japanese zero fighters from Rabaul could stay in the air above Guadalcanal for only fifteen minutes. Carrier based bomber range was barely enough to reach Guadalcanal. It was impossible to gain command of the air under such circumstances. The Japanese staff apparently did not take into account a possible American counter attack. Optimism was another "asset" of Japanese military planning.

After the American landing, the air forces from Rabaul launched an attack on the American task force in the waters around Guadalcanal, after which many Japanese planes had to make forced water landings. The pilots were picked up by destroyers. They were full of fighting spirit and did not mind sacrifice, but the overall result of this attack and those that followed were not good.

Shortly before the American landing on Guadalcanal, the 17th Army based on Rabaul had been studying plans for the attack on Port Moresby. The plan called for a landing at Buna on the New Guinea coast, advance over the wild and treacherous Owen-Stanley Mountains, then the attack on Port Moresby. The mileage between Buna and Port Moresby was 360 kilometers (216 miles), a distance to be covered by infantry entirely on foot.

The plan appeared unrealistic. Soldiers would have to carry food supplies, guns and ammunition. If the force consisted of 5000 men, three tons of rice a day would be used to allow each man 600 grams (1.3 pounds) per day. Each man could carry only about 50 pounds of rice. Since each soldier needed 600 grams each day, the volume of rice he would be able to deliver to the front would decrease in inverse proportion to the increase of distance the rice had to be transported. Suppose a soldier could cover 30 kilometers (12 miles) a day, 32,800 men would be required to feed the division once it reached the climax battle at Port Moresby, 360 kilometers away. For the resupply of ammunition and guns, more men would be needed. The plan was impractical.

Engineers and infantry officers were being sent to Buna to make a feasibility study in planning the campaign, but imperial headquarters in Tokyo also sent Lt. Colonel Tsuji, of Nomonhan fame, to visit the 17th Army. Tsuji requested the Port Moresby campaign be undertaken immediately rather than wait for the results of the feasibility study.

Taking this suggestion as the intent of imperial headquarters, officers of the 17th Army began immediate preparations for attack. Surprisingly, it was disclosed a few days later that Tsuji's request was merely a personal suggestion. The 17th Army resented Tsuji's interference. Tsuji's superior, Hattori, of Nomonhan fame, acted as mediator to smooth over differences. However, the 17th Army was unable to cancel the proposed campaign. An army of several thousand landed at Buna and began the advance toward Port Moresby. Each soldier carried enough food for a 16 day campaign (150 grams per day per soldier). The Japanese advanced to within sight of Port Moresby. They were starving and could advance no further. The Allied Forces quickly moved out after the retreating Japanese. Only a few survived. It was hell, produced by a concept peculiar to Japanese army leaders, in which, as always, common soldiers were the victims.

But let us return to Guadalcanal. When the Imperial Navy heard of the American attack, it regarded it only as a "reconnaissance attack" of a small force, not understanding it as the first step of a full-scale counterattack, despite 11,000 marines and 27 troop ships covered by a large task force, including aircraft carrier.

Imperial headquarters ordered a combined operation by the navy and army to regain the airfield. A Japanese fleet led by Vice Admiral Mikawa, in the waters off Guadalcanal, encountered the American fleet at midnight, August 8, 1942. The sea battle ended in total victory for the Japanese, with the American fleet driven from the sea, leaving American troops and supply ships undefended. Mikawa ordered his fleet to move away.

Mikawa's decision caused much controversy. If he had attacked the troops and supply ships he might have delivered a crushing blow, which probably would have changed the course of the battle for Guadalcanal. Mikawa was concerned with the American air attacks the next morning. The Midway defeat may have been on his mind. He wanted to be out of range as soon as possible.

There was another factor. The traditional view of the Japanese Navy was to sink enemy battleships and cruisers, but not troopships. General Togo's victory at Tsushima was immortal, but the philosophy behind it was outdated. Battles were now fought on land, sea and air. Only an integrated strategy could lead to success. Yet many Japanese admirals refused to accept this.

Another key issue was the Japanese lack of ability to evaluate the enemy's power, sum up the situation quickly and launch attacks at the right moment. We have already seen this in the battles of Nomonhan. If the Japanese Navy had followed up Mikawa's victory, using all available forces, the outcome would surely have been different. According to the record, Japanese air raids and Mikawa's victory caused a change in American strategy. The American task force, including carrier and supply ships, took refuge to the south, halfway through the landing of supplies.

At that time the Japanese Navy still had three carriers. Had imperial headquarters thrown full power into the Guadalcanal battle, there would have been a good chance of winning a major victory and repulsing U.S. counterattack; but the navy, which dared to run great risks in attacking Pearl Harbor, had become defensive and weak-hearted after the defeat at Midway.

Rabaul was too far to cover an assault. It required a task force, including carriers. Otherwise, the decision should have been to abandon Guadalcanal.

However, the imperial staff decided on half measures and was dragged into a battle of attrition. The air force from Rabaul made repeated attacks on the U.S. fleet. Impressive results were reported on August 10; but in truth, only one destroyer and one troopship were sunk. Imperial headquarters decided to conduct two parallel campaigns to capture Port Moresby, and also to recapture Guadalcanal using the Itsuki Corps of the 17th Army. Itsuki's force consisted of some 2000 men, divided into two parts. The first group of 900 was taken to Guadalcanal by six high speed destroyers, while the second was taken by troopship at a far slower pace.

Colonel Kiyonao Itsuki, well known as an expert in close combat and bayonet charges, believed a bayonet charge of Japanese soldiers would easily overrun American positions. Perhaps he did not know what had happened to Japanese soldiers when they charged the Russian positions at Nomonhan. On landing, Itsuki ordered the advance of his first group to the airfield. His scouting patrols were met by American patrols and were annihilated.

On August 20, the first group reached a point 10 kilometers (6 miles) from Henderson Field, the air base occupied by American marines. Itsuki ordered the attack for 6 p.m. across a narrow river. The American positions were on the other side of the river, manned by four battalions of Marines and three battalions of artillery, all fully prepared for attack. Itsuki ordered the charge across the river under fire cover of grenades. 900 men charged bravely, but American firepower was greater than expected; none was able to reach the American position. Soon, a sand bar in the river was littered with bodies of Japanese soldiers.

The Americans launched a counterattack, forcing the retreat of surviving Japanese forces. An American battalion moved to the rear, cutting off the retreating Japanese, while artillery showered with shells. The afternoon of the 21st, four American tanks joined the battle; by late afternoon, the conflict was over. Colonel Itsuki is said to have committed suicide, 777 soldiers were killed, 30 injured, and only 128 survived.

Of the ignominious defeat, little good can be said. Itsuki predetermined American strength at 2000 Marines, who would run away as soon as his men charged with fixed bayonets. He did not spend time to reconnoiter enemy positions nor did he wait for the remainder of his force, 1100 men. His patrols had been wiped out; therefore there would be no surprise. The result of his recklessness was like throwing eggs against a rock. This unreasonable set of tactics was, unbelievably, repeated by Japanese generals throughout the rest of the Guadalcanal campaign.

The second group of Itsuki's corps was still at sea during this battle. While they approached, the second Solomon sea-air battle broke out on August 24th. The Japanese task force, including three aircraft carriers, launched an attack against the American force, which included two aircraft carriers. One American carrier was damaged, a Japanese carrier was sunk by American attacks, and the Japanese lost 59 planes.

The defensive power of the American fleet had shown remarkable improvement. Radar had detected the Japanese planes well in advance of attack and enabled American fighters to cover the fleet. Anti-aircraft fire was deadly. The American air forces had the use of Henderson Field on Guadalcanal, making air control possible.

At this point, imperial headquarters in Tokyo should have reviewed the situation. American intentions were clear. This was no "reconnaissance" attack, but a clear move of an overall strategy with the ultimate target the Japanese home islands. The powerful American fleet was gaining strength and ability to fight. American firepower on land revealed the invincible Banzai charge was nothing but a myth, American marines were as brave as their Japanese counterparts. Japan should have realized the American fleet could no longer be beaten; Guadalcanal could not be regained.

Since victory or stalemate could be achieved only under optimum conditions, Japan had to change its operational policy from offensive to defensive. However, the Japanese military command had never learned to lose.

Neither imperial headquarters nor the 17th Army would accept defeat or a defensive strategy. They decided to reinforce the second Itsuki group under the command of Major General Kawaguchi. The force, although weak in artillery, numbered 6000 men. They were given rations for a two week campaign.

Kawaguchi's plan was to make a surprise attack from the rear at Henderson Field, which meant a forced march through jungles. The general did not take time to send out advanced patrols to reconnoiter. The deep jungle, never before entered by humans, proved an obstacle to advance; it took more time than planned to reach the point from which the all-out attack was to begin.

Kawaguchi discovered his brigade was too widely scattered to make an orderly, concerted attack. Although he knew little of the enemy's positions or the terrain over which his forces had to cross, there was no time to explore the situation. Food supplies were running low. Therefore, he gave the order to attack. All day and into the evening his men charged the Americans, but fierce fire prevented a breakthrough. After heavy losses, Kawaguchi had no choice but to retreat. It was not an easy or glorious retreat. Hunger was painful; the men ate little for five days. Heavy arms with the crest of the emperor were thrown away without thought.

Having learned nothing, imperial headquarters sent in the Second Division with heavy artillery, tanks and food, in what was to be a face to face confrontation. However, the Japanese did not have control of the air, and it was difficult to land forces safely. Bombings caused many casualties and destruction of food, supplies and military equipment. Since heavy artillery and supplies were less than expected, plans had to be changed; but the result was the same: the Second Division suffered the same fate as their predecessors, defeat in battle and slow starvation.

Imperial headquarters decided to send the 38th Division to continue the offensive, and dispatched Colonel Hattori to investigate. He saw the wretched situation, but refused to concede and ordered his subordinate, Tsuji, to continue.

On November 12, 1942, the 38th Division, along with all its artillery and a large amount of supplies was loaded onto eleven troop ships, to be escorted by a large naval task force. However, without control of the air, it was impossible for the task force to get to the island. A series of raids and battles took place, in which most of the troopships were sunk or damaged. None reached Guadalcanal. In addition, the Japanese Navy lost two battleships, one heavy cruiser and three destroyers.

At long last, imperial headquarters realized they did not have the power to recapture Guadalcanal, and by the end of February, 1943, the remainder of the 17th Army was evacuated from the island. Out of 31,404 soldiers, 10,652 returned alive. Some 3/4 died from starvation and disease; thousands who could not move themselves were given poison tablets or grenades to commit suicide and were left there.

The actions of the imperial staff and the staff of the 17th Army acted in a criminal manner. They sent soldiers to fight without proper food and military equipment. They made no provision for supplying the starving forces—conditions were so terrible, many reports of cannibalism were recorded. The army guided battles with scant information and ordered banzai charges that had little to no chance of success. At the end the sick and wounded were abandoned or forced to commit suicide.

Still, lessons went unlearned: these criminal acts led to similar tragedies of the Imphal campaign, the battles of the Philippines and Okinawa, in which soldiers again had to bear the consequences of mistakes committed by officers of the High Command. The secret history of Japan which has been withheld from the people helps to explain this.

As we shall see in the next chapter, slavery in the 7th and 8th centuries produced the idea of caste, and that it was not a crime to kill *hinin* (subhumans). This idea of "making men under men," with all its discriminatory precepts, was absorbed by the vertical society. When this was extended to international relations, with *ryo* (rulers) as the Japanese and foes as *sen* (humbled slaves), the innate views of the vertical society led Japanese soldiers to commit atrocities against millions of innocent civilians and thousands of prisoners of war.

After the war, Lt. Colonel Tsuji was elected a member of the House of Representatives. Tsuji's crimes and those of others like him must be made known to the Japanese people. The worst thing for Japan is to become isolated in the world by following false precepts and a false history.

Chapter Sixteen

Religion and Trade

The *Taiho Ritsu Ryo*, a code of laws promulgated in 701, divided Japan into two classes: *ryo* (ruling class or nobles), and *sen*, (the ruled, humble slaves). *Sen* were further divided into two groups: (1) those who resisted the T'ang Chinese and were left to starve in secluded mountain camps; (2) those who surrendered and were made slave farmers.

Buddhism was the national religion, and slave-farmers were the property of the Buddhist temples. The slaves were given rice seed in spring and forced to deliver harvested rice the next autumn or be killed. After turning over the yearly harvest, they were allowed to pick up the fallen ears to survive. As long as they raised food for the rulers they would be kept alive, but they were treated cruelly.

In *The History of Sanka*, Yagiri states that slavery existed in northern Japan for a thousand years, until the 18th century. The following of Yagiri's descriptions summarize slave conditions in the Edo period:

Names of privately owned slave farmers were entered into the census register of Buddhist temples for administration. In the domains of the shoguns and fiefs of the daimyos, *oobyakusho* (big farmers) bowed to local administrators, who owned the land and slaves, whose duty was to supervise and maximize rice production. The daimyo's revenue and samurai's salary were measured by the estimated amount of rice in a koku (about 180 liters). Japan was on a rice standard of exchange until the Meiji Restoration.

The *oobyakusho* followed slave tradition initiated in the 8th century by accomodating males and females in separate quarters, forbidding social contact between the two. The *oobyakusho* would freely avail himself of female slaves and impregnate them to multiply the labor force. In the 8th century, children were given the name *Hendo no Tami* and granted the privilege of living in caves covered with woven straw mats that kept out rain and wind. Slave women over thirty were set free and allowed to marry male slaves who had worked obediently and faithfully. A pair of male and female wooden dolls known today as *kokeshi* were fashioned, signifying male slaves with a serious wish to marry. These dolls are sold today in northern Japan as souvenirs at spa resorts. Until Tenmei (1781-1788), one could see slave women and horses sold at auction in northern Japan.

In the Edo period, slave farmers were nominally honored by being placed in the second rank of the caste system (samurai, farmers, artisans and traders). Yet this brought no change in their social standing; the farmers' lives were miserable; they remained near slaves until "liberation" by the American reforms following World War II.

The last four decades have been paradise for Japanese farmers. Fully protected by the government and legislators, they have enjoyed the good life. Eventually, they must face free trade, since the policy of a 100% ban on rice imports to Japan cannot continue. (In 1994 Japan was short of rice due to unusual weather conditions, and the government was compelled to approve emergency imports in substantial quantity. At the end of 1995, Japan ratified the Uruguay Round, and now a percentage of rice will be imported regularly).

Samurai ancestry reflected mostly Yottsu prisoners, with some Ya and Zoshiki who had also been confined to the mountain camps in the 8th century. Around the civil war age, to supplement their armies, daimyos drafted people from the mountain areas as expendable human shields. Those who survived battle later became members of the ruling class as shogun and daimyo, but due to their origin remained an enduring latent anti-imperial force.

Every shogun, the top level of samurai, tried to overturn the imperial court and make himself emperor. Masako Hojo, wife of Yoritomo Minamoto, defeated the imperial forces and put the court under complete control and surveillance, exiling all who turned against her. The Ashikagas reconciled themselves to being subjects of the Ming Chinese emperor, thus overriding the Japanese emperor. Nobunaga Oda's ambition was to enthrone himself as emperor. The court offered him a high rank, but he refused. Nobunaga demonstrated his military power at the imperial court to frighten the emperor and nobles, who were delighted when he was assassinated. Hideyoshi Toyotomi, the next shogun, killed a prince in an effort to become emperor, but eventually gave up his attempts out of fear of the curse of the prince's soul.

There would have been several reasons why the imperial household was not destroyed—among them: fear and respect for Chinese blood. It was widely believed that if an innocent man were killed, his soul would cause misfortune so serious that the usurper of the throne might be brought down. It was more profitable that the samurai utilize the authority of the emperor than kill him. The emperor had no military power, anyway.

Traders were ranked at the bottom of the pecking order, but they were originally the same people as the samurai. More accurately, some of the Ya who did not become samurai became traders. Therefore, the organization of trade houses was the same as the daimyos' and were anti-imperial. It is interesting to find that most Japanese trade names (wholesalers and retail shops) end in ya—like Meidiya, Sakuraya, Joshuya. This is traced to measures taken by Nobunaga Oda (1534-1582), a tragic hero in the civil war age who was killed just before accomplishing the unification of Japan.

Nobunaga Oda rose from Hatta Bessho, a Ya camp in Owari (now Gifu Prefecture). As soon as he gained power, Oda granted an exclusive business license to the Ya people. In order to show they were of authentic Ya, they added ya at the end of the trade name. After the death of Nobunaga, the exclusive license became null and void, and the Ya suffered many difficulties. Still, it seems true that the samurai and traders were relatives of sorts, and the Yas were in the majority.

In Tokugawa, each daimyo fief had its own police; no national police existed. Tadasuke Ooka, governor of Edo (Tokyo) in the early 18th century, set up a national police by giving powers to the Ya, who earned a living by acting in street performances and in vending.

Five main roads led from Tokyo to other important areas and cities of Tokugawa Japan, one being the Tokaido Road to Kyoto. Here the Ya set up police stations at key points, in order to keep close watch over the Yottsu living in the mountain areas, which had become nests of political unrest.

The system was convenient for Ya engaged in trade, enabling them to travel freely under police protection without obtaining passports, a great help in business. During the Edo era Ya businessmen worked hard and through free competition, built up financial strength to surpass the other classes. Rapid increase of agricultural and handicraft production from peacetime efforts helped develop shipping, another Ya business. Land transportation by horse was a Yottsu business.

In Tokugawa Japan, choice of occupation was limited by ancestry. Ownership of land, plowing fields, planting and harvesting rice, planting mulberries, raising silkworms and making silk were all reserved for the ruling class, those of Chinese and Korean ancestry. Farming was a key source of income for the ruling class.

On the other hand, jobs related to natural things, such as wild grasses and trees, nuts, honey, thread from cocoons of wild silkworms, stones, mountain soils and animals were assigned to the aboriginal races of the Ya and Yottsu.

Artisans such as stone cutters and masons, plasterers, china and earthenware makers, casting workers, gardeners, forestry workers, medicinal herb handlers and dyers were also of aboriginal ancestry. Furniture making and carpentry with Buddhist temples were jobs for people of Chinese or Korean ancestry.

Toward the end of the Edo period, the Tokugawa Bakufu initiated a policy of educating non-registered aboriginals, giving them jobs in carpentry, and causing a great deal of confusion.

The condition in which a few rulers controlled land producing the national wealth that was actually worked by slaves as cheap labor is similar to the postwar situation which led Japan to unprecedented economic growth and prosperity. There is a similarity in the relationship of the big manufacturing companies and their subcontractors and component suppliers. The roots of the control that exists today under the Keiretru in Japanese business may go back as far as this Edo era.

During the Ashikaga era (1338-1573) people of aboriginal ancestry, those who wanted trade licenses with the government or to serve as government employees, were forcibly converted to Buddhism and were upgraded to semi-humans, provided they repeated the name of Buddha one million times. Persons with Ami at the end of their names were among these people, like Kan Ami. Since these people came from anti-imperial groups, they were given only peaceful jobs in the arts and entertainments. They developed Japanese art and traditional culture—Noh performance, flower arrangement, tea ceremonies, and Japanese painting, for example. This discrimination explains why the arts were not much respected in Japan until the Meiji era, when the country was reopened in the 19th century, and visiting Europeans purchased Japanese lacquerware, porcelain and Ukiyoe paintings in appreciation of their artistic beauty. Only then did the position of artists and artisans begin to change, though discrimination continued.

It was not until the defeat in World War II that social discrimination against these artists was completely diminished and people paid them due respect. In my prewar childhood, actors, even Kabuki actors, were looked down on as Kawara Kojiki (beggars on the river shores).

Who were these Kawara Kojiki? Their origin dates back to 1107, when they were mentioned in the diary of a noble: "Stone-throwing battles have been customary since last spring." At that time slave farmers resented those of anti-imperial aboriginal prisoner ancestry because they did not raise anything. When hostility grew, the government decided to allow the slave farmers to throw stones at the prisoners one day each year, on May 5th, when prisoners confronted slave farmers on river shores, where stones were amply available. When the slave farmers won the stone throwing battles they took carp from the river and carried them back, impaled on bamboo poles. This is how the Boys' Festival of today originated.

Throughout the year, prisoners had occupied the river banks to secure advantageous positions, but the battle was only one day, therefore for the remainder of the year, the prisoners started shows and other entertainment businesses, which came to be contemptuously called Kawara Mono, or Kawara Kojiki. Court nobles despised these Kabuki actors.

At the bottom of society there lived many anti-imperial people of aboriginal ancestry who were placed under the four registers as outcasts. The meat-eating Yottsu were looked down on as subhumans by the Buddhist powers, and were severely oppressed. Fish eating by the Ya people was also looked down on.

Since the majority of Chinese and Korean descendants lived in southwestern Japan, discrimination for the anti-imperial and anti-Buddhist people was more severe there than for the same people in the Chubu, Kanto and Tohoku areas in the northeastern Japan, where the mass was composed entirely of descendants of aboriginal prisoner ancestry.

As the reader will recall, the oldest inhabitants on the Japanese archipelago were collectively called Zoshiki. Among these were E no Tami (E people), and the places they landed are marked with "E"—Edajima, Enoshima, etc. Edo (the old name of Tokyo) means gate - (*do* = "to") of the country of "E" people. Later Ya people arrived at these places, the names of which have the initial of "A"—Awajishima, Awa, etc. These people spread over the Pacific coasts. Apparently the Chubu area was the land of Ya people; to indicate it, the crest of Nagoya City is the number eight (ya or *hachi*) in a circle. Major inhabitants in the Tohoku area were Yottsu. All these facts are totally unknown to the Japanese people today.

Tsunayoshi Tokugawa, the 5th shogun, was a well-known and pious Buddhist ruler who did not permit the killing of living things. He was nicknamed Inu Kubo (Dog Shogun) because he protected ownerless dogs. In Japanese history, he was understood as a mediocre, arbitrary monarch who issued unrealistic orders because he was ignorant about worldly things. Tokugawa's true face was contradictory. He made Buddhism the national religion and cruelly oppressed non-Buddhist people, while simultaneously advocating the prevention of cruelty to animals. This policy ruined the lives of Yottsu engaged in skinning animals, tanning hides, and making leather goods, since when Tokugawa forced them to convert to Buddhism they could no longer do work relating to dead animals.

Traditionally, there had been one Jisha Bugyo (official in charge of religion, Buddhism and Shinto), but Tsunayoshi increased the number to four to enhance their activities. Those who refused to become Buddhists were sent into the same camps where their ancestors had been confined in the 8th century. As a result, hundred of thousands of people were exiled, since only a few were converted. Tsunayoshi would not tolerate even his Hatamoto (direct vassals of shogun), and hundreds of samurai worshipping Shinto gods were similarly exiled from Edo to ghettos.

It is briefly mentioned in Japanese history that Tsunayoshi ordered an annual examination of the people's religion, generally for the purpose of identifying Christians. However, this was not entirely so; the purpose was to identify Buddhists. Non-Buddhists were listed and confined in the place determined by the government.

If you should see a samurai movie of the Edo era, watch carefully for a scene in which the living quarters of the masses appears. At the entrance of two apartments built along both sides of a central street is a gate, often mistakenly thought to be for security purposes; its real purpose, however, is to prevent confined non-Buddhists of aboriginal ancestry from fleeing. At night the gates were closed and passage prohibited. Extra service duties were imposed on the aborigines in order to encourage their conversion.

Later, Tadasuke Ooka, one of the governors of Edo under Yoshimune, 8th shogun of Tokugawas, enacted a discriminatory law related to non-registered aborigines, stipulating they should not do up their hair in a topknot; the hair should be left untied and uncovered, in order that the aborigines could be immediately identified as pagans. While exploitation of farmers was dangerous because they could revolt and ruin the daimyo family, daimyos did not hesitate to exploit the hinin subhuman aborigines and make their lives as miserable as possible.

Tadasuke instituted a system to control the press in 1725, much earlier than Western countries. The system required an imprint as is done worldwide today. Names of writers and publishers were mandatory on imprints, and books had to be submitted to the government for permission to publish. No book advocating new theories or divergent views against the establishment were permitted, and violators were punished severely. A heavy fine was inflicted, particularly when the violation referred to the history of the Tokugawas. In today's world, this would be considered censorship.

Tadasuke was the founder of the national police, oppressor of anti-Buddhists of aborigine ancestry, and controller of thought and the press. It is he who is largely responsible for the Japanese people's ignorance of their history. He thought it advantageous to the Tokugawas that the people believe the fabrications of *Koudan* (storytelling, classical entertainment for the masses), dramas, plays and fictions supporting the shogunate.

Policies that keep the people ignorant and easy to rule continue even today; official history is modified to meet untrue stories of *Koudan* or plays. In Japan, even those respected as men of intelligence generally believe in *Koudan* history like brainwashed prisoners. The Japanese accept the misconception that they have a singular culture whereby only the Japanese can understand each other, sometimes, even without saying a word.

Contrary to his actual achievements, Tadasuke's image is that of an outstanding governor of wisdom and benevolence who put the welfare of the people above all else. This impression is so strong that every weekday in 1992 from 4 to 5 pm, Japanese could see a one hour televised drama related to Ooka's exploits. In each episode the hero shows his devotion to justice and protection of the weak, his extraordinary wisdom in settling difficult cases, his sympathy and love, and above all, his total loyalty and dedication to the Tokugawas.

The basic concept is that in Japan the ruler is good, and if the people work hard and loyally they will be recognized and rewarded accordingly, a feudalistic logic to justify a monarchy that is not always compatible with democratic ideas. It is ironic that the *koudan* basis of the television drama comes from translations of Chinese stories of a Chinese governor. Few people know this.

Several other samurai dramas are broadcast each week, all following a similar concept: the samurai of justice punishes evil with his sword and without a trial. The concept behind this is to maintain Ooka's views and policies today.

Will Japanese scholars of the 30th century write that in the 20th century the Japanese enjoyed wonderful lives ruled by an excellent administration under a symbolic Emperor, and that the people created samurai stories of Ooka and others in appreciation of *okami*, and therefore, the tv stories are fictions, but the people's thanks behind them are historical fact?

The reality of politics in today's Japan looks quite different. Political scandals, briberies to government officials, incompetence, irresponsibility and inefficiency of leaders—people not a part of the Japan, Inc. system are treated not unlike anti-Buddhist outcasts of the Tokugawa age. Even reading all the stories of human evil in the newspapers every day, the Japanese people have still not yet abandoned the creed that *okami* is good. As long as the emperor is there as the existing example of perfect, godlike man, the people will not accept that all people contain both good and evii, and that even *okami* can make mistakes. Slavery of a thousand years still influences Japanese mentality. Instead of fighting for their rights, the Japanese wait obediently, in anticipation that one day someone like Ooka on TV or a man like the emperor will appear and fix everything right.

In England it was agreed by 1689 that the King rules not by divine right but the consent of Parliament. The English people had become aware of the arbitrary use of power by their kings and found it necessary to check the monarch's power in order to protect their lives and civil liberties. The English learned they had to have earthly protection, since the protection of God was not always available; sometimes even earthly protection was flawed, due to human perversion; however, it was better to depend on people's wisdom rather than heavenly intervention. On this point the consciousness of the Japanese people is regrettably 300 years behind the British.

Some of the unregistered Ya people who along with the Yottsu fled into secluded areas in the 8th century when the Fujiwara family ruled Japan were Sanka, and in the 11th century, they were joined by some Khitan. However, the Sanka lived under strict precepts and kept their purity for a thousand years until the Meiji era. They did not mix.The Sanka are, for this reason, "pure" Japanese, and their descendants are now the only people who can testify to the T'ang Chinese conquest of Japan in the 7th century, the history of which should have been passed down as tradition.

In secluded mountainous areas, these people kept moving from place to place, so as not to be seen by villagers. A family moved as a unit and lived in a simple movable house called *sebri*, made of three pillars surrounded by curtains, built alongside the river. These units were more like a nomad *pao* (tent) than a house. The Sanka practice of using burnt stones in cooking is the same as the Polynesians and Hawaiians, indicating the Sanka were from the south. Similar to other south sea island people, the Sanka maintained a matriarchal society; women were the masters of the family, and monogamy was strictly observed. They had many children, so that one day they might have the manpower to beat the Fujiwara family who had driven them into the mountains (more about the cultural status of women in Japan's history will be discussed in chapter 18).

Yagiri recounts an intriguing episode about the Sanka during World War II. According to records opened to the public in 1983 at the Presidio Military Museum in San Francisco, the U.S. Army interviewed 6,000 Niseis of Sanka ancestry. These interviews took place at the Military Information Strategic Language School six months prior to the attack on Pearl Harbor. The interviews dealt with an investigation of Japanese history and traditions handed down from generation to generation by Sanka people.

Information gathered points in the same direction as Yagiri's view, that the Japanese were multi-racial origin and that the Fujiwara family that founded Japan in the 8th century was of Chinese ancestry.

Japan surrendered after the American atomic bombing of Hiroshima and Nagasaki. Were the bombings the true reason for the surrender? Or was there a latent fear of rebellion against the emperor institution by the people of aborigine ancestry who comprised 90% of the Japanese population, should the war be fought on the Japanese mainland? We may never know, but it is plausible that the emperor could have chosen to surrender because he knew he would have had no chance against potential rebels.

Yagiri tells us that in the Presidio Military Museum there is a citation signed by an adjutant of General MacArthur which praises, "The merit of the work of the secret warriors, the Japanese Nisei, who clarified the true history of Japan, which advanced the defeat of Japan, and as a result saved the lives of thousands of American soldiers." The Nisei soldiers of Sanka ancestry could have been more of a threat to the power of the Japanese Empire than the power of two atomic bombs, had they secretly landed on mainland Japan and contacted other Sanka people with the message, "Now is the time to avenge ourselves on the Fujiwaras and their descendants, the enemy for 1100 years, and build a new Japan with their Sanka blood."

We do not know what happened to the Nisei soldiers after the war; they might have opened the Japanese' people's eyes. The U.S.'s choice to use Hirohito for governing postwar Japan may be the reason the Nisei story is not stated in the history of World War II.

Today, the Sankas' descendants are engaged mainly in civil engineering and in the construction industry. Yagiri suspects their strong unity of blood has developed into the Japanese business practices known as Dango (to determine a successful bidder by private negotiations among the participants in accordance with turn, to be decided by the business circle in consideration of rank, share, and record of past performance). Dango is one of the subjects being considered by the Japan-U.S. Structural Reform Conference, but the roots of the problem are deep. Unless the hidden history of Japan is unveiled and the consciousness of the people radically changed, reform will be difficult. The Sanka people are about 15% of the total population now. If they would give up their secret life and open their history, it would no doubt cause the people to reflect on the importance of democracy and human rights, and thus would contribute greatly to Japan and the world.

Toward the middle of the 10th century, Khitan from Mongolia invaded Sung China, and in the 11th century they migrated to Japan. The Fujiwara family, descendants of the T'ang Chinese, hated the Khitan and treated them as *sen*, except for a few who were employed in the government. The rest were enslaved, killed or driven into the wasteland of "E" (the Kanto area).

Khitan in China tried to aid their countrymen by supplying weapons and food; Khitan in Japan revolted and were successful at first, but when problems in China forced an end to assistance, they were defeated. Some then joined with the Sanka, who by this time had begun to use steel knives cut from a full length sword. Each family was given a knife with the brand of Umebachi (five circles) on its grip, representing the informal shape of the Khitan crest.

The population of Japan in 1871 was said to be 33 million, which included about 380,000 aboriginals listed on the non-Buddhist register. In 1916, the population was listed at 55.6 million. The sharp increase was supposed to be mainly caused by the addition of non-registered people during the Meiji era, a registration spurred by the needs of the army due to casualties in the Russo-Japanese War; if more people had been available to be conscripted this could have prevented the large loss of life caused by the war.

The registration drive indicated there were over 10 million people not registered on any register: samurai, farmers, artisans, traders and non-Buddhists. Fearing anti-imperial forces might cause a rebellion, the government encouraged people to emigrate.

In Rome, it was said that a citizen owned 30-50 slaves and a noble had several hundred slave-farmers and slave warriors respectively. Yagiri estimates that the Japanese ruling class was about 4% of the population during the earliest registrations, with the rest slaves or non-registered.

Currently over 90 % of the Japanese population are descendants of slaves or non-registered. Yet the history of slaves is hidden completely. The origin of discrimination against Burakumin (descendants of aboriginal prisoner ancestry) has its roots here. Unfortunately, discrimination will continue until the complete clarification of Japanese history of slaves and non-registered is made known.

Chapter Seventeen

Buddhism, Shinto and Christianity

A report in the *Nihon Keizai Shinbun* (Nikkei newspaper), dated January 17, 1992, concerns American religious beliefs. According to a 1991 Gallup poll, 47% of Americans believe that God made man in his image, and 40% believe that God guides human evolution. About 90% believe that God created human beings. Only 9% of those questioned denied this idea. About 1/3 believe that every word of the Bible was dictated by God. Religion seems to be a strong influence on Americans, providing precepts which influence national behavior.

Were a similar poll taken in Japan, no doubt the people with "no religion" would be ranked first. The Japanese are indifferent to religion, (although they do not object to getting married in a Shinto ceremony, being buried in a Buddhist funeral ceremony, and married in church, because it is fashionable). Since Shinto, the oldest Japanese religion, is polytheistic, it was easier for the Japanese to tolerate other religions, such as Buddhism, and while religion may not play an important part today, in feudalistic Japan, religion was as important as it was in Europe.

A commentary in a Japanese newspaper, discussing the mideast crisis and the conflict between Jews and Arabs, mentioned how difficult it is to mediate between nations of different religions. The writer remarked that it was a great gift from heaven for the Japanese that the local gods of Shinto were impressed by the dogma of Buddhism and gave way to Buddha amicably without bloodshed. This comment reflects the general opinion of the Japanese that we worship God on various occasions, that the gods do not prevent us from paying respect to or even to accomodating other religions, which is far better than having an Almighty God who does not allow the existence of any other gods. The Japanese, it is thought, never shed blood over religion and had no religious wars; this makes us feel comfortable.

Unfortunately, the above opinion is based on ignorance of the true history of Japan. In ancient times people really believed in religion, which was more important than their life. Therefore, they would not abandon or change their beliefs so easily even for polytheism. The fact that Shinto mixed well with Buddhism is proof in itself that an incredibly strong power worked to accomplish the synthesis. The history of Shinto's oppression started earlier than the 7th century and continued until the Meiji reformation of the 19th century. It was a hard and long struggle with many religious wars and changes of rulers resulting.

In the middle of 6th century Buddhism was introduced from China via Korea. Before this, Japan's Paekche rulers worshipped the four Korean gods of Hirano and built national shrines to them. When Buddhist priests in black surplices, the vanguard of a Chinese invasion, arrived to propagate the religion, Buddhism became dominant; Chinese military forces occupied Japan, and the Fujiwara family promoted Buddhism as the national religion. Buddhist temples built in each province were used to govern Ya slave farmers. Each temple had its own armed monks and bell to summon people in emergencies.

The aborigines, ancestors of the majority of today's Japanese, had their own beliefs. Yas believed in Gi (originating in ancient Persian Zoroastrianism) or in the Inari belief that worshipped shrines painted in red. Zoshiki had their Schichifukujin belief (Seven Deities of Good Fortune). Yottsu had the Hakusan or Hachiman belief (White Mountain belief originating from north Korea) and worshipped shrines of plain wood.

It was believed that all disasters, such as earthquakes, typhoons, fires and plagues, were caused by evil spirits of the dead. The role of religion was to protect the people either by locking the evil spirit in a shrine or passing it on to the enemy through a spell. Shamanism, brought by migrants from southern areas, was prevalent in Japan.

In a well known myth, Ooanamochi no Mikoto peacefully handed his domain, Izumo, to Amaterasu Oomikami, allegedly the supreme goddess of the imperial household. In reality Ooanamochi no Mikoto was killed by Amaterasu's troops and Izumo was taken by her with military force. The proof of this is that Ooanamochi no Mikoto's soul is locked up in his shrine, guarded by the gods of Amaterasu, so that he cannot commit evil acts against his enemies.

Masako Hojo, wife of Yoritomo Minamoto and Queen of the Ya, had the same dream for three consecutive nights, a dream of a big bronze mirror rising from the sea in front of Kamakura. The third night a voice came from the mirror, saying: "I am Amaterasu Oomikami. I am chagrined at being shut in this shrine in the Chinese Taoist way. Masako, you are my rebirth. Attack Kyoto with your troops and avenge the wrong done to me. Believe it." Based on this vision, Masako declared, "I am the rebirth of Amaterasu Oomikami, and I am going to conquer Kyoto. I shall raise an army."

Masako sent her envoy to the Ise shrine to convey her pledge that she would take Kyoto; thus she raised an army of 45,000 strong in 1221. It was the Joukyu no Ran.

This is a mysterious episode. In Japanese history Amaterasu is supposed to be the supreme goddess of the current imperial lineage, while in Masako's dream Amaterasu told Masako to "avenge" the wrong done to her by the imperial household. The dream cannot be explained unless Amaterasu was the great Queen of the Ya, killed by pro-Chinese Wa who first built the Ise shrine at Yamato and shut her in; they then moved the shrine to the other side of the Isuzu River in Ise. The "I" in Isuzu and Ise means "barbarian," a symbol often used contemptuously by the Chinese for the land of the aborigines. In the *Nihon Shoki*, it is mentioned that a princess of Yamato was appointed as patron for the shrine; Yamato people were nothing but barbarians to the Chinese. It is possible Amaterasu was the leader of the Ya, if all these things are considered together?

It is difficult to reconstruct ancient history exactly. One way is to excavate the ancient tombs of the imperial household, and examine the bones to determine scientifically which race the body belonged to. Blood testing is effective and would probably prove all rulers were either Chinese or Paekche. However, the Japanese Imperial Household Agency does not approve archaeological research by scholars, as they disapprove of disturbing the sleeping souls of the imperial household; one questions whether the real reason for their reluctance is they do not want to confront scientific evidence that might indicate the Japanese are multi-racial, which might totally break the cords uniting the emperor and the nation. Archaeological study will show all famous priests and founders of sects were Chinese or Korean (except Nichiren, founder of the Nichiren sect, who was apparently from an aboriginal race). When the samurai were compelled to become Buddhists, they often chose the Nichiren Shu sect; this may be the reason why Sokagakukai (the association of Nichiren adherents) and its political party, Koumei To, is popular among the Japanese populace as an opposition party today.

During the civil war age there were many conflicts between Buddhists and non-Buddhists. For example, Ikko-Shu, a sect of the Jodo Buddhists, dominated the province of Echizen (now the Fukui Prefecture) and Kaga (now the Ishikawa Prefecture). They fought hard with neighboring daimyos and samurai believing in Shinto. In a book titled *Wars in Ka Etsu (Wars in Kaga and Echizen)* it is clearly stated that Buddhism was the great enemy of the samurai. Nobunaga Oda killed many Buddhists in the course of his attempted unification of Japan. In 1483 Nobunaga ruined Echizen and massacred 50,000-60,000 adherents of Buddhism. In Japanese history this event is attributed to Nobunaga's cruelty, but actually it was because of his belief in the gods as descendants of anti-Buddhist aborigines.

Hideyoshi Toyotomi, successor to Nobunaga who unified Japan in the civil war age, was also of aboriginal ancestry, but later became more favorable to Buddhists; aspiring to become emperor, he claimed to be of noble blood, which meant he was either T'ang Chinese or Paekche. The Buddhists donated huge amounts of money to him, particularly after he became possessed by the idea of invading China via Korea, and persecuted aboriginal descendants in order to maintain peace and order in the home country.

Tokugawas, who gained power after Hideyoshi, was clearly Shintoist at the beginning, but after the third shogun Iyemitsu, Buddhism became the family religion, because Iyemitsu's mother was from a Buddhist family. Later on, non-Buddhists were persecuted and confined to ghettos, a situation which continued until the Meiji reformation in the 19th century.

Religious wars in Japan ended with the victory of Buddhism, when it became the national religion under the Tokugawas, and was thereafter used to oppress non-Buddhists. Buddhism also had a history of discrimination: only Buddhists were human beings, while non-Buddhists were subhuman, their lives as insignificant as worms. All powers in Japan demanded the people's total obedience to the Buddhists. Unfortunately this history is not known to the Japanese, who had no chance to learn any lessons from it.

Just like the conflict between Buddhism and Shintoism, there were conflicts between silver and gold. Mt. Hakone in Kanagawa Prefecture was the border dividing Japan into two countries of different currencies. In central Japan to the west of Mt. Hakone, silver was the currency, while to the east it was gold. In the capital of Kyoto the Ninagawa Zaibatsu (financial combine) traditionally performed functions of a central bank and used the silver standard. Gold was merely a metal of ornament there and was exported to Ming China.

During the rule of Nobunaga, a liner service was opened between Sakai near Osaka and Macau. Then people started to realize that gold was money in countries other than Ming China. The people in the city of Sakai started trading gold to the Ninagawas, who soon discovered they could sell it for much higher prices in Luzon and Macau, although it was illegal to sell to any countries other than Ming China. Buying and selling gold and silver in the black market were so profitable that together with trading saltpeter and slaves, it made the city of Sakai very prosperous.

The rulers in this period, Nobunaga and Hideyoshi, knew the illegal trade was going on and attempted to switch to the gold standard. This change would have made it easier and more economical to buy saltpeter from other countries, but the Ninagawas opposed the idea. Nobunaga was killed in an explosion at the temple. Behind the scenes, the Ninagawas' silver financed Hideyoshi, who promised to support the silver standard. After several battles Hideyoshi unified Japan.

However, when Hideyoshi decided to invade Korea, he wanted to go over to a gold standard and use the vast amount of gold he had collected in Osaka Castle to pay for the cost of the expedition. The Ninagawas opposed this. The result was that the tremendous piles of gold bars remained in the castle. Even when Hideyoshi's son was locked in a death struggle with the Tokugawas for control of Japan, the gold was not touched. The Tokugawas pledged to the Ninagawas they would keep the silver standard in western Japan.

Most Japanese do not realize that saltpeter, the major material used in producing gunpowder, was the key to victory in war. Saltpeter is not produced in Japan but is imported from foreign countries. Nobunaga, Hideyoshi and Iyeyasu, as well as other daimyos, concentrated their energies on how to secure supplies of high quality saltpeter. Without it, any daimyo's destiny would be crushed by an enemy who had access to it.

The Jesuits held the key. Since coming to Japan in 1549, the missionaries, through contact with Portuguese traders, controlled the importation of saltpeter, which came to Japan from Macao on Portuguese ships. The Jesuits used money from sales to finance their missionary work in spreading Christianity throughout Japan. Many daimyos converted to Christianity in order to gain more favorable access to saltpeter. Between 1553 and 1620, eighty-six daimyos were officially baptized, and many more were sympathetic to the Christians.

Louis Froez, a Jesuit wrote, "When I went to see Nobunaga for permission for a priest to live in Japan and for freedom to propagate the Christian faith, he carried a tray of foods himself to feed me and presented me with clothing made of silk and of white hemp cloth. Everyone was surprised by the extraordinary favor shown me." It was only in this period the number of Christians increased dramatically. The reason is obvious—saltpeter. However, most Japanese do not follow this view.

The Japanese do not like the idea that victory or defeat in battle depended upon superiority in manpower, firepower or money. In our history, clan alliances were seldom considered as a strategy to win a war. Instead the simple success stories of Koudan are popular. A lord went through hardship to win the war, managing his subjects as one body. Another popular plot was the faithful samurai achieved victory by dedicating his life to his lord.

This attitude of relying on emotional and spiritual elevation rather than an objective study of victory based on an evaluation of power, military strength, and strategy, has prevented the Japanese from discovering the true history of Japan.

The Tokugawas, after destroying the Toyotomis in 1615, took a series of actions to close Japan to foreign visitors. In 1637 the Shimabara no Ran rebellion broke out, which in Japanese history is explained as a rebellion of 38,000 persecuted Christians and oppressed farmers against the daimyos of Shimabara and Amakusa. Shiro Amakusa, a Christian, was the leader of the insurgents, who were besieged in the old Hara Castle and resisted stubbornly from October 1637 to February 1638. In February, Tokugawa Bakufu forces launched an all-out attack using 120,000 troops, while Dutch ships bombarded the castle. It is believed only one person, a painter, surrendered to Bakufu forces, and that all the rest died in the battle.

It would be more exact to regard the Shimabara no Ran as a farmers' rebellion, not a Christian revolt against persecution. However, the Bakufu used the rebellion as a pretext for further persecution of Christians. In 1641 the Bakufu built Deshima, an artificial island where only the Dutch were allowed to settle and trade; the remainder of Japan was closed to the outside world.

For proof that the Shimabara no Ran was not a religious revolt, two pieces of evidence should be examined: first, several kilometers to the south of Hara Castle is an old harbor, Kuchi no Tsu, which was a Jesuit concession. Rebel forces attacked the storage depot, killed the Jesuits and other Christians, and took saltpeter and arms to use in their uprising. It was said the Dutch offered their ship as an act of revenge for the action of the rebels. Secondly, the Vatican paid little or no attention to this rebellion or to the "martyrdom" of the rebels, clearly indicating that the Vatican did not view this as a religious rebellion.

One further point of interest should be noted: it seems that Tokugawas intentionally kept the painter, the lone survivor of the uprising alive on purpose, so that he could paint a picture of the battle. His painting, which still exists, shows the insurgents' flags on the castle walls. The Bakufu used this as evidence of a Christian revolt; but closer examination shows a puzzling depiction: Catholic and Protestant flags are interspersed; however, Catholics and Protestants would never have joined together at this time in history, since there was bitter hatred between the two. The sensible explanation is that the Bakufu wanted proof of a Christian revolt, so they commissioned the painting, but they were ignorant about the situation that existed between Protestants and Catholics at the time.

At the outset of the rebellion the Bakufu were optimistic about a quick victory, believing that no untrained mob of Christians and farmers could go against the Bakufus' trained samurai. However, their all-out attack on January 1, 1638 failed to capture the castle. Shigemasa Itakura, Bakufu commander-in-chief, was killed in battle, and Bakufu troop casualties reached 4,000 in that day alone.

The Bakufu appointed Nobutsuna Matsudaira, a member of the shogun's council, supreme commander, and sent a large army to complete the job. It was a shock that even using 120,000 men in heavy bombardment from the sea, it still took two months to take the castle.

The length of the siege proved that even an untrained army could be taught to fight if they were armed with guns and powder. The use of weapons and saltpeter taken from Kuchi no Tsu made it possible for the rebels to hold their position for such a long time. The Bakufu did not want other daimyos to learn these facts, because it might encourage opposition. Therefore, they massacred all the rebels, including women and children. Citing the rebels' religious fanaticism, the Bakufu used the painting as evidence of a Christian revolt.

However, this presented a serious warning to the Tokugawas: "don't allow access to saltpeter." They decided to grant the Dutch a monopoly of foreign trade between Japan and the outside world, and the Tokugawas as a result gained monopoly of the saltpeter trade. Nukeni Gai (smuggling) was prohibited and severely punished.

Often in Koudan stories, trading houses were destroyed by the government on the charge of smuggling antique jewelry, but actually the Bakufu were not really concerned about this; their sole concern was to stop the smuggling of saltpeter and firearms by the daimyos. By closing Japan, they kept the powder to themselves until the Meiji restoration; the Tokugawa Shogunate fell when the monopoly was broken.

The powerful Satsuma and Choshu daimyos obtained saltpeter and arms from abroad after Japan was opened by Commodore Perry in 1853. In January 1868, an allied army of Satsuma and Choshu, armed with modern weapons, defeated 30,000 Tokugawa troops at the battle of Toba Fushimi. The reason for the victory was simple: gunpowder used by the Tokugawa forces often misfired because the saltpeter stored in the Bakufu warehouses for long periods of time was wet. Yoshinobu, the last shogun, soon realized he could no longer fight reform. He made his peace with the rebel clans and the imperial court. This decision saved the Tokugawa family, who remained among the Japanese nobility until the end of World War II.

Let us return to the period before the Shimabara no Ran. It should be noted that there was great tension between the Imperial Household and the Tokugawa Shogunate. The Emperor Gomizu-no-o married Kazuko, daughter of the second Tokugawa Shogun Hidetada in 1620, a union which seemed to cement friendly relations between the Shogunate and the Court. However, an affair called Shi-e Jiken shattered the friendship.

The Tokugawa Bakufu prohibited the Emperor from granting the right, at his discretion, for highly ranked Buddhist priests to wear the purple surplice, but the Emperor ignored the order. The Bakufu then canceled the Emperor's grant. Emperor Gomizu-no-o became angry and abdicated the throne.

The Emperor's 6 year-old daughter was enthroned as Empress Myojo. Gomizu-no-o, maneuvering behind the scene, proposed to issue an imperial order to the other daimyos to subjugate the Tokugawa Bakufu. The Tokugawas uncovered the plot and sent tens of thousands of troops to Kyoto to control the Court. Under these circumstances, Gomizu-no-o could not issue his imperial order to the daimyos. At about this time the Shimabara-no-Ran broke out, which the Bakufu proclaimed to be a local Christian rebellion. Had it become known as anything but this, such revolts could have spread with imperial connivance and support.

The fact that many Japanese men and women were sold as slaves to the Portuguese during the civil war period is not discussed by Japanese historians. Men were sold to the Portuguese colonies in India and Malaysia. Good looking women were sent to Europe, where women were in short supply due to the witch hunting of the Inquisition. An imperial edict issued by the Portuguese King on March 12, 1571, relating to the importation and treatment of Japanese slaves, attests to this situation. Macao in this period was the great distribution center for Japanese slaves. Nobunaga's massacre of several thousand Buddhists was considered by the Portuguese a waste of human resources.

There are other reports about these Japanese slaves. Soho Tokutomi, publisher and journalist (1863-1957), quoted in *The Modern History of the Japanese Nation*, the words of Yuki Omura, Secretary of Hideyoshi: "Black ships brought several hundred Japanese men and women into the harbors of Goto, Hirato and Nagasaki, and carried them away in chains in the bottom of the ship. It was a miserable scene, resembling hell."

A report of 1603 from Goa, India, to the King of Spain, said:

"Here we have only a few Europeans. We use the Japanese slaves as soldiers to defend our forts. They are a warlike race and use arms to repel the natives."

Why were so many Japanese sold as slaves? The answer is simple. The Christian Dominicans traded them in return for saltpeter from Macao. When the Tokugawa Bakufu closed Japan, the export of Japanese slaves was ended. However the Tokugawas hid much, which seriously influenced Japanese character over the next 200 years.

As we have seen, Japanese history was fabricated, hidden or destroyed to meet the demands of the imperial government. These facts still present a serious peril to Japan and to the world today.

Chapter Eighteen

The Japanese Woman

It is generally believed in Western countries that Japan is a male dominated society, though it is noted that the status of women has greatly improved since the war, and that the trend toward woman's economic independence has strengthened their social standing. In Chinese and Korean cultures, the predominance of man over woman is traditional, but for Japanese Ya and Yottsu, the predominance of woman over man is in the cultural heritage.

Aboriginal rebel armies which rose in northeastern Japan in the 8th century, shaking the T'ang Chinese dynasty in Yamato, consisted of many clans, each commanded by a bold female leader or *okami* (woman general). Female leaders trained male corps, but dissatisfied with men's fighting spirit, organized special corps of women only. Their brutality frightened the government soldiers. Defeated armies who did not surrender were driven into confinement in secluded mountainous ghettos. Here, women leaders controlled their clans with strict rules, which helped them survive life in the mountains.

Female proprietors of Japanese inns, restaurants, and pubs today are called *okami*. In ancient Japan these businesses were controlled by the Ya. Owners of geisha houses were also called *okami*, and the matrilineal family is still maintained in these sectors as a cultural heritage. The word *okami* is phonetically the same as the *okami*, (ruler such as emperor or shogun), and it is not mere coincidence that both indicate a person in power.

Great and beautiful tales of love and romance among noble men and women in the imperial court, such as the *Tale of Genji*, are valuable literary works for us today. However, historically only a handful could afford such romance. Privileged conquerors' lives were made graceful and comfortable only thanks to the service of nearly 100 slaves per family, thus they had the leisure to become involved in courtly love affairs. At least nine out of ten people in Japan today are the descendants of these slaves or of the prisoners in mountain ghettoes who were not allowed to experience human feelings of love between man and woman, a fact which most Japanese do not know.

Life in the mountains was severe; survival under conditions of starvation was the first thing a leader had to overcome. At the same time, it was important to have a reserve of healthy children ready to defend the integrity of the clan. Personal feelings counted for little. Marriage between families was set by either the leader or the parents. As decades went by, it became more difficult to identify the original clan of a bride or groom, and investigation into family lineage became an important part of a potential marriage. The woman of Ya ancestry had to marry a Ya man (only later when the Tokugawas allowed it did marriages between Ya and Yottsu take place). The tradition of arranged marriage is still maintained within Ya and Yottsu society today, though the origin has been forgotten.

The lives of enslaved women were no less miserable than those captured in ghettoes. They were not allowed to refuse the demands of their T'ang Chinese and Korean masters, and had no choice but to give birth to children of mixed racial origin. They brought up their children, but were never legitimatized by their masters. Perhaps this is the reason we call ourselves *shomin* (illegitimate people), even under today's democratic system.

The idea that Japan was ever ruled by T'ang Chinese and Korean in ancient times is new and amazing to most Japanese. However, this explains many things; for instance, every time tombs were excavated, those buried were found to be either Korean or Chinese.

What happens when one group conquers another? Official Japanese history tells us nothing about the Chinese conquest of Japan. However, in the Spanish conquest of Mexico, the Spanish conquistador Cortez massacred the royal families and nobles of the Aztecs. As a result of Spanish intermarriage and liaisons with the Indians, many mestizo resulted. It is hard to imagine that the Chinese conquerors did not do the same thing in 8th century Japan. In Mexico it is obvious due to difference in skin pigmentation of the people, and there is no way to hide it. However, in Japan we are unable to identify original races by color, and it became convenient to obscure the truth.

The life of Sanka women was always difficult. Some wandered in the mountains and made *sebri* (temporary cottages) along river banks;

some settled in town secretly. The Sanka had strict rules to keep themselves hidden from the government and the public. It was most important for them to keep their blood pure and to increase their number to be able one day to avenge what the Fujiwara family did to them in the 8th century. Women controlled men with regard to drinking and sex, preventing them from disease and alcoholism. The role of women was so important in deciding the Sanka fate that the women also regulated the marriage system and customs. It is amazing these people could live for 1,000 years completely hidden from the government, maintaining their racial independence.

Masako Hojo, who married Yoritomo Minamoto, head of the Yottsu people, was one of the most remarkable ladies in the history of Japan. In the 12th century, Yoritomo made an alliance with the Ya against the Heike (Taira) family, and after Heike power was destroyed, established the Kamakura Bakufu. After Yoritomo's death, the Hojo family ruled Japan, using Minamoto shoguns as figureheads. When the imperial court declared war against the Bakufu in 1221, Masako's army of 190,000 men defeated the imperial forces in May of that year, in what was seen as her revenge on the Fujiwaras as a Ya woman.

During the civil war age women showed courage and resourcefulness by fighting as bravely as men. To appear more formidable, they shaved off their eyebrows, painted horrible, frightening ones with ink, and dyed their teeth black to scare enemies when they opened their mouths. Female daimyos and samurai proliferated until after the age of the Tokugawas, when female succession was prohibited.

Daimyo wives controlled food storage and family finances. Since foods were stored in the northern, cooler section of the castle, a daimyo wife was often called *Kita no Kata* (the north lady) with a mixed touch of awe and respect. Wives sometimes lent money to their husbands, charging high interest rates to finance a battle; and ofttimes, women were considered valuable as hostages. The image of the Japanese lady sighing from grief due to a tragic lost love caused by an arranged political marriage is romantic but inaccurate.

When guns were introduced into Japan, female gun corps were organized in the Tachibana Han of Kyushu, who proved women and even children armed with guns and ammunition could make stronger troops than stout samurai with conventional arms. This hurt the samurais' pride, and as a result they deemed the use of guns dishonorable. In the Shimabara no Ran, the great rebellion during the Tokugawa reign, mobs of farmers, women and children, well armed with guns and gunpowder, held out for five months, from October 1637 to February 1638, against powerful attacks by large samurai forces of the Bakufu.

The Shimabara no Ran began as a protest by farmers of the Shimabara/Amakusa areas (now the Shimabara Peninsula of Nagasaki Prefecture and the Amakusa Islands of the Kumamoto Prefecture) against severe taxation policies of the Shimabara Han. These areas had formerly been governed by the Konishi and Arima families respectively, until the Toyotomis were ruined by the Tokugawas. Both the Konishi and Arima were Christian daimyos whose retainers became *ronin* (lordless samurai) providing military leadership in the farmers' rebellion, in response to the secret rescript issued by the abdicated Emperor Gomizuno-o to overthrow the Tokugawa shogunate. (Gomizuno-o, obliged to marry the daughter of Hidetada Tokugawa, the second shogun, was compelled to abdicate when his son from that marriage was seven years old). When the Bakufu forces eventually suppressed the rebellion, they killed all rebels, including women and children. In order to conceal the fact that the imperial court backed the rebellion, in an attempt to overthrow the Tokugawa shogunate, the Bakufu announced the Shimabara no Ran was a Christian rebellion and used it as a pretext to stamp out Christianity in Japan.

The Shimabara rebellion spelled the end of Japanese contact with the West, when the shogunate closed the country and monopolized the importation of saltpeter. Smuggling saltpeter was dealt with harshly. When the martial art of kendo became popular at the end of the Edo era, masters of swordsmanship were loathe to admit that men with swords could not win against women with guns.

This idea was adapted by the Japanese World War II army, and made military leaders foolishly enact banzai charges, which led to the unnecessary deaths of many young men. Frighteningly, this concept is still alive today. TV samurai heroes, masters of kendo, always defeat villain-gunmen by throwing a knife faster than a speeding bullet. On the positive side, guns are not considered a man's weapon, which keeps Japanese communities free of privately owned guns.

Guns were introduced in Japan during the witch hunting age in the West. Believing that the great leader of the witches fled to the east, the Pope ordered the militant Jesuit order to hunt them down, at the same time propagating Christianity to the yellow skinned races. The Jesuits built a base in Macau, where they stored saltpeter, the main ingredient of gunpowder. In Europe, Chilean saltpeter with much higher explosive power was replacing conventional saltpeter, which was dumped by the army and sold in the east, where the Jesuits used the profits to pay the expenses of their mission.

Soon the samurai learned the power of guns; saltpeter became a magic ingredient for victory in war and every daimyo desperately wanted to obtain it for his survival. Aboriginal men and women were hunted out of the mountains and bartered for saltpeter. Attractive young girls were sold for a good price, since in Europe women were in short supply from the witch hunts. Japanese blood today runs in Portuguese and Spanish veins in significant percentage.

The tradition of the great witch who fled to the east is still alive. Yagiri alludes to books which advertise, "Let's take a flight to the country of witches and try to find out...if witches' genital organs really open horizontally." The Japanese are proud of the nickname given for the women's Olympic volleyball team, "Oriental Witches."

Woman's power reached its peak at the age of Kasuga no Tsubone (originally the office of the mistress of the shogun of a rank allowed to visit the imperial court, later mistaken as a proper noun). In this case it refers to a specific woman, who lived from 1579-1643 and bore a son by the first shogun, Ieyasu Tokugawa, who became the third shogun, Iyemitsu. As mother of the shogun, she was given specific powers: none of the Tokugawas' vassals could manage her or other ladies in the apartments of the shogunal palace under her patronage. She controlled the Bakufu ministers as servants. Through her influence, her sons from a former marriage were all promoted to high positions. In traditional history she is described as the nurse of Iyemitsu, but this is wrong; she was his mother, as recorded in a secret book kept in the library of the Tokugawas, according to Yagiri. This woman was a daughter of Kuranosuke Saito, who saved the life of Ieyasu by assassinating Nobunaga. In return, Ieyasu made a secret promise to make her his mistress, and if a son was born he would be made shogun. In the civil war age, virginity was of no particular importance; Ieyasu did not mind making a divorced woman his mistress—her experience of easy deliveries was more important to him.

The religion of the Tokugawas was originally Shinto, but during the reign of Iyemitsu, they became Buddhists. The mother of Tsunayoshi, the fifth shogun, was Korean, born in Cheju, and a devout Buddhist. Tsunayoshi made Buddhism Japan's national religion. Buddhism was introduced from China via Korea, both countries being "men first" races. After Kasuga no Tsubone died, the "men first" concept rapidly took over, and women were prohibited from becoming daimyos. Onna Daigaku, the text of ethics demanding women abide by feudalistic morals, was widely adopted in the Han and in private schools by the 19th century, resulting in women's power being drastically cut. The current graceful image of Yamato Nadeshiko, obedient to husband, devoted to family and virtue, was formed in the period leading up to the Meiji era.

The fate of women in the countryside was cruel. Priests had the right to rob a woman of her virginity before selling her into prostitution, where she would be forced to serve numerous men until death. In the family of the daimyo or samurai, all female servants were vassals of the lord; if the lord wanted a female servant's chastity she could not refuse.

A noble woman married to a daimyo often chose to remain childless; instead, she would offer a husband her maids as mistresses, and adopt a resulting offspring as soon as it was born, thus avoiding the high risks of death by childbed fever, and providing a successor at the same time. For this reason, it was forbidden that female servants should make love with any man but the lord. Relations between master and servants in trade houses and storekeepers was the same as that of daimyo and his vassals. Amorous love affairs sung in *joruri* (ballad dramas) or played in theaters concerned only the few of the ruling class.

As the cotton, yarn and spinning industries became the core of the Japanese industrial revolution at the end of the 19th century, many female workers were employed by factories in adverse labor conditions. The women worked twelve hours a day for very low pay. Many died of lung disease, fatigue and overwork. Young daughters of tenant farmers were sold by brokers into houses of prostitution in order to save their parents' lives. Their miserable situation led to the socialist movement. The first women's political organization was initiated in 1911 by the incorporation of Seitosha, a publishing company under the leadership of Hiratsuka Raicho, which issued a magazine for ladies titled *Seito* (blue stocking). After the company was dissolved in 1916, another association demanding woman's suffrage was established in 1920 (New Women's Association—Shin Fujin Kyokai). In 1924 the League for the Attainment of Woman's Political Rights (Fujin Sanseiken Kakutoku Kiseidomei) was formed. Fusae Ichikawa, a famous leader, was an active member of the Diet until recently. One more association of working class women was instituted in 1925. The Taisho era (1912-26) lasted but a brief time.

Under the Showa era, which began in 1926, the lives of tenant farmers worsened. In the first universal suffrage election in 1928, to the surprise of the government, eight communists won seats in the House of Representatives. To suppress communists, the government enhanced the Act of the Maintenance of the Public Order, which had been enacted three years before, and red hunting became a predominant activity.

Economic depression and political corruption caused an unprecedented coup d'etat of the imperial army on February 26, 1936, in which 1400 officers and soldiers participated and several ministers and senior statesmen were killed. The instigators demanded the emperor's direct intervention to reform corrupt politics and save the farmers from their plight. Even though the emperor's resolute attitude caused the coup d'etat to end in failure, his personal effort within the Meiji ideology and political system could not stop the tide of militarism and ultra nationalism. As they grew stronger, women's standing slipped further, until women came to be seen only as instruments to breed men for the military, or as objects of men's sexual desire.

The Japanese do not have the perception of Christian original sin. We have no conflict of soul and flesh, and historically the ruling class was tolerant of men's love affairs and of womanizing even after marriage. Emperors, court nobles, shoguns, daimyos, samurais and rich merchants were free to have mistresses. When a nobleman traveled to a local place, it was not unusual that the head of a good family in the village would have his daughter attend the nobleman in his bedroom, hoping that a pregnancy would result, providing a baby of noble blood. In a vertical caste society, marriage or blood relationships were the only the possibilities for a family to improve its social status. An attractive young girl played an important role in the family; familial ups and downs often fell on her shoulders or depended on her moves.

When the Meiji system was initiated, ministers, generals, and owners of big businesses could enjoy both power and women to their heart's content, relieved of responsibility to be moral leaders for the people, leaving that cross to the emperor to carry. The new system said "womanizing is an ability of man." On the other hand, wives were now expected to be chaste and not jealous of a husband's love affairs.

In the military there was and most probably still is no guilty feeling to buying a prostitute; the concern is only hygiene and cleanliness. The army is a gathering of tens of thousands of young healthy men with natural sexual desires, a common problem of the military worldwide, particularly in wartime. Yet one can imagine the suffering and despair of prostitutes compelled to their fate. It is painful to read *The New York Times'* July 12, 1992 report of Japan's other war crimes, i.e. sexual enslavement of Korean women during World War II. The *Times* blames the Japanese: "Some 20 million people died in the Pacific War, 17 million of them victims of Japanese aggression. Yet Japanese text books and popular culture still emphasize how Japan suffered." To most Japanese, devilish acts of the imperial military are unbelievable, for one simple reason: we have never been informed of them. History books do not tell the facts concretely, but contain stories of the bravery of soldiers who fought with all their might for the emperor and nation.

Surviving soldiers know exactly what happened, but they do not speak. My own special knowledge of the true history of Japan as well as of the harsh fate that befell our aboriginal ancestors allow me to appreciate the truth. The Japanese are human beings; all people are both good and bad. However, the Japanese government's position is, "We are a glorious single family country with a benevolent, peace-loving emperor who as big father has led us morally from the infinite past. Only for a brief period of twenty years to 1945 were we maddened by the military, which led us into aggressive wars and unspeakable actions. It was our fatal mistake. But from our uniquely clean history, it cannot happen that our fathers did such cruel and dirty inhumane acts."

The emperor may make words of apology in his speech. The prime minister may follow them, but words are not enough. And as *The New York Times* continues to accuse, "Half a century later, Tokyo still resists acknowledging other appalling wartime crimes. Until it does, Japan's efforts to play a more active role in Asian affairs will provoke distrust." We will return to this issue again later.

Today, young girls of south Asian countries are being brought into Japan illegally by yakuzas, paralleling experiences of the Ya women of the 8th century. In the 20th century, lucky girls can go home with a lot of money, but the essence is the same. On the other hand, many rich Japanese young "witches" travel to the U.S. seeking dissolute nights of international experiences. These ladies are contemptuously called "Yellow Cabs" because they let anybody ride. They come back home to marry Japanese men, pretending innocence. If the husband is not as good as expected, they get divorced in Narita as soon as the honeymoon is over. This is called a "Narita divorce."

Japanese women have contributed to Japan's postwar economic success with their tremendous energy; women now work in almost all sectors of society, and it may not be long before we have a female prime minister. However, Japanese women need to realize what a good life they are currently enjoying, compared to the past. Unlike Ya women who had to marry whomever was designated by the woman leader, today's Japanese woman enjoys freedom. The fate of race, clan and family is no longer on her shoulders, as in former ages in which there was no room for sentiment. In the past, if a woman loved someone, she was not allowed to show it because she might be required to play a much more important role for the country or clan. Today's Japanese woman is free to make her own decisions. Women have come a long way.

Part Three

POST-WAR POLITICS AND ECONOMICS

Chapter Nineteen

Constitutional Monarchy vs Democratic Republic

Japan's constitution is commemorated as a national holiday. It was announced on November 3, 1946, enforced on May 3, 1947, and contains five major concepts:

1. Democracy (the nation is sovereign).
2. Pacifism (the famous Article 9 stipulates that Japan has renounced war).
3. Respect for human rights
4. The emperor's status as symbol
5. Separation of the three branches of government

It is widely known that General Douglas MacArthur, Supreme Commander for the Allied Powers in the Pacific, with his staff at General Headquarters (GHQ) drafted the constitution and presented it to the Japanese government in February, 1946. Masayasu Hasegawa describes the details in his book *The Constitution of Japan*, (Iwanami Shoten, 21st edition, Tokyo, Feb., 1991).

The U.S. government sent its reform policy for the Japanese government to General MacArthur as early as January 7, 1946. The policy directed MacArthur to establish a legislature to represent the Japanese electorate, and added that the emperor institution established under the Meiji constitution did not conform with U.S. views on the new constitution.

Based on that directive, Gen. MacArthur gave his staff three principles for establishing initiatives in the new constitution:

1. The emperor is at the head of the state (this does not mean he is the official "head of state"); succession to the imperial throne is hereditary; the emperor's obligation and power shall be exercised in accordance with the constitution and correspond to the basic will of the people as stipulated in the constitution.
2. War as a sovereign right of the nation is renounced: Japan renounces war as a means of solving international disputes and maintaining safety; Japan shall entrust her defense and protection to the sublime ideal which is ruling the world now; Japanese army, navy or air force shall not be permitted, nor the right of belligerence by any Japanese forces.
3. The Japanese feudalistic system shall be abolished.

After GHQ drafted the constitution according to General MacArthur's three principles, it was sent to the Japanese government, which issued its first draft on March 6, 1946. This draft was then submitted to the 90th session of the Imperial Diet, convened on June 21. In Gen. MacArthur's draft, the first article stated: "The emperor's position derives solely from the sovereign will of the people and from no other sources." The Japanese government's draft expressed: "The Emperor is to be the symbol of Japan and the unity of the nation based on the nation's supreme will." Though the difference was slight, the Japanese version was ambiguous as to who was the sovereign.

During the Diet's deliberation, the Far Eastern Commission in Washington, D.C. intervened, resulting in the final article adopted by the current constitution: "The Emperor shall be the symbol of the State and of the unity of the people, deriving his position from the will of the people, with whom resides sovereign power." Together with the preamble, "We, the Japanese people...do proclaim that sovereign power resides with the people and do firmly establish this Constitution," it is clear that the people are the sovereign. However, according to Hasegawa, there is still a problem left, to wit: the difference between "people" (*Jinmin*) and "nation" (*Kokumin*). In Gen. MacArthur's draft the "people" were sovereign, while the current constitution says that "the nation" is sovereign. (However, it must be noted, "the people" is still used in the English version). "The people" is the republican concept that opposes any monarchy; it does not include the emperor and nobility. "The people" with whom the sovereign power resides agree to position the emperor as a symbol, but this does not mean that "the people" accept him as one of "the people." Japan is more a "democracy with a symbolic emperor."

On the other hand, "the nation" includes the monarch as one of the people, meaning that the emperor is one of the sovereign. The concept of "nation" is the principle by which the monarchy is made constitutional, clearly a political system called a "constitutional monarchy," which is different from Gen. MacArthur's idea. Of course, "constitutional monarchy" can be almost as democratic as republican, by limiting the number of privileged men to as few as possible. Since the emperor is defined as the only man with special privileges, the constitution makes the Japan's political system the most democratic constitutional monarchy in the world, even though confusion exists regarding definitions of the "people" and "the nation."

Article 4 of the Constitution provides: "The Emperor shall perform only such acts in matters of state as are provided for in this Constitution, and he shall not have powers related to government." Articles 6 and 7 define these acts and powers exactly. Article 6 provides: "The Emperor shall appoint the Prime Minister, as designated by the Diet. The Emperor shall appoint the Chief Judge of the Supreme Court as designated by the Cabinet."

Article 7 provides: "The Emperor, with the advice and approval of the Cabinet, shall perform the following acts in matters of state on behalf of the people: promulgation of amendments of the Constitution; laws, cabinet orders and treaties; convocation of the Diet; dissolution of the House of Representatives; proclamation of general election of members of the Diet; attestation to appointment and dismissal of Ministers of State and other officials, as provided by law; and of full powers and credentials of Ambassadors and Ministers; attestation of general and special amnesty, commutation of punishment, reprieve, and restoration of rights; awarding of honors; attestation of instruments of ratification and other diplomatic documents as provided by law; receiving foreign ambassadors and ministers; performance of ceremonial functions."

The emperor's acts in matters of state are limited to those enumerated above, and he must have advice and consent of the cabinet. Actually, the emperor's functions have been expanded beyond constitutional limitations. Though he remains a symbol, somewhere between his specified constitutional duties and his private life, the emperor performs semi-constitutional functions. For example, visits to local cities and foreign countries in rituals and ceremonics of state under the name of royal diplomacy fall in this capacity. The government has purposely arranged for his appearances as often as possible, so that the people will appreciate him as a special man above the nation and government, and he is treated with deep reverence and respect by the Japanese media in all public affairs.

The restoration of National Foundation Day on February 11th created the same effect on the Japanese public. In his book *The Constitution and the Emperor Institution*" (Kabushiki Kaisha Iwanami Shoten, 1990), Kouichi Yokota describes this national holiday as based on imperial myth rather than history. Now sponsored by the Prime Minister's office, the Ministry of Education, the Ministry of Home Affairs, and the Ministry of Foreign Affairs, the national holiday commemorates the mythical accession of Japan's first emperor, Jimmu, according to the account of the oft-rewritten *Nihon Shoki*.

The annual celebration in 1990 was attended by Prime Minister Kaifu, government officials, the President of the House of Councilors, the Speaker of the House of Representatives, and various diplomats. At the occasion, Bunpei Ohtsuki declared: "I am glad to celebrate the day of the accession of Emperor Jimmu, which dates back to the age of Ki Ki." (*Nihon Shoki* and *Koji Ki* collectively).

Clearly this annual ceremony continues to foster the ideology that the Japanese nation was founded on the accession of the first emperor, Jimmu. The Prime Minister and the nation praise and pay respect to the current emperor in this celebration. Despite recent scandals that have tarnished the image of Japanese politicians involved in bribery, under the current constitution the prime minister is the top official and representative of the nation in Japan's democratic system, but a contradiction exists, in which the image of the emperor in Meiji ideology is steadily reviving. To the people today, despite his limitations outlined in the Constitution, the emperor is the sovereign head of the state, and the celebration of National Foundation Day as an historical event has paved the way for his restoration to an inviolable position.

In similar manner, the government guides school education, so that the current view of Japanese history remains unchanged from the prewar imperialistic view. The two decades preceding the defeat in World War II are dismissed as a short but unfortunate period of madness caused by ultra-nationalism of an otherwise peace-loving people. Some extreme right movements advocate the revival of education based on the Rescript of Education of the Emperor Meiji, and the official teachers' manual for compulsory education requests that teachers teach that the emperor is in the center of the nation and must be venerated as having a special existence.

The government continues its arbitrary interpretation of the constitution, and is building a more conservative constitutional monarchy. Are we going back to compulsory selfless loyalty to a divine figure again? Arbitrary interpretation has caused a gap between the spirit of the current constitution and today's political system. A particular example of this gap exists in the discrepancies in Article 9. The emperor's performance of so-called "official duties" beyond the limit of acts in matters of state such as "royal diplomacy" is another matter. The government had pushed such policies for the sake of economic recovery and winning the cold war. But now that the war is over, to continue unconstitutionalities is intolerable. Currently voices demanding revision of the constitution are gaining power, for reasons that the climate has changed or that the constitution was written by the U.S.A. One worries that if the government can freely do anything it wants, such as make arbitrary or broadly interpreted laws, whether it is no use to make any new laws at all. This situation may have been created by the remains of feudalistic ideas in Japanese society that *okami* (rulers such as emperor, shogun, government, employer) thought of laws and regulations as merely tools to control the people, which the people were resigned to accept.

The Japanese imperial household is often compared with the English monarchial system, but they are quite different. There are few myths and fabrications connected to the foundation of the present British royal household. Except in its earliest days, the British monarchy was subject to control of a parliament. Before God, the British monarch is a man or woman like any other man or woman.

British history details many conflicts for power: the Norman conquest, civil wars, wars fought in France, defiance against arbitrary monarchial rule, revolutions, the beheading of a king, a commonwealth, and finally constitutional monarchy: a 2,000 year history exposes every essence of human nature from the most godly and sublime actions to the most devilish and subhuman ones. History records a struggle between the British monarchy and people for democratic reform and establishment of dignity and human rights. The present British system required painful bloodshed and political compromise, and took a long time to establish. One can definitely learn from British history what their nation has come to stand for.

These values are reflected in politics through democratic procedures which the British established, using the wisdom acquired from their long history of experience, good and bad. The position of the British monarch is crystal clear, with no room for doubt that the monarch is a human being like any other person. The reverence the British people hold for their royal household is an agreement based on honesty, fostered by a realistic view of a history marked by conflict, but manifested in a human desire to find solutions.

One of my British friends summed up the essence of this conflict as follows: "The path of progress for monarchy in the West has been a combination of legislation to place government and finance totally in the hands of the people, while making the monarch the figurehead of the values of the nation."

"The modern monarch, to the Western mind, must be totally above political affiliations or control. This is a matter of public trust, as well as security against the monarchy being used for political purposes contrary to the welfare of the people and the world at large."

We see evidence of this historically, in Britain:

* Magna Carta (1212): The English king promised not to seize property or imprison any subject except according to the laws of the land.
* The British Parliament: Parliament is composed of two houses, the House of Lords representing nobles, and the House of Commons representing commoners. In the 17th Century, parliament successfully established its supremacy over the king after two revolutions.
* Bill of Rights (1689): The king rules not by divine right but by the consent of parliament.
* Act of Settlement (1701): The crown's ministers are responsible for the acts of the sovereign (i.e., the behavior of the king is considered a matter of public importance).
* Reform Act (1832): Actual sovereignty belongs to the people as represented by parliament (the sovereign cannot gang up with parliament against the people.)
* In the last coronation in 1952, many symbols of the tradition of divine rights were contained in the ceremony. The queen was anointed with oil in a very brief but secret part of the rituals. Under her throne was a stone that was once believed to confer its power on the kings of Scotland. It cannot be said that the British royalty is entirely detached from ancient rituals, but the degree that they exist is accepted and enjoyed by most British as pageantry and tradition. The feelings are that those rituals belong to the people, not to the monarch who only plays a part in them. Prince Charles once called the monarchy his "job".
* In recent years, the royal family has been subject to various bodily attacks. Nevertheless, they have actually increased their public appearances. The monarch is a figurehead and a replaceable human being; the needs and expectations of the people come first.

Now let us look at some of the differences between the British royal family and the Japanese imperial household. The British are aware of the turmoil and suffering that were necessary to achieve their democracy. Unlike the Japanese, they did not seek solace in the imagery of a godlike, benevolent king dedicated to their welfare. Rather, they had to fight for their freedom, independence and human rights. Their national values are rooted in recollection of that struggle, so that their monarch is the figurehead of values symbolizing victory in the fight to establish democracy. It was the strength of these values that united Britain to withstand the fierce attack of Nazi Germany.

The British monarch is completely separated from religious functions. God rules over everyone with no special privileges for the monarchy in the United Kingdom, while the Japanese emperor plays the role of a god, a special man above the people, even today. The direct influence of Christian precepts in government may be less effective in today's British politics; however, attitudes based on Christian morals are reflected in British national policies through democratic procedures which have been established over a long history.

How are morals and precepts reflected in Japanese culture today? From personal experience, my own values stem from my primary education based on the Rescript of Education of the Emperor Meiji. This foundation was enhanced by the Cadet School of the Imperial Army, with the emperor surrounded by the national belief in Shinto at the center of my consciousness.

After the war, it was declared that the emperor was just a man, and the national belief in Shinto was prohibited. Religion has since been separated from politics and education, with freedom of religion assured. Unfortunately, no other religion could replace the former combination of emperor and Shinto; thus this freedom has made the Japanese irreligious. Typically, the Japanese exercise a religious potpourri in their family structure by getting married with a Shinto-style wedding or a Christian wedding in church, then choosing to be buried at death with a Buddhist style funeral. Being atheistic or irreligious, the Japanese have to find moral precepts from parents, ancestors, predecessors, the elderly, and the one man above all others, the Emperor.

When the current constitution was written, the Far Eastern Commission's intent was clear: to thoroughly demilitarize Japan. There was no consideration that Japan might ever be expected to participate in any future international military operations; pacifism and prohibition on the use of violence under any circumstances was the predominant view in Japan. The Japanese did not participate militarily in the Korean and Vietnam Wars. These were not "our" wars. Protected by the U.S. under the Security Treaty, the Japanese accepted the role as a U.S. ally given political and financial support and the defense of U.S. military bases on their mainland.

The Japanese supported the U.S. cold war ideology and contributed financial support to relieve the U.S. of some of its overseas financial burdens, but were not prepared to send troops in international peacekeeping operations. Japanese were frustrated when the country's $12 billion donation for the Gulf War was not fully appreciated, because the country sent no military forces. Under international scrutiny, Japan finally sent soldiers to Cambodia as a part of the U.N. peacekeeping operation, but without a clear understanding of why. As the Japanese media suggested, it is dangerous to accommodate ourselves to international opinion without good reason. Japanese soldiers could face a situation in which substantial casualties would result. There is no guarantee that the U.S. military protection under the Security Treaty with Japan will continue permanently, even if Japan wishes. Japan may face a situation in which she would have to defend herself alone, like it or not. Therefore, when a Japanese soldier faces the danger of death, the cause must be clearly defined.

For what values are Japanese willing to die? How will we weigh the values of democracy, freedom, independence, equality and human rights? Do we value the system Westerners built up with their blood and from which they have derived so many benefits? We must be able to answer all these questions.

Most probably no Japanese soldier is now willing to die for the emperor. But as we have seen, the emperor is moving away from a legal, constitutional, symbolic position toward a position of great father/spiritual leader of a single family nation, or as it were, back to the Meiji ideology. What will happen in the future if the prohibition against the use of armed forces other than for self-defense is removed from our constitution? Should the constitution be so amended, abolition of the emperor institution would make sense, for the emperor institution is the diametric opposite of democracy; Japan is unique to combine the two.

Together with the abolition of the emperor institution, the imperialistic view of Japanese history, which was concocted for the political purpose of supporting the emperor institution, should also be thoroughly destroyed, replaced with one aligned with human nature. Japanese must clearly recognize that democratic values are essential to our country to secure prosperity, and to contribute to the world as a powerful member of free nations; and the Japanese should be willing to defend democratic values at the cost of their blood, if necessary.

Chapter Twenty

Isolationism Supports Imperialism

Japanese history has been arbitrarily altered and fabricated for political purposes. For a period of about 1200 years, since the first edition of the history books, *Koji Ki* in 712 and *Nihon Shoki* in 720, until the defeat in World War II in 1945, it was impossible for scholars to study Japanese history freely and scientifically. It is noteworthy that the oldest books were written in the letters of T'ang China. (In Japan the letters are called Han China, which may be an example of another political consideration). Japanese history is written in a foreign language that could not be understood by most of the people, much like the U.S. wrote Japanese history in English at the time of the postwar occupation.

The *Nihon Shoki* was considered infallible; in cases where local history was contradicted, views were altered to meet *Nihon Shoki* ideology. Old books containing views different from the official one were burned; scholars who established new views that helped rulers justify their power with plausible excuses were rewarded with extraordinary promotions, and scholars who wrote anything to spoil the rulers' reign were punished severely.

Tadasuke Ooka's policies kept the people ignorant of truth, so the government could create a history and ideology to make it easier to rule. Ooka's methods have proven to be so effective they were followed by succeeding governments. Neo-Confucianism encouraged the Bakufu system, while religious suppressions and forcible conversions to Buddhism occurred. The people had no way to defend themselves against this assault, as weapons and supplies were under government control. Yet some kept their racial identities until the end of the Tokugawas' reign by secretly maintaining their own beliefs.

Then came the Meiji Reformation, integrating the nation under the emperor system. Anything to suggest conquest of foreign power or slavery was opposed to the image of the emperor, who was billed as the great father of a single family country. Besides, the Meiji government was suffering from a shortage of revenue and bent their knees to the Tokugawas, who offered donations of tremendous amounts of money to the government, upon the pledge that history of the Tokugawas' reign would not be questioned. If the government had encouraged scholars to find the truth, it would have helped to piece together many clues and allowed us to approach the history of an enslaved people, as well as those discriminated against, such as the Eta Hinin (dirty subhuman) and Sanka. However, the Meiji government was too busy implanting the Meiji ideology into the Japanese people's minds. Meanwhile they took over the Tokugawa Bakufu's policy of not letting the people know anything that might contradict the Meiji ideology; particularly with regard to the imperial household; freedom of study was denied scholars, and no one was allowed to question the emperor's divinity.

Only during the past half century after Japan's surrender has there been freedom or opportunity for scholars to reveal Japan's true history of enslavement by foreign powers. However, the government still does not encourage investigation, and the structure of Japanese vertical society itself is a deterrent to publishing new ideas that deny predecessors' views, a feat achieved through control of professors in gov- ernment schools, using authority to decide promotions and other such treatment.

Obviously, there has been strong government manipulation of the media, prohibiting any program that denounces the current emperor system, and promoting occasions of imperial presence to impress the fatherly image of the imperial household. Furthermore, right wingers sponsored by the ruling Liberal Democratic Party were mobilized to threaten scholars who might publish dangerous opinions, thus no government scholar has expressed any theories to oppose the governmental view. Their cowardice brings peril to the Japanese nation.

Pressure has been brought on private students of history as well, by ignoring their ideas, by media boycott, by putting a label of communism on them, social punishments which have worked to stifle any germination of opposing theories. The government will explain that it has been necessary to mobilize all means available to maintain the current emperor system as the backbone of the country in order to defeat communism and bring economic success to Japan. In fact, there were a few scholars who advocated the materialistic view of history. However, they soon disappeared from the media when the American GHQ started oppressing communism.

Therefore, our true identity has never been recognized, due to multilayered cover-ups of fabricated and glorified histories written for political purposes; thus, the Japanese have never been able to set real national principles of behavior. It was not important while the U.S. remained as our guardian and protector.

It has never been important for Japan to have her own values and principles until recently, since the fall of communism, when our relationship with the U.S. changed. The mutual objective to cooperate in the fight against communism has been lost, leaving only economics in the spotlight. Now the U.S. appears as the antagonist to stunt Japan's further economic expansion. Japan cannot expect favors from the U.S. she previously enjoyed now that she is considered a competitor. She is now being pressed to take a higher role, rather than just donating large sums of money to meet international obligations based on her own decision, using her own judgment for the first time since World War II.

During the period of the cold war, Japan understood that she and the U.S. would have to share the fate of an atomic war that could result in World War III. Japan relied upon American strategy, and it was more important for her to play a limited role in economic activities as a faithful member of the Western countries to fight against communism together. Although there were oppositions of left wing parties against American policies domestically, the Japanese government succeeded in suppressing them with a new emperor system, a rehash of the Meiji ideology, in the process toward economic success.

The Japanese do not have any perception that the concept which made Japan so successful economically and drove off communism contained elements incompatible with democracy. Americans were tolerant, accepting it as a peculiarity of Japanese culture, so long as it served their needs against communism. But since the fall of communism, the U.S. has perceived peculiar elements of Japanese capitalism and business practices and how they affect a mutual economic relationship. This has become the root of American distrust and friction. Though revisionists have sensed a need to address the problem, until now, neither nation has been able to pinpoint this source of ill feeling between the U.S. and Japan.

The essence of Japan's self-contradiction lies in her need to use the strength of the emperor system with precepts inherent in the Meiji ideology to provide unity for her self- determination; yet Japan's values are founded on false precepts based on myths created by a history that cannot hold up to international scrutiny, which would reveal that Japan's ideologies are in opposition to Western values. This in turn would increase friction between Japan and the West. Japan will become isolated in her desperate efforts to save her businesses. That effort, unfortunately, will be construed by the West as an economic invasion.

In such a case, does the Japanese individual have close friends in the West with whom anything can be truly understood from the heart? Unfortunately, very few, since our ideas are closed to Westerners. The negligence of Japanese to openly reflect on real ethical and moral values, particularly in relation to our past history, has kept us from making true friendships with the West. As a result, Japan is becoming increasingly isolated within the world community. Japanese decisions are based on misinformation and a mythological history which cannot be relied on to guide Japan in an international society not necessarily friendly to her. Japan's perception of hardship incurred by this situation will create a snowball effect forcing her into a nationalistic and imperialistic course again.

On the other hand, if Japan wants to stay in Western society and keep her prosperity in a free market, then she must change her social constitution that allows the government to dictate by means of *gyosei shido* (government control with no legal provisions), and by scaring people with threats.

Politically, the change would mean a switch from the current consititutional monarchy under a symbolic emperor system to a democracy with a symbolic emperor, going back to the spirit of the Japanese constitution, which will amount to another war against feudalism, totalitarianism and nationalism. It will require Japan to change her whole system and ethos. Mentally it will be a revolution to liberate the Japanese from supporting a "man above men" vertical society expressed in imperial myths and fabricated history. Unfortunately, the more strongly we move ourselves toward democracy, the more resistance will arise from the right wing, to whom liberation from old ideas means discarding national pride, which they believe would undermine economic success and ruin the nation.

This is a serious "to be or not to be" for Japan. If Japan shifts the cause to the outside world, it will lead to isolationism, a proven forerunner to imperialism. Revealing the true history of the Japanese people can get democratization started anew. A shocking view like Yagiri's can help bring the Japanese out of the mass hypnotic trance they have been in since the Meiji era. Shock from the outside world has not worked. Even defeat in World War II did not bring the Japanese out of their delusions. Japan should throw away its wrongful pride along with its fabricated history and face the truth head on with full knowledge of its history of slavery.

Article 9 of the Japanese constitution reads: "Chapter II, Renunciation of War: Article 9. Aspiring sincerely to an international peace based on justice and order, the Japanese people forever renounce war as a sovereign right of the nation and the threat or use of force as means of settling international disputes. In order to accomplish the aim of the preceding paragraph, land, sea, and air forces, as well as other war potential, will never be maintained. The right of belligerence of the state will not be recognized."

If the above article is interpreted based on common sense, it is clear that the constitution prohibits Japan from having any war potential and that Japan has renounced her right of belligerence, even for the purpose of self-defense. But based on the U.S. demand to reduce her financial burden for the safety of Japan year by year, Japan's self defense force has continually been strengthened. The broad interpretation of "self-defense" once started, never stopped, and has led to the creation of a significant military power over four decades, although it should also lead to an in-depth examination of current laws.

At present two opposing law systems co-exist, one being the law system established by the Constitution based on the anti-war and anti-fascist principles of democracy; the second stemming from the Treaty of Mutual Corporation and Security which led to a military alliance between the U.S. and Japan, and eventually to the powerful Japanese self defense force. It is only natural that these two systems conflict and confuse the Japanese people.

The value of loyalty to the nation will have to be questioned again after having been disregarded for a long time. The socialist party has even denounced the self defense force as "tax thieves;" servicemen had no choice but to endure this undue humiliation. One cannot expect loyalty from young Japanese risking their lives while the nation humiliates them at the same time.

Japan's under-developed democracy is still influenced by *okami* (emperor, shogun or sometimes government and its agencies). The *okami* has always been good and right since the seventh century, when the Chinese conquerors set themselves up as *ryo* (nobles). After World War II, the Japanese made General MacArthur and his GHQ the *okami*. However, the U.S. has since slipped from that position. Without the *okami* who formerly directed us, it has become extremely difficult for Japan to make proper judgments.

When the Gulf War broke out, Japan could not determine which side was right. Despite the fact that the control of oil was vital to her economy, she hesitated to take a position. Eventually she offered $12 billion in aid to help liberate Kuwait, but it was not appreciated, and Japan was shocked to find her name missing from an American newspaper advertisement published by Kuwait, thanking allies who supported the effort against Iraq.

In 1945 a new democratic Japan was born, completely different from the great Empire of Japan, and yet for the Japanese, perhaps it is still easier today to die for a god-like emperor than for democracy, in which one must prepare to give his life for those with whom he disagrees, dislikes or even hates. Regrettably, Japan is not yet fully democratic. Only when we awaken to our bitter but true history and tradition, can Japan and the West begin to understand each other.

Chapter Twenty One

A Materialistic View of Japanese History

When ultra-nationalism and militarism were suppressed by the U.S. occupation forces, communism made rapid progress in Japan. Communism had a much longer history in Japan than did democracy. The roots of Japan's socialist and communist movements go back to the early 1880's, when social and labor problems were arising as a result of rapid industrialization.

In 1897, Fusataro Takano, after returning from the U.S., organized a labor society. In the next years the Association of Socialism was established. Soon after the National Railway Union went on a strike. In 1901 the Social Democratic Party was formed under the direction of Sen Katayama, Shusui Kotoku and Iso-o Abe. The government met this move with the Security Police Act, which banned the party the day after it submitted an application for registration.

As the Russo-Japanese War loomed on the horizon, government oppression against labor associations and socialists intensified. In 1903, the socialists formed a new association, *Heiminsha* (the common people's company), and published a newspaper, *Heimin Shinbun* (the common people's newspaper). Their point of view was radical, considering the political climate of Japan at the time. They rejected violence, advocating peaceful revolution by democratic means. During the Russo-Japanese War, the newspaper sent a letter to the Russian Social Democratic Labor Party, saying: "Due to imperialistic ambitions, the Japanese and Russian governments have rushed into war. However, our relationship with you as comrades remain unchanged. We are not your enemies." In solidarity with Japanese Socialists, the Russian Social Democrat Labor Party bulletin responded with a pledge to continue fighting Tsarism and to oppose the war.

That same year, 1904, Sen Katayama, Japanese representative to the 2nd International Convention of Communists in America, shook hands on the platform with the Russian representative. They agreed on close cooperation of both parties to oppose the war and act to overthrow the arbitrary rule of both countries.

The government tightened its control over the socialist movements by dissolving the Association of Socialism in November, 1904. The newspaper was banned and Heiminsha was dissolved in 1905. The socialists did not renounce their activities, but organized the Japan Social Party, which advocated socialism within a legally approved scope. Further oppression came in 1910, when a Socialist group belonging to the faction of Shusui Kotoku attempted the assassination of the Emperor Meiji. They were arrested in a mountain hideout during bomb testing. The government made maximum use of this case by arresting several hundred socialists and trying twenty-six of them, along with their ringleader, Kotoku, on charges of high treason. The trial was held in the Supreme Court behind closed doors. Twenty-four men were sentenced to death, Shusui Kotoku and eleven others were executed soon after sentencing, but due to criticism from London and Paris, death sentences of the other twelve were reduced to life imprisonment.

The high treason case may have seemed to stifle the communist movement in Japan forever, but it actually did not. In 1914, World War I broke out, and Japan joined the allies. During the war Japan enjoyed a booming economy, but in 1918 was hit by an economic panic in which many banks and trading companies went bankrupt. The tough economic times encouraged socialist ideas, and in 1922, the underground Japanese Communist Party was formed illegally. In 1923 the Great Kanto Earthquake destroyed most of the city of Tokyo, causing serious unrest, and the life of the masses became more difficult. Communism spread quickly throughout Japan, even in the face of ultra-nationalism and militarism.

The February 26 coup d'état by the imperial army in 1936 was an important step in the military's attempt to gain greater power. Many officers taking part in the coup claimed they had risen to save tenant farmers from a miserable life. To right wing factions, the emperor was good but his advisors were wrongdoers who failed to govern in appreciation of the emperor's great mind. Therefore, the ministers had to be removed, to bring the government under direct control of the emperor. For the communists, absolute monarchy and monopolistic capitalism were the cause of all evil; capitalism had to be destroyed by a people's revolution. The two ideologies were complete opposites, but their aims were the same. There was a point of contact between left and right. Both messages appealed to young people's sense of justice. The ideology of Marx and Lenin attracted students because it was more logical and intellectual than the ultra-nationalism of the right wing.

It was no wonder that communism seemed to flourish in Japan when the American occupation forces liberated communists from prison and showed them a sympathetic attitude. Communist ideas were more familiar to the people than those of democracy. The Japanese intelligentsia who had been quiet during the war now spoke out for communism, charging that the emperor, monopolistic capitalists and the military were the villains. This picture was easy for the masses to understand. To those who had been forced to endure the greatest hardships during the war, the idea of overthrowing the national system by revolution seemed attractive. A communist state gave hope for equal opportunity.

Led by communist leader Kyuichi Tokuda, mass demonstrations were held on Tokyo's streets. On May 1, 1946, the first Japanese May Day demonstrations were held, followed by a number of "Give Me Rice!" demonstrations, demanding the government provide more food. It seemed as if a communist revolution was about to take place. In some demonstrations, the emperor was accused of responsibility for the war and for leaving many soldiers to die in foreign lands. A placard held by one of the demonstrators read, "You, the subject, starve! I, the emperor, have a full stomach!" The demonstrator was arrested and accused of lèse-majesté, although he was probably more guilty of defamation than lèse-majesté. The strong language of the placard indicated the hatred of people against the emperor.

Although communists were a small minority, their vitality and philosophy excited the Japanese and helped bring attention. Once a labor union came under the control of communist organizers, it became political and militant and did much damage to a company's profits.

Following the war, many leftist scholars began to paint the emperors of ancient Japan as vicious despots who oppressed and exploited the people in order to fulfill their own desires. A materialistic view of Japan's history quickly dominated historical interpretation, as all historical records were reinterpreted and twisted to fit the new materialistic views. Using this new interpretation, a call went out, "Destroy the emperor institution."

Some reinterpretation was right and necessary, but it was a pity that too much twisting and manipulation of records made most of it valueless. However, many Japanese remained faithful to the emperor. Those who had been in a slavish state for a thousand years, indoctrinated by the educational system of the Meiji and ultra-nationalism of the Showa, could not change their creed overnight.

Hirohito made tours to encourage recovery, in which thousands welcomed him fervently. Although he had denied his divinity in 1946, many still worshipped him as a living god, and crowds would sit down on the road, a tradition from feudal times, as he passed by. Enthusiasm was so great that GHQ suspended the tours in 1948 at the request of the Soviet Union.

The government and establishment were relieved by the people's overwhelming support of the emperor institution. 83% of the people were affirmative, while only 13% were against, according to a public opinion poll taken in April, 1946, right after the presentation of the government's draft of the new constitution.

The silent majority resented the strong words of the communist demonstrators' placards. Traditionally, they feared the Russians. From the Japanese point of view, the Russo-Japanese War had been caused by Russian aggression in Manchuria and Korea. The Japanese remembered Russian brutalities in Manchuria toward Japanese civilians and events following Japan's surrender in World War II, when the Russians sent surrendered Japanese soldiers to Siberia for forced labor, causing tens of thousands to die of malnutrition and disease. As a result most Japanese distrusted the Russians as well as the communist agitators in Japan.

The Japanese responded enthusiastically to the appeal of democracy brought by U.S. occupation forces. Many reforms were made under American guidance, in which a set of American laws were legislated to ensure a democratic system. However, democratic values such as individual independence, equality and human rights were foreign to the Japanese. Even the American way of business was neither well understood nor accepted by Japanese companies, despite the fact that the U.S. was Japan's biggest single customer. Japanese liked the rich American way of life, but certain values were beyond our understanding. Americans could lead the Japanese to democracy with the emperor as a symbolic leader under the new constitution, but they could not really change the Japanese way of thinking.

Three powers clashed in the nation: the communists were less in number but with much sharper edges; the traditional right-wing majority was clinging to the emperor institution; and Uncle Sam was the new *okami* of the country. The U.S. disarmed Japan and democratized the political system. To do all this peacefully the U.S. decided to use the Japanese *okami*, the emperor and emperor institution, with necessary modifications. The emperor was exempted from prosecution as a war criminal and allowed to remain as a symbol, although his position was completely different from that in the Meiji constitution. One wonders if the average Japanese realizes the obvious distinction between the emperorship in the Meiji constitution and the current one. In 1986, the 60th anniversary of Hirohito's reign was celebrated. The period of his reign for twenty years under the Meiji constitution was an entirely different emperorship.

After the defeat of Japan, the world's political and military situation changed quickly; the honeymoon between the U.S. and Soviet Russia broke down, as the two superpowers stood in opposition, dividing the world into free nations and communist countries. It was a battle between two principles. As the cold war turned hot in Asia with the outbreak of the Korean War in 1950, the U.S. responded with policy changes. Japan's position shifted from a defeated county atoning for war crimes to an ally. Japan and the U.S. now shared a common goal to beat communism. Japan offered the U.S. important bases for U.S. troops in the Far East. Earlier, General MacArthur announced that the new constitution did not deny Japan the right of self-defense. Two weeks after the war began, he had the Japanese government organize a police reserve. A purge of communists from government offices and key industries followed next. A peace treaty was concluded in San Francisco in 1951 with 48 allied nations of the free world, in which Japan's independence was restored, and her position established as a member of the free nations. In addition, her economy was strengthened by the U.S. desire to use Japan as a base and buy Japanese supplies. In return the Japanese were expected to maintain peace and order and prevent communist infiltrations and sabotage.

This was clearly a fight between American democracy and Russian communism. Under opposing principles of the two superpowers, which way would the Japanese decide to live? Among a minority of intelligent people, there were serious believers in communism even in prewar days, and they agitated the masses skillfully. University students, government employees, employees of the national railways and post offices were mobilized for big demonstrations against American imperialism and the Security Treaty between Japan and the U.S.

The Japanese majority disliked Russia and communism. But it would not be correct to say that they believed firmly in American democracy, as we had never studied or understood it. Traditionally Japanese faith was pointed to a person, not to principles. So the principles of the American *okami* were made *tatemae* (the official view) to please the American *okami*, while the Japanese simply chose traditional way in *honne* (true mind). One needs the values he truly believes in when he fights against anything. Thus, the symbolic emperor institution was established upon the rehashed Meiji ideology within the framework of democracy the American *okami* had built.

The special procurements by the U.S. forces for the Korean War encouraged managers of private companies. The economic boom made them more ambitious in expanding businesses, and they became earnest supporters of the new emperor institution. Their efforts were soon rewarded with success. Communists quickly disappeared from labor unions. Persistent strikes for political purposes were gone. Conveyor belts started turning out products for export to the free nations. Japanese industrial growth was beginning.

The communist students' and government workers' strikes and movements lasted much longer. When the Security Treaty between Japan and the U.S. was revised in 1960, Anpo Toso (anti-security treaty demonstrations) reached their peak. On January 19, a new security treaty was signed in Washington. When the Japanese government presented it to the Diet on February 5, it met opposition from the socialist and the communists parties, who both boycotted Diet proceedings. The ruling LDP became irritated, and on May 19th, adopted the Security Treaty Bill by voting alone under guard of 500 policemen in the assembly hall of the House of Representatives.

The transfer of the Bill to the House triggered even stronger opposition movements, with big demonstrations around the Diet day after day. On June 15th, demonstrators of the National Federation of Students' Self Government Associations rushed into the Diet Building, clashing with police guards. One woman died and many others were injured. The Diet was occupied by 330,000 demonstrators just prior to the treaty's automatic approval date of June 19. That day was the peak of anti-treaty sentiment. After that, communist power gradually ebbed, helped by Japan's economic success.

This was, in other words, a battle between two opposing views, the materialistic view and the rehashed imperialistic view. The former offered communist and socialist grounds to deny the emperor insti- tution, while the latter served to defend the symbolic emperor institution. When communism fell in Japan it did not mean the victory of freedom and democracy, but was merely the confirmation of a return to traditional values wearing the new Western faces of pacifism and dem- ocracy. Both views serve political purposes and are wrong; democracy can stand only on truth.

Chapter Twenty Two

Mysterious Country—Miraculous Growth

It is a fact that Japan's economic success was miraculous. In 1945 Japan was defeated, her cities, industries and economy in ruins. Today Japan is one of the richest nations in the world. In 1991 her gross national product was 423,565 billion yen, ($3,400 billion U.S. dollars), about 13% of the world GNP. Only the U.S. has a greater share of the world's GNP (about 24%). Japan's per capita income was $19,035, compared to the U.S. per capita income of $17,379 (1990 figures).

Japan's net external assets reached $129.8 billion at the end of 1985, making her the world's number one creditor nation. In 1990 Japan dropped to second place behind the newly reunified Germany, but regained the top position in 1991. (These statistics are based on *The Japan Almanac*, 1993, published by the *Asahi Shinbun* newspaper).

In 1992, Japan's trade surplus reached $100 billion. The U.S. is Japan's largest customer, buying about l/3 of Japan's total exports. Japan imports about 22% of the total U.S. trade exports, a situation that has created a huge trade imbalance of $40-50 billion every year in Japan's favor, causing serious friction between the two countries.

Japan's contribution to the international community has largely been limited to financial aid to developing countries and to various international organizations and activities. Her official development assistance funding was about U.S. $13 billion in 1993, number one in the world. Her contribution to the United Nations made up 10.8% of the budget, second only to the U.S. (*Japan Almanac, op. cit.*). For the Gulf War, Japan donated U.S. $13 billion, but was sneered at by international society for offering only financial participation. This criticism was unfair because it was a significant sum of money for which the Japanese people bore an extra tax burden.

The Gulf War caused a nationwide debate about the importance of contributions not only in money but in manpower. Japan later took a step forward by dispatching 1800 soldiers to Cambodia in the United Nations peacekeeping operation, sending Japanese troops overseas for the first time since 1945, an epoch-making event. It was the government's view that this mission conformed to the provisions of Article 9 of the Japanese constitution.

Japanese behavior in international society is sometimes mysterious and beyond Westerners' comprehension, a view which seems to revolve around the fact that the Japanese government looks impotent, timid, slow and even idiotic in responding to international political and military issues, while Japanese businessmen are so competent, aggressive, efficient and clever in the world markets. Discussion between the Japanese and American governments on economic issues have been going on for the last twenty years, but surprisingly little progress has been achieved. Difficulty in negotiating makes both sides feel uncomfortable.

Japan has been going through a serious depression, which has made everyone nervous and somewhat discouraged. Wealth amounting to US $1000 billion evaporated between 1990 and '93 from the real estate and stock market crashes, spelling the end of Japan, Inc. and Japanese Style Management. A soft landing of the Japanese economy would have been possible if the government had adopted the right policies, but the government did not realize we were in a structual depression of a totally different nature from past ones. Instead, the government claimed this was just a recession that free economies experience from time to time, one that would soon end.

Now, finally the Japanese realize that Japan needs to change her economic system. To cure the disease, one must detect the focus and extract it. In this case, it means to extract Japan, Inc. Japan has to die for a new Japan to be born. It has happened before; it happened in 1945; it can happen again. Not only the economic system, but everything must be redone. It will take time, and meanwhile Japanese businesses have been undergoing real hardships.

Nevertheless, no one has taken responsibility for causing such a serious situation. None of the LDP leaders committed hara-kiri for this unprecedented economic crash; none of the high ranking government officials resigned. No bank presidents resigned or assumed bad debts. It is traditional that in Japan, ministers and officials take responsibility only to *okami*, not to the people. Similarly, bank presidents will not answer to shareholders but to *okami*. Historically, Japanese leaders have seldom been brought to account for irresponsible actions. No leaders were held responsible for the disastrous policies that led to World War II and subsequent defeat. Would such a government be able to assume responsibility in international negotiations and commitments? It will only produce friction in international relations and invite isolation.

Who has ultimate power in Japan? In *tatemae* (principle), the prime minister is supposed to have it. He is designated by the Diet, then appointed by the emperor on behalf of the Japanese people in accordance with Article 6 of the Constitution. In actuality, the prime minister has usually been the president of the Liberal Democratic Party. As a result the LDP has ruled in postwar Japan. The prime minister is elected in a democratic system and there is no doubt he is our legitimate representative. To some, he is also the head of state. (Some people insist the emperor is the head of state, but he performs only limited acts in matters of state). The prime minister is the leader of the nation, deciding what course Japan is going to take.

However, someone else sitting behind the scene holds real power. He can have the Diet designate whomever he wants to be prime minister, and manipulate him as he likes, though he has no legal ground to do so at all. His power simply derives from money. This makes all LDP leaders absorbed in a money game, rather than working out good policies for the people. For the last thirty years, politicians, government officials and businessmen have built up a triangle of interests. Few foreigners realize the structure and system of our Japanese plutocracy.

In the postwar political evolution, Kakuei Tanaka is considered the initiator of the plutocracy. After he resigned the position of prime minister due to scandal, he continued exercising power as "the shogun in the dark," with his tremendous political resources and vitality. He developed a huge money machine to pump up donations from business and industry. In return, businesses expected favorable treatment in the allocation of budgeted projects under *dango*, (in which the winner of a bid is pre-determined in a private meeting) or obtaining approvals and licenses to enter new fields. Tanaka turned politics into a business. His political party was made a *kabushiki kaisha* (corporation). He was the sole owner of the company with his money. The members who submitted and pledged loyalty to him were guaranteed to win elections, with financial aid from the party. Those who served loyally for a length of time were given promotions as ministers.

Tanaka rewarded government officials who did his bidding by giving them positions in private or semi-governmental corporations after their retirement from government posts. In case some of them wanted to become Diet members he gave them full support. These Diet members are called *zoku gi-in* (Diet member active in the field covered by a particular ministry). They all joined Tanaka's faction and became his *kobun* (followers), enhancing his political power. Under the system it was inevitable that politics would become corrupt.

In 1976 the Lockheed scandal unexpectedly came to light. Tanaka was arrested and charged with bribery. Yet he remained the "shogun in the dark" free on bail until he was disabled by a cerebral inaction in February 1985. The Lockheed scandal was disclosed in a public hearing of the Multinational Business Subcommittee of the Securities and Exchange Commission, opened by U.S. Senator Frank Church on February 4, 1976. The directors on the board of Lockheed Corporation testified that the company had paid tremendous amounts of money to Japanese ministers and influential politicians for many years and also paid several million dollars to Yoshio Kodama, notorious ultra-nationalist, employing him as a secret sales agent to sell F104 jet fighters to the Japanese Self Defense Force. It was the biggest international scandal involving an ex-prime ministers. A great number of ministers and politicians were also involved.

Noboru Takeshita was a *kobun* of Tanaka (follower in his faction). He betrayed his *oyabun* (boss) and took most of the members of Tanaka's faction when he organized his own faction. He succeeded Tanaka's money machine/system and made it even bigger and more powerful. We can peep into the inner workings, thanks to a report of *The Shukan Post*, a weekly magazine, which says: "Takeshita has been dominating the Shimane Prefecture...which has been his electoral district for the past twenty years. Most members of the city, town and village councils belong to the Takeshita faction. The same applies to the key staff of the prefectural government, as well as the agricultural and local welfare commissioners. All civil engineering and building contractors belong to Takeshita. Hotels, restaurants, even stationery shops cannot oppose Takesita since their business will be hurt. In Shimane it is a taboo to criticize Takeshita openly."

Takeshita maintains strict control over civil engineering and building trades. In public bidding, a successful bid price is preliminarily decided for the object in the bid based on the cost calculation by the government agency. The price must be kept strictly confidential to outsiders. However, prices were leaked to *dango* meetings by key staff of Takeshita's office. (A *dango* meeting is one in which a group of bidders meet secretly to determine who will get the bid. Although it is illegal, it is a widespread business practice peculiar to Japan). In return for privileged information, the successful bidder is to donate 3% of the total contract to Takeshita's office. In the Shimane Prefecture, there are construction projections valued at 100 billion yen annually. This means that 3 billion yen ($24 million) is pumped out by the Takeshita machine as political donations.

Using funds collected in this manner, it stands to reason Takeshita should have reached for the supreme power. In 1987, he succeeded Yasuhiro Nakasone as Prime Minister. He secretly threw money around the members of the LDP as well as to members of the opposition parties, often in a casual and non-political manner so as to avoid the charge of bribery. It is also said Takashita keeps a record of the birthdays of departmental managers' wives in the Ministry of Finance and has been a Santa Claus for these people. His money machine grew too big to hide from view. When the Recruit scandal was revealed in 1988, it was discovered his personal secretary was involved, and Takeshita was forced to resign as prime minister. Notwithstanding, he succeeded in getting the LDP to nominate one of his *kobuns*, Sosuke Uno, as prime minister. The Uno administration lasted for only one month until Uno was forced to resign because of involvement in a sex scandal. Next, Takeshita picked Toshiki Kaifu to be prime minister. Takeshita ruled Japan, as "shogun in the shadow," by remote control. When Kaifu tried to dissolve the Diet and call for general elections, Takeshita objected; Kaifu was removed from office. Takeshita made Kiichi Miyazawa the next prime minister. Miyazawa was the last of the LDP prime ministers.

The Recruit Scandal presents an interesting picture. Hiromasa Ezo-e is the central figure in this saga. After graduating from university, Ezo-e founded a small publishing company and produced a magazine which provided complete information on job opportunities. The publication proved enormously popular with students seeking jobs. Later Ezo-e published another magazine providing office workers wishing to change jobs with information about opportunities in other companies. This venture was also successful. Ezo-e decided to expand to other business sectors, and established a subsidiary, Recruit Cosmos, to operate in real estate. He was again successful and the subsidiary grew quickly. Ezo-e moved to expand Recruit's operations, this time into remote computer services (time sharing services) and information network services (resale of high speed digital lines).

In the course of the new venture, Recruit was required to obtain numerous approvals and licenses from various government ministries. Ezo-e needed to make friends with persons in high position who would help his company obtain permits quickly. He worked out a plan. He would sell shares of Recruit Cosmos to his powerful friends prior to going public. Shares of a company which went public would rise sharply after their initial listing on the exchange, perhaps ten-fold or more.

The plan was obvious. In return for removing obstacles to Recruit's getting a license, Ezo-e's friends acquired stock and sold it for a much higher price, making a handsome profit.

Ezo-e was even kind enough to provide friends in need of loans with generous financing, in some cases without expectation that the loan would ever have to be repaid. In a few months' time the powerful friends would reap huge tax free profits. Ezo-e did not believe this plan would be construed as bribery. He made the deal available to about sixty people in various positions—politicians, government officials, mass communication, and business.

Ken Ohtani lists the names of persons who cashed in on special deals in his book *Japanese Style Management on Trial.* Important politicians include: ex-Prime Minister Yasuhiro Nakasone, Chief Cabinet Secretary Kousei Fujinami; Michio Watanabe, Kimi Watanabe; ex-Finance Minsiter; Kiichi Miyazawa; ex-Prime Minister Noboru Takeshita; Deputy Chief Cabinet Secretary Ichiro Ozawa; Katsuyuki Fukuda.

Despite the sensational report, none of the above politicians except Fujinami were prosecuted. The reasons given were that their secretaries made the deals without informing the bosses. It was technically difficult for the prosecution to prove the price of the shares would always go up, leaving expected profits in the hands of the suspects. Ezo-e awaits trial on bribery charges; Takeshita was forced to resign as a result of the ensuing scandal.

A more recent scandal involving Sagawa Tokyo came to light when an ex-chairman of Sagawa's board filed suit against Hiroyasu Watanabe, ex-president of Sagawa, for breach of trust. It appears that while Watanabe was the president, Sagawa gave guarantees amounting to 400 billion yen (about $3.3 million) to banks to repay loans made to related companies in case of default. These guarantees were made without approval of Sagawa's board of directors. It has been reported that Watanabe got kickbacks of no less than 2 billion yen (about $17 million) from these companies. Watanabe made many political donations to the LDP and to Diet members individually in order to obtain his approvals and licenses and also to get facilities from the Ministry of Transportation for the expansion of Sagawa's transportation business.

Among the contributions was one for 500 million yen ($4 million) to Shin Kanemaru, then Vice President of the LDP and Vice Prime Minister. Kanemaru was arrested and prosecuted for violations of the Political Fund Control Act. Surprisingly, in an informal hearing and judgment, he admitted receiving the contribution, and paid a fine of 200,000 yen (about $1700), the maximum penalty provided by law. Kanemaru resigned his Diet seat and all of his other positions in the party (he had been Takeshita's right hand man and chairman of the Takeshita faction).

In the prosecutor's report of the Watanabe case, an astonishing story was related. It said: "I (Watonabe) had dinner with Kanemaru, who was concerned that Takeshita might miss his chance of becoming prime minister because of an anti-Takeshita car campaign by the Kominto party of ultra-nationalists. He asked me if I could do anything about it. I replied, 'Perhaps I could ask the Inagawa-Kai (a Yakuza [mafia] group) to intercede and act as intermediaries in stopping anti-Takeshita demonstrations.' Kanemaru agreed to this and indicated I was their only hope.

"On October 5, I was asked by Kanemaru to come to the Tokyo Prince Hotel. There I met with Kanemaru, Takeshita and Ozawa. Takeshita informed me that he was hesitant about informing Tanaka, his former boss, that he was planning to run for the presidency of the ruling LDP. (Takeshita had organized his own faction, taking a major part of Tanaka's faction away, done without obtaining Tanaka's consent; Tanaka was very angry at what he regarded as Takeshita's betrayal).

"I told Takeshita whether the Kominto would stop their campaign against him or not depended upon his making a 'respect call' to Tanaka and I asked him to do so next morning. Takeshita agreed.

"After Takeshita succeeded in becoming president of the LDP, I was invited to a restaurant on October 29. Kanemaru and Takeshita jointly thanked me for my support and efforts. I felt very proud about it." (Becoming president of the LDP was actually the same as being named the next prime minister).

In his testimony before the Diet, Kanemaru denied he had attended any meetings with Watanabe, claiming that probably his secretaries had the meeting with Susumu Ishii, boss of Inagawa Kai, to ask him to act as intermediary to the Kominto. What Watanabe wants to say is obvious. He was trying to explain why he had to give financial guarantees to the banks for the companies owned by Ishii, the notorious yakuza (mafioso), even though these companies were in poor financial condition. He may not have realized the seriousness of what he said, but the sensational report in the newspapers that a yakuza was involved in the appointment of the Prime Minister of Japan put the whole nation in hysteria.

When Takeshita was called to the Diet for testimony, he insisted that the yakuza had played no part in his becoming Prime Minister or in the formation of his cabinet. However, the majority of the nation believes there is much truth in Watanabe's story.

In spite of bitter criticism and overwhelming demands for his resignation from the Diet, Takeshita ignored them, determined to remain in the House of Representatives. But his power and prestige were significantly damaged by the scandal. Karemaru was forced to leave the Diet; Ozawa organized his own faction, taking forty-four members away from the Takeshita faction. These three top politicians are related by marriage and were once proud of their unity. But this unity is now a thing of the past. Takeshita's money machine has been seriously damaged. Yet he still believes he can repair his image and make a comeback in the future.

Despite exposure of obviously unethical, if not criminal, activity on the part of LDP leaders, LDP members still accept large contributions day after day from similar sources and feel no guilt or compulsion to stop accepting the money. And it will still be a fact that the one who has the best money machine will become prime minister.

At one time Prime Minister Miyazawa made Americans angry by stating, "Americans are lacking a work ethic." He is totally wrong. Ethics is not an American problem; it is our problem. "Japanese politicians are totally lacking in ethics."

The focus of LDP members is raising money from business. Businesses in turn use politicians for obtaining government projects or licenses to conduct business profitably, and government officials are given numerous benefits by politicians in return.

Chapter Twenty Three

Internationalization

We have seen how in the Japanese plutocracy, political bosses in factions of the ruling LDP collect money from businesses. The boss who does the job best reaches real power. Even if he should lose the position of prime minister, it is not a vital problem; he can still exercise power from behind the scenes as "shogun in the dark," as Takeshita did. It may be more advantageous for him to stay out of the limelight; since he has no official power, he can receive even questionable donations without much fear of being prosecuted for bribery. He can also remain free from administrative failure. He can simply replace his robot prime minister when necessary.

Politicians seek money and status. In every faction there is a long line of politicians, each waiting his turn for promotion to ministerial rank, particularly to juicy ones such as the Ministry of Finance, Transport or Construction, which have big budgets and strong influence on businesses. These are excellent opportunities for the politician to strengthen his fundraising ability and acquire constituents who will pledge themselves to be absolutely faithful whether the politician is right or wrong.

Government officials want regular promotions and security in retirement. They want the Diet to approve large departmental budgets with yearly increases. They want their department to cover wider jurisdiction. Bosses of the ruling LDP control these matters in and out of the Diet. Therefore it is important to maintain cozy relationships with powerful politicians of the ruling LDP by cooperating in fundraising operations, which will favor policies advantageous to certain business sectors, or grant authorizations and licenses to businesses in accordance with requests. Competence of a ministry in granting authorizations and licenses is useful in controlling businesses with *gyosei shido* by the *okami* (government directives without legislation).

Businesses provide ministers and government officials with positions in private companies after retirement. If government officials are faithful to LDP rulers, an easy and comfortable life is guaranteed for the rest of their lives. Executives of large businesses, particularly in key industries, have been relieved not to have wasted shareholders' money on large donations. As long as they keep sponsoring the LDP bosses, the party remains in power, and as a result their money and interests are protected. Whenever problems arise, they can go to the bosses and ask for help, and the LDP will be more than happy to oblige. Government controls and regulations, barriers blocking new entries to a sector, are welcomed by established insider businesses, since this avoids competition, enhancing their bottom line.

A shameless tripartite oligarchy dominated the Japanese people for nearly three decades, until the arrest of Shin Kanemaru, ex-Vice President of the ruling LDP, on suspected tax evasion, in March 1993. Up until this time, oligarchs were solely absorbed in pursuing their own interests, paying little attention to the interests of the people.

The ruling LDP has always followed a policy favoring the farmer, and Japanese farmers have usually supported the LDP. The two made common cause to defend "democracy" from communism during the cold war. Vestiges of feudal ideas still persist among farmers, and it is comparatively easy to buy their votes. It is said that if Diet members send farmer constituents congratulatory telegrams for weddings, wreaths at funerals or at the opening of new shops, offer job help and guided tours of the Diet, and entertain them with a fine *obento* (box lunch), the farmers will continue to support them.

The farmers are not used to voting for principles or ideas. As a matter of fact, farmers enjoy subsidies and protection far in excess of their number and the taxes they pay. Prohibition of rice imports under the Staple Food Control Act is one of the privileges they obtained due to the support of the LDP *zoku* members—Diet members specializing in representing interests of certain business sectors, for example *Yusei Zoku*; *Yusei* means Ministry of Posts and Telecommunications, and *Yusei Zoku* means LDP Diet members who specialize in taking care of the interests of businesses controlled by ministries such as Television and Radio Broadcasting and Digital Networkings. The ministers presumably receive political donations from those businesses.

The ruling LDP has paid little attention to people who lack money, offering nothing to upgrade the quality of their lives, to policies lowering prices or to encouraging competition in markets such as land and housing. Instead of applying anti-trust laws, the government has allowed the Fair Trade Commission to overlook illegal business practices such as *dango*. In Japan, business profit has always been given priority over people, particularly on the consumer side. All of these factors have helped the economic bubble to inflate enormously. When the bubble bursts, the common people will be hurt badly.

Corporate employees, both white and blue collar, have fared better. Although the government has paid scant attention to the betterment of workers, management has. They have developed a system based on paternalism, which in turn is based on the illusionary concept that a company is a family—the president is the father and the workers his children. The children will share in the profits of capitalism in return for totally surrendering to management for their lifetime. This paternalism has its roots in the old feudal system in which the loyal samurai pledged himself to his daimyo. To fight against communism, the LDP backed the idea of a symbolic emperor as great father of the country, which has been a strong prop for management in the effort to convince employees of the worth of Japanese Style Management. In a sense, this is a kind of slavery packaged in paternalism.

Corporate employees are excellent taxpayers, since taxes are deducted by the company from salaries. The current sharp progressive income tax system encourages a low basic salary, accompanied by nontaxable subsidies in housing, food and entertainment, a system which leads to increased dependency on the company and its paternalistic policy. Japanese labor unions are organized company by company rather than in a horizontal labor union of workers with similar jobs across different businesses and industries. When Japanese Style Management took root, labor unions belonging to private businesses refused to continue their unified struggle with communists and socialists, but said good-bye to politics and became cooperative with management. It was more important to get a bigger share of the pie from the high growth of the Japanese economy.

However, the political struggle of students, government and corporate workers continued much longer. The cold war forced people to make choices. One was to accept the politics of the LDP built on the symbolic emperor institution of rehashed Meiji ideology, Japanese Style Management, and right-wing yakuza organizations, which controlled the lowest elements of society. It was unfortunate that sincere efforts to study American democracy and achieve a Japanese version were stifled in the cold war. For the ruling LDP and the government, it was easy to put a label of "reds" on those who criticized efforts to restore the authority of the emperor, and to reject them from leading positions.

Under the circumstances, the United Red Army incident, known as the Asama Villa Siege, broke out in February, 1972, and shook the nation. Five members of the Army, including a woman leader, took a hostage to a villa, where riot police laid siege for more than a week. Two policemen were shot dead trying to save the hostage. The event was televised nationwide and everybody watched closely until the Red Army members were arrested. It was later discovered that they had hung 14 comrades and buried their bodies in the mountains. The siege became one of the most notorious incidents in postwar history. The final sentence of death for the ringleaders, including the woman, was confirmed by the Supreme Court in February, 1993, twenty years after the event occurred. This ghastly and brutal case caused students and corporate workers alike to lose sympathy for the left-wing struggle against the U.S., and after the end of the Vietnam War in 1975, the government clamped down; Communist and Socialist influence in Japanese society was weakened remarkably. Actual benefits from economic success encouraged the people to keep voting for the LDP. However, this long monopoly of power has inevitably fostered oligarchy and plutocracy; the people of Japan do not like the LDP anymore but have not found any party to replace it.

The worst news of 1993 was the arrest of Shin Kanemaru, Vice President of the ruling LDP and Vice Prime Minister in the Nakasone cabinet. The public prosecutor seized more than six billion yen ($50 million dollars) worth of unregistered bonds, cash and gold bars from a secret safe in Kanemaru's house. Tax evasion is a serious crime and challenges democracy. In addition Kanemaru appropriated "black" money, illegally donated by various businesses and businessmen, for political funds; probably included in this were bribes paid to him directly. Apparently Kanemaru had a big money machine similar to Takeshita's—the civil engineering association and construction companies in his Yamanashi Prefecture electoral district made donations in tremendous amounts. Kanemaru showed a complete lack of ethics and morals, and his actions caused serious distrust of politics throughout Japan.

If the Japanese could have admitted that men make mistakes and that men in power are apt to do evil things, they would have devised more effective ways to check the conduct of politicians. If they had studied history, they would have realized despotism and money ruled the politics of feudal Japan. But they imagine old Japan was cleaner, and think Japan will be all right again if the *okami* of the good old days returns.

Are only politicians so unethical? You will recall the *shikidai* installed in the entrance hall of the samurai house. It was for the daimyo's secretary to judge by the sound if the visitor put enough gold on the *shikidai* for asking his master a favor. If not, the secretary would not let the visitor see his lord. The visitor was required to *iro-wo-tsukeru* (put more gold) till the secretary said yes. The expression *Iro-wo-tsukeru* is currently used with the same meaning in daily business, though the people do not know the origin.

In feudalistic society everything was settled with gold (or with silver in western Japan), including political alliances between families and marriages, even if they meant interracial and inter-ethic unions. The real picture is totally different from the established image of a stoic samurai as written in Bushido or illustrated in TV samurai plays understood as Japanese culture. In fact, the Japanese of the past may very well have been even more unethical than the Japanese of today. The precepts of Buddhism and other Chinese teachings were merely tools of power to rule the people. However, modern Japanese are blinded by glorified stories and believe our ancestors were all men of justice with much higher morals than today, and are proud of it as a part of our unique culture.

The Meiji ideology was concocted to found modern Japan under the emperor institution, with devotion to the emperor a supreme value. However, in the end, the idea proved fatal. Blind loyalty to a ruler is dangerous. During the wars too many lives were wasted for this cause. Ultimately, the people became fed up with the bloody principle; they saw death and found it ugly, not beautiful or glorious. So after the surrender, the new constitution offered the symbolic emperor system to the people, and the Japanese faced a choice to keep traditional vertical society with Hirohito on top under the protection of a new American *okami*, or to set up a truly democratic state on the same principles and values as America. This historical option has not really been recognized by the Japanese.

Now we do not have to commit hara-kiri when we blunder; for a country which renounces war, old bloody values are no longer necessary. To make money, the principle of capitalism is enough. Capitalism requires no national values; capitalism is international. All difficult and painful decisions were made by the U.S. The Japanese were to follow the decisions of the American *okami* without a clear idea of their own economic interests.

It is a pity that the sincere pursuit of democracy was mixed up with anti-communism. All political parties except the communists are determined to preserve the current emperor institution, because it is the only method to govern the people with feudalistic ideas under a democratic system. When General MacArthur announced Japan had the right of self defense, the self-defense force was organized and the question of bloody values revived as a reality.

The question, "What cause do we die for?" must be answered. Certainly it will no longer be "for the emperor." Then what is worth defending at the cost of lives? Democracy? Our history tells us that the benevolent emperor, our great father, is our center and guides us correctly. We have not been taught any experiences that convince us of democracy. We have no values such as freedom, independence, equality, fraternity or human rights in our traditions and culture.

There are no stories of the people rising to protest the feudalistic lord for his abuses of power; there are no samurai heros to protect the rights and interests of the people against the arbitrary rule of a shogun with military power. We have no Robin Hood, which must be unique in the history of the world. What we do have is useful in implanting into the mind of the masses the idea that the government under the emperor institution has traditionally taken good care of the people.

The uniqueness of Japanese history can be construed as artificial. However, it is difficult to prove: history dates back thousands of years, and there are not many source materials to tell us what happened. What about modern history after the Meiji Reformation? Here we can see the facts clearly. However, the Japanese government is not active in clarifying the truth about what we have done and who is responsible. The government tries to explain World War II and the wrongdoings of the imperial army as a result of madness that captured the Japanese at that time. We do not realize how little we know our history.

Would the soldiers of the Self Defense Force be able to die for democracy in the same way American soldiers have? Unless the soldiers are shown the values of democracy in historical evolution, they will not be prepared. A military lacking fighting spirit is wasted, however superior their weapons may be. Unless the majority of Japanese come to share this view, which derives from Yagiri, Japanese soldiers will not be able to fight for democracy.

Dying for democracy is not easy. For the Japanese, it was easier to die for a deity that personified the emperor than for an ideal like democracy. Loyalty in itself is a fine trait, but loyalty to false gods and evil ideas leads to disaster. However difficult it may be, it is vital to make Japan a truly democratic nation, the value for which the people are willing to die. It is the first step for Japan toward internationalization.

Japan must share the same values of democracy as the U.S. if she wants to become a member in good standing of world society. A spiritual revolution and full accounting of history is necessary to achieve this.

Chapter Twenty Four

Old Rules vs American Reforms

On the day of the surrender of Japan, August 15th, 1945, most Japanese felt relieved. While radios and newspapers cried for a decisive battle with U.S. forces on the mainland, loudly insisting this would bring eventual victory, the majority of people—save for a few fanatics—felt Japan had no chance of winning the war, and that everyone's fate was to die. Desperation soon changed to hope and brought vitality to the hungry and tired people dressed in rags who stood gazing at the ruins of their towns.

Of course, people were afraid of being occupied by foreign forces. What would they do to us? They might retaliate, but what could we do to protect ourselves without weapons after we had surrendered? There was no other choice but to entrust our lives to the new rulers. As veteran American soldiers who had experienced dog fights with Japanese soldiers on the Pacific islands first came in with the smell of powder, there were a few unhappy incidents such as rapes, but military discipline was maintained generally well. After they were replaced by fresh soldiers sent directly from the U.S., there were no major problems, and the people's fear of atrocity by the occupation forces vanished.

After the first contact with American soldiers, some Japanese threw away traditional values. The first internationalists to test American democracy and way of life were prostitutes called *pan-pan*. Men, particularly defeated soldiers, were more timid. Those who survived desperate combat and hunger in southern islands stood absentmindedly just staring at *yamato nadeshikos* (glorified name of Japanese girls) proudly walking on the Ginza arm in arm with American soldiers.

Those who had played leading roles in the war kept silent, cowering in corners. The structure of Japanese life was changing quickly and irrevocably. What had been bad and criminal was now good and had to be emulated. Under such circumstances GHQ came out with various policies in rapid succession in order to democratize Japan. Here is a list, together with relevant events:

- August, 1945: dropping of atomic bombs on Hiroshima and Nagasaki
- U.S.S.R.'s declaration of war
- Acceptance of Potsdam Declaration
- Emperor's broadcasting of rescript to end the war
- Landing of occupation forces and General Douglas MacArthur
- September, 1945: signing instrument of unconditional surrender
- Issue of General Headquarters first directive
- Arrests of war crime suspects
- Visit of Hirohito to GHQ to see General MacArthur
- October, 1945: GHQ's directive for democratization (freedom in speech about the emperor, release of political criminals, abolition of thought and political police)
- General MacArthur's demand for 5 major reforms to Premier Shidehara: (liberation of women, encouragement of labor unions, democratization of education, abolition of secret inquiry, judicial system, and structural democratization of economy)
- Abolition of the maintenance of the Public Order Act
- GHQ's directive to prohibit militaristic and ultra-nationalistic education
- GHQ's directive to purge militarists and ultra-nationalists from educational concerns
- November, 1945: founding of Japan Socialist Party
- GHQ's directive to dissolve the Zaibatsu (huge financial clique)
- Founding of the Liberal Party, December 1945
- 4th meeting of Japan Communist Party
- GHQ's directive to make land reform
- GHQ's directive to separate the state from the Shinto religion
- New election law for the House of Representatives, including suffrage for women
- Trade Union Act
- January, 1946: rescript to deny deity of the emperor
- GHQ's directive to purge militarists from public offices and to dissolve ultra-nationalist groups
- Arrival of the first ship for the emergency import of food from Manila

- February, 1946: General MacArthur's three principles of Japan's new constitution (actually more like an amendment to the Meiji constitution)
- Presentation of the government's draft of the new constitution to GHQ
- GHQ's refusal of it
- Issue of moratorium ordinance (new yen issued)
- Emperor's visits to the prefectures in the Kanto area to encourage the nation, starting from Tokyo
- March, 1946: announcement of the government's final draft of the new constitution
- May, 1946: opening of International Military Tribunal for the Far East
- Speech of Dean Atcheson, U.S. representative to the Allied Council for Japan, against communism
- Demonstrations in demand of more rice ration under the leadership of left-wing parties (the people were nearly in a state of starvation; see Chapter 22).
- General MacArthur's statement to ban riotous demonstrations
- Appointment of Shigeru Yoshida, Liberal Democratic Party, to Prime Minister
- June, 1946: Chief Prosecutor Keenan's statement in Washington, DC. that there would be no indictment of Hirohito as a war criminal
- Premier Yoshida's reply at the House of the Representatives in discussions on the new constitution that Japan renounced war even to defend herself, as well as the right of belligerence
- July, 1946: approval of Far Eastern Commission on fundamental principles of Japan's new constitution
- September, 1946: approval of the new constitution by the House of Representatives
- October, 1946: final approval of the new constitution by the Diet
- The second land reform
- November, 1946: Promulgation of the new constitution
- January, 1947: new Imperial House Law
- Gen. MacArthur's directive to stop general strike planned by the Joint Strike Headquarters of all government labor unions
- March, 1947: Fundamental Law of Education
- School Education Law
- April, 1947: first election of prefectural governors and city mayors
- Labor Standard Law
- Antitrust Law

- Local Autonomy Law
- Election of the members of the House of Councilors
- General election of the members of the House of Representatives
- May, 1947: enforcement of the new constitution
- July, 1947: foundation of Fair Trade Commission
- August, 1947: GHQ's limited approval of private foreign trade
- October, 1947: Chief Prosecutor Keenan's statement that Hirohito and business leaders are not responsible for the war
- National Civil Servant Law
- Amendment of Criminal Law
- December, 1947: New Police Act (localization)
- Economic Decentralization Law
- Dissolution of Home Ministry
- January, 1948: Army Secretary Kenneth C. Royall's speech to position Japan as the wall to block communism
- February, 1948: Far Eastern Commission's adoption of the directive to disarm Japan
- April, 1948: Maritime Safety Agency Law
- July, 1948: New Criminal Procedure Code
- New Code of Civil Procedure
- November, 1948: the judgment of the International Military Tribunal for the Far East—25 defendants found guilty
- December, 1948: GHQ's announcement of 9 principles for the stability of Japan's economy directed by the U.S. government
- Execution of ex-general Tojo and 6 others
- March, 1949: The Dodge Line, a special economic policy aimed at balancing the Japanese budget and spurring economic recovery
- April, 1949: GHQ fixing single exchange rate of 360 yen to one U.S. dollar
- June, 1949: foundation of Civil Liberties Commission
- August, 1949: Dr. Shoup's recommendation of taxation system reform
- January, 1950: Gen. Mac Arthur's declaration that Japan has the right of self-defense
- June, 1950: outbreak of Korean War
- July, 1950: General MacArthur's directive to set up Police Reserve Force (later renamed the Security Force and eventually the Ground Self-Defense Force) and to increase the strength of the Maritime Safety Agency
- August, 1950: General MacArhtur's directive to dissolve Zen Roren (Federation of All Labor Unions)
- September, 1950: Red purge; cancellation of purge of ex-government officials

- October, 1950: Cancellation of purge of ex-military and naval officers
- April, 1950: U.S. President Truman's dismissal of General MacArthur
- September, 1951: San Francisco Peace Conference
- Peace Treaty with 48 free countries
- Security Treaty between the U.S. and Japan
- April, 1952: restoration of independence

The Cease-Fire Agreement was reached between South and North Korea in July, 1953. The Japanese economy, having been brought back to life by U.S. special procurement for the Korean War, was ready to take off soon. From the above chronological table, one can trace changes in American policy toward Japan during the period of occupation.

May 3 is a national holiday in Japan, commemorating the enforcement of the new constitution in 1947, which was adopted by the Diet in October of the previous year. *The Price of a Constitution*, by Tetsuya Kataoka (Hoover Institute, Stanford University), written in English, reveals a great deal about the establishment of the constitution that saved the emperor and the emperor institution. Most interesting is the author's claim that there was manipulation of history, which he calls "standard history". He says: "In 1952 John Foster Dulles, special consultant to Secretary of State Dean Acheson, persuaded the State Department to set in motion a 'psychological program' for creating a new ideology to combat Marxism. Edwin O. Reischauer, distinguished Harvard historian of Japan, and his fellow Japanologists were entrusted with the task. In the hands of the academics, however, efforts went beyond a 'psychological program' to a search for a new paradigm of Japan's modern history. The concept of modernization, a slightly milder affirmation than nationalism, was the answer. In the new history based on that paradigm, Japan was no longer the semifeudal oppressor and aggressor as the Marxists said it was. Instead, it was the leading modernizer and the first to introduce constitutional democracy in Asia; far from deriving from innate native traits, Japanese militarism was now viewed as an aberration in an otherwise uninterrupted flow of 'continuity'; the concept of feudalism was replaced by 'tradition' or 'early modernity;' and the secrets of Japan's success were sought in its tradition."

Kataoka continues: "...John Foster Dulles's call for an anti-Marxist ideology has produced a paradigm and a history—which I choose to call standard history—based on it. Standard history reflects the interests of the parties who constructed the new Venice. Douglas MacArthur was interested in maintaining the myth that the Japanese people had freely willed the constitution. He had to conceal the fact that he wrote it, that he saved Emperor Hirohito in exchange for the emperor's acceptance of it, and that the emperor was not quite so free of responsibility for World War II as he had to insist at the time in order to consummate the exchange."

Occupation and manipulation of history inevitably coincide. That is a common point in both the Chinese occupation in the 7th century and the latest American occupation. Conquerors always like myths that justify and glorify them; it is the effective way to strengthen effects, and paint the vanquished foe to look good. Who dictated Article 9? It is understood in the "standard" history that Shidehara, then Prime Minister, put the article into the new constitution in a meeting on January 24, 1946. The truth is that General MacArthur dictated to the Prime Minister his principles of the revision in that meeting. Shidehara is characterized as an idealist to have worked out the renunciation of war; he merely accepted the role to save the emperor.

A touching story about Hirohito's first meeting with General MacArthur widely believed among the public is another myth created to benefit both the emperor and the general: on September 27, 1945, Hirohito went to GHQ in the Daiichi Building, which stands on the other side of a moat facing the imperial palace. Kataoka states in his book: "According to MacArthur, the emperor surprised him by offering to 'bear sole responsibility for every political and military decision made and taken by my people in the conduct of war.' It is also said that the emperor offered to abdicate in due course." It is generally understood that Hirohito's attitude to take the entire responsibility as an absolute monarch and his resolution to protect the faithful from possible retaliating punishments or executions, even at the sacrifice of his own life, impressed the general greatly, and was enough to change his prejudice toward the emperor, and to become friendly to him.

This episode built in "the standard history" makes the general a hero of a glorious American victory over an atrocious foe who, at the end, saved the life of the heroic monarch from the tragedy of defeat. It justifies, describing the emperor as a sublime and deserving man. Nothing could offer better grounds to restore the emperor and emperor institution, which was in serious discredit because of defeat, than a story telling the character of the emperor—so noble and heroic that even the enemy commander respected him after only one meeting. It gained the people's confidence that General MacArthur revealed the story in his own memoirs, while Hirohito kept silent in good faith to his promise with the general.

There are many versions of the historic meeting between MacArthur and Hirohito. One is in "Memoirs," found in a collection of short essays entitled *News Archaeology*, by Naoki Inose, written from August 1991 to August 1992 for the weekly magazine *Bunshun*. Inose describes the meeting, based on MacArthur's recollection, as follows: "MacArthur was afraid that Hirohito might start appealing to him not to be prosecuted as a war criminal, but the fear was proven groundless ...Hirohito said, 'I am here to submit myself to the judgment of the states you represent, since I am solely responsible for all decisions and acts made by the people both in military and political situations in conducting the war.'"

However, John Gunther, the well known American journalist, records Hirohito's words differently in his book about MacArthur: "In the first meeting Hirohito expressed his regret for the war and added he had wanted to stop it. MacArthur asked why he was unable to do so if the truth were so obvious. Hirohito replied brusquely: 'My people love me very much. So they should have sent me to a mental hospital till the war was over if I had opposed to the war and endeavored to maintain peace. If they did not love me they would have cut my head off without hesitation.'"

Katsuzo Okumura, an interpreter, made a five page memo of this meeting and submitted it to the emperor. The Ministry of Foreign Affairs must have the copy, but it has not yet been made public. Approval was not granted in a request for disclosure. However, for reasons unknown, it is printed in a book titled *The Emperor and his War Responsibility*, by Yuzuru Kojima, published in 1988: "'I wanted to avoid this war with all my might. I regret to my utmost it resulted in war.'" There are absolutely no other words. This makes one doubt what MacArthur wrote in his memoirs. The words of the emperor are straightforward, carrying his sincere regret that he wanted to avoid the war but failed. On the other hand we find him explaining this situation with a slightly different nuance in another memo called "The Monologue of the Emperor," recorded on June l, 1946, in which he states that he did everything within the criteria of a constitutional monarchy. This may well have been done in preparation for the possible prosecution by Allied Forces to the International Military Tribunal for the Far East. It tells that an explanatory story was in the process of being made to save the emperor from prosecution. The Okumura memo seems the more likely truth; unfortunately the touching scene is merely a fiction that was deliberately created for the interests of both parties. One suspects General MacArthur decided to save the emperor and preserve the emperor institution from the beginning of the occupation. His desire was to make the occupation a great success and his name immortal; he realized he had to use the emperor in order to achieve this ambition. Once he said the emperor was as mighty as one million troops. It is ironic that the man who wrote the constitution to prohibit political use of the emperor made utmost use of him to achieve his occupation plans.

MacArthur practically took the emperor hostage. At that time the major concern of the Japanese government and political leaders was to save the emperor and preserve the emperor institution. They were compelled to obey the directives of General MacArthur absolutely. His strategy was right and we have seen his remarkable success. Of course the most brilliant achievement was the new constitution, which was written exactly as MacArthur dictated. He succeeded in democratizing Japan with a popular sovereignty and symbolic emperor. He also succeeded in demilitarizing Japan permanently with Article 9. Many other democratic laws were transplanted from the U.S. to insure penetration of democracy into the life of the Japanese. General MacArthur did his job well and the Japanese government responded to his guidance well: this is the way we understand standard history.

However, grave consequences have been produced. Certainly it was effective for MacArthur to manipulate the Japanese government and politics at his will. By having Hirohito on his side as a hostage, resistance of other leaders was eliminated, plans for reforms more easily carried out. But this allowed the preservation of "a special man above all men and rules," the vertical society and feudalistic ideas. One may argue the emperor is only a symbol in the new constitution, but it is clear he is much more than that to the Japanese. Everybody in Japan is equal but the emperor. Everybody venerates him; otherwise you are not a Japanese. The emperor is at the top of the vertical society; only under such a system using his authority can we make decisions. In Japan if everybody is equal, nothing can be decided.

Kataoka quotes President William McKinley's speech in his book: "No imperial designs lurk in the American mind. They are alien to American sentiment, thought and purpose. Our priceless principles undergo no change under tropical sun..." Analagously, no democratic ideas ever emerged in the Japanese mind. They are alien to our sentiment, thought and purpose. Based on a thousand years of tradition, the Japanese people believe that when the emperor "appoints" political leaders to government positions, these leaders automatically gain a share of the emperor's accumulated wisdom. To us, the emperor embodies our principles. Other principles such as democracy are only secondary. Our principles change, depending upon the situation, but the emperor remains unchanged at all times.

Kataoka has clarified what price America paid for a constitution, while I have pointed out what price the Japanese have paid. Our price is more intrinsic than America's, i.e., the extra burden on the U.S. military budget from Japan's freeriding eventually worsened the American economy.

Japanese attitudes are different from those of Westerners. We are not well trained in democratic ways to make decisions. Our system is both socialistic and feudalistic, and we have not made due effort to study and learn American democracy and practices. What we now must do is reflect upon ourselves more deeply and radically.

Chapter Twenty Five

"You Can't Fight City Hall"

Shortly after the successful conclusion of his first goal of the occupation—the implementation of reforms necessary to demilitarize and democratize Japan—General MacArthur was compelled to change policy in order to cope with changes in the military situation in the Far East. GHQ, whose staff set communists free from Fuchu prison, became the oppressor and acted to purge them from public office, while withdrawing nationalist purges. Oppression of communists became stronger after the outbreak of the Korean War.

Now the U.S. policy was to rearm Japan, to make her the wall to defend against communist invasion. The Japanese reaction to rearmament was cool. We were fed up with bloody ideology; our memory of narrow escape from death was still fresh. We had little desire for the same agony, even to defend the new *okami*'s ideal. We were not ready to die for the principles of democracy which were foreign to us.

For Japanese leaders it was convenient to put more effort in restoring the authority of the emperor and reshaping the Meiji ideology in the mold of democracy. For the U.S. it was good to have Japan stabilized politically and economically. As a result they could expect Japan to become a well established military base for American troops fighting against communism in Asia. If the emperor institution were to fall, Japan would become a communist nation, a loss the U.S. could not afford. For the Japanese establishment, the emperor institution helped preserve the vertical society with which they traditionally governed the people.

Under the new constitution, sovereignty resides with the Japanese people. Our political system and laws are perfectly democratic, thanks to the reforms by MacArthur and the U.S. government. But what about the people? Do we believe in democracy and its values wholeheartedly? Are we willing to sacrifice our lives to defend them? These points must be clarified, because it goes without saying democracy fundamentally rests on individual attitudes.

According to *Constitution and the Emperor Institution*, by Koichi Yokota: "At a radio broadcasting investigation conducted on December 23, 1945, 95% of the people supported the emperor institution." Yokota has some reservations that the investigation was incomplete, yet it is surprising only 5% were against it when the authority of the emperor was so discredited by the defeat. Yokota continues: "In fact, farmers working in the fields alongside the railway prostrated themselves on the ground and worshipped (the emperor) as soon as they noticed his special train approaching on November 13, 1945, on a trip to Ise Shrine to report the defeat to his ancestors enshrined there. It was the same when (the emperor) visited the Tama Imperial Mausoleum in a suburb of Tokyo on November 17 of the same year. The people still venerated him very much."

The lesson to be learned is that when an ideology is planted in a person's mind and followed for a lifetime, it is difficult to change. Even after a defeat which exhausted the people of Japan and discredited the old regime's principles and values, the emperor was still revered. In our way of thinking our emperor was always good, always right, like a god. The evil was caused by the people who advised him. After these evil advisors were replaced with good people things would go well again. It is obvious that the Meiji ideology made us think this way, in blind deference to the emperor institution. That deference is derived solely from historical knowledge about the imperial family perpetuated in school textbooks. Hirohito remained Hirohito, unchanged in our hearts, even after August 15, 1945. Principles and values of a regime can change in the long run, but the emperor will be the same for thousands of years to come. We do not want to destroy this vertical society with the emperor on the top, in which persons in higher positions control people in lower places.

Yokota wrote: "After he declared himself a human being in January, 1946, (the emperor) started touring local cities and villages throughout Japan, with a visit to Kanagawa Prefecture the next month to encourage people depressed by the defeat. (The emperor's) visits were welcomed with great excitement, and the tour was continued up to 1954, with interruptions during 1948 caused by GHQ directive in response to Soviet protest in fear of a nationalist revival. This contact with the people was effective in establishing a friendly image of the emperor among the people. He was no more the living god of prewar days, riding on a white horse to be worshipped. The new constitution made him a symbol." In a survey made in April, 1946, after the announcement of the final draft of new constitution, 85% of the people supported the symbolic emperor and only 13% opposed (*The Mainichi Shinbun Newspaper*, May 27, 1946). On November 3, 1946, at a mass meeting of Tokyo metropolitan residents held at the Imperial Palace Square to celebrate promulgation of the new Constitution, 100,000 citizens sang *Kimigayo* (which the government insists is the Japanese national anthem; however, there is no legal ground, and the Japanese Socialist Party opposes for reasons that the text wishing the emperor's reign to last forever is inappropriate for democratic Japan), and cried, "Banzai!" to the emperor and empress.

The people are unaware of the secret political trade-off made between the Supreme Commander of the Allied Powers and the emperor over their heads. Also they are not aware that the "standard" history they believe true is merely a fiction created to save the emperor. In order to keep the people blind, the emperor was skillfully and politically used; history was fabricated to cover the truth and maintain the myths. In spite of the democratic appearance of current society, the continuation of the emperor system has left much of the feudalistic and authoritarian aspects of Meiji ideology in the consciousness of Japanese individuals.

History repeats itself. The Meiji reform is no exception. It is said that the restoration of imperial prerogative was the cause of that reform. However, this is merely *tatemae* (the official excuse). *Honne* (the true motive) of powerful Hans like Satsuma, Choshu, etc., was to overthrow the Tokugawas, whose power was remarkably weakened in the course of negotiations, to open the country to foreign powers and to make their lord the new shogun. It was not their purpose to liberate the people from slavery and establish a modern democratic state; the emperor was merely a tool to keep the cause on their side and retain power in their hands.

Mutsuhito was enthroned at the age of fourteen in January, 1867, after the sudden death of his father, Emperor Komei, who was in favor of peaceful restoration by means of the union between the imperial court and the shogunate. One can guess that this was the final solution for most Kuges (court nobles) who had looked down on samurais as *sen* (humble slaves) since the time when Chinese invaders founded Japan in the 7th century. The radical, ambitious young leaders of Satsuma and Choshu Hans who rose from the lowest class of samurai were hoping to make their lord the next shogun; but ironically, the lord of Satsuma was in agreement with peaceful restoration, and thus the emperor's sudden death was convenient for both powers.

History says the emperor died of small pox, but rumors persist he was assassinated. Holding young Mutsuhito, the clan of radical Kuges and Satsuma-Choshu samurais put their plans to overthrow the Tokugawa Bakufu into practice. Yoshinobu, the last Shogun of Tokugawas, offered to return power to Mutsuhito on October 14, 1867. Responding to the situation, the court accepted at once. On the same day a secret rescript of Mutsuhito to overthrow the Tokugawa Bakufu was issued. It was withdrawn immediately but troops of Satsuma and Choshu were already approaching Kyoto, the nation's then capital.

They also mobilized the power of Ya and Yottsu descendants, promising to liberate them from Buddhist oppression when the restoration proved successful. (This oppression had been initiated by the 5th Tokugawa Shogun Tsunayoshi, with his policy of making Buddhism the national religion). People cheered and danced their way through the streets of Kyoto and Osaka, hoping for the revolution to begin. While Japan was in a state of turmoil, revolutionary Kuge and Satsuma-Choshu carried out the coup d'etat on December 9, 1867.

The new government, led by Meiji Emperor Mutsuhito, was immediately established by the radicals. Yoshinobu, the Shogun, was forced to give up the Shogunate and return his fiefs to the emperor. The coup angered pro-Tokugawa Hans, and in January, 1868, the Boshin Civil War broke out. The new government army was made up of troops from Satsuma and Choshu. The imperial troops defeated the Tokugawa-Bakufu forces at Toba Fushimi and then marched down to Edo, where they overwhelmingly crushed the remaining Tokugawa Army.

Yoshinobu swore allegiance to Mutsuhito and evacuated his Edo castle. He confined himself to his family lands in the region of the Mito Han. However, pro-Tokugawa Han resistance continued until May, 1869 in northern areas of Japan. Ya and Yottsu who had been promised religious freedom worked hard for the imperial forces during the Civil War. Government commanders wanted to banish the Tokugawas to insure that Emperor Mutsuhito's central government would have sole power to govern Japan as united states.

At the outset of the revolution, the Satsuma-Choshu alliance wished to remove the Tokugawas and select their own lord as Shogun, who would, in turn, appoint loyal samurai *rojues* (ministers of the Shogun). The alliance had expected to exercise actual power on behalf of the Shogun and the emperor; however, plans were changed in the course of the revolution.

Many of the Satsuma-Choshu leaders were from the lower class of samurai. A peaceful union of imperial court and Bakufu would have left them little chance for advancement and power. Therefore they brought about the coup d'etat and Boshin War. Afterwards, all daimyos lost their power and became direct subjects of the young emperor, to whom they were obliged to return their fiefs and serfs. The daimyos' Hans were changed to prefectures. Former lords remained temporarily as honorary governors, however, were dismissed almost immediately when new governors were sent by the imperial government. The survivors of Satsuma-Choshu leaders became ministers of the imperial government, and fully exercised power over ex-daimyos and newly appointed governors. Their objective was achieved.

For a period of over 260 years, Japan was ruled by the Tokugawas through the Bakufu (central government of the Tokugawas) and a feudalistic system was perfected. What sort of life did the Japanese have in that period? First, Japan was a vertical society with the Shogun at the top. The Shogunate was supported by the Bakufu, the military arm of the Shogunate. Under the Shogun's control were the Hans of daimyo families. Each Han was a miniature vertical society with a hanshu (feudal lord) at the top. Japan was in essence divided into some 300 nearly independent countries (the Hans).

The shogun commanded all daimyos and samurais, and was the absolute ruler of Japan. As a formality, each shogun was appointed by the emperor. The Shogun had a large army of his own vassals. His monopoly control of saltpeter deterred the daimyos from plotting to overthrow the Bakufu. The result was a long period of peace and order under an arbitrary monarchy.

All hanshus were compelled to submit to the authority of the shogun and swear total allegiance to him as their ruler. His direct vassals, the *hatamoto samurai* (*hatamoto* means "at the foot of the standard in his camp") and *gokenin* (samurai of lower rank) pledged absolute loyalty to him. However, within his own Han, the hanshu was the absolute ruler. He had a local government to rule his Han. Everyone in his Han was required to pledge loyalty and obedience to him rather than to the shogun.

The same principle was applied to vassals and employees of the *hatamotos*. Their loyalty was to be directed solely to *hatamoto*, their own master. This system was extended further to the world of merchants and artisans. In the vertical society everyone had his direct master to whom loyalty was directed. The principle in the master-servant relationship was established as a supreme value in the morals and precepts of the scholars of Confucianism and orthodox Neo-Confucianism serving the Bakufu. The program was useful to defend power and fix the hierarchy. The Shogunate of the Tokugawas was supposed to exist forever. Vassals and daimyos would also have perpetual power, as long as they were faithful to the Tokugawas. Farmers, merchants, artisans, and others of the lower classes would serve the higher-ups to make their lives comfortable. Only Buddhist priests were placed in a special category due to the religious beliefs of Iyemitsu, the 3rd shogun, and all succeeding shoguns. The Buddhist belief in ancestor worship also aided the Tokugawa rule.

Ya and Yottsu people were considered outcasts. One's standing and vested rights were fixed permanently and the master-servant relationship was linked by strong loyalty. The salary of a samurai was fixed in accordance with the rank peculiar to his family. However capable and hardworking a samurai might be, his advancement was limited by family rank; success beyond one's station could only be achieved via the underground way. For example, bribing a senior with gold, becoming related through marriage to a high standing family. It was also effective to offer a beautiful girl as mistress to the lord, which might result in getting an office in the Bakufu or Han's government, for which an additional allowance was paid. In any case it was most important to be always liked by seniors..

The same methods were open in other phases of society. Rich merchants became *gokenin* (low class samurai) by buying the right. A samurai could take a wife from a rich merchant's family by having a samurai family adopt the merchant's daughter. Some Ya people bought the merchant's register and became good citizens of Edo. Money always talked.

The highest position one might hope for was that of Karo (minister of the daimyo) or counselor. This was where the real power lay. In reality the system caused a dual power structure that resembled a constitutional monarchy. The lord was never held responsible for misgovernment; the ministers took the blame. They were not responsible to the people but to the lord.

One of the most striking examples of moving up in a society is the story of *Otama no Kata* (the Concubine Otama). Iyemitsu, the 3rd Tokugawa Shogun, was on a trip to Kyoto in the summer of 1626 to attend an audience with Emperor Go-Mizuno-o. While traveling, he saw a beautiful young boy prostrating himself near a bridge. Iyemitsu, a homosexual, ordered his attendants to bring the boy to him. He fell in love with the boy and brought him back to Edo Castle.

After two years "the boy" surprised everyone by becoming pregnant—proof that "he" was a woman. The *rojus* of Bakufu were taken aback, since they had not investigated the "boy's" birth carefully, a boy being unable to have a baby who might succeed the Shogunate. They found out the "boy's" family had originally come from Cheju Island in Korea. The Bakufu kept the birth a secret, but sent the "boy's" family back to Cheju with a great deal of gold and silver. The Bakufu assigned a family owning a vegetable shop as adoptive parents. The adoptive father was made a samurai with a salary of 500 kokus (a koku is a unit of weight equal to 5.12 U.S. bushels). The money that came from the sale of rice provided the samurai with his salary. At this point the woman was made *Otama no Kata*, and the birth announcement was made. This baby became the fifth Tokugawa Shogun Tsunayoshi at a later date. (You will recall only Chinese or Korean Japanese were considered qualified to be the sovereign in Japan).

As soon as her son became the Shogun, Otama brought the remaining members of her family back to Japan. Otama made her cousin a Buddhist priest and built a large temple for him. She exercised great power as the mother of the Shogun and did not spare any efforts to make Buddhism the national religion of Japan.

The success story of *Otama no Kata* is one of few exceptional cases. Most people were fixed for life in the vertical society in terms of place, home, occupation and master-servant relationship. At times a daimyo was ordered by the Bakufu to change fiefs with another daimyo. The people of the Han remained where they were; only the daimyo and his vassal samurais moved. In the city of Edo, gates in front of tenement houses confined Ya and Yottsu people. At night the gates were closed to prohibit inhabitants from leaving. Normally occupation was preliminarily determined by birth and there was no freedom of choice. One had to live with the same people under the same master doing the same thing for as long as they lived. One's rank and standing was permanently fixed and there were few chances to move upwards.

In such a society the most important thing was to be as much like everyone else as possible. Once you angered someone, you could never guess what disaster might result. It was of no advantage to be conspicuous, since this often led to suspicion and disfavor. You should never defy your superior, especially in public. If he felt insulted by you, you would certainly feel his wrath at some time in the future. It did not matter if you were right or wrong. You always had to present an ambiguous attitude in difficult situations so that you could change your position if the situation developed in an unexpected way. In such a society you were required to live carefully and prudently, to strictly observe all morals, precepts and customs. You could not fight city hall. You could not say no too clearly without the possibility of punishment.

The most important thing was to please your superiors. In order to demonstrate loyalty to superiors you would work long hours and present gifts. These feudalistic concepts are well represented in today's society. For example, Japanese are used to work long hours. And as President Clinton remarks, "Sometimes the Japanese 'yes' is 'no.'" We are not used to saying no bluntly to a senior, even if he was in error. We will say yes at first, and then wait for a proper chance in hopes that he will recognize his error. At times Westerners have called Japanese "liars" on this account.

The emperor always had power to appoint the shogun and to give offices and rank to daimyos. This was merely ceremonial, since the imperial court had no military power. The revenue of the Tokugawas Shogunate was about 4 million kokus, while that of the court was only 30,000 kokus. However, the powerless emperor and his court survived all changes of power from the first appointment of the Sei-i Tai Shogun (great general who conquered the barbarians) in 1192.

The imperial system was saved for the same reason that General MacArthur saved Hirohito. The emperor had no troops, but if the Bakufu should attempt to overthrow the imperial family, the emperor could be the toughest of enemies by issuing rescripts to other powerful daimyos to overthrow the Bakufu, who would then face endless and costly challenges from the daimyos. The emperor's appointment finally legitimatized the shogun's power to rule, though it was a matter of formality only. Suppose a shogun killed the emperor to become ruler of Japan? This would cause chaos. First, it was believed that the vengeful soul of the dead emperor would cause a horrible disaster to the shogun. Second, the vertical society would collapse because its focal point, the emperor, would be lost. The emperor was irreplaceable. Without him the vertical society could not exist. If the emperor were not present in his position above us, the rest of us would see no differences among people and as a result would refuse to follow the rule of others. Bloody warfare among powerful daimyos would have continued for a much longer period. It would have been a great tragedy for the Japanese people. However, this type of bloody, prolonged conflict could have brought democratic ideas to Japan at its conclusion, as happened in England.

For the leaders of the Meiji revolution, it was important to preserve the vertical society and to be seated close to the throne in order to exercise power. It was also necessary to make Japan look modern to Western powers, so that she would be recognized as an independent nation. The Meiji constitution was strengthened, giving legal ground to the emperor as a modern monarch. The principle of loyalty in the master-servant relationship was changed to a more modern version, and a "standard history" was written to unite the people under the emperor's rule.

Had General MacArthur eradicated the imperial family, Japanese society would have disintegrated resulting in bloodshed and civil war, and most likely Japan would have become a communist state.

There were merits in the Meiji reforms. Japan could quickly become the most powerful state in Asia, with modern armament and industries. She was able to win two major wars, the Sino-Japanese War and Russo-Japanese War. Japan solidified her independence and joined more advanced states of the West as an equal.

Defeat in World War II presented an excellent opportunity to democratize Japan. However, the deal between MacArthur and Hirohito, followed by the cold war and the Korean War, spoiled the opportunity. At present the average Japanese is satisfied with the vertical society and the symbolic emperor institution because of the unprecedented success of Japan's improved living standard. Thus, the Japanese are not making any great effort to achieve a truly democratic society. Instead, the Japanese insist upon a "unique culture" as our defense to the Western inquisitors.

The origin of the vertical society goes back to the *ryo* and *sen* codes set forth by T'ang Chinese and Paekche Korean conquerors from the end of the 7th to the beginning of the 8th century. The title of this chapter, "You can't fight city hall" is an American saying. The original in Japanese says *Nagai mono ni wa makarero*, literally: "Be obedient to the one with long hair." Long hair means the T'ang Chinese with a pigtail. These conquerors, far away from their motherland, founded their own country, in which nearly one hundred *sen* (slaves) served a *ryo* (noble) to make his life comfortable. As a result, the capital was called *Togenkyo* (paradise). And as much as the nobles' satisfaction rose, the misery of slaves worsened in equal measure.

The history of Western countries illustrate people's resistance against tyranny and their struggles for self- determination and human rights. We have similar situations in Japanese history, however our history of conquest and slavery is hidden from the eyes of the people. 1,000 years have made us numb to the discomfort of the vertical society. Regrettably, we still carry the servile spirit of "adapt to the ways of the master" even today.

Chapter Twenty Six

Old Values vs New Policies

In the first chapter of his book *Christian's View of Life*, author Hidenobu Kuwata, D.D., a Japanese Christian priest, introduces Soren Kierkegaard's view of the relationship between God and man. Kierkegaard insisted man should not ease God's commandments selfishly like the Pharisees. However, it is impossible to completely carry out teachings such as the Sermon on the Mount or the commandment of love, no matter how hard we try. If we take the commandments seriously, we have no choice but to become desperate and consider suicide, since we cannot measure up to such high standards.

But Kierkegaard pointed out that another choice exists. Since humans are unable to keep God's commandments perfectly, we should admit sin in a sincere manner, after we have done our best, and then submit ourselves to God as we are. Kierkegaard's view concludes that a man cannot overcome egoism by his own efforts alone. This he says after rejecting Pharisaism.

Since the end of World War II, we Japanese have been living Pharisaic lives. Up to August 15, 1945, we faithfully tried to carry out precepts imposed on us under a set of national values created for the Meiji emperor institution. The national ideal of dying for the emperor is so severe that many Japanese find it impossible to follow. The command of the emperor was absolute and had to be carried out at any cost. Loyalty and obedience to the emperor was the national precept, the supreme value to die for. Everyone was urged to dedicate himself selflessly. Spirit was a great value, while money was of no value. Morals were clearly set forth by Mutsuhito in the Rescript of Education, and the precepts of glorified bushido were emphasized to supplement them.

The Japanese wholeheartedly endeavored to live according to these precepts, even in the extreme situation of war. Although it was not even easy to observe them while we were winning. However, as catastrophe was nearing, it became impossible to carry out the commands and to hide the decline of morals.

The earliest conspicuous change was seen in the battle of Guadalcanal, the imperial army's first experience fighting with American troops from the mainland. The commander of the imperial army thought that American soldiers would surrender immediately, once they made a violent charge. But conventional tactics were hopeless in front of the Americans' fierce firepower, which was far beyond our imagination.

Lower class officers realized intuitively all attacks were going to fail, so they chose banzai suicide charges rather than take the blame for failure. On the first day of allout attack, they took the lead in charge and most died. In the concept of glorified bushido, it was an honorable death in battle, but in actual fact, it was suicide to escape duty. Japanese soldiers, sick, starving, and without heavy artillery, were as desperate as their officers. They were commanded to fight, but could not. Some stayed in foxholes with rain water up to their waists. Some gave up, and hid in the jungle. Some attacked fellow soldiers and took their rations; some even resorted to cannibalism and ate the flesh of friends' bodies.

If staff officers had made a more precise reconnaissance of the enemy and honestly reported the actual situation at the front to imperial headquarters, and if the supreme commander, Hirohito, had ordered the troops to withdraw from Guadalcanal earlier, it would have saved a lot of lives of promising young men. Unfortunately the order to withdraw came too late. Meanwhile the soldiers repeated futile allout charges, with more waste of life. An enormous volume of blood was shed in the same pattern in New Guinea, in Imphal, etc., until the surrender of Japan. The generals and their staff have never taken responsibility for the strategic and tactical errors they committed during World War II. Our national values sank in the sea of blood.

The new symbolic emperor institution is nothing but Pharisaism. Pharisees were self-content with their superficial dedication to Christianity. The Japanese of today enjoy a good life and are self-content with the childish ideal of pacifism. We refuse to take responsibility in international military affairs, using the constitution of peace to shield ourselves, while Americans and other Westerners support a free international society with arms. We do not recognize we have left them the detestable, inhumane job to stake their lives in combat and kill enemies. Traditionally the Japanese intelligentsia was sympathetic to the left and rather antagonistic to the U.S. In particular, they were critical of the Vietnam War. We did not attempt to learn what democracy really was and never tried to develop it earnestly.

The U.S. government was ambivalent. It hoped Japan would rearm sufficiently to help U.S. operations as a military ally. At the same time it feared prewar ultra-nationalism might revive and ruin democracy. The Japanese people had sighed with relief when the long bloody war came to its end in August 1945. We had given our best for Hirohito, the Supreme Being in the emperor institution, an institution alleged to have existed for a few thousand years. Why was it necessary for us to take up arms again to defend an idea called democracy which had only recently been forced on us by foreign powers?

It is well known that Prime Minister Yoshida resisted the pressure of the U.S. government for rearmament and kept Japanese military forces strictly within the frame of self defense. There was very little danger to Japan of a war of self-defense, since she was fully protected by the U.S. under the Security Treaty. As a result, the Japanese government was released from responsibility in international politics and military affairs, and was not required to make decisions on the use of force.

It is the old logic. The *okami* prohibits the people from carrying arms; then we have no trouble making decisions whether to use them or not, and taking responsibility for the result. The Japanese like it that way.

As Japan became a superpower in world economics, she wanted honor and respect. At the same time the world has started looking for Japan's due contribution to international society rather than just money. When the Gulf War broke out the Japanese government did not send forces in collaboration with the coalition, on account of Article 9 of the constitution. It was out of the question to use military power, even to defend Kuwait against Iraqi Invasion. Renunciation of war is a golden rule which could not be broken even for the emperor; thanks to the U.S., whose protection enables us to feel safe from the possibility of foreign invasion. As a result the Japanese felt justified in limiting their contribution to money.

The Japanese wanted to make sure the U.S. action was right. Since there was no absolute standard of judgement, some doubted. We did not want to be involved in the war even though it was clear that the Japanese economy would have collapsed if the oil supply were disrupted. On one hand the Japanese leaders feared it would spoil the relationship with the U.S. if we neglected demands for financing the war. But to make a donation we needed the *okami* to authorize the action. If the United Nations *okami* approved military actions of the coalition, it was all right.

The same argument was repeated when the UN requested Japan's participation in the peacekeeping operation in Cambodia. The LDP and the government pushed the bill through the Diet, insisting Japan should play a more important role suitable to her economic position in international society. It was suggested that if Japan did not join with the West in the effort, she would become isolated and lose the world's good will. The Japanese Socialist Party used delay tactics; however, eventually the vote was taken and for the first time in nearly half a century, Japanese military forces crossed an Asian sea and landed on foreign soil.

This is not a question of politics and diplomacy, but morals, values and principles. What shall I do when I am attacked by a villain and my life is in danger? Shall I fight back and kill him to defend myself? Or shall I refrain from fighting back and give him anything he wants, including my life? What shall I do when I see somebody else is about to be killed by a hoodlum? Shall I try to help him, or run away? Or call the police, knowing it will be too late?

This argument lacks reality in Japan. In a vertical society where the people are closely controlled by the *okami*, the situation is not likely to happen very often. In Japan, gun control is very strict. Only police and servicemen are permitted to carry guns. All others are prohibited by law from carrying lethal weapons. Unless I am involved with *yakuza* (Japanese gangsters), attempts on my life will be almost nil. Japan is protected by the U.S. and it is unlikely any country will attack her, knowing the U.S. will defend her. Under the circumstances the majority of Japanese have no perception that Japan may be invaded or will face the question of "kill or to be killed" in reality. *Bunkajin* (people in academic and artistic careers) speak idealistically of Japan's determination to be a peaceful, unarmed nation. They have never thanked the U.S. for their military protection with the nuclear umbrella. In fact, these people are rather antagonistic to the U.S.

Japan has been able to play the role of a peaceloving state with an idealistic but powerless policy enjoying the happiness of the Pharisee for half a century. When North Korea declared it was withdrawing from the Non-Proliferation Treaty, a Japanese professor commented on TV, "Japan must make more effort in persuading North Korea to give up the attempt to produce nuclear bombs through peaceful negotiation. Japan has been appealing to destroy all nuclear weapons and we shall keep up our activities until it is actually done."

Will belligerent North Korea listen to the professor's appeal? Any one believing so is naive. North Korea may listen to what the U.S. says, for it has nuclear arms. It is international common sense, only the Japanese do not understand it. No doubt our professor would insist that killing in self-defense is wrong. What about attack by a villain? Which choice is he going to make in the question of "kill or be killed?" It is a sin to kill a man. Therefore, one must refuse military service, in order to be faithful to the teachings of God. This is Japan's Socialist Party's position. The conscientious objector can exist because someone else is performing the awkward work of killing enemies by risking his life. Similarly, Japan's Socialist Party can be idealistic because the U.S. has pledged to protect Japan with its nuclear umbrella. The socialist is only transferring trouble and responsibility to others.

The Socialist can spend his life without the agony of Kierkegaard, but the Christian has to take responsibility for his actions. Hidenobu Kuwata says, "There are three things in life where we are unable to reach decisions using reason, which can only be arrived at by faith and through our own inner voice. The first concerns morals—what is right? How can we really know? Next is hope, regarding future events; third is the belief in God. All of these are uncertainties, yet we cannot avoid facing them in life; the only way we can handle them is to believe in our own inner resources and then make choices. Believing in God goes beyond mere thinking about God philosophically, and encompasses taking risks in the course of our lives."

No matter how much we may deliberate and agonize, each choice is a gamble; we have absolutely no means of knowing in advance what action God will consider right until Judgment Day. Our only course is to trust in the "still, small voice" within. This is the meaning of belief in God; it is not merely interpreting the words of the Bible superficially, but realizing them intrinsically and profoundly in our lives.

Before I read Hidenobu Kuwata's book I misunderstood Christians. I thought the Bible was a sort of manual that would always assure the correct action in accordance with God's will in every circumstance.

The majority of Japanese are not religious; however, thanks to Einstein and other physicists, we all have enough scientific knowledge to recognize that a great power beyond our comprehension has created us and the space around us. After enormous efforts to discover the true essence of life, it has been revealed in quantum theory that the ultimate micro state is uncertainty. It appears we have no choice but to live with this uncertainty, and act according to the best dictates of our conscience. On this level, the Japanese are living a life not that different from the Christians'.

On the personal level, after living life to the fullest, I wish to have few regrets when I close my eyes forever. This hope mandates that I should be the master of myself as I live. My values and training, together with whatever added knowledge and experience life has afforded give me resources to use when making decisions. "Do unto others" is a principle of my life, and yet in an extreme situation, I am still unsure I will be able to follow this noble precept to overcome my ego.

If individual decision is reflected in making national decisions through a democratic system, decisions of the Japanese government will be essentially acceptable to the U.S. Unfortunately, in actuality there is distrust, revisionism and even fear, causing serious frictions between the two countries. What is the reason?

The Japanese face two opposing values: emperor and democracy. We can die for one value but not for two values opposing each other. This contradictory marriage of emperor and democracy has caused the nation to lose centripetal force. Japanese slavish mentality to obey whatever decision the *okami* makes and ignorance of true history have caused this to happen. Moderate right wing political and business leaders hope to restore centripetal force by strengthening the emperor institution, to once again cause young Japanese to have the guts to stake their lives for the nation. They think it will help clean up the current plutocracy, as well as solve the problem of sending military forces abroad as our international contribution. They also want to revise the current constitution to make the emperor the official "head of state," (although he is already treated so as a fait accompli). They believe if the emperor is in the position of supreme commander, it will encourage the Self-Defense Force and hopefully enable men to die for the country again.

This attempt will fail, because the Japanese cannot abandon democracy, the tremendous benefits from which we have enjoyed for nearly half a century. Can we, then, totally abandon the emperor institution? Or can we make it compatible with democracy, like the British?

Chapter Twenty Seven

New Wave in Politics

"Was what Japan did in World War II different from what the western nations did to underdeveloped countries in Africa, Asia and South America? The western nations colonized and exploited people. Perhaps we joined in the game too late and disturbed the world's established order. We had to fight against the entire world and were defeated. However, what we did was essentially the same as what western nations did. Why were we the only ones to be blamed? Is it because the color of our skin is not white? If people of color commit crimes in Western society, they will be punished severely, but if caucasians do the same thing, people are more tolerant, and often the perpetrator escapes from punishment. We have nothing to be ashamed of! Why do we have to apologize?"

The moderate right wing, perhaps comprising most members of the Liberal Democratic Party and business leaders, believe the above explains Japan's position in World War II. That, together with the standard history that Hirohito was against imperialism and tried his best to avoid the war within the limits of his constitutional monarchy, has removed the sense of having committed crimes from the conscience Japanese nation. A bit of *yamato damashii* (samurai's traditional fighting spirit, willing to give his life to his lord and state) is essential for the Japanese, in order to make positive international contributions, such as dispatching the self-defense force abroad for peacekeeping operations, in which they will face the danger of incurring inevitable casualties.

The establishment thinks Japan's greater international contributions, not only in money but "sweat," or possibly in "blood," will put Japan in a more favorable position in world society.

The trade imbalance is a problem which has to be solved for both the United States and Japan. But the Japanese still believe the U.S. demand can be evaded. They want to stop the rise of the yen in order to save the export industry. However, in *honne* (true mind) they have no intention of carrying out comprehensive reforms quickly, as they think it would destroy the grounds on which Japan's current prosperity is based. The cold war is over, but they have not gotten rid of *amae* (dependence) on the U.S. yet.

The Japanese populace does not recognize the seriousness of the trade imbalance. People feel we work harder and produce a more attractive product at competitive cost. Americans like our products and buy them in large quantity. On the other hand, U.S.- made products are not as attractive as ours. The population of the U.S. is double ours. Our buying is naturally much less than our selling, which brings us a trade surplus. It is always good to work hard and save money. The U.S. demand is unreasonable. Maybe the U.S. is merely trying to damage our economic power.

This resembles the situation preceding World War II. We lost that war, but this time we must keep winning the economic war. The *okami* is always right; foreign power is wrong; we are right and America is wrong. The two ideas interact.

Historically, Japan's expansion via military force began in 1895, when Japan made Taiwan (Formosa) her first colony, with the victory in the Sino-Japanese War. In 1910, Japan annexed Korea, and in 1931 added Manchuria, the biggest gain in her imperialistic adventure, which compelled her to withdraw from the League of Nations two years later. Greedy with success, Japan invaded northern China, where Japanese troops repeated aggressions for several years, which developed to allout war in 1937. Dazzled by brilliant military gains of the Nazis at the initial stage in Europe, Japan concluded a triple alliance treaty with Nazi Germany and Fascist Italy, which led straight to World War II. Stuck in the mud of war with China, Japan was gradually exhausting. In 1940 and 1941 Japan invaded north and south Indochina (Vietnam), in order to secure war resources. As a consequence, the U.S. government froze U.S.-based Japanese assets and banned export of oil to Japan.

The details of processes the imperial government underwent until the final decision to go to war with the U.S. are vividly illustrated in a book titled *Gozen-kaigi (Council in Pre*sence *of the Emperor)*, by Junpei Gomikawa. The Army could not resist the temptation of enormous gain in case the Axis won the war. Deluded with false hope of a Nazi victory, warlike factions of the Army advocated war. The Navy was hesitant. In *honne* (true opinion), the Navy opposed the war, but could not say, "We lack the power to beat the American Navy, and Japan will be defeated." The Navy's budget used to be bigger than the Army's for building warships. As samurai abiding by bushido, the Navy could not confess it would be defeated by the U.S.; the closest they could admit was to say, "For the first couple of years we will be able to fight with the American fleet pretty well; however, as time passes we will no longer be able to guarantee victory."

It was clear to reasonable people that in the long run Japan was no match for the U.S., that it was impossible to overcome the amazingly big difference in industrial strength and war resources. Even the most radical Army staff saw that Japan could not force the U.S. to submit. But nevertheless, the warlike Army made up a paper plan which it presented at the Third Council, held on November 5, 1941, putting forth the following strategy: the Navy pledged it would be able to fight the U.S. Pacific fleet pretty well for a couple of years. It might not be feasible to destroy the enemy fleet completely, but it should be possible to keep the vital defense circle around Japan to build up invincible positions against the U.S.. If we occupied South East Asian and Oceanic regions we could secure war resources such as oils, minerals, rubber and food supplies; then it would not matter how long the war continued; we would not be exhausted. In the long run there would be an optimum moment to talk peace with the U.S. on terms favorable to Japan. Most important was to start the war immediately. Further delay would cause a more serious shortage of oil, and before long our war potential would be gone; then Japan would be compelled to submit to the U.S.

The Navy demanded the government give full assurance of minimum essential war resource allocations, for example, iron, steel, nickel, bauxite, tin, and rubber for the first three years. The ministers promised whatever quantities requested. It was all nonsense, but removed the reason for which the Navy kept saying no to the war. In the end, the Navy gave in and agreed to go to war.

The last Council meeting was held in Boardroom East-1 of the Royal Palace on December 1, 1941. Present were Hirohito, Tojo, the Prime Minister and the Minister of Home Affairs and the Army; Togo, the Minister of Foreign Affairs; Kaya, Minister of Finance; Shimada, Minister of the Navy; Iwamura, Minister of Justice; Hashida, Minister of Education; Ino, Minister of Agriculture and Forestry; Kishi, Minister of Commerce and Industry; Terashima, Minister of Posts and Railway; Koizumi, Minister of Welfare; Suzuki, President of the Board of Planning; Sugiyama, Chief of General Staff of the Army; Tanabe, Vice Chief of General Staff of the Army; Nagano, Chief of Naval Command Department; Ito, Vice Chief of Naval Command Department; and Hara, President of the Privy Council. These leaders started the war that brought disaster to people in and out of Japan. Yet only three of them committed suicide at the defeat of Japan, while they forced hundreds of thousands young soldiers to die under the precepts of bushido.

Hirohito held prerogative as supreme commander of the Army and Navy. He was the only one who could stop the war. He was the sole person in the room who was absolved of responsibility for the warmaking decision and held harmless for the consequences. It was most strange. He usually kept silent, allowing the Prime Minster to conduct the Council. The last *gozen-kaigi* was merely a formality, with Prime Minister Tojo concluding the meeting on behalf of all advisers with the pledge to Hirohito that they would do their best to satisfy him in executing the war. According to the memo taken by Sugiyama, Hirohito nodded assent for all explanations, and looked convinced. He left in a good humor. All who attended signed consent to the decision to go to war. Sugiyama and Nagano jointly asked Hirohito's imperial sanction for the order to carry out the initial campaigns. It was granted immediately.

From the above, Hirohito looks like a puppet; however, he was actually not. Prior to the Council he was given ample opportunity to study the issues. He had access to full information and briefing from his ministers and staff. He could ask all details and figures, request amendments or reject plans. If he was determined to avoid war, it would have been possible to do so. There is no way he could escape from war responsibility other than being released from charges of war criminal by the International Military Tribunal, for political reasons. He is responsible for: (1) commencing the war of aggression; (2) all war crimes; (3) the defeat of Japan. This is entirely separate from the Tribunal.

Hirohito carefully examined risks and the possibility of discontinuance of the imperial throne with the advice of confidantes, assuming Japan's defeat. In the process of reaching a decision, his concern was focused on his major priority, the throne, which in all cases should be safeguarded, as it is the emperor's supreme duty to secure the throne that has been passed down from generation to generation since the infinite past (for a thousand years, actually). The emperor was glorified and worshipped.

One cannot help feeling betrayed; during this time, soldiers drafted from the nation were dying at the front in China in absolute obedience to the Emperor. In these discussions, the people did not exist. We were like robots to obey any orders of the *okami*. If the imperial government demanded, "Go to hell", we did so. Our life was cheaper than a rifle bearing the imperial chrysanthemum crest. Men were drafted into the Army by just mailing a post card. The tradition of our enslavement since the 8th century was still alive.

Given this attitude of the Japanese government toward its people, the fate of those in the colonies and conquered lands was self-evident. Despite the slogan "Mutual Prosperity in the Great East Asian Region," the real policy was to steal resources needed for war, including labor and food. Atrocities and disasters people in the region incurred during World War II were predetermined in the *gozen-kaigi*.

Japan made a surprise sneak attack on Pearl Harbor on December 7, 1941 and World War II was initiated under the most irresponsible and random war plan. *The New York Times* on July 12, 1992, ran an editorial, "Japan's Other War Crimes," relating the sexual enslavement of Korean women during the war. "Some 20 million people died in the Pacific War, 17 million of them victims of Japanese aggression. Yet Japanese textbooks and popular culture still emphasize how Japan suffered," the *Times* commented. Despite suffering, loss of life, and destruction of property, Japanese war leaders have never been judged guilty by the Japanese people in the last 50 years. Yes, war criminals like General Tojo and six others were executed, but this was by judgment of the International Military Tribunal, the conqueror's verdict, not ours.

On August 9, 1993, Morihiro Hosokawa formed an eight party coalition cabinet, driving the Liberal Democratic Party out of power after a 38 year monopoly, in a new wave in politics. The Prime Minister admitted in his first press conference that World War II was Japan's aggression, and expressed his deep condolences for all the victims. He is the first prime minister to officially admit as much. His frank attitude is welcome, but mere speech is not enough. Policy should materialize, including reasonable compensation. At the same time there must be special efforts on the part of national and private scholars to review Japan's modern history so that we can face the facts and reflect. This time there will be no fear of glorification, because it will be objected to by scholars in neighboring countries.

The right wing immediately repudiated the prime minister's view. They said, "Millions of drafted men who dedicated their lives to the nation in action will be very sorry to hear this." Since we have neglected to make a precise accounting of World War II in 50 years, such arguments can still arise. We have never clarified who is really responsible for the fatal decision to open fire. What drove Japan to go to war politically and/or ideologically? We might have to go back as far as the Sino-Japanese War of 1894 to find out the roots of our expansionism.

Which leaders were really responsible for the defeat of Japan? Was General Tojo a war criminal? Who else? Soldiers and officers judged war criminals by allied military courts were executed or imprisoned on the spot, right after the war. Apparently some innocent men were found guilty, due to misconceptions of confused witnesses. All soldiers look alike. Contrarily, some war criminals escaped punishment. We should endeavor to identify them, restoring the honor of the innocent, while naming the true criminals. We must re-examine all facts, so that we can judge who made mistakes, who committed crimes and what caused them to do so.

The Western nations won and we lost! Why did the West win? Why did we lose? What differences exist between Japan and the West? This must be clarified. Protesting against atomic attacks on Hiroshima and Nagasaki does not help. It happened because we challenged the U.S. to a war. Whom shall we hold responsible? The imperial government of Japan or the U.S.? It is self-evident.

The European nations' penetration and invasion of Asia, America and Africa commenced following the development of ships and the art of navigation at the end of the 15th century, with Christopher Columbus, Vasco da Gama, Ferdinand Magellan, and others. In Japan the civil war age was about to open at the end of the 15th century. Rifles were first brought to Japan in 1543 and soon after came the age of Nobunaga Oda, Hideyoshi Toyotomi and Ieyasu Tokugawa.

The Portuguese were first to come to the far east, then the Spanish. They expanded their colonies eastward up to Macao through India, westward to Central, South and North America and to the Philippines in the 16th century. In the next century the Dutch, British and French followed, colonizing India and East Asia as well as North America. During the 19th century the Great Powers dismembered Africa and reached Ch'ing China, which had taken a national isolation policy.

The British defeated Ch'ing in 1842 (the Opium War), took Hong Kong and gained privileges in China. A decade later the War of the Arrow broke out and again the Ch'ing submitted to the military powers of the British, French, Russian and Americans. In 1854 the Tokugawa Bakufu of Japan concluded a peace treaty with Commodore Perry of the U.S., who had appeared off the coast of Uraga with his black ship fleet a year before. The Meiji Restoration was achieved in 1868. Only a quarter century after the Meiji Restoration, Japan defeated Ch'ing China in the Sino-Japanese War and took Formosa.

At this point the Great Powers, Russia and Japan, started dismembering China by leasing territories and spheres of influence. The Germans leased the Tsingtao area, the British the Weihai region, the Russian Ta-lien and Lueshun in Liao-tung, the French the Chan-chiang region (Kwang-chou-wan). In 1898, the U.S. annexed Hawaii and took the Philippines from Spain. The U.S. showed its concern over European/Japanese dismemberment of China by setting up the Open

Door Policy to grant equal opportunity and guarantee the territorial integrity of China. Russia's advance to the south soon clashed with Japan's interests, and the Russo-Japanese War broke out in 1904. Japan annexed Korea in 1910; World War I broke out in 1914. Chiang Kai-shek established his government in China in 1927. Japan invaded Manchuria in 1931.

The expansion of Western nations was made possible by the overwhelming military power which they acquired by the development of science. Why did it occur in Europe? The reason may well be European rationalism, which developed into humanism, born in Italy in the 14th century, which brought on the Renaissance.

In politics, absolutism prevailed, and in economics mercantilism, during the 16th and 17th centuries. Western democracy aided the rapid development of science and technology in England and brought on the Industrial Revolution, helping to make British military forces stronger than any other country in Europe. An overflowing national energy and production directed the English concern to underdeveloped areas to achieve increased national wealth. Exploiting colonial people was certainly against British values, but Western nations had not yet overcome national egoism.

Here we face the cultural differences between Japan and the Western nations. In Japan nothing similar to rationalism, liberalism or democracy was developed, even after 1945. The Japanese people never needed them. In Britain the monarch acted in an autocratic, arbitrary, selfish and often extravagant manner, so the people rose up to fight the king. The result was a gradual move to limiting royal power and achieving liberal democracy. The details of this long process are clear to the English people and make up a set of values and principles for the nation to follow.

In contrast, in Japan the *okami* (whether emperor or shogun) is supposed to be the venerable father who takes care of the children with his great mind, benevolence, and virtue. The people have no reason to be against the *okami*; we should be thankful to him. The people are made to believe "standard" history through education and are ignorant of their true history of merciless enslavement. The Japanese think Western thought is fine, but not indispensable, as is as our emperor institution. "Look! Even the *okami* of *okamis* (General MacArthur during the occupation) was so benevolent he presented a democratic system with an emperor."

From the Kamakura Bakufu (1192) to the Meiji Restoration (1868), samurai governments (bakufu) of the Minamotos, Hojos, Ashikagas, Odas, Toyotomis, and eventually Tokugowas, governed Japan. All of these families except the Ashikagas originated from enslaved

Japanese aborigines. However, their concern was focused on holding power as long as possible by suppressing any influential daimyos who might contend. To justify their power, all shoguns depended on the emperor's authority. It was a society of authoritarianism in *tatemae* (formalities), but might in *honne* (actuality).

Even in the late Edo period immediately preceding the Meiji Restoration, Western thought did not penetrate Japanese life. The people were controlled to every last detail of daily activity, and there was no room to receive such thought. Possession of weapons was prohibited. The idea of a sovereign people was out of the question. Loyalty and dedication to rulers was absolute. Non-establishment people were discarded, often left in reservations to starve. In such a society, human rights could never be a value. There was no principle save the concern for maintaining power.

Under these circumstances, science could not flourish. Rational thought was rejected, as it might teach resistance against power. Without independence and freedom, no creativity can develop. The government saw Japan was no match for Western military power. A samurai's courage to charge with traditional swords meant nothing before Western guns. So Japan imported Western scientific knowledge and technology and adopted policies to develop industry. However, it rejected Western thought as dangerous to the emperor institution.

The people were merely a means of production and service to the ruler, which is expressed well in the familiar Japanese words, *Wakon Yousai* (Japanese mind with Western technological knowledge). All not useful to the ruler were to be discarded.

What would a nation with such an idea about their fellow countryman do with colonial people or a country it occupied? What did Western countries do? The purpose of invasion by Western countries was wealth; therefore, as far the aim was fulfilled, there was no necessity to use military force against the people.

As a matter of fact, Western thought was transferred to colonial people by education for elite natives or by personal contact in local life, and it enlightened the natives about different ideas and cultures. In Indochina French influence is evident. In Hong Kong, Singapore and India, the British way is remarkable. In the Philippines, American democracy left a much stronger influence than the old Spanish. The Philippine people hated Japanese domination and many joined with guerrillas to fight against Japanese troops during World War II, in cooperation with the U.S. Army.

The Japanese purpose was no doubt wealth too, whatever banners the government might have been raising. But in order to take from the colonies, it followed the same path as in the homeland, by extending the vertical society of "man-above-men-rules." Locals were positioned at the bottom, below the lowest class Japanese, and ordered to serve the masters by offering everything they had. To elicit loyalty, the Japanese ruler forced local people to speak Japanese, believe in Shinto and worship the emperor—all completely different from the Western way. In essence, it was no different from enslavement in 8th century Japan.

Having tasted success with the conquest of Manchuria in 1931, the Japanese Army set their next target—northeastern China, and began an invasion (1937). This adventure developed into allout war with China (1937-45), in which more than 3 million Chinese soldiers (including guerrillas) and 7 million civilians were killed by the Japanese Army. These figures do not take into account the millions wounded, raped or forced into labor in mines and factories. During wartime more than 200,000 Korean soldiers were killed in action and hundreds of thousands conscripted as slave laborers. In addition, there was the sexual enslavement of tens of thousands of Korean girls. In the Philippines about 50,000 soldiers and guerrillas plus 1,000,000 civilians were killed. Altogether, the total number of deaths of Chinese, Korean, other Southeast Asians and Oceanians is estimated as many as 18,000,000 plus. Of the Japanese 1,550,000 soldiers and 660,000 civilians were killed. (*New Japanese History*, by Saburo Iyenaga and Kiyotaka Kuroha). This enormous loss of life was the result of Japanese aggression.

In World War II, most of the Western countries were suddenly invaded by the Nazis and had to go to war in self-defense. Great Britain declared war against the Nazis after the latter invaded Poland. The U.S. joined after Pearl Harbor. In these two countries, the war was decided in Parliament or Congress through democratic process. But in Japan it was not so. The *okami* and a handful of ministers could start such a disastrous war in which 20,000,000 people were killed, based on a foolish war plan. The fewer the leaders, the more mistakes will there be. This submission to the *okami* opened the way to the war. Anyone who refused to submit was kicked out as a *hi kokumin* (non-Japanese), and individuals were not free to defy the authority of the *okami* by expressing opposition.

The essence of the above-described society remains unchanged in Japan today. The risk in defying the system is losing profits or interest. The problem is milder than in the past; however, it is the same.

The Japanese must recognize that democracy and the emperor institution are incompatible. We have to choose one value, either the emperor institution or democracy. If the true history of Japan is revealed to the populace, the majority will choose democracy. The Japanese have to get rid of feudalistic remains in their thinking. Vagueness, ambiguousness, non-committal ways must be replaced by clear, plain rules and agreements, so that there will be no room left for the *okami's* "special consideration", "pity" or "broad interpretation" in application. If the *okami* makes unreasonable demands, we should stand up and speak out against it. It is no good to escape into the world of *do* and shut ourselves in.

We must spend more time studying modern thought—rationalism, liberalism, democracy. What nation do we want to be? Keep asking these questions and we will find answers. In appearance, the solutions may not be much different from the current system, but the substance will be completely new. If this is done it can change the whole nation. Big government based on *okami* will end and reforms will be made. With deregulation will come free, competitive markets, creating a better life for all, and Japan will achieve honor and respect in the world.

This means a radical change in polity, and contains the danger of disintegrating Japan. Without devotion to democracy and a fight against the emperor institution, meeting our goals will be difficult. But we must do it. It is the only way to really apologize for what Japan did in World War II to the tens of millions of innocent people in the world, and allow Japan's rebirth as an essential member of world society.

Chapter Twenty Eight

Anger and Despair

Jack Edwards' book *Banzai, You Bastards!* is referred to in Chapter 33. Edwards, a sergeant in the British army, was taken prisoner in Singapore, and spent three years in a Taiwanese forced labor camp until freed by the U.S. army in 1945. He accuses the Japanese of insisting only on how they suffered from the war, rather than reflecting on what they did to others.

Edwards declares the samurai ethics (bushido) are abnormal. A samurai losing on the battlefield has only two choices—be killed in battle or commit suicide; under no circumstances is he allowed to surrender. Based on this ethic, the Japanese soldier believed anyone who surrendered was not a samurai. When Jack Edwards surrendered he was therefore looked down on by Japanese soldiers.

The International Military Tribunal for the Far East revealed that the Japanese army was involved in the massacre of six million civilians. How many Japanese know that this figure is approximately the same as the number of Jews murdered by the Nazis in the holocaust? Japanese must realize that it was against this backdrop, and against people obsessed and ruled by the abnormal ideas of bushido, that the atomic bomb was used. The use of the bomb saved more lives than it took, and removed more pain than the pains the Japanese military caused and planned to cause. Of course, not all Japanese should be held responsible for atrocities, and probably many Japanese did not believe in the ethics of bushido. However, all Japanese supported the military, which did believe in it.

World peace movements and anti-nuclear groups today use annual commemorative events in Hiroshima and Nagasaki as opportunities to demonstrate the horror of war to the world community. Japanese authorities have cleverly turned those events to advertise how Japanese continue to suffer from aftereffects. They are trying to make the former Allied Forces appear criminals.

In addition, the Japanese Ministry of Education is trying to justify the atrocities of the Nanjing (Nanking) massacre by explaining that it occurred spontaneously under extremely confusing circumstances. Japanese aggression against China and in the Pacific is explained as an "advance" or as "expansion of territory" in Japanese school texts. Moreover, the text implies that the main evil lies with the West and not with Japan.

Atrocities committed by the Japanese during the war have never been fully investigated, and most of the perpetrators have been left unpunished. Some have become billionaires and are enjoying a life of luxury, while their victims are left without any form of compensation. The German government is shouldering its responsibilities to civilians killed or tortured during the war by paying compensation to this day. The Japanese attitude can never be regarded as correct.

Jack Edwards concludes that those who died and those who survived Japanese military prison camps with extraordinary courage and fortitude must be given due dignity and respect by the Japanese. He wishes he could forgive the Japanese, but the nightmares will not go away until the day he dies. None of us should be allowed to forget the ordeals caused by the Japanese military. Edwards' detailed descriptions of how he and his comrades were ill-treated point out evil in the Japanese heart, and show how ignorance of history, misunderstanding of human nature, and blind belief in fictitious ethics can lead to dreadful consequences.

Former British prisoners of war are taking legal action against the Japanese government, demanding compensation for the ill-treatment they underwent in the camps. Rather than 60 billion U.S. dollars being paid to Japanese farmers as compensation for allowing imports of rice, Japan should pay whatever amount required for compensation to former British prisoners, enslaved Korean girls and any other people to whom we must apologize.

In his first general policy speech at the Diet following his eight party coalition victory in 1993, then Prime Minister Hosokawa admitted World War II was a war of aggression, and expressed apology to the nations concerned. The speech caused great controversy in the Diet, since the LDP insisted that not all Japan's acts were of aggression. LDP member Shintaro Ishihara, author of a controversial book, *The Japan That Can Say No*, was especially critical of Hosokawa. Ishihara classified the countries with whom Japan fought in World War II into three categories:

1. China and Korea, to whom Japan's aggression brought great disaster.
2. The U.S., Great Britain and the other Western powers whose colonialist interests in Asia collided with Japan's interests.
3. The Soviet Union, which broke a treaty of neutrality.

Ishihara questioned to whom Japan's apologies should be addressed. Howasaka replied Japan must apologize to those classified in the first and second categories, but not to Soviet Russia. Ishihara agreed on China and Korea and on no apology to the Soviet Russia; however, he objected to the apology to the U.S. and its allies, claiming these countries committed imperialist acts similar to Japan's; they have not been questioned as to their responsibilities merely for the reason that they were the victors.

Hashimoto, the controversial and powerful LDP member who replaced Murayama as Prime Minister and Chairman of Japan's Bereaved Families Association, introduced the feelings of some "bereaved families:" "Was my husband, my father or my child one of those wicked aggressors? It can't be true!"

Self-reflection on Japan's responsibility in World War II has made little progress beyond excuse-making and justification. It is time to discuss the "republic" of Japan seriously—but regrettably, no political party is taking up the issue. The U.S. as a true friend of Japan should give us a hand to help study real democracy. Pressure to open Japanese markets to Western business through trade negotiations is fine, but the U.S. must realize when it demands deregulation and a free market economy, it is demanding a radical change in Japan's polity, i.e. from the emperor institution to a republic.

History is replete with examples of people venturing into unknown lands to take advantage of new opportunity. It occurred in Europe, Asia, Australia and the Americas, practically everywhere. As indicated earlier, Hitoshi Takeuchi's view is that "new" mongoloid people ousted "older" mongoloid people, pushing them to the extreme ends of the Japanese islands (they are now known as Ainu and Okinawaian people); Tomeo Yagiri says migrations of several different ethnic and racial groups to Japan continued until the 12th century.

The evolution of the Japanese people is in many ways similar to that of the British people. Eventually Paekche (Korean) and T'ang Chinese gained power over aboriginals and established a central government to rule the entire Japanese archipelago. Similarly, many ethnic groups were mixed in the United Kingdom's evolution: aboriginal peoples; then Celts, Picts, Scots, Angles, Saxons and Jutes migrated from the European continent. Invasions of Vikings and Normans followed. Groups commingled, intermarried and combined to produce the modern Englishman and Scot.

There are clear differences between the histories of Japan and the United Kingdom. First, there is little to no attempt made to conceal British history. People know they have evolved from an ethnic mixture. Events both good and bad are stated and reevaluated in the light of historical analysis. Monarchs are treated as human beings with human virtues and vices. The struggle of "the people" against monarchical power is well documented and recorded. History is a study based on factual interpretation.

Contrarily, Japan's history is based on the fictitious myth of a single racial and ethnic people with a deified emperor whose lineage is fabricated to seem "unbroken from the infinite past." These myths, created for political purposes, instilled "standard" history in school text books. Anything not conforming to the revised *Nihon Shoki* has been rejected by the government. Undemocratic ideas have been used to preserve the vertical society in which government can more easily rule the people. Historical studies in Japan are political campaigns rather than rational or scientific studies.

Gosai-in was charged with plotting against the Tokugawas Shogunate and confined in a shack for 20 years. Tsunayoshi, the 5th shogun, declared himself "emperor" and set up an imperial "court" in his Edo Castle. The emperor in protest transcribed the *Rikkoku Shi* (collective name of six history books edited between 720-887 AD, the oldest of which is the *Nihon Shoki*). The *Nihon Shoki* was reedited several times as power changed hands. The present version, edited by Katsumi Kuroita, an historian with imperialistic views of the 1930's, is based on materials written by Emperor Gosai-in in the 17th century.

Gosai-in's transcription is kept in the library of the imperial palace. It is not known which version of the *Nihon Shoki* Kuroita's was transcribed from. The original does not exist; only several pieces of wooden plates bearing old transcripts remain. We have absolutely no means of knowing what was actually written in the original. There is no guarantee to admit Kuroita's version is right. The confinement of Gosai-in is concealed in "standard" history. It is also concealed that Tsunayoshi oppressed Shinto to promote Buddhism, and had everyone call Edo castle the imperial court. In a society that makes one man at the top as perfect as a god, whatever facts spoil that image must be suppressed. This principle rules Japanese society from the imperial household to presidents of banks.

Ideas such as rationalism, liberalism, democracy and human rights developed in Britain over several centuries. These ideas oppose imperialism and colonialism. In the 18th and 19th centuries practical economic advantages overrided humanist ideas, but eventually humanist ideas were extended to the colonies, who have since become independent. Unfortunately, humanist ideas had limited exposure in Japan. It was only after the Meiji Restoration that they were introduced to the Japanese intelligensia; soon after, the government suppressed them as dangerous to the emperor institution. As a result they never took root in Japan.

To Westerners, it might appear that democracy is established in Japan, but this is only *tatemae* (outward face), while the rule of *okami* at the top of the vertical society is honne (the true face). The Japanese masses were indoctrinated with *okami* ideas based on a code enacted in the 8th century. Since then, vertical society has consistently developed downward, making men below men. The people followed this feudalistic system for over a thousand years up to the 19th century. After the Meiji Restoration, indoctrination was continued by the government for nearly eighty years under the reigns of Emperors Meiji, Taisho and Showa (Hirohito). The Meiji ideology made it a supreme value to willingly die for the emperor, who personified the nation with his body. This concept was first directed for the defense of Japan's independence, later in wars of aggression. The creed of *okami* has survived World War II.

It has not been possible to really establish democracy in Japan. You cannot democratize a nation using the *okami*, which is radically against democracy. While the U.S. expects Japan to democratize, this means Japan must remove the *okami* idea and system. Would the *okami* agree to remove itself?

So-called "royal diplomacy" is proof that the vertical society is living. From time to time, the emperor of Japan has apologized to heads of neighboring countries for the "unhappy past." From the Japanese point of view, the apology offered by the highest personage of the state should be accepted by other nations. But will other nations accept Japan's apology unless the *okami* is removed? It was the *okami* who began war and brought tremendous disaster to other nations. It would be a better apology to the West if Japan would remove the *okami*.

Japan has two systems contradicting each other, one democratic, the other undemocratic and still carrying the guts of Meiji ideology. Jack Edwards will forgive us only when we have completely removed the undemocratic *okami* system. Democracy is a system for minimizing mistakes. Democracy, at least so far, is the best man can do. As Winston Churchill said, "Democracy may not be perfect, but it's the best system we have."

Part Four

A PERSONAL JOURNEY

Chapter Twenty Nine

Hard Times

August 15, 1945 was a fine summer morning. Together with my comrades, I was engaged in digging a large tunnel-type air shelter at a small hill behind the Cadet School of the Imperial Army in a village situated about 10 kilometers north of Nagoya City, when we were instructed to assemble at 12 noon in the auditorium, fully dressed in uniform, to listen to a very important announcement to be made by Emperor Hirohito himself.

We stood at attention and listened to the radio, trying to understand what the emperor was saying, but no one could catch even a word, due to heavy noises on the radio. After the broadcast ended, the schoolmaster, also unable to understand the message, gave a speech imbuing us with fighting spirit, saying we should work harder to be able to give counterblows to the American forces and win the final battle on mainland Japan, where the Americans would be invading shortly, after they took Okinawa.

We returned to work on the hill that afternoon. An air raid alarm sounded. When I saw a B-29 bomber flying straight toward us and heard the sound of bombs falling through the air, I jumped into a foxhole and covered my eyes and ears to protect them from damage. The bombs hit a factory that produced ammunition right in front of the school, causing a big explosion followed by fire. Fire squads were unable to reach the fire to extinguish it, and it was left to burn and smolder for several days. The bombing did not cause any damage or casualties in our school, but I remember that day clearly as the end of World War II.

That evening, the commander-in-chief told us the broadcast at noon was Hirohito's rescript of surrender to the allied forces. We were dumbstruck. That night, I quietly walked down to the non-commissioned officers' room to eavesdrop on the radio broadcasts. Now I heard the Emperor's voice clearly, "However it may be hard to bear..."

For a couple of days I felt unrest in our school, and heard rumors that a group of cadets insisted on continuing to fight despite the order to surrender. They were going to attack a nearby arms depot to obtain necessary arms. However, the fuss calmed down in a few days. Of course, I was deeply disappointed by the defeat of Japan. My hope of being a good soldier was gone, but I was young and I felt a new hope coming.

At 6 p.m. on August 27, our school was officially dissolved. We were given a send off by the staff as we made our final departure, and were driven to the Nagoya station by trucks. The long summer day had ended, and the station was beautifully illuminated by lights as brightly as the day I had arrived one and a half years before to begin the school. Blackouts were no longer necessary. I felt Japan's defeat in my heart. As I crawled onto a crowded freight car bound for Tokyo with a heavy knapsack and trunk full of rice and soybeans the school provided, I wasn't sure how long it would take to get home, because of the heavily damaged transportation system.

As the train began to move with the sound of a thud, memories of my life in the school flashed across my mind. With deep emotion, I recalled the day I first put on the uniform of a cadet, the hard but exciting training and marches, the pain of operating without anaesthesia, unbearable hunger, and the dedicated faces of my comrades. This was only a short period in my life, but I will never forget it.

Above all, I recalled the horrible experience of suffering through an American bombing raid, when I experienced the fear of dying for the first time in my life on a Sunday in November 1944.

I had been granted permission to enjoy a holiday in downtown Nagoya City. While there, the air raid alarm sounded. I decided to go back to school. The American bombing began the moment I arrived at the train station. Quickly, I jumped into a shelter on the street with several other civilians following. A mix of incendiary and normal bombs fell from the sky like a rain shower, making peculiar sounds, exploding successively as they hit the ground, causing fire in buildings on the street. The shelter kept me safe. I came out when the last wave of bombers left the area. Nagoya was covered with thick smoke; it was as dark as night, and I could see nothing but red flames shooting out of black smoke. Railway service was interrupted. I was picked up and returned to school in our school truck late that evening.

This was my first encounter with the American Air Force, and the beginning of a series of air attacks on the city of Nagoya as well as industrial complexes producing military airplanes 25 km north of the city. Since our school was situated in between Nagoya and the complexes, we saw numerous B-29 formations flying over almost every day. From the foxhole on a hill at the back of our school at night, it was a spectacular scene to see the city of Nagoya in flames, while up in the air, Japanese fighters were attacking B-29's. I could see shining red dots, tracer shells shot by Japanese fighters at the B-29's, going through like meteors. Soon the city was completely burned flat. I was excited by imminent danger, but did not feel real fear for my life this time.

I don't remember the date exactly, but it was a night in late spring, 1945, when my pleasant sleep after the day's work was interrupted by faint noises. Someone was moving around in our bedroom. Through the corner of my eye I caught a glimpse of a comrade in combat uniform. There was nobody else in the room. I asked what was going on. The comrade replied that everyone had taken refuge at the sound of the air raid alarm. Surprised, I jumped up and put on my uniform, grabbed my rifle and ran down the stairs. At the barracks exit, I paused, dazzled by bright light shining on our training ground. I thought it was a flare. By this time, carrier-based American fighter bombers were attacking us. In the sky I saw a melee of Japanese and American planes. In order to get to the assembly point in the woods at our school's northwest corner, I had to cross an area of several hundred meters where there was no cover to hide if I were shot at by the planes. I felt the shadow of death hanging over me as I ran across the ground at full speed. No planes attacked me and I joined my comrades safely. If this had been a drill, my blunder would have caused my comrades and me, in joint responsibility, to be severely punished. However, since this was the real thing, I was received warmly by the commander with a blessing.

My fear was much stronger in this second incident, perhaps because I was alone. Although I had been educated to be prepared to die for the emperor, once I was caught in terror I wondered what would happen to me. I doubted that I would ever be able to do as my father had. I don't know how long he had to wait alone until his ship sank or how long he was consciously afloat afterwards.

I don't know exactly what made my father choose death—loyalty, bushido, anger, despair, love of family and nation—but in any case, I admired the determination he maintained, bearing the terror of death for a significant length of time. This thought remained in my mind for a long time. If the war had continued a half year longer, I most probably would have died in battle on the mainland. Sitting in the darkness and listening to the thud of the train, I felt I was heading for a new life, having been liberated from the spell of death.

My train made repeated stops, arriving at the Tokyo terminal after a twelve hour trip. Compared with today's bullet train which takes only two hours, this was much longer and tougher. I usually got off at Ofuna station, several stations before Tokyo, to change to a train bound for Kamakura, which would have saved me two hours, but this time I decided to go to the Tokyo station in order to take a look at the capital with my own eyes. The station remained safe, though quite deserted. I could see a few buildings—the Marunouchi building, the central post office, and a few blocks away, the red brick Mitsubishi building. Most of Tokyo, however, was flat and reduced to rubble. I was sure that in my lifetime, Japan would never recover from ruin, and that though I had escaped death, my future was gloomy.

After a short look at Tokyo station I took the train to Kamakura. It was here I had stood with my father's urn to receive condolences from the city of Kamakura in February after my father's naval funeral. I was an honorable little soldier determined to follow his father in service to the emperor and nation. Kamakura remained unchanged. There was no trace of bombing. I started walking home with my heavy load of rice and soybeans. Food was valuable in a civilian's life and I struggled to bring it back to my mother. On the way I met a friend on her bicycle who offered to take the food home for me. Since it was a very warm day I thanked her very much. My home stood as ever; my mother was waiting for me, as always.

I don't remember how I spent my time until October, when my school reopened. The only thing I recall is a visit to my uncle in Kofu where I had fresh grapes from the vineyard to fill my stomach. The beginning of my new life wasn't so bad yet. However, the Japanese newspapers that had always praised us for fighting against the American forces in wartime, now changed their attitude abruptly by 180 degrees, initiating a campaign in admiration of democracy, condemning the military clique and professional soldiers as the incarnation of evil that brought unprecedented disaster to the Japanese people. My mother and I, the widow and son of a professional navy man, were to have all the blame and criticism of the world directed at us.

I went back to the Seijo Middle School in Tokyo and studied until I finished the 5th year of middle school in the spring of 1948. The Japanese educational program was being changed to the American system of 6-3-3 from primary to high school, but in my case I could choose either the old 6-5 system or the new. I chose the former because I had to work. During this two and half year period my life was not so bad under the protection of my mother, although I was always hungry. Food shortages were bad, rations skimpy, delayed and even canceled. Our diet was terrible. We ate the remains of soybeans after the oil was extracted. We made something resembling bread from bran and a little flour that was even worse than chicken feed. Once I had American military rations. The main dish was canned pork chops and beans. It no longer seems exciting at all now, but at that time it tasted like the most delicious meal I had ever had in my life.

Young boys like sweets, but nothing was available. I looked for names of sweets in my dictionary to recall dim memories of tastes I had enjoyed in the good old days. I read a name, for example, Anpan, then the explanation, "a roll stuffed with Japanese sweets." I could smell the faint flavor of poppy seeds on the roll. I sighed from longing for *muhmuh* eclair, a slender-shaped cream puff which I hadn't the pleasure of eating for a few years. One day my friend and I found a bottle of tablets. They tasted sweet and we finished the bottle. Later we found out they were digestion aids, and we were more hungry than before. I don't remember where I first met American soldiers who had been my mortal enemy just a couple of months before. I worked one summer at an American base to earn money. American soldiers were friendly, and I was very attracted to the smell of their dining room.

Soon after the war ended, my mother's bereavement allowance was abruptly cut off. We had to live on savings. The national bonds my mother had bought in good faith out of my father's salary became waste paper. In January, 1946, emergency food supplies were imported to prevent the people from dying of starvation. In February, emergency monetary measures were enforced. All bank deposits were frozen by the government and cash in hand was exchanged for new yen notes issued by the Bank of Japan. I am sure shrewd businessmen were able to rescue some of their fortunes somehow. However, my mother, a simple housewife, lost her life savings. She had thought she had enough money to pay for my education through the university, but it turned into refuse only six months after the surrender of Japan.

My mother took anything that could be bartered for food to the farmers around Kamakura. Her beautiful kimonos and obis (belts) were all consumed in my stomach in less than a year. She told me two interesting episodes about these times. One day she was standing on a crowded train struggling with a big, heavy bundle of food on her back. Suddenly, she was relieved of the burden. Looking behind her, she saw two young American soldiers holding the bundle in their hands. They kept smiling at her until the train arrived at the terminal. She was very happy and said "thank you" to them. It was the first time in her life she had spoken English to any foreigner and she was pleased the Americans understood it. Another day she was again on a crowded train when two American soldiers boarded. They made a speech to the passengers in English. Not understanding, everyone kept silent. The Americans pulled up all the seated men, allowing the women to sit down in their stead. My mother got a seat. At over 90 years of age, my mother told me these stories with a fresh memory and a grin.

The U.S. is a nation of principles. American forces brought a set of national values to Japan and attempted to convince the defeated people of their values. The occupation was accomplished in good order with few exceptions. In my town, a laborer working for the Shinto shrine Tsurugaoka Hachiman Gu was shot to death by an American guard on duty at night, the only unfortunate affair that happened in the peaceful city of Kamakura. At first citizens were extremely tense when Americans appeared, but they were soon relieved by observing the Americans' behavior, and became friendly. I think the Americans had a sense of mission. To my eyes they appeared full of confidence in themselves as well as in their values. They could do everything right.

People were thirsty for literature and arts after the long government control of freedom of speech. In order to satisfy their ardent desire to learn, various books, Western and Japanese, were published, as if the floodgates were broken open. I still keep those books of coarse paper printed in old style type. Whenever I take them out I remember those dark days with nostalgia. Having started with Japanese literature and philosophy, I went through German, English and French. It was desultory reading. For instance, after I covered the major classics such as *The Tale of Genji*, I went down to the contemporary works of Osamu Dazai, Yukio Mishima, via Souseki Natsume, Ougai Mori, the famous writers in the Meiji era. In philosophy I read Kitaro Nishida, Hyakuzo Kurata and Kiyoshi Miki. In foreign literature and philosophy, I was strongly impressed by French existentialism, represented by Jean-Paul Sartre, though I went through Shakespeare, too. Of course I could not miss Immanuel Kant, the great German philosopher, nor Johann Wolfgang von Goethe, the greatest German writer.

They were too difficult and I did not understand what they really meant, but after reading so much, the values in which I believed in my childhood were buried away. I was looking for something to replace them with. Perhaps I was merely looking for another *okami* whom I could serve with the same total dedication and dependence as the emperor. My soul was drifting. Although I was unable to find an instant solution to my problems in those books, they helped me a lot in later years when I encountered Western culture as a businessman.

I had nothing to live for and I had no money, but I was going to be a man soon. It was only natural that I started questioning the meaning of life, and at the same time, began having strong sexual feelings. While still a student, I fell in love for the first time. My girlfriend looked so charming to me, fair complexion, with large beautiful eyes. She was sweet and graceful. Her presence was somewhat like a queen with a cheerful egoism and touch of innocent childishness. She often made everybody laugh with unexpected humor and esprit and I wondered from where she had picked up such funny ideas. Her family environment was similar to mine. Her father and relatives had all been in the service and her living after the war was as tight as mine. I wrote her a letter expressing my feelings for her, and proposed a date. I waited in Hibiya Park, and was rewarded. She appeared on time. The first words she uttered were, "Here I am, as you specified, exactly at 1:30 p.m., March 14, 1948." She made fun of my excess exactness in setting a date and added she liked my letter. We went to a concert in Hibiya Hall and enjoyed an orchestral play of Tchaikovsky's *Pathetique* in the gallery.

We had further dates and exchanged letters for a length of time. I was in love, but I could expect nothing—I was a student with no money or job, and the precepts of bushido to despise acts solely to gain money and profit in the temporal world still held me bound. What I needed was to find an honest job and realize the value of making a peaceful living rather than reading books. However, I could not afford to go to a university, which was the only way to become an elite employee of the government or a private company. I had no particular talent or skill. I could not guarantee my love a decent life. I have no doubt she loved me as much as I loved her but it was not a match for marriage. I lost my first love when she married another man from a rich family. When she and I parted it was raining. In my life, I will never forget her eyes as she looked at me, showing her wordless love. Sometimes I wonder what my life would have been with her had we married. At that time, I was mentally a prisoner of war, just like my ancestors who had been confined in secluded mountain prison camps in the 8th century. I had no way out yet, no way of knowing that I would have a job essentially as a human shield in Japan's economic war similar to my ancestors' role, when they were hunted out of the mountains in the 8th century, as their only method of survival.

My mother was struggling to make a living. She had to work, but work for a nearly middle aged woman with no special talent was limited. She had no choice but to take any job offered to her from time to time. She worked as a waitress, maid and housekeeper. She hid her past. Twice she was given proposals by men she worked for. In both cases the men had wives who were very ill. They offered to pay my tuition which would allow me to graduate from the university. My mother turned them down and changed jobs. After I finished the five year middle school course, I was employed by a small foreign trade company in Tokyo and we moved there, where my mother would be able to find a job more easily. I started as a mail boy in the company because I could read English.

This foreign trading company was established with a capitalization of 195,000 yen, when American GHQ approved the resumption of private foreign trade by Japanese in August, 1947. Its main business was to export toys and various sundries to the U.S. Each sales agreement with a foreign buyer had to be approved by GHQ, and upon receipt of a letter of credit or cash in U.S. dollars, an export declaration was submitted for approval for shipment. In order to fix the price of an export, an application was submitted to the government agency, accompanied by a cost calculation and a case by case exchange rate for U.S. dollars was determined. This system was continued until April, 1949, when the fixed rate of 360 yen to a U.S. dollar was decided. After I finished my mail room work I was in charge of obtaining export licenses. I was required to go to the Board of Foreign Trade daily with the export documents (the Board of Trade became the famous or infamous Ministry of International Trade and Industry— MITI).

The export items were primitive and labor intensive products, such as mechanical toys, Christmas lamps, and other sundries. As an assistant, I often went to toy factories for inspection prior to shipment. We were supplying a cheap product at a cheap price. A lot of women worked the production line. Our inspection standards were quite loose and we often found faulty products. Many of the approved products were poorly finished, and I wondered if Americans would really buy them. We packed them in cartons first, then in wooden cases, marked them with black ink and loaded them on the trucks for transportation to Yokohama.

When I got used to my job, the company was kind enough to provide me with a two room house for my family as company housing for minimum rent. One room was three *tatami* mats (6'x9', 54 square feet). The second was a 6 *tatami* mat room (9'x12', 108 square feet). In addition there was a kitchen and a toilet. My mother asked my grandfather and grandmother, who had been living in the countryside, to come and live with us. Living was very tight but we enjoyed our family life shoulder to shoulder for the time being. Unfortunately, it ended all too soon by the bankruptcy of the company in 1951.

Chapter Thirty

Drifting Soul

One of my former managers established his own company to take over the export business and I joined him. I worked hard in hopes that one day I might become a manager, but my ambitions soon collapsed, because in less than a year this company too went bankrupt. I found a job as a clerk typist in the U.S. Army's furniture and carpentry depot. In the beginning, I was afraid my English wasn't good enough to communicate with the American soldiers. However, it was fine. American soldiers and Japanese colleagues around me were all very kind and helpful in my daily work.

On the U.S. base there was a Pepsi Cola warehouse where we could buy Pepsi for 5 cents, but I soon learned there was a way to have it free of charge, simply by breaking the bottle after drinking and having it disposed of as breakage. My mother found a job as housemother in the dormitory of a pharmaceutical company and I lived with her. My grandfather and grandmother moved in with one of my uncles.

I made friends with an American sergeant in the office. He was black and married to a Korean girl. He was looking for a house and I helped him. There were always plenty of Japanese homeowners advertising in English newspapers looking to rent to Americans, because the rent was very attractive. My American sergeant's housing allowance was US $150 per month. An income of 54,000 yen per month was enormous to the Japanese at that time, and everyone welcomed my telephone inquiry to take a look at his house. But upon seeing the prospective tenants, the homeowner's attitude changed and ended with polite refusal without exception. This was the first time I had been exposed to racial discrimination. I doubled efforts and finally succeeded in finding a place for my friends. The sergeant appreciated my help and took care of me well. Since the couple did not smoke, he let me have their entire monthly allocation of cigarettes at the cost he paid in the P.X., a good deal for me, because I could sell them to Japanese for a much higher price on the black market. The sergeant also let me buy American products from the Sears catalogue, which was a dream for a Japanese. His assignment was short, but I remember him well.

While with the U.S. Army, I experienced my first American Christmas. My life was improving, but I was concerned about my future. Once the American Army decided to go back home or go to some other place I would lose my job. I wanted a more stable life, with opportunities for promotion. One day by chance on the Ginza, I met a German, a member of the board of directors of the former trading company where I had first been employed. He remembered me well. He had recently become a partner in a German trading house, and offered to arrange a job for me. He wrote me a letter a few days later and told me I was employed. This encounter changed my fate drastically.

During my service with the Japanese trading company I learned about two things, drinking and women. At a company party at the president's house in Kamakura, I was offered alcoholic drinks for the first time in my life. I drank sake too quickly and by the end of the party was dead drunk. I passed out and the next morning found myself lying in a strange room. One of the senior employees kindly took me to his house. This was the beginning of my career in drinking. Once I tasted alcohol, I could not stop.

A cashier in the company, an ex-navy pilot who barely survived a kamikaze suicide attack, became my best friend in the company. Both of us worked till 8 p.m. every night, always creating some excuse. Exactly at 8 p.m., we finished the work, he took out 300 yen for each of us from the cash box as our dinner allowance for overtime. Grabbing the money, we went out in downtown Shimbashi, where tiny shacks selling goods from the black market and illegal bars and pubs were crowded side by side.

Shochu (Japanese gin made from potatoes) was being sold illegally for 50 yen. It was officially served as tea in a teacup to cheat the government control of alcoholic drinks. Occasionally a controller checked the pubs, but his inspection schedule was preliminarily leaked to the pub operators. The guests were required to be quiet. When he came in, the *okami*, the proprietress of the house, gave him an envelope, and he normally disappeared quickly. *Tonkatsu* (pork cutlet) was the most expensive meal we could afford. Around Shimbashi station today, I can find several bars and pubs still with the atmosphere of those days, and occasionally I make a sentimental journey to some of them.

Not knowing how to use my excess energy, I often discharged it in reckless fights with other drunken men. My partner was an ex-navy pilot and we were both very strong. One night we had pork cutlet with several glasses of *shochu* and both of us were high. We were on our way to Shimbashi station to go home, carrying the cheerful atmosphere of the pub with us, talking and laughing loudly. As we passed the entrance to the station, a man came from the other side. He didn't avoid me and I didn't avoid him. When we collided in the middle of the entrance, I gave him a lead off blow that triggered a big fight. For several minutes, about twenty people were exchanging blows until the station staff took control.

Sometimes unbelievable things happen in life. One night my seniors took me for drinks after work. With several glasses of *shochu* and food, everybody was inspired and someone said, "Let's have a good time." In high spirits, we went to Yoshiwara, the traditional amusement center in Tokyo. It was my first experience with a woman. It was not as fantastic as I had supposed, and I was rather disappointed. But at the end, I was surprised we did not have enough money to pay for the entertainment, and I was left in the house as a hostage until my seniors could come back to settle the account. Next morning one of them came with money, and I was released. Later I learned they went into the president's room, and in postures of "attention," reported what happened. When the president nodded his approval, everybody made a deep bow, then submitted I.O.U. vouchers for signature to take out the necessary cash to save me.

My job was export clerk handling all shipments. An older Japanese departmental manager with long experience in Chinese trade taught me the basics of foreign trade. He would spend one hour before business hours every morning with me. His training helped me in my whole business career.

By this time, Japanese industrial growth had begun. Japan was exporting light machinery, such as sewing machines, bicycles and small electric motors. Exports to South America, especially to Brazil, were growing at a fast rate. Since the Brazilian government did not permit importation of complete sewing machine heads, we received import licenses for parts only. I had to adjust unit prices to make the commercial invoices correspond exactly to the amount of the license. It was a painstaking calculation and I was given a hand operated mechanical calculator to do the job efficiently. It was my first encounter with a calculator.

We imported various industrial machines made in Germany to Japan. The company represented many first class German manufacturers. A lot of German coal mining machinery was imported free of import duty and sold to mining companies. German heavy chemical technologies, particularly in making rayon and plastics, were licensed to Japanese manufacturers. The quality of German steel was superior to Japanese at that time, and was sold to Japanese industries in large quantity. Items of import later changed to automatic packaging machines, typewriters and electric calculators, reflecting the growth of the Japanese economy.

Foreign trade was severely controlled by MITI (the Ministry of International Trade and Industry). In order to import machinery of foreign manufacture, you had to obtain an import license from MITI. A condition of approval was that the particular machinery could not be made by Japanese manufacturers. My German company imported a bright annealing furnace, state-of-the-art equipment for the electric wire manufacturing industry. The furnace was patented in Germany and the German manufacturer enjoyed good business internationally.

One day, MITI banned the importation because a Japanese maker had begun producing a similar furnace, infringing on German patent rights. The German manufacturer was furious. They stood to lose a very good market because their products were illegally copied by the Japanese competitor. The protest by the German company led MITI to correct the situation later, but this episode shows how tight MITI's control was. The Japanese government was determined to aid the progress of Japanese business and industry by any means.

While at this company I fell in love with another girl. We had many dates; we went to movies and had drinks and snacks afterwards; we made excursions out of Tokyo together. We were very happy. Our relationship was known to everybody in the company and they expected we would sooner or later marry. Our love was very hot. But I had problems to overcome. My mother was working as housemother at the pharmaceutical company, and I could barely make enough to share a room with her. I was living hand to mouth. I had no opportunity of promotion in this company. I was just one of the clerks to handle simple office work and I could not expect a good salary. If I could have found a way to improve my situation, I would have proposed marriage without hesitation.

I had learned about drinking and women; it was now time to turn to learn a third sin: the thrill of gambling caught me, mah jongg and horse racing, in particular. I had beginner's luck and won a great deal of money on my first bets. I dreamed of making a fortune. However, lady luck soon turned against me. I lost heavily and found myself buried in debt. I could find no way out. My love affair came to sudden end when she left me and married another man.

Only much later did I realize that the idea of needing an income to make her happy before marriage was wrong. It was the *okami* idea in myself, the result of an elite education in the cadet school. If I did my best for her, it would have been all right. I should have asked her to share my life. The emptiness in my heart grew. I became addicted to the three sins of drinking, women and money. I wanted money desperately. I borrowed from whomever was available. Money was never enough. My mind was completely devastated and I needed a lot of alcohol to numb my conscience. I accepted vendors' invitations to entertainments. My life was like walking continually on a tightrope high above an arena. For money I could have done things that would have landed me in jail. I was always worried, haunted by fear and conscience. Those were the darkest days in my life.

Unexpectedly, soon after my love affair was broken off, I was transferred to the Osaka Branch and appointed acting manager, which gave me hope to start a new life. I took my mother with me. I went to the horse races during the New Year holidays, taking part of my year end bonus, about 17,000 yen. At the end of three days of betting I had about 200,000 yen. I was able to clear all the debts I had incurred before moving to Osaka. I took over all branch office accounts, expecting to expand business significantly with the sale of electric calculators, the latest products government offices and large business companies were adopting to revolutionize their office work. But I failed. My business experience up to this time was a sort of brokerage for large companies without much risk. But the sale of calculators was a new business for me and I was caught in a trap because of my lack of experience.

Sales of the machine went well, as a matter of fact, but elated with success, I overdid it. One of the dealers was a crook. He signed for a large order of machines, then became suddenly insolvent. I tried to locate and attach the inventory to secure the receivables. My head office sent me an Italian businessman well experienced in this kind of trouble to take command. We found the warehouse where the inventory was stored and went there to negotiate. Suddenly a few gangsters appeared and snatched us away in a car. We were confined in a house and forced to write a check at gunpoint. The Italian wrote a check and the yakuza took it to the bank to cash it. Upon confirmation of cashing, we were released with the inventory. I tried to sell the machines directly to end users, however, in the end, it resulted in significant loss.

This scandal happened just before my marriage. I was introduced to a girl by one of my acquaintances. After several dates I made up my mind to marry her. I proposed and she accepted. The wedding ceremony was performed in Shinto style. An informal and simple wedding party was held at a public facility on November 27, 1963, at a very reasonable cost. Only relatives and a few close friends of both families were invited. A couple of my relatives were kind enough to perform a Noh dance for us. The wife chanted while her husband danced. It was a small but heartwarming party not to be compared with the spectacular wedding parties of today, which are very much spoiled by commercialism.

Our honeymoon tour was a trip to Kyushu. We enjoyed our visit to Nagasaki, Unzen and the national park at Mt. Aso, where famous spas are abundant. When we returned to our apartment, a letter transferring me to Tokyo was waiting, a demotion caused by the scandal. The first memorial service for the crew of my father's ship the Shinano was conducted by Yamagishi that year. Yamagishi kindly sent an invitation to my mother, but she had no money to go down to Kure, due to my marriage.

My wife was a schoolteacher, and she had to take care of her class untill March of the following year, so she remained in Osaka and I returned to Tokyo with my mother, where I was now manager of the technical division of electric calculators. I was surprised by the prices in Tokyo. While I was away in Osaka for five years prices had gone up sharply. With the help of my uncle I was at last able to rent an independent house, though it was an old cottage, in Koganei, a satellite city around Tokyo. This was the start of a new life, commuting to Tokyo on super crowded trains for one hour every morning and evening for the next thirty years.

When my wife rejoined me in Tokyo she was already pregnant, and I became a father in the summer of 1964. The delivery was delayed due to this being a first birth, until finally, late one night, my wife was in labor. Early the next morning I ordered a cab and took her to the hospital. On the way her water broke. I was very upset because I knew nothing about having a baby. My first baby was a girl. It was strangely sweet and touching to hold her in my arms. I will never forget her smile of total reliance on me. Our house was small and old but had an indoor bathroom, although it was primitive. It was the first time since leaving Kamakura, twenty years before, that I was able to enjoy the luxury of an indoor bath with my family. I was happy but my business life was still gloomy.

My new job back in Tokyo was to manage the service department for electric calculators made in Germany and Italy. They were made with iron gears and an electric motor to rotate them. The quality was not first class and breakdowns at customers' offices occurred often. There were constant complaints that machines repaired by servicemen failed right afterwards. I strengthened the servicemen's technical training to improve their repair technique. In order to raise employee morale, I introduced a new evaluation system of annual performance for salary review and bonus incentives as well as for promotional standards. In this private German company these points were neglected and left at the discretion of a German technical manager without clear rules, which spoiled morale.

In order to work out a stimulation and motivation package, I needed to acquire more exact accounting knowledge, and decided to take a night course at a university. Company management did not show much interest in my idea. Competition was getting more difficult as the Japanese market had became important. Some European manufacturers decided to establish their own companies to control distribution in Japan directly, leaving out independent agents. Management's concern was to secure as many distribution rights as possible to keep the company profitable.

Japan was changing drastically. Ikeda, then Prime Minister, took aggressive economic policies under the slogan, "Let's double our income." Japanese businesses were enjoying a series of unprecedented booms and everybody was benefiting from the high rate of economic growth. The *Shinkansen* (bullet train) was built and construction of highways started. In 1964, the 18th Olympic games were held in Tokyo. In 1967, Japan's GNP was ranked second in the Western world. A new era was drawing near, and I thought I should be able to play a more important role. My foresight was correct.

Chapter Thirty One

Dark Days Before The Dawn

While I was looking for an opportunity that would bring meaning to my life, Japan was enjoying the great economic growth that has been called the "Miraculous Recovery from the Ruin of Defeat." From 1955-65, mining and industrial production increased 430%. The average gross national product growth was just over 10% per year for that same period. Although Japan suffered a short recession in 1965, GNP continued to increase by more than 350% in the next 8 years (1965-1973). As a matter of fact, the GNP growth rate between 1955-1973 reached 10½% per annum.

I left the German trading company in the fall of 1965 after 13 years of service, a period of time which roughly corresponds to the "Miraculous Recovery" of Japan. However, as an employee of a small private foreign company, my life was not directly influenced by national progress. For the first ten years, government efforts for economic recovery were concentrated on key industries, such as iron and steel, electric power, mining and railways. As the shipbuilding industry was a priority, the government provided shipbuilders with funds at low interest rates.

In 1954, this special interest rate caused a scandal involving cabinet ministers and political leaders. Prime Minister Sato was accused of taking bribes from Showa Denko, a Japanese corporation. For the first time in Japan's modern history, the Minister of Justice exercised authority over the public prosecutor, and stopped him from arresting the Prime Minister, an action which saved the rule of the Liberal Democratic Party. The affair shook the foundation of separation of powers between the three branches of government. However, the decision was rewarded when in 1956, Japan's shipbuilding industry became number one in the world. Japanese industries recovered quickly from then on. Having laid the groundwork, over the next ten years, the Japanese economy expanded into many industrial areas, including consumer durables.

What sort of role would I play under such circumstances? I was struggling to find a new direction, but looking back, I realize my fate was already determined. While working for the German company, I had become an expert in electric calculators, a star product in the office machine field. I was good at English, aware of Western culture, and my knowledge and skills, while not perfect, were sufficient for business purposes.

The role I was fated to play was essentially the same as my ancestors in ancient Japan, a sort of "human shield" to fend off enemy flying arrows, using two swords, one in each hand, in the battle's advance-guard. Before my big chance came, however, I had to go through one final ordeal.

When I received retirement money from the company, I immediately headed out to the race track, dreaming the same thing that happened when I was transferred from Tokyo to Osaka several years back would happen again. Unfortunately, I lost my entire stake in a single day. I was in debt and had no income to support my family other than unemployment insurance. A friend introduced me to a company where I became employed, but the company went bankrupt three months after I joined. I was desperate.

A unique, domestically manufactured calculator had attracted my attention at the Tokyo Business Show. It operated on the same logic as a computer, with on/off relay components performing the same function as "0" or "1" in the computer. In the early 1960's there had been a report of a transistorized electronic desktop calculator successfully developed in the U.S. and the UK. In Japan, two well known international companies, one in cameras and another in electric consumer durables, announced the same kind of calculators in 1964. The relay calculator manufacturers also announced an electronic calculator model in the fall of 1965. The age of electronics had arrived, and I knew Japan would play an important role in the field. I presumed the calculator company would want to market their products worldwide, and would need personnel who knew calculators and foreign markets. I was right; they were indeed looking for someone like me. I suggested sending offers to my business connections in Europe to determine interest in the product. Casio, the then small, unknown calculator company, would await replies from my sources before hiring me.

Then, less than three weeks later, I received unanimously positive replies from my friends in Europe, and was finally hired by Casio as first manager of their foreign trade department. My job was to market the most up-to-date product of the new electronic age worldwide. It was March, 1966; I was 35 years old, and for the first time, had a job I could be proud of. I would make this opportunity a success. It was my war.

Before the advent of electronic desktop calculators, world markets were dominated by mechanical calculators manufactured by American and European makers: Friden, Monroe, Merchant, SCM Hamann, Dhiel, and Lagomarsino were leading brands. The calculators were made with iron gears and levers; the principle of calculation was the same as hand operated machines, except that an electric hand motor drove the mechanism. These foreign made machines were imported by Japanese agents and distributed throughout the country. There were electric adding machines, multipliers and full four function machines.

Price depended upon function. The price of a four function machine was around 400,000 yen, while a printing calculator was more expensive. Dhiel, a German company that made printing calculators, at that time seemed invincible. 400,000 yen was a heavy price, and only government offices and big companies could afford the machines.

In the two years after the electronic desktop calculator was announced, ten manufacturers were in and out of Japan, using different systems: a cathode ray tube display was first adopted by foreign manufacturers but proved too expensive; then a nixie tube display was used. Using the nixie tube, Casio developed a display system to show only the entered number or answer in the calculation sequence, and this system became the popular method among manufacturers.

The company finished its export model in 1966. That July, I took five units to the National Office Machine Association Convention at the Palmer House in Chicago. Since the machines were delicate, they had to be carried into the plane cabin by an electronic service engineer by special permission of the airline. The reaction of American dealers was excellent. Many inquiries were received, but we had no proper distribution organization yet; the purpose of showing the machines in Chicago was merely to assess the market. The model exhibited was a basic 4 function calculator with a 10 digit capacity, a constant and a memory, and it weighed about 5 kgs. In the 1980's, a handheld basic model with an even better function, weighing only 150 grams, was sold for only US $4.99 in tens of millions of units per year. In 1966, the original machine's retail price was supposed to be US $1200. One dealer commented, "If we can sell it for $500, it will be a fantastic business."

The Chicago trade show was my first overseas trip. Travel to foreign countries was strictly controlled at that time. First, one had to buy

U.S. dollars. I was requested to submit an application to the Ministry of Finance with a letter explaining who I was, the purpose of the trip, and if it would bring revenue in dollars to Japan later. I visited six government offices, the Ministry of Finance, the Ministry of International Trade and Industry, the Ministry of Education, the Ministry of Foreign Affairs, the Economic Planning Agency and the Bank of Japan. After all this I received US $3075 in cash and traveler's checks for a fifty day trip, to include visiting European countries following Chicago. Credit cards were not yet available and all expenses—communications, ground transportation, hotel accommodations, meals—were to be paid with the allotted dollars.

Casio's size was still relatively small, with annual sales from April 1965 through March 1966 just under 1.2 billion yen (US $3.33 million at the then prevailing exchange rate of 360 yen to the dollar). It was a very important investment for the company to exhibit the product at the show, and to make a market survey, accessing the market's vast, hidden potential. The Western world was totally unknown to us. My job was to carry back as much information as possible.

I was confident our products would be well accepted and that business would grow rapidly. My objective was to make the company number one in the world. To add encouragement, many colleagues came to see me off at the airport, and in loud voices, shouted "Banzai!" at the boarding gate. I appreciated their gesture, but it was a bit embarrassing. As my plane was going to take off, I felt the pressure of the responsibility that was on my shoulders. "I've got to win," I said to myself. Enjoying a deluxe steak dinner, my expectations expanded as I considered strategies and approaches. This was, I thought, like war; I would have to win or the company would die. Perhaps my father had a similar feeling when he made his departure on the Shinano's maiden voyage.

As the long flight was about to end I could see the North American continent spreading below me. It was huge far beyond my imagination. The American way of life was a dream for all Japanese; the U.S. was like a bright shining star, and everything American was superior. I thought if the Japanese had known the gigantic size of America, we would never have gone to the war. Ignorance can be a tragedy.

I landed in Vancouver, B.C. It was a Sunday, a dry day in British Columbia, and so I was compelled to spend my first memorable North American night without a toast. After a few visits to dealer prospects in Vancouver, I continued east to Toronto, and from there flew to New York, where I met the staff of the US subsidiary of a Japanese trading company (Sogo Shosha) with whom I had contacts in Tokyo. We had a series of meetings about the possible distribution of the product in the U.S., and I learned from them that American business practices were entirely different from Japanese. To do business in the U.S., it was absolutely necessary to have legal knowledge. If the company should become involved in adverse legal entanglements, we would miss the opportunity of success, no matter how good our products were. A word of caution was advisable.

Workfree weekends and holidays were a pressure for me, since no progress could be made in business. But on the other hand, everything in New York was new and interesting. I took walks on streets, looking up at the skyscrapers lined up on both sides. The scenery was strange. In Tokyo we had no skyscrapers yet. One day I went to the Radio City Music Hall, where I enjoyed a film starring Audrey Hepburn, followed by a stage show. In one of the acts beautiful dancers (the Rockettes) staged a famous scene in which American Marines were putting up the Stars and Stripes on Mt. Suribachi in Iwo Jima. All the Americans I met were so friendly they made me forget the war, but it was a lesson to me: I should not forget that we had been the defeated enemy twenty years ago.

Life in American hotels was quite comfortable, except for bathing. The Japanese way of bathing is to dip the entire body into plenty of warm water to relax. I tried various positions but the American bathtub is too shallow to accommodate. Tipping was a problem because in Japan we do not have the habit. I had to calculate quickly in my head, and in most cases I gave too much. Food was expensive. Breakfast ranging from $2.00 to $2.50 plus a 10% tip was out of my budget. The price of meat was much cheaper than in Japan, to my satisfaction. I became used to having a sandwich for lunch, since I could save both on time and money. My favorite was corned beef. I loved the enormous thickness of the corned beef in comparison to the paper thin ham of a Japanese sandwich. In the evening I mostly had Chinese food. It was the least expensive and most familiar to me other than Japanese. At that time there was only one Japanese restaurant in downtown New York, and the price was prohibitive.

Placing my order with the waiter was sometimes a problem, and I probably often appeared stupid. When I was embarrassed, my American friends helped me. Life in the U.S. was much more friendly and easier than I had imagined.

With many unforgettable experiences and a great deal of business information, I left New York for London at the beginning of August. I was going to see my old German friend, who was well informed on the European calculator market, and to have a look at the situation myself. I visited my friend at his home in Zurich and discussed possible distribution of the products in Europe. We came to an agreement on strategy. I promised that I would ask the company to employ him for European operations. After I returned to Japan, the company approved my plan to open a liaison office in Zurich, and did appoint my friend manager for European distribution.

The first export of our electronic calculators was made to Australia, upon my return from Europe. The distributor, a subsidiary of a large US office machine manufacturer, was eager to get the product into the Australian market earlier than anyone else. We were still reluctant to sell products outside Japan, beyond the reach of our own servicemen. Product reliability had not yet been established. We did place a small fan inside the body. As soon as power was on, the fan would turn, cooling the electronic components, preventing heat buildup that could cause malfunction. Ultimately we could not resist the Australians' enthusiasm, and agreed to let them have the machines on trial. Our fear was founded. Reliability became a serious problem, and all the machines had to later be replaced at no cost to the distributor. To us, this was a small business that ended unsuccessfully, but actually, it brought an unexpected serendipity at a later date, in 1970. The Australians liked the way we treated the problem and when the management staff of their U.S. parent company visited them they told them about us. The U.S. parent company was planning to market electronic calculators on an OEM (Original Equipment Manufacturer) base and was looking for the proper manufacturer. The company contacted us and we came to an agreement. Thus, trust fostered in settling trouble led us to a big business.

In April, 1967 a new model was exhibited at the Hannover Fair, and in September, we concluded an OEM agreement with another American company. Business started rolling quickly, and I was busy organizing Casio's Foreign Trade Department. The first problem I encountered in Europe was the power of distributors. When I set up the Zurich office, we were the third Japanese company to market electronic calculators in European markets. The Japanese manufacturers who preceded us were both internationally known big companies who had already picked off the number one and two calculator distributors in each country; only third level distributors were left for my choice, which meant we would have to remain number three in market share. One might think there would be a way to become number one based on the product itself; however, experience shows that is next to impossible.

Misfortunes never come one at a time. There was trade friction among European manufacturers of electric calculators. Their sales had declined sharply and it was now clear this would become a serious problem between Japan and Europe. Our Ministry of International Trade and Industry did not want trouble with Europe so in industry circles they made *gyosei shido* (to oblige businesses to follow their instructions without legislation of laws) to voluntarily restrict the export of electronic calculators to Europe.

Export allocations were given to manufacturers according to percentages of their total export from Japan the previous year, a system which protected preceding manufacturers. It seemed impossible to reverse the market share as long as these restrictions were in effect. However, advances in technology made it possible to develop an entirely new product, personal calculators, a different category. The products were small, light, easy to use, and inexpensive, around $40-50. And the market size was much larger than the business market. We could talk about thousands of millions instead of tens of millions. Sales channels were changed from dealers to consumers. This caused a lifting of restrictions and put everyone at the starting gate again. We were in luck.

The OEM agreement with the giant American office machine company was ready to be fine tuned. For this, I had to spend three and a half months in New York, meeting their lawyer in Rockefeller Center almost every day. My American attorney and I came to a complete understanding of each other in the course of negotiations and became good friends. On September 15th, 1970, the agreement was finally signed. My lawyer congratulated me with tears in his eyes and a bill for $20,000, a sum which made me do a double take. But I soon found it meant very little, compared to the profits that resulted from the agreement.

The quality standards demanded by the buyer were very high compared to our standards. It was necessary to translate the agreement into Japanese and distribute copies to all factory managers and engineers in order to tighten quality controls. If we failed to meet the standards set forth in the agreement, the company would incur great losses. This improved the quality and reliability of the products dramatically. Improvements in production technology made it possible to mass-produce high quality calculators in huge quantities, and sell them in the vast international markets without fear of claims or a heavy burden of sales after service net. Our OEM business expanded greatly in just a few years' time, contributing to our growth and bottom line.

The development of a consumer calculator changed the market totally and opened up the golden era of new electronics. My dark days of struggle were finally ending, and I was going to enjoy a series of great successes in international markets. Looking back, I find the most significant management decision was the change from relay calculator to electronic calculator in 1965. It is difficult to give up a successful technology, yet the company decided to go for a new technology when the market showed signs of change. It was the right decision.

One cannot escape from destiny or tragedy. European electric calculator manufacturers were so good at mechanical electric calculator manufacturing technology that they dominated world markets. They had large investments they could not simply throw away. They delayed decisions, and once they missed the chance, there was no way to catch it again. None of them survived the new electronic era.

Ironically sometimes it is not weakness that causes failure, but success. If Japan should fall, it will be because of her success and merit—the loyalty of the Japanese to the emperor, to the president of company, to seniors. All that made Japan a successful economy could hurt her at the end of the day.

Chapter Thirty Two

New Age of Electronics

The 20 years in which I worked for Casio was the beginning of the age of electronics. New technology began with transistors and diodes on printed circuit boards, which soon developed to integrated circuits (IC), first from small scale, then to very large scale integration (VLSI). In the summer of 1972, Casio announced the first in the world 6 digit extended display handheld calculator capable of addition, subtraction and 12 digits in multiplication and division. It was approximately 7" x 4" and weighed less than 2 pounds. Gimbel's in New York was the first retailer to sell this model in the U.S, and on opening day, a long line extended around the block. The first model was sold for $59.95. Phone calls from all over the world—from department stores and discounters who wanted to sell the product—came in the entire day at the company's U.S. subsidiary (established in 1970). It was wonderful but we had a big problem.

Our production plan was 50,000 units monthly, an enormous quantity compared with past records. We had thought it was realistic in view of the extraordinarily low price, but the 6 digit capacity was a concern—could we really sell that quantity? To hedge the risk, the company concluded an original equipment manufacturing (OEM) agreement with an American company to cover a certain percentage prior to production. The product was very well accepted by worldwide markets, and we found production far short of demand. I was pressed hard by distributors but had no way to comply with their requests; the gap was too big. In such a contract, the seller wants to make sure the buyer takes products regularly without fail, while the buyer wants flexibility, including a right to cancel orders without compensation, if possible.

With the strength of our new product, I could obtain a contract favorable to the seller. The American OEM buyer naturally took all allocations and offered to take more. Ironically, contract provisions making the OEM definitely take the products turned out as barriers for diverting certain quantities to distributors of their own brand name. I had to wait for an increase in production and meanwhile I had to take all the blame.

Seeing the great success of the world's first personal calculator, I was convinced we would be number one before long. The markets we created were vast and we could not afford giving anything away to competitors. (As mentioned in the previous chapter, we came into the market third, and in voluntary allocation were fixed there; but in consumer markets we were first and free. I thought it was a matter of sales net which had to be reorganized to cover consumer channels.)

Company sales were growing rapidly, from only 1.2 billion yen when I was first employed in 1966 to 10 billion yen when the company went public four years later. Capital was increased quickly, too. The company's stock listing on the Tokyo Securities Exchange remarkably helped improve our financial position. At the same time, a new factory was built to increase production. Product quality and reliability improved remarkably by new quality control measures. Preparations to challenge the number one position had been started; now we would make it happen.

Becoming number one was our raison d'etre. The position brings advantages in business: vendors give number one the best terms and prices; inventions and new technological information are automatically offered first. Circumstances work favorably for number one.

The balance sheet of our U.S. subsidiary was improving with the sales of consumer models, but despite efforts, European sales did not show satisfactory growth. My attention was focused on the European markets. It was essential to find powerful distributors who trusted me and were willing to invest heavily in marketing. I thought it best to distribute and market the products myself in one of the European countries to prove my strategy worked fine and was profitable. I was going to demonstrate how to sell; it was the shortest way to become number one.

Market research convinced me to establish a subsidiary for experimental distribution in the U.K., and also to locate our European headquarters there. At that time, our market share in the U.K. was very poor, but since I spoke only a few words of French and German, English was convenient. My plan was approved by the board. I was appointed director in 1972 and had served since then; yet I had to find a partner of Western nationality.

Through the OEM business with an American company I became acquainted with a sales executive stationed in London. He was Irish-American, married to an English lady. I was impressed by his executive leadership and extensive knowledge about calculator products and markets, and thought he was best qualified to run the U.K. subsidiary and European headquarters. I made contact with him and we met in the U.S., where we discussed terms of employment and came to an agreement. He was appointed managing director and I positioned myself as resident director of the parent company in charge of strategy and coordination. We worked together for three years; he became my lifelong friend, and in fact assisted a great deal in writing this book.

After all preparations were in order, I left Tokyo for London in July, 1975. My American friend was waiting for me. We went to a solicitor's office and bought a company off the shelf, but ran into immediate difficulty when we tried to rename it to that of the parent company in Japan. As the English had registered the name of our choice some time before, it was illegal to use the name. As a result, we were compelled to start operations with the logo of our parent as a trade name. We resolved the problem by the end of the year, when my American associate arranged to have the registered British company name transferred to our subsidiary.

We temporarily rented a small room at Great Sutton Street, with five persons, our American managing director, his secretary, two other Japanese and myself as staff. The managing director had several English friends engaged in the sale of office machines whom we contacted one by one. When I explained we planned to sell millions of calculators and become number one in U.K. markets, to some, our plan seemed speculative, and they were suspicious of its feasibility. By October we came to agreements with each of them, and a small but excellent sales force was organized. They immediately commenced calling on prospects for our first Christmas sale. Meanwhile, the first shipment of about 70,000 calculator units had arrived in London.

Our strategy was to maximize sales per head with "best value for the money" prices. Aggressive pricing, and sales through major multiple chains such as W.H. Smith, Dixons, Boots, Curry's etc., were the key. However, to my regret, none of them was selling our calculators. We made special offers and explained our policy that "best value for the money" pricing would assure quick movement over the counters to consumers, leaving good net profits as originally planned, due to no inventory losses. Quantity discount was carefully built into our pricing. We did not want the major stores to buy too much and build up excess stocks. We wanted them to sell as much as they bought in a month and come back with an empty stomach. When we said "sell," it meant the products were actually sold to the consumer.

Buyers' common fear is loss from disposing of dead stock, sometimes even below cost. Losses could be heavy. Lack of information on release of new models often made buyers commit blunders. To make room for launching new models, from time to time, manufacturers made special offers for current models which some buyers grabbed for the attractive price. Then about the time the stores were ready with products in hand they would see big advertisements in the papers and learn that new models with better functions were being released at much lower prices. Special deals turned out losses and it soured the buyers.

The parent company was well-known for launching hit models quite often in short intervals. It was also the price leader. The cost of calculators went down sharply at annual rates of 30% and doubled the markets year by year. Buyers found our products attractive and exciting, but their fears increased since there was no orderly marketing.

While official distributors were selling few calculators through dealer sales net, conventional sales outlets for office machines, parallel importers were selling briskly into consumer retail channels at random. The prices of our calculator were competitive today, the shops could enjoy a good profit, but perhaps tomorrow they would have to take losses by dumping stock. Buyers could stock products today but might find it impossible to do so tomorrow. All machines were flown in by air, an expensive means of transportation, but better than losing money through price erosion during transportation by sea. Our products were sold to consumers without proper guarantee and after sales service. Markets were in chaos and buyers could not escape the nightmare of seeing ads of competitors across the street offering the same calculators for much lower prices than theirs.

This was the prime reason major chains did not take our product. My efforts were focused on how to eliminate elements obstructing sales. I told buyers I was the resident director of the parent and fully informed of future lineup; I would be able to hold them safe from damage incurred in coordinating sales and production. To endorse my words, we gave price protection for a reasonable period. I emphasized the relationship between the stores and ourselves should be that of reliable partners in selling and marketing our products. Good communication and cooperation were essential. I pointed out, "If you trust me or not is no matter. The result will soon tell where the truth lies. Why not test my words?" To be really competitive in the market, particularly against parallel importers' pricing, we were compelled to work on paper-thin gross margins. The lowest priced model was pound sterling 4.95, an epoch making price for a state-of-the-art electronic calculator at that time.

Consumers reacted as expected. The first U.K. Christmas campaign wound up a huge success; the shipment from Japan sold out. Although we did our best, most of the major stores did not join us. We had to depend upon sales of small and medium sized stores who could move faster.

It took great power to turn into first gear. Our Christmas sales success set us on the right track. Our encouraging balance for the six month period up to the end of fiscal 1976 was plus minus zero. The English proverb says, "Perseverance prevails." The Japanese proverb says, "Sit on the stone for three years." Continuous efforts to put our products into chain stores were duly rewarded in two years, and our sales increased dramatically. We stuck to our original policy, and by the end of the third year gained buyers' trust and came to a complete understanding with them on our way of business.

We saw tremendous growth in sales. By the end of 1979, our marketshare had increased from a few percent to 23 percent. 780,000 calculators were sold that year. Sales forecasts became most important. In order to sell more, we had to stock our warehouse with more products. But prices were still eroding quickly. If we bought too much from Japan we would lose a great deal of money. Lead time was several months from placing an order to the arrival of products at our London warehouse. We had two major sales events in a year: back to school and Christmas. The products for the back to school campaign should be shipped by the end of April at the latest and for Christmas by the end of July, meaning orders had to be placed by the end of December and March respectively. Once the products were imported, they needed to be sold out via any means possible.

Profitability of the subsidiary was dependent upon the accuracy of a purchase plan covering at least six months ahead. It was my responsibility to provide Japan with this plan so they could program production. I was required to foresee sales of about 3,000 products over the six month period precisely based on an objective evaluation of the products vs. markets. A combination of both a rational and scientific approach as well as insight to forecast potential evolution in markets such as "expansion price down" was very important. But above all, I would point out, the guts or fighting spirit of the manager was most important. In order to become number one, we had to import enough quantities into U.K. However confident of the plan I was, I still was afraid of buying too much, which would result in big losses. It was a big gamble; I bore the pressure. In essence, my role was similar to that of my ancestors who dashed at the enemy, fending off flying arrows with two swords in each hand, as human shields in the civil war age from the 15th to the 16th centuries. If successful, I might become a samurai with armor and weapons stripped off bodies I killed in war, and eventually even become a daimyo if I were lucky enough.

My plan was based on at least a dozen "ifs:" if the parent R & D could develop new models in scheduled time; if the factory could produce at estimated cost without trouble; if competitors could not launch better models for lower prices; if there was no earthquake in Tokyo, no war, no general strike in the U.K....if, if, if...no one could be sure if we could maintain the original plan. But to become number one, I had to gamble with a will of steel. If I made one mistake, the subsidiary could be mortally wounded.

Worldwide markets were expanding tremendously. Our parent company was growing fast. Sales in fiscal 1976 were just under 45 billion yen. In six years they were up 2.8 times. This extraordinary growth was made possible due to the quick progress of semi-conductor technologies, which brought down prices of components sharply and also enabled remarkable product diversification. For instance, in the early days after the advent of integrated circuits, there was no room on a chip to accommodate complete circuits for both functions of percentage and square root, in addition to four functions plus one memory. There was serious debate as to which function to be selected, either the percentage key or the square root key. At our head office in Tokyo, I joined a heated discussion over the issue. We reached our conclusion as morning light beamed into the conference room. Before long, technological developments made it possible to produce chips of much greater capacity and to design smaller, thinner calculators with much more sophisticated functions, such as scientific calculators, at much lower cost.

In order to become number one in the fierce "electronic calculator war," as Japanese journalists termed it, in which forty major manufacturers were fighting worldwide, we took an aggressive strategy to penetrate into all channels available—chain stores, stationary and electronics shops, department stores, discounters etc., as quickly as possible with a plan to obtain a marketshare of over 50% in each channel. Also, by increasing the number of models and categories, it was possible to increase sales fast.

The best-value-for-the-money pricing policy based on minimal percentage of gross margin and maximum sales per head was firmly maintained by the subsidiary throughout the time I was in London. During back to school and Christmas season, our advertisements coordinated with the plans of major chain stores to maximize impact on

British consumers. For that purpose we provided all accounts with 3% cooperative advertising allowance on the amount of purchase, sharing 50% of advertising costs.

Investment in our trademark paid off very well. In several years, it built up a strong brand image of number one across the country. Our products were able to compete very well against southeast Asian markets. Our marketshare rose year by year and exceeded 50% in 1983, the eighth year after our foundation. Just a year later I returned to headquarters in Tokyo. My original plan was to finish my assignment in three years and then go back to Japan, leaving everything to my American partner. However, I had to change plans since Tokyo management requested his transfer to an American subsidiary, and he left the U.K. in 1978. I took over his position and control of European markets, which prolonged my stay in London till the spring of 1982. A joint managing director system of British and Japanese succeeded me.

During my assignment, three more products were added: electronic digital watches, electronic cash registers and electronic musical keyboards. I employed sales managers and sales forces specializing in each product and organized new divisions, all of which were supervised by a British general manager. The last fiscal year of my term, annual sales exceeded 10 billion yen for the first time. Also for six consecutive fiscal years, I could show reasonable net profit after taxes on the balance sheets, the most remarkable results among the company's three overseas subsidiaries.

I was very lucky. Here is one episode to indicate it. Electronic digital watches were first developed by the parent company around 1974. First generation watches were too big, thick and expensive. Liquid crystal display was employed to tell time but no one knew for sure how long it would last because only a few years had elapsed since it was developed. By 1978, drawbacks were improved significantly, and new functions added, such as calculator, chronometer, water resistant and multi-display times. Markets were expected to boost dramatically in 1979.

The parent R & D had developed several new models. I saw samples and was convinced they would be sensational sellers in the U.K. I thought it was a marvelous opportunity, and had the marketing staff plan an extensive TV advertising campaign for Christmas sales. Normally TV commercial broadcasting was scheduled beginning at the end of October and continued through mid-December. To make sure consumers would understand the new products' features, I decided to make a two step TV campaign: first, a light campaign in September, with the main campaign in November and December. I coordinated major chain stores to place their newspaper advertising campaigns at same time.

The first alarm came at the beginning of June. Tokyo proposed to cut down 1/3 of the quantities allocated to us due to initial difficulty in production. I urgently requested Tokyo stick to the original plan, in view of our commitments with TV and to our major customers. Everybody was complaining, including the domestic sales division, U.S. and German subsidiaries. While I was still begging for supplies, I was shocked by a sudden notice that delivery would be delayed by a few months. If I took the entire shipment by air, they would arrive barely in time for the last TV campaign we had planned. September was nearing. I did not know what to do. I could ask the major multiples to stop advertisements but there was no way to cancel the September TV campaign. A substantial amount of money was going to be wasted. Then kamikaze (the wind of god) blew and pulled me out of the predicament. The TV labor unions went on strike and there was no broadcasting during September. Although our watch supplies were tight, nevertheless, our Christmas campaign was a great success.

Our U.K. operation was fine, but on the European continent the situation was quite different. I made a mistake. I should have made more effort to look for reliable and financially sound distribution partners on an exclusive basis in each country, in order to carry out the same strategy that had proven successful in the U.K. But the difficulty in finding proper distributors, particularly in large countries like France, Germany, Italy and Spain made me look for an easier way. In a small country, it is not so difficult to find a distributor with enough power to cover entire markets. I had no problem, for example, in the Scandinavian countries, Belgium and Holland.

Big and decentralized, Germany was typical. It is very difficult to find nationwide distributors in Germany. There was no other choice but to distribute ourselves. So we established a subsidiary in a joint venture with a Japanese *sogo shosha* (general trading company), our first joint venture in Europe.

In other large countries where I could not find a good distributor, I tried non-exclusive distribution by multiple distributors, but results were poor. I spent three days a week traveling in Europe in an effort to improve sales, but it did not work. In April, 1976 European sales hit a record low, a shock that was enough to make me stop smoking. Things always have two faces: I was permanently liberated from the smoking habit.

I made up my mind to change policy. I said to myself, "Do what I am really convinced of so that there will be no regret left in my mind if

I have to die as a human shield." I stopped the multiple distributor system right away. The system was against the European mentality. I decided to find reliable partners however much time it might take. Since headquarters was convinced of the multi-distributor system it was not an easy decision to make.

I started reorganizing the European sales net immediately. It took several years, but in the 1980's efforts were rewarded. I appointed forty distributors country by country for four products and had long conversations about marketing policy. Success in the U.K. made my arguments convincing, and eventually complete understanding was reached. Sales went up gradually and steadily. Meanwhile, I learned the European way of doing business. Changes were slow to take hold, but once they started moving they would keep going steadily until one day they would be done. Once a brand was established, consumer loyalty was much stronger than in the U.S.

From the beginning, I thought there would be no problem carrying out my strategy in the U.K., because I controlled my staff; however, later I learned I was wrong. It made no difference to convince employees or independent distributors of my strategy. I now believe independent distributors are better than subsidiaries if the right ones are selected. It is their own business; they have a stronger motivation. It goes without saying the character of the manager counts.

My marketing philosophy in short is to consistently give consumers maximum satisfaction in the best value for their money, presenting a wide range of products for their choice. The perceptive consumer will find the concept behind the products sooner or later. Whenever I see a big discount like 50% off, I imagine the manufacturers' marketing concept is wrong somewhere. The list price has been artificially jacked up high; therefore after the 50% discount the relationship between price and value comes into balance. My idea is to sell out products at "best value for the money" prices from the start so that it will not be necessary to dump dead stock later; taking losses before they really come up assures a reasonable profit.

During the electronic calculator war, the major chain stores could enjoy profits 8% above average on our products because of our pricing. To realize my idea I needed the shortest possible distribution to reach retail, and I found the chain stores were the right channel. Some managers think it is dangerous to work on a thin profit margin. My experience is the opposite. It is more dangerous to work on a high gross margin and sit on inventory. If sales go well on the strength of "best value for the money," product will flow from the manufacturer to retailers without interruption, leaving everybody—component suppliers, sub-contractors, manufacturers, distributors and retailers—reasonable profits.

In my philosophy, management must be creative, including R & D, production and sales executives. This means directors and executives must be independent thinkers, allowed freedom in conception, encouraged by management.

Japan's postwar economic success was brought about by the initiative of creative entrepreneurs free from constraints of the vertical society, who were able to commercialize inventions and technologies developed by Western nations during the war. Some, like Sony, were great successes. But many failed. In the ruins of war these challengers had nothing to lose. They could not but charge as "human shields," without regret. These entrepreneurs' challenging efforts met with faithful dedication by employees made to believe in the idea of the "family" company. It is often said that it is the Ministry of International Trade and Industry who has made Japanese business and industry so successful. I disagree. While the government protected against foreign competitors, what actually led to success has been the entrepreneurs' creativity and traditional values of the vertical society employees have held. We have done it, not the government.

Time flies like an arrow. Entrepreneurs who became successful daimyos have passed away or gotten old. The basic inventions and technologies which gave Japanese industry such wonderful opportunities have now been used up, causing a serious slowdown in economic growth. New innovations are yet to be seen. Because of blunders in economic policy, Japan's financial system is in danger. It is Japan's turn to contribute to the world in return for the success she has enjoyed so much. This will be difficult. Everyone cries Japan needs radical change; yet nobody realizes this means a complete change in polity.

Chapter Thirty Three

The British Way of Life

My life in London began in July, 1975. The weather was fine, and though I did not realize it at the time, a blessing to a middle-aged oriental stranger who had come here to establish a distribution company. Only after I had fully experienced the English weather did I understand, and come to know why British people yearn for tropical climate so much. Long daylight hours was an adjustment. In Japan the sun sets before 7 p.m. even in summer, and I am tuned to feel relieved of work when it gets dark; my day is then over, and I can enjoy a glass of beer to conclude it. But in Britain, the sun never went down, which constantly said "Work!" to me. It also made me feel a bit guilty to drink alcoholic drinks in daylight.

Lunch at a pub was a new experience. Our first office in the cleaning company soon became too small and we moved to another one in the city. Only a few steps across the street was a pub where all of us had sandwiches and a half pint of lager or bitters for lunch. The Japanese do not drink at lunch except on special occasions when entertaining guests. Alcohol in the daylight made my head dull. It took me a couple of years to become adjusted and impervious to it. When I saw a pub was full of people grasping mugs, high on beer Friday afternoons, and realized they had just cashed a week's pay at the bank and came straight here, I wondered if people in U.K. worked only four and a half day weeks.

Japanese society has been traditionally generous to the drunk. At parties, too much drinking is usually overlooked. In izakaya (Japanese pubs) drunken people can be found laughing or crying loudly, sometimes quarreling and fighting. I found Europeans are not as tolerant as the Japanese; they are much stronger against alcohol. I once saw a Swedish friend imbibe five *go* masu of sake four times in less than an hour. (Masu is a traditional square shaped wooden measure used for drinking cold sake. Five *go* is about 1.6 pints. Sake, as the reader may know, is rice wine with approximately 16% alcohol content). Cold sake tastes sweet and is smooth to drink, but will get to you suddenly sometime later. Strong as the Swede was, he crawled back to his hotel. It was the only occasion I saw a European get really drunk in public.

The Japanese have a substance in the body called aldehyde, which when combined with alcohol, forms acetaldehyde, which causes terrible hangovers the next morning. Westerners do not have this substance. It was curious to me seeing people waiting in a queue for the opening of pub in the morning. I was also amazed at the government's control of the sales of alcoholic drinks. At certain hours of the day sales of alcohol at pubs, bars and restaurants are prohibited, and shelves selling alcohol in department stores and supermarkets closed. When my friends and I finished a round of golf and wanted to make a toast, we were forced to drink milk, if the timing was bad.

Physical differences between Japanese and Westerners appeared in various phases of life. The Japanese main diet is rice. Rice takes longer to absorb in the bowels, and our bowels are much longer than those of Westerners, our feces more voluminous and stronger smelling. Some Westerners find this unpleasant; this kind of thing could be the seed of trouble. Westerners say Japanese smell fishy, but we can't smell ourselves; to us, Westerners smell of meat and milk. These differences come from the main diet of each culture.

My family was due to arrive in the spring, and for nine months I was going to live the life of a bachelor in London. I rented a small flat on George Street, on the second floor, or in the English way, the first floor. Right below my room was a Japanese restaurant. It was convenient, but a quick lunch in a Japanese restaurant cost 2.00-2.50 pounds, while it was only 50-52 pence at a pub. Japanese dinners were enormously expensive, so I decided to cook myself.

Electric rice cookers, in which just a push of a button cooked the rice, were widely in use, but I found this awkward, since I had never used one before. Due to my military school training, I could cook rice with a hango (military rice cooker), so I had put it in my luggage in anticipation of need. I pulled it out and tested it on the electric heater (usually charcoal or wood fire is used) and found that strong heat from the 240V heater was excellent for cooking rice. My skill in heat control cooked California rice to my taste very well. Cooking dinner started at 9 pm, and my Japanese staff joined me every night in my small kitchen. To let rice steam for a while, the cooker should be turned upside down when finished. The best way to time it was to hit the cooker with a spoon and listen to the sound. If it was clear, the rice was ready for serving. My neighbors were to hear mysterious sounds every night. One of us, our chief cook and bottle washer, could make only one dish, Chinese fried vegetables with eggs. We all had to keep this menu until our bachelor life ended.

Along Finchley Road was a Japanese food store where we went every Saturday to shop for the tastes of our homeland. At business lunches I would test all kinds of European drinks and dishes. I wanted to study the European diet. In wines, I began with German Rhine and Mosel whites, then went on to claret and burgundy, and to Spanish and Italian wines when I was traveling around Europe. In cuisine, I liked Italian the best; pastas and fish were wonderful. Next best were French, then Spanish. I found both Indian and Chinese cuisines very good in London.

London had a couple of Japanese bookstores in which I could never resist the temptation to aimlessly browse, and I could hardly wait for the delivery of newspapers, air freighted from Japan, that arrived at our office. News from home was most welcome. Any place I could connect with Japanese culture was an attraction to me. I felt a close connection whenever I was near the offices of Japan Air Lines or Japanese banks. Perhaps I was unaccustomed to life in a foreign country, but I could not live apart from Japanese culture. On one hand, I wanted to become more acquainted with Western cultures, but surprisingly, when I questioned myself about Japanese culture, I found I lacked solid knowledge. This made me start looking for my identity and roots.

There was an undercurrent of anti-Japanese feeling in British society stemming from World War II. The courteous British did not show it in their faces, but I felt it occasionally. Once, for no reason, an old woman on the street suddenly shouted at me, "This is my country, not yours. Get out!" For a moment I was astonished, but I guessed that probably she had lost her dearest son or loved one in the war against Japan. I felt totally helpless and quickly left in silence.

Anti-Japanese sentiment has gradually faded away as time has passed. However, the memory of humiliation and hatred will not be completely wiped away. The *Asahi Newspaper* of September 13, 1993, reported that 12,000 British ex-prisoners of war who survived severe forced labor in Japanese army camps demanded compensation from the Japanese government for the inhumane treatment. During World War II, 57,000 British soldiers were taken prisoners of war and sent to mines in Taiwan and other locations for forced labor. According to British records, only 37,500 returned home after the war; the rest died in concentration camps.

The camp situation is well described by Jack Edwards in his book *Banzai, You Bastards!* Edwards was a prisoner of war at one of the labor mines in Taiwan. In the preface to his book, Edwards refers to "bushido" as abnormal precepts for warriors. (see chapters 27–28.)

Japanese Prime Minister Hosokawa of the non-Liberal Democratic Party expressed apology for the inhumane labor camps of the Japanese army, but refused British ex-prisoners of war demands for compensation, for reason that the case had been settled between the two governments after the war. This angered the British greatly. It is not merely a matter of money; nor can this issue be settled by lip service. We Japanese must deliberate what in our natures allowed us to commit atrocities; the same deliberation must be applied to the matter of imposing sexual slavery on Korean women, as well as to forced labor of Korean and Chinese civilians, and to the massacres of innocent people in many countries.

What Jack Edwards says in his preface is very clear to me: "We were not human beings to the Japanese army." Remember that vanquished and enslaved Ya, Yottsu and other aboriginal races (Japanese *shomin*—masses) were considered subhuman in the caste system established by the 7th century conquerors. Aboriginal people were treated in the same way that Jack Edwards was treated by the Japanese army. The despotic rule by *okami* and slavish mentality of the masses have expanded downward over a thousand years, and this society formed in the mind of people has survived, despite modernization of the political system.

A slave will have to live like a slave till he dies. The best he can do is to cheat the master, and his only sense of power comes from tormenting whomever is weaker than himself. Modern Japan defeated China, annexed Korea and Manchuria. Aggression continued. Colonial people, the occupied, and prisoners of war were placed below Japanese subhuman, the lowest caste. There was no dignity of the individual, no privacy, no human rights, only absolute obedience or severe punishment, including daily beating. The life of a prisoner was the same as a worm's. Jack Edwards' British culture fostered liberalism and democracy and produced a set of national values based on independence, freedom, equality and human rights, which clashed violently with the reality of subhuman life in the camp.

A true apology will look into the intrinsic cause of atrocities. Without self-reflection, apologies in words alone, whether by prime minister or emperor, will sound hollow and only serve to reactivate old hatreds.

In the beginning, I knew nothing of English culture and the British way of life; I was merely one of many busy executives walking the streets of London, whose concern was focused on establishing sales and stabilizing subsidiary operations. If a fateful encounter with Tomeo Yagiri's books had not happened, I would still be leading an ordinary businessman's life today; but Yagiri's books altered the course of my life entirely, causing me to change jobs and to write this book.

One day, tempted as usual, I entered the Japanese bookstore near Picadilly Circus and searched the shelves. Yagiri's *Turned Over History* caught my eye. I flipped through a couple of pages. "Defeat in Hakusuki-no-e...occupation of Japan by T'ang Chinese forces...the Fujiwaras...enslavement of aboriginal races..." Several phrases excited me and seemed so interesting I bought the book and took it home.

This first book so thoroughly captured my mind that I sought out Yagiri's other works one after the other. The author clearly and logically answered my questions about Japanese history. For example, Ya were "boat people" in today's terms, who drifted the seas to arrive on the southern coast of Japan. Their motherland was ancient Persia; they first moved to Malaysia, Vietnam and southern China, then to Japan between 200-100 BC.

Some settled along the shores and became fishermen. From this origin fishmongering and running fish restaurants became their hereditary and exclusive occupation. Their diet was fish. *Sushi*, an open sandwich of rice and raw fish, is typical.

A point I often wondered about was why women's power was so strong in family businesses of this kind, despite Japan being predominately a male-oriented culture. Yagiri points out that in the Ya society, women were dominant. In the society of bees, the queen rules the worker bees. The Ya's was a similar society; therefore Hachi (bee) was another name. The Ya revolt was called *Houki* (uprising of *Hachi*). *Hachi* has another meaning, "eight." It is also said that T'ang Chinese called them *Hachi* because they had eight vowels in their language. Another explanation is that T'ang Chinese called them *ba* or *pa* (eight in Chinese; also means "stupid").

It is no wonder that like a worker bee, the Japanese worker today submits his paycheck to his wife, who gives him pocket money. Strong control by women, particularly of foods, was vital to survive the hard life in the mountains, and helped keep men from disease, alcoholism, gambling and syphilis (after it was brought into Japan by Westerners). In modern Japan, company employees are willing to work till late evening even when there is no work to be done. After finishing work they go to pubs. Why? From Yagiri's point of view it is to escape from the wife's strict control.

Why are Japanese married in Shinto weddings and buried in Buddhist funerals? This traditional mixture goes back to the oppression of Shinto by ancient rulers when the *okami* forced Ya and Yottsu to convert to Buddhism. No Japanese asks this simple question about an incomprehensible custom; Japanese people do not know that Japan had religious wars in the past.

The Japanese are amazed at the 2000 years of religious wars in the Middle East. But *Gi* of the Ya and *Jin* of the Yottsu have survived one thousand years of oppression in Japan, surely enough to prove how people were faithful to ethnic religion. It was unfortunate that religions were unified in national Shinto; education in the Meiji ideology cut off the roots of our original races. Furthermore, the shock of defeat in World War II made the Japanese religiously numb.

I accept Yagiri's view that our ancestors were enslaved by T'ang Chinese invaders in the 7th century, although he presents only one direct proof of T'ang Chinese occupation: General Guo's report to the empress of T'ang China, contained in Tse-t'ien characters, a copy of which was said to be used to brainwash Japanese prisoners of war in the Sino-Japanese War in the 1930's and 40's by the communist army.

As to circumstantial evidence, among the most powerful is the *Nihon Shoki*, written in Tse-tien characters and Chinese grammar. Why was the official history of the nation written in the language of T'ang China!? (In Japan, Chinese characters are called *kanji* - Han's characters—but we can suspect this was to hide the origin). Why were all court systems suddenly changed to T'ang Chinese style in the 7th and 8th centuries? Why is Chinese culture so dominant in Japan? Civilization is transferable from one race to another, but not culture, unless the people move physically. The overwhelming remains of Chinese culture indicates that T'ang Chinese ruled in ancient Japan. They had a much higher civilization than ours at that time; the stronger ate the weaker.

If archaeological and anthropological studies of ancient tombs of emperors and nobles are allowed by the government, it will disclose our true history, because the bodies interred would be Chinese and Korean.

My agreement with Yagiri's historical analysis relieved me of the tension I had when first coming into contact with the Western way of life, a tension derived from the traditional Japanese view of history instilled by my education, to wit: "Japan is a mono-racial family country, led by virtuous great father emperors in an unbroken line from an infinite past. Throughout history, Japan has always been a peaceloving country of courteous, gentle and agricultural people, except for one disgraceful period—World War II." Japanese pride made me nervous when faced with Western culture, particularly humanism and rationalism, through which Westerners had liberated themselves from the myths of their past a long time ago.

My anxiety resembled the Christian's agony on the point that one cannot carry out the teachings of Christ literally. For Christians, Kierkegaard pointed out the third way. But for me it was a question either to become non-Japanese by denying the whole story or keep to the Japanese creed. Could I deny? The emperor of Japan is like the pope in Roman Catholicism—perhaps more so.

Yagiri indicated a way. For the first time, I could liberate myself from bias, become free and tolerant of other cultures. My love and attachment to the Japanese culture was doubled and tripled. I was able to share feelings of the defeated in the history of the U.K. and elsewhere, and associate with anybody freely without prejudice.

Yet not everyone was friendly to us. A friend who lived in the same building had his traveler's checks stolen from his room. A few nights later my room was robbed. Returning at midnight, I found my door ajar; everything in the room had been overturned. It was obvious a thief had broken in. I was unable to sleep that night, fearing the uninvited guest might return through the broken door. My overseas experience made it a habit to carry all valuables with me, so my sole damage was a carton of Japanese cigarettes. I reported the incident to the police the next morning and an investigator visited me. Hearing that the thief took only a carton of cigarettes, the investigator asked if I had any documents pertaining to industrial secrets. I heard nothing further, but the building caretaker left. I learned he had been providing tenant information to the thief.

My family arrived at the end of March, 1976. I had rented a three bedroom semi-detached house facing Helenslea Avenue at Golders Green, an upwardly mobile residential area in northwest London. The house was handsome, furnished for the convenience of foreign tenants; my children were happy it was larger than our house in Tokyo, but the rent was high, over 200,000 yen per month, and there were problems whenever we required plumbers or electricians. Since my wife spoke no English, I had to handle these troubles, but I couldn't understand cockney.

In winter, the central heating system did not work either on the ground floor or first floor. An English husband would be used to handling these things, but unfortunately I was not. Another headache was the inadequate capacity of the hot water reservoir. Japanese use two to three times the hot water English do. After we lived in the house for two years, I looked for a newer residence. It was difficult to find, but after a long search I did locate a comfortable, relatively new place near the crossing of Finchley Road and North Circular Road. We settled down there till my family went back to Tokyo in 1982.

My children were admitted to Wessex Garden School in Golders Green, the eldest daughter to the 5th grade and the twin boy and girl to the 2nd grade. They did not speak English at all (in Japan, English education starts in junior high school) but a few Japanese pupils who had come to London earlier acted as interpreters and helped my children in class. Despite my initial apprehension, everything went fine; my children enjoyed school. The English have a school lunch program and the sweets served were particularly attractive to my children. At home they always watched TV, and to my surprise, started catching onto English in a few weeks' time. By the end of the year they spoke it well. Once they understood what the teacher was saying, lessons were easy; they had no problems. On Saturday they went to a supplementary Japanese school so that they would not forget *kanji* and Japanese education. The following year a Japanese school was founded; my children changed over, as this was on the home country school system, thus they would have no trouble adjusting when they returned to Japan. It was a rather short time for them to have learned in an English school with English friends, but it was an unforgettable experience for them.

Soon after my family arrived in London, I took them on a short trip to Penzance during Easter holidays. We went out to Land's End and other places with beautiful scenery. When my family arrived at an old, beautiful church on St. Michael's Mount, the church service was in progress. I wanted my children to see it, and asked if we might enter the church, even though we were not Christians. I expected refusal, but they admitted us. I was deeply impressed by the devoutness of the people and felt myself a pagan from the far east.

That summer I took my family to Paris. Since there was no custom in Japan to take vacations, this was my first one-week holiday with my family. Since that time, I took my family to various places in Europe every year. In 1979 we traveled to Scotland and visited John o'Groat, thus reaching both ends in the west and north of the U.K. In six years we not only enjoyed many beautiful landscapes but also learned the history and culture of many countries of Europe. It was expensive for me but necessary for my children.

I think it was the sense of living in a foreign country under the rule of a different race that united my family more tightly than in the home country. Even small equipment problems at home strengthened the family union. The British way of life was an entirely new experience for all of us. In Japan, I left my home in early morning and returned at midnight. Exhausted, I spent Sundays idling or went out for a round of golf with my colleagues in the company. (Saturdays were half-day work days. In the 1970's big companies started to make two Saturdays a month full holidays, and towards the end of the 1980's most of them made all Saturdays holidays). Like my fellow executives, I was absorbed in business 100%. I had no time for my children; everything was left to my wife. As a matter of fact, I knew nothing about domestic chores until London. It was a new world I was living in and I was changing gradually. Time with my family increased and I became more open in showing affection.

Near my first house in Golders Green was a beautiful Jewish synagogue, and on Saturday, through the window of my house, I watched pious Jewish people gathering to pray. All the men had terrific black beards and wore black hats, and the ladies were dressed up. Since I'd had no chance to see so many Jewish people at one time in Japan, this made an extraordinary impression of religion being vividly alive, in contrast to Japan, where religion is dead. The former residents of my new house were also Jewish; Jewish charms were left here and there in the house.

I was feeling cultural frictions in daily life, yet I never had any political fears. I saw the people were independent and free. Politics were stabilized, from a long history of liberalism and democracy. At first the Labor Party was in power and its socialistic policy reflected in the taxation system. The English joked, "We would pay 101% tax if we worked any harder and were any more successful." Sharp progressive taxation punished hardworking people and managers were discouraged from attempting ventures.

Many capable businessmen left the U.K. for the U.S. Smart but poorer people found a way to fight back. Some earned money in the black market while receiving unemployment allowances from the government at the same time. The morale of workers deteriorated and every day one read news of strikes. Another joke was the number of strike days at a factory of well-known British automobile manufacturers was more than its annual working days. Government workers went on strike too, as did firemen. What would happen if a big fire broke out! Worse was the garbage collectors' strike, with streets flooded with stinking garbage. The people were suffering from the so-called "English disease" until Iron Lady Margaret Thatcher made her dramatic debut in 1979 with determination to cure the disease. In a book titled *New Circumstances of The U.K.*, Kiyoharu Nagai states: "She judged the cause was that British industries had lost the competitive edge against the U.S. and Japan in international markets. She stripped off government protections against foreign competitors and privatized government-owned businesses...gave up the policy of throwing state money around for stimulating the economy, and pushed monetarism to restrain the money supply. She challenged inflation by making government smaller. As a result, inflation, which reached its peak of 22% right after her advent, was brought down to 3.7% in June, 1983....bankruptcy increased drastically; in 1983 it increased by 24% compared with the previous year...The government just let businesses go bankrupt, rendering no help, which increased unemployment...In January, 1986, 3,400,000 people did not have jobs, while 1,500,000 were jobless before her advent." Underground fares went up sharply. In Britain, commutation expenses are borne by employees; the increase had a serious influence on family budgets, and we lost a few employees who picked up jobs nearer to home for this reason.

Nagai continues: "To cure the English disease, Thatcher believed it essential to lance boils thoroughly, and she ordered industries that did not pay cut, such as coal mining. Strikes broke out. It had been a pattern that the government made compromises with unions...But the iron lady hung on firmly, and the number of strikes decreased..."

The income tax rate was cut to 50% maximum and the "Value Added Tax" system was introduced. Tax reduction was good news to me. Regarding VAT, I had to work all night immediately prior to enforcement day in order to review the pricing of 3,000 products. Because of her drastic measures, Mrs. Thatcher became unpopular with the masses; Conservatives were going to lose power in the next election. But the Iron Lady was lucky: the Falkland War broke out in 1982, and British victory saved her and the Conservative government. I saw her on TV daily and heard her speech in the House on my car radio. She quit in November, 1990, the day I arrived in London on a business trip. I respect her for the guts she showed to carry out the unpopular plans in which she believed. I wish we had statesmen like her in Japan.

With interest I noted that a woman's position in British society is not as high as I had expected, in spite of the fact that the British had a queen and a woman prime minister at the same time. I also felt that the British had a similar way of thinking as the prewar Japanese in certain aspects. I also took note of classes in the society. I found all working class people were very kind and warm, even to a stranger like me, though their cockney often puzzled me. I remembered the same kind of Japanese people I met in my prewar childhood. In Japan today most of the people are university graduates and highly intelligent, however, to my regret the warmth of the heart is gone.

Life in London was pleasant. I took my family to Windsor Castle, the Tower of London, the British Museum, famous galleries and concert halls. We went shopping at Harrod's, Selfridge's, Fortnum & Mason's and other sophisticated stores along Regent Street, Oxford Street, Bond Street and New Bond Street. My wife and I were invited to casinos, horse races and dog races. We could see many sporting events—golf, cricket, football, rugby, darts. I even had a chance to see the royal wedding parade of Diana and Charles. Gorgeous fireworks were displayed celebrating the royal wedding a night before. Heavy traffic jams on the way home exhausted my car's battery, an experience shared with many others that memorable evening.

London became my second hometown. In January, 1982, my family returned to Tokyo. At the end of March, some 200 friends from the U.K. and other European countries attended my farewell party held at the Dorchester. When I was driving back home, suddenly uncontrollable tears came, as I realized this was farewell to my life here in London, a life that had come to mean so much to me. The next day I left Heathrow, with a big card of messages from all the employees in the company. This card is my great treasure. Certainly London was the best time of my life. Those days will shine in my memory always.

Chapter Thirty Four

The Dreams Return

April, 1982, I was back in Tokyo. My children were admitted to Japanese schools with no problem. To accommodate a growing brood, we built a bigger house. It was completed in June and my family was happy to move in.

Everything seemed fine at the beginning. Everyone in the head office seemed friendly to me. However, soon I started to feel a sense of incongruity. In London people were independent, free and equal, serving as one organ. They recognized human weakness in each other and worked based on that premise. In Japan, people were submissive to the company, vassals striving to meet their superiors' wishes. The pecking order was absolute and loyalty the measure of evaluation.

In *tatemae*, people are to be good, and trust is the rule, but in *honne*, distrust actually rules. In Japan, there is no real organization based on an exact job description, and the "check system" does not work well. Therefore, in order to make sure subordinates will cause no trouble, superiors control them closely, even to details of their private lives.

I was reminded of the words of one of my English friends, who when asked what part of his Japanese experience he disliked the most, replied that he felt most Japanese executives tried to force him to be subservient and to surrender initiative. Before I went to London this was beyond my perceptions. Now back in Tokyo I felt it first hand. I did not want to surrender to anybody. What I wanted was a job I could execute on my own responsibility. My position in the company was very high. I was Executive Managing Director of the board and General Manager of the Foreign Trade Department. However, in actuality my job was merely an assistant to the chief executive, despite confidence attained from my London experience that I could do more. My achievements proved my marketing and management capabilities, but my present position was a disappointment to me.

I sought a new challenge by volunteering to take over the struggling systems division. Since the products were new to me, I had to study a great deal. I felt, however, my goodwill was not appreciated nor my sense of responsibility rewarded with due delegation of authority.

Looking back to those days now I realize I made a mistake. In Japan a Han needs only one lord and everyone is vassal to him. The lord wants everyone loyal to him directly. It is not like the organization of a Western company where each job is clearly assigned to each employee who is employed to perform it, for which responsibility and authority are duly given to him. I felt it impossible to apply the vision and marketing strategy I had cultivated in London. Respect of subordinates was not based on my capability in a specific sector of business, but loyalty to the lord. My job got to be somewhat like a chamberlain. It was not what I wanted. I resigned the company in 1986.

In Japan there is no free labor market, particularly for executives. Each company (Han) regularly employs fresh graduates (vassals) each year under a permanent employment system. Most employees work there until normal retirement at 60, when they are transferred to a subsidiary for another five years or so.

One starts from a position somewhat like an apprentice. Year after year, loyalty and achievement as "a subject of the Han" will be evaluated by superiors, leading to gradual promotion to managerial positions. With a little bit of luck one can rise to a position of opportunity, in which loyalty and achievement will be noted directly by top management. If one is lucky, he can eventually become a board director. His salary will be increased in accordance with his position and length of service. At the beginning his salary is less than the amount he should be paid. However, with annual increases he will be overpaid towards the end of his career. If he quits the company halfway he will lose it all.

I set a worldwide sales net which would produce an annual profit of several billion yen for the company over many years to come. Yet my salary did not reflect this. Had the company offered to pay me a much higher salary or bonus, it would have benefitted me little, due to Japan's progressive taxation system. Therefore, if I wanted to enjoy the full benefits, I had to stay for the rest of my life. The company would control my life this way. But I wanted to live an independent life to my own satisfaction.

Little by little, changes were taking place among the young people. The first tendency was to quit a company and start one's own business. Then head hunting companies appeared. Manpower companies joined the market to supply temporaries, although the market was limited compared with the U.S. The company for which I worked for 20 years was listed on the Tokyo stock exchange. Each company had its own salary and promotion system as well as different welfare systems, such as housing programs. All companies discourage job changing. Had this been the U.S., perhaps I would have been in a position to expect several offers from other companies or head hunters. But here it did not happen.

The system makes it difficult for employees to change jobs and at the same time for companies to obtain competent executives and specialists at market prices. Under the circumstances, in July, 1986, I chose to establish an international consulting company. As I announced this, one of my friends introduced me to a digital duplicator manufacturer who was starting up overseas sales. That company became my first client.

The president invited me to join the board. I was employed again. My dreams returned. I knew I could achieve remarkable success for the company. I started activities by participating in international exhibitions to find good distributors and dealers. In Europe I arranged for the company to participate in the Hannover Messe and in the United States the National Office Machine Dealers Association's exhibition. Xerox type copiers, except for expensive high end products, were not built for heavy duty use, whereas people did high volume copying with them, causing frequent problems. It was a nuisance to call servicemen every day. Besides the cost of copying was high.

The digital duplicator is built for heavy duty use; cost per copy goes down in proportion to the number of copies; therefore, it is best for high volume copying. Using digitalization, the operation is fully automated with the press of a button. Its price is in the range of sophisticated copiers. As I expected, it caused a sensation and I received many inquiries.

However, before starting to export on a large scale, it was necessary to polish the products. Concept development, product design and engineering, manufacturing and quality control had to be improved to meet international levels. While this was going on, I looked for a good distributor. When I say good distributor I mean a person to rely on as a partner. An independent distributor with adequate financing capacity is best. But in a big country like the U.S., it is difficult to find a qualified one. Prior to my joining, the company had already built a subsidiary in the U.S. which had been used for market research. I decided to initiate distribution through that company. Since the new products announced in the NOMDA convention were so popular, many applications for dealerships were received. I served as non-resident president of the U.S. subsidiary myself, frequently making trips over the Pacific.

It was clearly not possible to continue commuting from Tokyo to Boston for any length of time. I was looking for a president to run the U.S. subsidiary. I also needed experts and specialists in international business in the head office. I was in the process of organizing an efficient export division. It was a hectic time for me mentally as well as physically.

In appointing a distributor, agreement on products' present as well as future marketability is essential. It was a super sales job to convince a candidate of the potential business he could expect. Once he was prepared to make the necessary investment to maximize sales in his territory, we could come to terms. Of course, ways to reduce investment risk had to be taken. His sales net was uneven; it was almost impossible to improve the weak part, even given our products' strength. The endeavor required investment of money and manpower over the long haul. Without management and dealers' full cooperation, it would be impossible to build up a country's sales net.

Pricing was another point. Many managers thought it safe to take a high profit margin for their companies. However, my "best value for the money" philosophy was that pricing to ensure a quick sell-out was safer and more profitable; managers willing to take initial losses would make the company profitable eventually. Good communication with dealers on concept and strategy was most important.

When products lose competitiveness in the market, sales will slow down and inventory will increase. Price reduction becomes necessary. How much to reduce is a question. One is apt to reduce a little, then wait to see what happens, hoping things work out all right. If that is not enough, another price reduction ensues. But this gives no impact, and eventually the loss will grow even bigger. However, if a drastic price reduction is made from the beginning there will be enough power to move the products quickly. The first loss is always the best loss. This is the same as military tactics in a battle. You read about the Guadalcanal battles in which the Japanese army committed mistakes by throwing its strength to the front little by little. Theoretically this is the same as taking losses in business.

I covered Europe and other free countries with distributors. I found a Brit whom I arranged to become president of the U.S. subsidiary. He did a fine job, forming a dealer sales net and establishing a firm foundation, which enabled me to devote more time to other markets.

In European markets, my old friends helped to find good distributors, and business was expanded smoothly. I achieved remarkable success in two major markets, Germany and France, by means of M & A. The export division's sales had been a little over 200 million yen when I joined. Since my command, they jumped more than 10 times the first year and kept increasing. The remarkable international expansion stimulated domestic sales, and healthy growth was seen. I was appointed Senior Managing Director in charge of all sales and planning. My efforts centered around making the company profitable in all phases of production, including both logistics and sales.

The company went public. Profits increased year by year. In the U.S. subsidiary, a change of president occurred, to encourage further sales expansion following initial ground work. In five years sales in international markets increased 100 times. The company's financial status was excellent. On a special incentive trip program, I welcomed all major American dealers at our head office in Tokyo. I was thankful to the president of the company for giving me a free hand to exert my full power and talents. My dreams had come true. I was very happy. On the other hand, my frustration was growing. It seemed that Japan remained in a state of mass hypnosis and was digging its own grave in international relationships.

I had given much thought to my father's death, to the vainglorious cause to which he devoted his life, to Japan's motives for World War II, and to the incomprehensibility of Japan and the Japanese to most westerners. For the first time, I began to think I might contribute something to enlighten others on these matters. I wanted to write a book; but clearly, time was an obstacle. I would not be able to accomplish my goal without quitting the company. I resigned in June 1991, and immediately began writing this book. To support my family, I resumed international consulting on a part time basis.

Just before my resignation, Japan's economic bubble burst, causing tremendous damage to the country's wealth. When signs of impending trouble were emerging in the stock and real estate markets, the Japanese government did nothing to prevent catastrophe. The Bank of Japan and the Ministry of Finance should have lowered interest rates, but did not. They should have removed controls over the money supply, but did nothing. The Japanese economy crashed. Ten trillion dollars of wealth vanished in less than two years; the vitality of the Japanese economy faded away.

Consequently, inherent contradictions in Japanese Style Management became evident, emerging much earlier than even I had expected. While Japanese Style Management was considered an absolute, I had long held the system in doubt, but no one listened to me. Now that sales of Japanese companies declined or remained flat and profits reduced sharply, former critics admitted the system was no longer suitable. The key word for Japanese businesses became "restructuring," and its focus was to cut swelling personnel expenses. Continuation of permanent employment and the seniority system, the basis of Japanese

Style Management that demanded employees' lifetime loyalty to the company, was in serious danger.

If Japanese companies abandoned this system, employee loyalty would suffer. Over the past half century, Japanese companies, particularly manufacturers, primarily made improvements of Western innovations. For such works, loyalty was the most valuable asset. Now, Japanese companies badly needed creativity and innovation to stay competitive.

There were other problems, stock price for one. If the Nikkei average plunged too low, profits on stocks owned by Japanese banks and insurance companies would erode. These companies had huge bad debts to depreciate. The total amount of bad debts of all banks, nonbanks and housing corporations was published at over U.S. $270 billion, but the amount was believed to be four or five times higher. The fund enabling banks to write off the huge debts was the profit on stocks they had in possession. Selling could cause a crash, destroying Japan's credit system and leading to monetary panic.

The Ministry of Finance controlled banks and insurance companies with *gyosei shido* (guidance without legislation), not to sell the stocks in the exchange markets. After severe criticism, some of the banks sold. As a result, the Nikkei average reached a critical level.

The government spent over U.S. $270 billion to boost the economy, but nothing happened. The money was spent mostly for construction and civil engineering. Huge amounts were spent for roads, renovating fishery harbors, river improvement works, museums and gymnasiums, benefitting general constructors, but failing to provide opportunity for new ventures. Money was spent for reviving inefficient businesses, which, in the principle of free trade, must die out. Businesses should take the initiative to be profitable, cut personnel and change the pay system. Obviously there would be a flood of unemployed.

Let us look at this problem from the position of the shareholder. Banking management wants to write off bad debts with profits obtained through sale of stocks. But the money belongs to shareholders. How will management take responsibility for such heavy losses? In the United States, management who acted in this manner would be fired.

Shareholders must be informed of the true picture. Negligence is a breach of trust and a misrepresentation to public investors. But in this country it is surprising the Ministry of Finance, the okami, dictates to the banks to make window dressing settlement of accounts by concealing the true amount of bad debts. This is a national crime. Under such circumstances is it right to pay bonuses? What about executives and directors?

Let us examine this problem from the employees' point of view.

Their income has been reduced drastically. At the peak, many employees worked as many as 100 hours of overtime a month, providing a large additional source of income, which many budgeted from to pay car installments. Now there is no more overtime work. Even more serious is the bonus system, which has been drastically reduced. For instance, the bonus Japan Air Lines paid to its employees was 33% less than the previous year.

During the bubble economy, Japanese employees were used to receiving bonuses equal to approximately six months' salary. Bonuses are paid in June and December, roughly 50:50. It is generally understood that a bonus of up to two months salary every half year is guaranteed, so it is in effect part of the salary which is paid six months later. Why does the company pay it later? There is no clear reason. One interpretation is that employees (children) tend to spend all the money they earned in a month and do not have enough savings when needed. So the company (father) will hold a quarter of the monthly salary for six months and pay it out at the end. From the employees' point of view, it would be better to be paid a full salary every month. If they quit halfway or the company goes bankrupt before June, they won't get the bonus. It is unfair.

The remaining bonus equal to approximately one month's salary in half term is said to be subject to company results and paid upon evaluation of the individual's achievement. If this portion is an incentive, the amount due employees pursuant to the incentive scheme must be fully paid irrespective of company results, since non-executive employees are not liable for it. If this portion is profit sharing, the amount due will vary in accordance with company profit. If profit is zero, it will not be paid. For the average employee, it is too much to bet one month's salary on the fate of the company. A more reasonable profit sharing program should be worked out. (It is incomprehensible why we pay a bonus to government officials).

Bonuses for board members is taxable as profit and is clearly profit sharing. Japan Air Lines' directors are not supposed to be paid a bonus when the company takes a loss. However, most board members are also company executives, and entitled to deferred salaries as well as what ever amount is due under incentive schemes. Renumeration for board directors is low when risks and gains are compared; it is not enough to motivate capable persons. Can shareholders expect good result from such directors?

There have been no discussions between management and labor unions, nor management and shareholders. The management system has been left deliberately obscure, giving managers more power to control employees at their discretion.

If Japanese industries want to be competitive in world markets, there is no choice but to abandon Japanese Style Management and adopt Western Style Management. In addition, costs will have to be cut. Shifting production to Southeast Asian countries is a must. This has already started, with Japan having increased its investment in overseas plants and equipment by 28% in the first half of 1995 alone. China and Vietnam are emerging as attractive venues for Japanese-based offshore business.

Even if all these things are done, how many can survive if protective measures by the *okami* are still in place? Japanese Style Management based on a rehash of the Meiji ideology worked in the fight against communism. The emperor system was convenient for the Japanese government to control the people. But now to cope with severe reality, we need a new principle to replace the conventional one. We must destroy the idea of the vertical society; otherwise democratization of Japan cannot be achieved. Without this, our future is dim.

For the Japanese, the coming economic war will be as hard as World War II. Do we have the guts to go through the ordeal? We must be independent and use creative thinking, to defy traditional authorities and the establishment. We can only hope the younger generation will rise to the challenge. However difficult it may be, someone has to do it.

Part Five

A CALL FOR RADICAL CHANGE

Chapter Thirty Five

A Vertical Society: The Corporate Foundation

As the reader now knows, the origin of Japan's vertical society goes back to the Chinese invasion in the 7th century. The T'ang first established themselves in western Japan, then gradually expanded into the eastern and northern territories in the 8th Century. The conquerors divided society into two classes: *ryo* (court nobles), and *sen* (humble slaves, comprised of all other races—Ya, Yottsu, Zoshiki, Silla, Kogoryoe).

To control his slaves, a master chose one reliable slave in the group and made him head man. Only the head man was allowed to marry slave women, who were then set free from sexual service to the masters and allowed to have children. This slavery is the probable cause of a number of trends peculiar to the Japanese that have continued even today.

First, without the *okami*, the Japanese do not know how to make a decision, particularly when it requires sacrifice. Under democratic rule in which everyone has equal rights, the Japanese needs someone to play the role of *okami*. An *okami's* decision is final, and everybody must obey it. This makes governing easier.

Second, it was only natural that all slaves should wish to be the head man. If a *sen* was built into the establishment, normally a concession was granted by the master, although social standing remained low. To receive a coveted position, any means—military force, political marriage, gold, etc. were used. As soon as someone of lower caste was absorbed into the system, he would hide his birth by fabricating a genealogy, and look down on people in the class to which he had formerly belonged. Discrimination persists today in Japanese society.

Third, slave resistance was such that slaves would cheat whenever possible. This mentality remains today in the Japanese perception of tax. Fourth, the slaves' desire was to be the same as others; and slaves could not say no to a master—obedience and endurance were absolute requirements. All these modes still remain in today's Japanese society and have become our characteristics.

"I know it is not easy to achieve this plan. But the company needs it by all means. Let's achieve it with our effort and sacrifice working late at night or even on holidays!" When the president (*okami*) of the company speaks this way, employees follow him without objection, though they think the plan is unfeasible in *honne* (true mind). "I can't fight city hall!" This way of thinking is alive today in business and has helped managers of Japanese businesses and industries in achieving results.

However, the government's efficiency in executing its plan plummeted as a result of the postwar change from an almighty *okami* to a symbolic emperor. For example, fifteen years after the opening of Tokyo International Airport at Narita, second stage expansion is still stuck due to the stubborn opposition of left wing sponsored land owners. This, in the face of repeated requests by many nations and airlines to expand facilities and runways to accommodate more passengers and airlines. Landowners oppose the government decision because they are against capitalism for political reasons, and there is little or no room for negotiation. No politician is willing to take responsibility for action to the benefit of the majority. Even now we are daunted by harsh slavery. The coward's mentality was passed down from generation to generation, and at present we have little or no stomach to solve difficult problems ourselves, so accustomed are we to ceding final decisions to our master. When it has to make a decision to force sacrifice from the people, the government needs *gaiatsu* (pressure from overseas, mainly from the U.S.).

Whenever anything goes wrong, the *okami* at the top is never to be questioned or held responsible. The *okami* is always right and beyond reproach. It is always the wicked subjects around him who cause the problem. Examples of this are seen in many historical events. The Japanese have never accused Hirohito for responsibility of the disasters that World War II brought to the people. Surprisingly, we have not bothered even to look into the responsibility of his "wicked subjects." We claim the International Military Tribunal for the Far East victor's trial, but we have not tried to clarify who is responsible for the failures and mistakes which brought us such disasters, even half a century after defeat. The Yasukuni Shrine problem is, for example, not yet settled.

The origin of racial discrimination in Japan also began in the 7th century. It was generally recognized by the Japanese intelligentsia and the ruling class till the Meiji reform that only nobles of either T'ang Chinese or Peakche (Korean) blood had the legitimate right to rule Japan. In fact, the Japanese people lived under a system of racial and ethnic discrimination for 1000 years.

The history of past discrimination was concealed as top secret. The war with China in 1894-95 was a must in order to gain independence from the historically subordinate relationship of Japan to China. The annexation of Korea in 1910 was likewise necessary in order to destroy all evidence that might suggest the true origin of the imperial family and court nobility.

As the Empire of Japan acquired new territories in neighboring areas by military aggression, Japan's vertical society was expanded downward, adding Koreans and Chinese to the bottom below the Japanese subhuman caste. It made the Japanese *shomin* (masses) feel better to look down on former masters. This ethnic outlook was supposed to have been corrected after the defeat of Japan in 1945, but there still remains an undercurrent of discrimination, for the postwar Japanese government has not completely denied the old Meiji fictions, causing ill feeling and the isolation of Japan in Asia today.

In ancient times, T'ang and Paekche masters not only looked down on Japanese aborigines as uncivilized and stupid, but also discriminated against them for religious reasons. The Buddhists made great efforts to convert the aboriginals to Buddhism, and a new sect with a more easily acceptable dogma was specially developed for them.

As time passed, some people rose from slavery and were successful at improving their lives. They concealed their origins and joined the establishment. For example, the Tokugawas must be a family of Yottsu blood. The first shogun *Ieyasu* was no doubt a Shintoist and Shinto is the ethnic religion of the Yottsu. Ieyasu was deified as *shin kun* (monarch of deity) and enshrined in Toshogu (shrine to enlighten the east). However, with the 3rd Shogun Iyemitsu, the family was converted to Buddhism, and the 5th Shogun Tsunayoshi adopted the policy to oppress Shintoists.

To evade oppression, many daimyo and samurai families of Yottsu or Ya ancestry were compelled to hide their origin by forgery and conversion to Buddhism. Successful merchants and artisans, duly registered with Bakufu as good citizens, did the same thing to defend their interests. However, the poor masses, shut up in special districts or ghettos in secluded places along rivers without bridges, had no means of evading oppression and were discriminated against by people of the same origin as *oni* (devils). This unfounded contempt and discrimination is still seen in Japan today with the problems of *burakumin* (people of humble blood), who incur disadvantage in employment and marriage.

A nobleman in ancient Japan is estimated to have had nearly a hundred slaves. Michinaga Fujiwara (966-1027), regent of 9-year old Emperor Go-ichi-jo, left a *tanka* poem: "It's my pleasure to find this world mine. My satisfaction is like the full moon that has no want." Any such person would wish his paradise to continue for *banzai* (10,000 years; forever, metaphorically) or *Sazare ishi no iwao to naru made*.

The latter is a phrase from *Kimiga yo*, a song composed in the Meiji era, which the government insists is the Japanese national anthem, to be sung at national ceremonies. The left wing opposes this because: (1) the phrase is not proper for a democratic state; and (2) there is no legislation officially declaring this the national anthem. *Kimiga Yo* means "Your Majesty's reign" and *sazare ishi no* means "Your Majesty's reign be continued forever." In June, 1993, a controversy arose whether the *Kimiga Yo* should be played at the wedding ceremonies. The *Kimiga Yo* was played after all.

The T'ang Chinese invaders of the 7th century were men of lowly birth, and it was an unexpected fortune that they could found their paradise on the far eastern frontier. One can appreciate their wish to keep the ruling position as long as possible, and understand why the Chinese idea of the Mandate from Heaven (any Chinese emperor lacking the virtue of a benevolent rule is to be overthrown by any person who has received a mandate from heaven) or the legality of revolution were not brought to Japan by the invaders. Furthermore, the idea of an imperial unbroken line of emperors in which no replacement was possible was emphasized. As a descendant of slaves, personally, I do not wish to sing "Your Majesty's reign be forever," although I consider myself a conservative, far from any left-leaning philosophy; yet singing this hymn to the emperor sounds too ironic to me.

Racial mixing caused by the conquest of one group by another of different ethnic stock has occurred often in world history, where a dominant group attempts to either wipe out or enslave the conquered one. In the 1990's in the former Yugoslavia, we have a perfect example of this under the name of "ethnic cleansing." A similar thing happened one thousand years ago in Japan. However, the Japanese shomin who have been made to believe in *okami* stories, regard the Serbian and Bosnian atrocities as just a savage foreign case.

Indeed ignorance creates a tragic comedy. In spite of events that occurred in the war, the Japanese people stick to the doctrine that they are essentially good and have always been an agricultural mono-racial, mono-ethnic people believing in peace, in harmony with nature and the rest of the world. We think our history is unique and we should be proud of it. And it must remain that way; otherwise, our vertical society will collapse.

In Japan the only people who have maintained purity of blood are Sankas. The Sankas are supposed to know the true history of Japan from their traditions. I am sorry that none has spoken up: "I'm a Sanka and proud of our history." If that history became known it would certainly put an end to the vertical society. The Sanka are probably afraid of oppression and discrimination, and one can understand their fear; they had to endure a thousand years of oppression up until the American occupation. At last they have been given an opportunity and they have made a success. They feel they cannot afford losing it.

"The fact that there are only few mentions of wars and conquests in ancient Japanese history is the best proof that Japan was a peaceful paradise." Is this view of Tsuda and Yamamoto correct? The same situation can happen in a society where the people are controlled by a ruler. Our ancestors had no choice but to surrender to conquerors if they wanted to survive. All were put under close watch by the head man who was wholeheartedly loyal to the master. Secret information and false charges to master and headman by fellow slaves were a daily matter. Speaking up was dangerous. People developed special ways of communication, called *hara gei* and *aun no kokyu*—forms of non-verbal communication.

Those who did not surrender to the masters were exiled to ghettos named *bessho, sansho, kaige* etc., and were isolated by surrounding rivers without bridges, left to die of starvation. If they came out of the ghettos, they were immediately killed by farmers, which caused no legal problem, since they were subhuman. The history of these "subhuman peoples" was discarded by the government because they deviate from descriptions of standard history, (*KiKi* (*Kojiki* and *Nihon Shoki*). Only a few of these traditions remain today. Yet if we read the remaining materials carefully with insight, we can discover enough clues to reconstruct the truth. The study of local history is most important, yet government scholars have neglected it, since if they advocated a different view, criticizing their predecessors, it might endanger their future position in academia.

The people keep silent. Superficially, Japan is a paradise, as the ruling LDP claims, rich and clean, intelligent and peace-loving—no unemployment, no violence, no shootings, no drugs, no crime. It makes a sharp contrast to the US, where people are the masters of the country, and every factor of human nature shows freely and openly as a result of individual independence.

What will Japanese historians write about the 1990s several hundred years hence? They may say, "Look! The emperor institution stands firmly for three thousands years with no change. How long will sick American democracy be able to stand?"

Japan's system to restrict occupation by race continued until the Meiji reforms. Artists' social standing used to be low; for example, kabuki actors were contemptuously called *kawarakojiki* (beggars on the shores of river). Grave keepers for noble families were probably the originators of the art of Japanese porcelain; the custom of slaves following masters to the grave was abolished in time, replaced with *haniwa* (dolls made of clay) being placed in the grave with the master. Grave keepers cremated bodies of people of the same race and used the cremation fire to produce the dolls and ceramic ware (porcelain); the art of china was the byproduct.

Everyone in the clan followed occupations predetermined by the master; all were resigned to accepting their destinies. No one was allowed to show originality in creativity. An artisan painted the same designs and patterns throughout his lifetime. He became absorbed in the work of drawing a line, in the use of color, or producing stylized beauty. Even today, this is the reason why Japanese start learning the arts and performances by studying style and pattern. This situation produced the idea of *do* (way of living) in our culture.

We have *do* in everything: *gado* (the way painters should live); *shodo* (the way calligraphers should live); *shonin do* (the way businessman should live); *sumo do* (the way sumo wrestlers should live); kendo, judo, bushido, etc. *Do* means road to lead one to a satisfaction in group life to which Japanese devote themselves. The individual was to dedicate himself selflessly to his work and not appear to be outstanding.

Lives were under complete control and restriction, with no privacy, independence, individual success or originality. Total concentration on a given job, however, opened a spiritual world in which one could enjoy freedom and independence—for example, write a stroke of a Chinese character with a brush on a sheet of paper with great concentration as though one's life depended on it was a way to reach spiritual perfection. Teachers in *do* initially teach the styles and designs; the rest is one's own fight as to the depth of concentration he can achieve, how to train the will and elevate the spirit. All this is deemed essential to higher perfection. It is the Japanese concept that the degree of one's spiritual perfection will determine the quality of workmanship.

"Handmade" is a key word in the current marketing of consumer products. People like it much more than "made in a state-of-the-art, fully automated and computerized factory," and are prepared to pay a higher price for products advertised as "handmade". Take the example of *unagi kabayaki* (grilled fillet of eel with sweet soybean sauce). Japanese prefer that the fillet of eel be grilled over a charcoal fire by an aged cook, hopefully the proprietor himself, with deep wrinkles on his forehead, which proves his skill and experience. It will taste much better than the mass-produced *kabayaki* coming out of a fully automated production line. "Handmade" by a man of perfection in spirit has a traditional value rather than just a taste.

Suppose I join in a *do* society: my life will be dedicated to become a master in the *do*. The direction I am going to go is clearly set. If I keep walking on the *do*, eventually I will arrive at my destination. I have no fear of being lost half way. Perfection in spiritual concentration will cause a state of absolute selflessness. There I will gain complete freedom in physical motion. If I am in *ga do* (painting) I can draw an ideal line with a brush freely and creatively. If I am in *ken do* I will be able to cut off the head of an enemy as easily as I cut tofu (bean curd). If I am in *yakyu do* (baseball) I will be able to mass produce home runs. Only hard training makes such extraordinary concentration possible. As my technique improves it will be appreciated in society, but more important and more intrinsic is the spiritual perfection that causes me to do fine things. Even if my skill reaches the level of great master in the *do*, my income may not be necessarily much better than the poorest one in the group. Income is unimportant. It is strictly a world of self-satisfaction. Within the realm of the *do* I will be highly respected because of my level of spiritual perfection. The progress will move me closer towards *satori* (ultimate understanding of the meaning of life). I will be even more respected as I get older and lose physical skills. It is no doubt the only way for me to be liberated from the temporal destiny of slave, and join in the spiritual world of freedom and independence.

Sumo wrestling is Japan's national sport and one of the most representative parts of Japanese culture. It is also a *do*. The constitution of the Sumo Association has many items reminiscent of feudal customs, although it is clothed in postwar modernization. In order to become a *yokozuna* (grand champion), a sumo wrestler is required to attain a certain plateau of spiritual perfection in addition to winning a percentage of his matches. A problem would have been created if Konishiki, a Hawaiian sumo wrestler, had an unquestionably good number of wins to be recommended as a *yokozuna*. If he were not recommended, it would have inevitably invited controversy over racial prejudice. Actually it is not racial discrimination, but more resistance in the Japanese mind, a doubt as to how far a foreigner whose culture is completely different can reach spiritual perfection in *do*; one wonders how a person with freedom and independence can totally submit himself to the authority of *do*.

Akebono, the first American *yokozuna*, Grand Champion of sumo, said to Western journalists at a press conference in the American Club, "I wrestle. The Association takes care of the rest." This is the philosophy of *do*: "I, the slave, concentrate on the work given by the master.

The *okami* (master) takes care of the rest." A similar idea is seen in the relationship between Japan and the U.S. Japan is used to concentrating on efforts to win international economic competition under the rules of the American *okami*.

The philosophy of *do* may not necessarily serve a man with freedom and independence. In a democratic system one can freely exert his own creative power and participate in political fights to change the system without fear of suppression.

To live in the vertical society of prosperous Japan today is not always unpleasant. It can be very comfortable, once one is resolved to the authority of *okami* who sets the rules to follow in an escalator system. I get on the escalator and it automatically takes me up till the end. *Okami* sets the course and once I am on it; it is no good to get off course halfway because I will lose what I have gained till then.

It starts as early as education in kindergarten. I must go to a good school if I want to be successful, and it is best to enter a famous school with a complete course—kindergarten, primary, junior high, high school and university, all of which belong to the same management. Then I can graduate university on the escalator without much effort, provided my records are average. Or I will also go to *juku* (a private class to help pupils get ahead) as soon as I start primary school, in order to win the exam competition. Sixty percent of 6th grade pupils in primary school go to *juku* and study till late night, eating fast foods instead of having dinner with their family.

In order to pass examinations, I need to memorize hundreds of thousands of "right answers." I am not in a position to question or doubt the answers. By the time I graduate university I will be a standard Japanese; I will have the same view of emperor and emperor institution as others. I believe the Japanese creed. I will be admitted to the vertical society and can have a good job in government or in a large business corporation, where I will spend most of my life until I retire. This is another escalator and it will take me to the top if I keep riding it. The escalator for government officials will take me to the office of administrative vice-minister, the highest position in a ministry. Then I can choose my second life. I may run in an election as an LDP candidate to become a Diet member and take care of the businesses I formerly controlled, or I could be employed by a large private business as a board director to help gain permits and licenses from the ministry for which I served.

It will not be much different in large private businesses. Starting as apprentice, with a bit of luck, I can be promoted to a board director on the escalator if I keep riding it. I must get along well with my superiors and should not make any big mistakes. Average ability is good enough to assume an executive position. Management of a big company does not require special talents or entrepreneurial guts, because the company itself is on the escalator system provided by the government. Take Japanese banks, for example. The Ministry of Finance protects them from bankruptcy with heavy regulation barriers. For example, the fees banks charge for various services are set by the ministry at a level where the weakest bank can be profitable. For management of a top rated bank to show a huge profit for the shareholders requires little effort. On the other hand, it was reported that each of the ten top Japanese banks at the end of March, 1993, had more than $10 billion in bad debts as a result of careless loans made to businesses during the booming economy of the 80's. This amount roughly corresponds to profit before taxes these banks can normally earn in the course of several years. It is whispered among economists that the actual amount of bad debts is much more than that. Sooner or later the banks will have to sell the shares of companies who are their customers. Since the banks invested a long time ago, the sales will provide profits to cover losses, but at a loss to shareholders. No manager or government official has taken responsibility toward the people who lost their investments as a result of the government's poor economic policy. The interests of the people have been ignored, as usual. The bad debt problem has become very serious, shaking the fundamental credit system of Japan.

Yet these high-ranking officials and managers will be honored as good citizens who have made significant contributions to the nation. Medals will be solemnly given in ceremonies attended by the emperor, and the decorated will be invited to the imperial garden party.

Japan's postwar success has been achieved by the rush of grassroots companies like Sony and Matsushita, who were put off the escalator system and left in open competition. They are rather minor sectors in Japan's total economy, but their advance led Japan to unprecedented prosperity. The managers of these companies are just like the daimyos of the civil war age. They too started as human shields. I am proud to have fought in the front as a human shield to make one of the companies, Casio, number one in the world, and to have fought together with many comrades, Japanese and foreign alike, who contributed to building today's Japan. The tripartite oligarchy (politicians/government officials/business leaders) have fully enjoyed the fruits of success we brought. But in the eyes of *okami* the rights and interests of *shomin* (the people) do not exist and the people are not getting their due share of prosperity. Japan is the same as one thousand years ago.

Chapter Thirty Six

Secrets of Success in Japanese Style Management

What is the secret of Japan's economic success? And what is the substance of so-called Japanese Style Management? If a foreigner wants to successfully penetrate the Japanese market, what policy should he follow? If he wants to be successful in a Japanese company, how should he behave? These questions are not easily answered. To fully appreciate Japan's successful economic growth, it is essential to understand the depth of the Japanese spirit.

The U.S. special procurement for the Korean War kicked off three consecutive big waves of economic booms. By the end of the 1950's, Japan had built up a solid base from which further expansion could be made in the future. H. Ikeda, president of the ruling Liberal Democratic Party, became Prime Minister in 1960. His comprehensive policies to prompt economic growth were fostered by his timely slogan: "Let's double our income." Prime Minister Ikeda's ideas were quite popular among people who had been suffering. For the first time after the defeat people had hopes for better life and they were ready to dedicate themselves to overcoming any obstacles that stood in Japan's way.

An enormous volume of blood was shed for the values of the Meiji ideology. The people detested bloodshed. The Americans brought in a new set of values—democracy, freedom, independence, equality and brotherhood. Though Japan's leaders pushed the new ideas enthusiastically, the immediate concern of the average Japanese was with eating, rather than freedom. National Shinto was prohibited, leaving a void. Mutsuhito's rescript of education was turned down. The Japanese lost precepts to guide themselves in this new "godless democracy."

Communism was more familiar to the Japanese than American democracy. It appealed especially to students, labor leaders, unions and the intelligentsia, and gained power despite the government's suppression after the outbreak of the Korean War. During the cold war communists succeeded in stirring up anti-American sentiment in Japan. Prime Minister Ikeda came out with his slogan amidst the storm of protest against the Japan-U.S. Security Pact. The left-wing claimed the Pact violated the Constitution. Indeed, there are two contradictory streams of laws, one deriving from the Constitution, the other from the Security Pact.

On June 15, 1960, students broke into the Diet building, counterpart of the Capitol. Many were wounded when protestors clashed with riot police. For three days, 330,000 demonstrators in the streets of Tokyo protested against the Pact.

To counter the communist movement, conservative leaders realized they needed a productive work ethic to inject at the production line. What was available? Religion had been abandoned and was impotent. The only choice in combating communism was to rehash the old Meiji ideology to suit the postwar situation. The emperor should be the central figure of the nation, but with the pacifism of the Constitution that endorsed "no more bloodshed". (As a matter of fact, the government refused U.S. demands for full rearmament and maintained the policy of limiting arms to the minimum for self-defense. Japanese diplomacy has been carefully conducted with the principle of "peace").

The emperor's authority was considerably damaged by defeat and ensuing criticism, especially from the communists. Although the emperor's functions are restricted to acts in matters of state provided for in the Constitution, the government made a broad interpretation, encouraging the emperor to act in private and semi-constitutional functions in order to increase his public presence. The government managed to make these functions appear democratic and peaceful.

This strategy to steadily magnify the emperor's authority was a great success. Hirohito practically came back to the position of head of state and sovereign monarch despite constitutional provisions. In the late 1950's, there was attempt by conservatives to revise the constitution to make Hirohito head of state and sovereign monarch "officially." This was not possible, but "official" revisions are no longer necessary because the purpose has been achieved de facto.

The images of bloody madness, militarism and ultra-nationalism were detached from Hirohito, and he became the nation's central figure to lead Japan to economic growth. The Japanese people have been conditioned not to question or doubt the *okami*, and traditional values were more familiar to them than democracy. They wanted prosperity and peace rather than sophisticated conceptual discussions. Accepted by the people, the new emperor institution defeated communism as the first step towards Japan's prosperity.

This establishment of new a emperor institution revitalized historical values, such as loyalty of subjects to monarch, which was used to reinforce loyalty of employees to employers. Factory productivity improved. No doubt this was Hirohito's greatest contribution to Japan. In social relations, loyalty and obedience have remained standard in measuring performance and determining rewards.

A subtle change from "democracy" with a symbolic monarch to a constitutional monarchy resembling that of the Meiji has been effected. The Japanese have been stuck with a constitution that cannot function on their behalf, for it is not based on democratic principles of equality. Because of the old values embedded in Japanese society, Japanese liberalism and capitalism are different from American or British. Western people see the Japanese have made an overwhelming success with different economic rules than theirs, but find it difficult to praise the success without reservation. This is the cost the Japanese now pay for the "miraculous" development.

Every segment of Japanese society needs a man like the emperor. All levels begin by making a man special, with glorification accompanied by myth. We often say, "Oh, he is a *tenno* (emperor) in xxx company (or ministry, etc.). You should not be against him." This position of *tenno* is given by the preceding *tenno*. To be nominated as the next *tenno* one has to totally submit oneself to the preceding *tenno* and serve him faithfully and selflessly for a long time until his approval is granted. The approval is given on evaluation of character, knowledge and ability, but most important is loyalty to the preceding *tenno* and spiritual perfection in traditional values such as *do*. Results are important, but secondary. A vertical chain of submission has been established:

- The emperor (great father figure over Japanese family)
- The president of the LDP and its members
- The prime minister with his cabinet and officials
- Presidents and directors with executive officers and managers of *keiretsu* companies (capitally related companies linked by loyalty to a parent company)
- Workers

Though the people are supposed to be legally equal, this vertical structure in practice overrides any equality conceived in the constitution. As great father of the country, the emperor is above the people and sets an example. The president of a company is not only a technocrat or organ to maximize profit for shareholders, he is also in a position to set an example for his children and the employees under him, in both business and private life. In this context, every company president is a small replica of the emperor within the domain of his company.

To be successful in a Japanese company, it is essential to realize these two points: Japan is a vertical society and the Japanese are loyalty oriented people. When an opinion is presented at a meeting it is more important who stated the opinion than how good this opinion may be for the company. Free debate by independent and equal members is seldom exercised in decisions. Employee evaluation is based on loyalty. A performance pay system rarely applies within the Japanese business structure because the concept is too selfish, in Japanese thinking. An employer looks upon his employees as his children. As a good father he will love them all equally.

A Japanese employer thinks: "Though my children have different capabilities and performances, it is a minor difference compared to the importance of their equal loyalty to me. As long as they have done their best to be loyal to me I will treat them equally. In appreciation, I do not make a big difference in any subordinates' salaries or bonuses. Money is not nearly as important as the love I give my workers. And with this love, as a man set above them, I can move them to their best productivity."

The idea of making a company president the father of his family of employees has worked well to save Japan from communism. This same relationship extends to the parent companies and *keiretsu* companies over their divisions. This loyalty method connecting father-employer with family-employees as a means of determining rewards for employees has created an effective bond between management and employees and has improved productivity significantly. In sales, where individual performances can vary, there has been some dissatisfaction. But salesmen are essentially against communistic ideas, it has been no problem.

This loyalty-based evaluation system is the backbone that supports the company family system. There is a myth about "permanent employment" in Japanese companies. Many believe Japanese management will not lay off employees even in financial difficulty. The company family system has fostered this legend because no father would kick his children out of their home just because of hard times. The LDP, as a capitalist political party, has encouraged the idea of father-employer with permanent children employees. It certainly helped the government financially in saving welfare and unemployment funds.

On one hand the LDP's policies brought votes from workers as well as abundant donations from business and industry. Employees were gratified by job security; employers were content with government aids that offset the cost of maintaining the permanent employment system in a climate of high growth rate. LDP leaders were able to enjoy easy lives, and could afford being absorbed in power games without outside interference. It seemed to be a good system...if it was not set against Western rules and values.

It is well known that the renumeration to Japanese managers is very low compared to American standards. Of course, a father should not be selfish or greedy. But Japanese managers are willing to accept lower renumeration from a different perspective. In 1949, Professor Shoup of Columbia University was sent to Japan to advise the government about its taxation system. As a result of his suggestions, a steep progressive income tax was adopted in which it was often a disadvantage to get a raise in pay because one's net income in a higher tax bracket could actually decrease. It was more advantageous to keep the income relatively low. It was also convenient in refuting the communists' logic that managers got a high income by exploiting workers. It also enhanced the "father and family" image and made the position of president sacred. How would founders and entrepreneurs be rewarded for success? They could become billionaires by selling shares when their companies went public, due to a special capital gains exemption. Other directors and executives were given fringe benefits that made their life comfortable; however, it made their dependency upon the companies stronger.

The reader must have many clues about how to be successful with Japanese management. The first thing you must do is to find out who is the *jitsuryokusha*, the ultimate decision maker. You ask, "Who will make this decision?" The answer is always the same: "Next meeting." In actuality, the *jitsuryokusha* has already made his decision before the meeting, and *nemawashi* (obtaining consent of important members individually on certain issues before the meeting) has been done. So when the matter is brought on the table for debate, there will be no opposition. The *jitsuryokusha* can adjust interests among parties with power and all will agree as he wishes. Of course he can provide his subordinates with significant advantages or disadvantages regarding their current and future position and treatment.

The *jitsuryokusha*'s faction is composed of *kobuns* (followers), who are informed of his intention beforehand and will steer the meeting to produce the decision according to his will. The term *kobun* is often used among gangsters, like, "He is a *kobun* of *yakuza* (Japanese Mafia)."

In a company there are usually two or three factions challenging the presidency and the *kobuns* of the faction that have succeeded will stand to benefit from the victory as a matter of loyalty.

It is not so easy for outsiders to find out who has real power, because he may be hiding behind someone else. Titles in a Japanese company are not always significant. "Chairman" could be just an honorary symbol like emperor. "President" could be a dummy. Often the *sodanyaku*, a consultant or advisor on the board, could be the real decision maker. In many cases he is the semi-retired founder of the company. Title alone does not necessarily give someone full authority to make decisions. It is important to study the history of the company and family names. Establish as many friendships as you can in the company. They will provide you with vital information about the current power situation and what is on the mind of the *jitsuryokusha*. Don't say no to an invitation to an after-hours office gathering at a pub for drinks with your *kacho* (section chief) or your *bucho* (department manager). It is an excellent occasion to obtain information and deepen your relationship with them by showing your faith. You may become a *kobun* of a powerful *bucho*. You must find out who is the ultimate decision maker. Then concentrate your efforts to find out how to gain access to him. Join his faction and become known to him personally so that he may identify you and hopefully like you. To become a *kobun*, you must be prepared to surrender yourself almost like a slave. Forget about yourself. You no longer exist. Dedicate yourself to the benefit of your boss.

Second, you must serve your boss with utmost loyalty and sincerity. Do not cheat. Even if you are sure to get away with it, never take advantage. Show your appreciation for what he has given you. Under no circumstances drive him into a corner. Never spar with him. If he makes an error, be sure to cover up for him even if you incur damage yourself. It will always pay off later.

Third, work long, hard hours. Come to work at least a half hour early, attend morning assembly without fail. Sing the company song in a louder voice than anybody else. Don't go home before your manager has left for the day. Volunteer to work overtime. Never refuse to work on a holiday no matter what you have scheduled with your family. If you are in a managerial position, you will not be paid extra compensation for overtime and holidays. That is why it is the best opportunity to show your dedication to the company. Of course you love your family and they are important, but you should act as though your boss and company have much greater importance. When you work on a holiday don't directly broadcast the fact. You must be discreet, and wait for the right opportunity to let it be known indirectly.

Fourth, don't object or argue with your boss in an open meeting. You may bring up your argument as a gesture to show your eagerness to participate in the discussion. That's sufficient. Read your boss' expression carefully. If he does not seem to like your idea, drop it right away. By all means do not let him feel insulted. To avoid making mistakes, it is better to keep your opinions and beliefs to yourself; in fact, it is best to have no particular opinions or strong beliefs. Accept your boss' words without question. Any principle you hold dear could backfire, especially if you are an international businessman. It is more convenient to deal with Americans today, Arabs tomorrow and Chinese next week, with no regard for personal beliefs and principles. Better to concentrate on making good business for the company.

Fifth, apply the same attitudes in your private life. Listen to your boss when he advises you about his own view of life. Hear with patience and eagerness, even if he seems silly and foolish. If his wife needs help with anything, it is the best opportunity to show your loyalty. Always accept when he invites you to play golf. Run ahead of him to find his ball when he hits it into the rough. Praise his good shots and sympathize with his misfortunes. To show your consideration to his family, send nice gifts twice a year.

Finally, if you speak Japanese, marry the president's daughter and become a Japanese citizen. If you observe all the above for thirty years without fail, you stand an excellent chance of being the next company president. If you fail, you have only yourself to blame. This similar relationship between bosses and workers exists in all aspects of Japanese society, i.e. government, academics, medical practice and law firms. A typical example of this relationship can be found between the boss of a faction within a political party and his *kobun* members whom he controls by providing with funds and administrative positions. It is the same between parent companies and *keiretsu*. Remember Japan is not a democratic society of independent, free, equal people. Business circles are closed to foreigners unfamiliar with the structure described in this chapter.

All this having been said, I must now qualify the above recommendations as being somewhat disgusting to me. I worked in an international area, and consequently did not have to do much that was against my will. In a similar vein, most American executives cannot become board directors of a parent company in Japan. Although an American might rarely be president of a Japanese subsidiary in the U.S., the president is usually Japanese. Japanese management is aware that Americans will not endorse the ground rules described in this chapter. Consequently, Americans are kept out of management. It is not a question of nationality or ability, but acceptance of rules of loyalty in the vertical structure.

Japanese employees who work selflessly in a company are not ultimately rewarded that much. Although Japanese companies have become extremely rich, employees remain in a rather poor environment. What happens to the children of the "family" after they have been so loyal to their father? Typically, an employee in his late 50's will find himself staring out his office window with no work on his desk. Gray-haired warriors who fought at the front in the economic war as "human shields" are now being disposed of one by one, held in limbo, waiting for a post in subsidiaries or related companies. After 40 years of faithful service, they must work for their family in a new company, still under the strain of loyalty. Their income is not enough to retire. They face the high cost of living. It was expensive to educate their children. Their taxes are high, their pensions low. Many still have a mortgage to pay. This is a new style of slavery, born of the same tradition of the vertical society. Employees dedicate their lives and the company responds with a "throwaway" tradition at the end. Though we live in a modern industrial world, employees in Japanese companies today are much like our ancestors who were hunted down from the mountains and made slave-soldiers to be used as human shields in battle. Today they fight in economic wars, but the outcome is much the same. They must use, like slave soldiers, two swords, one in each hand, to fend off enemy arrows. Few fortunate survivors may become *karou* (minister of the lord, director) and luckier ones even a *daimyo* (president).

Today, due to a longlasting depression, the Japanese economy is in danger of collapse, and Japanese workers are scared of being dismissed. Masters in this country will always settle the problem at the sacrifice of their servants. Their principle is to have no principle.

Chapter Thirty Seven

Pride Goeth Before A Fall

During my years of service with Japanese companies, much praise was given to Japanese Style Management because of the tremendous success of Japanese companies. Rapid growth was brought on by favorable conditions, including the government's strong protection and support, and a hardworking workforce that was loyal and obedient to the company. In this chapter I will give you a true picture of Japanese Style Management, based oN first hand experience over more than two decades.

Economic growth in Japan began as early as during U.S. occupation after World War II. The U.S.'s first objective was to demilitarize Japan so that she would never be able to cause further trouble in the world. Hirohito was used as "a man above men," for governing smoothly. This relationship is well indicated in the current constitution and gave the *okami* concept a way to survive. The godlike *okami* never commits any mistakes, proven in the imperial family, who made the long history of Japan unique in the world.

Any acts that spoil this conception should be concealed, even down to fabricating history. These are the features of the vertical society, in which the emperor is positioned at the top, essential to the Meiji ideology. With the American-inspired constitution, the only difference was that dying for the emperor was no longer necessary, due to Japan's renouncing war.

During the occupation, the U.S. made various reforms, including enforcement of labor laws as early as 1945. At the same time, *zaibatsu* (giant financial combines, such as Sumitomo, Mitsui, Mitsubishi, etc.)

were dissolved. The U.S. policy was to extract the power of *zaibatsu* that supported militarism.

Communism was then very popular. Communist leaders freed by the Americans were welcomed as heros who had not forsaken their anti-imperialist beliefs despite government oppression. Sympathizers in GHQ encouraged communists. To many Japanese, the semantics of communism were synonymous with democracy.

By the time the war came to its end, the Japanese people had lost properties and were living in air raid shelters that barely kept them dry from rain. In rags, pained by hunger, people wandered aimlessly through the streets. The war's end had robbed them of their reason to live, which ironically was to die for the emperor. Ex-soldiers repatriated from southern islands where they had fought not only fierce battles but hunger, found their homeland dominated by two sources of business: the black market and prostitution.

People were devastated, without hope for the future. The Japanese economy faced a crisis whereby half the population could have died of starvation. Then Japan's fate took a sudden turn. In 1949, Nationalist China fell and Communist China was born. Recognizing a serious threat, the U.S. quickly changed its policy. Japan was to be made the main base to support U.S. forces in the Far East.

In 1950 General MacArthur declared that Japan's constitution does not deny her right of self-defense. In June, the Korean War broke out. GHQ had the Japanese government organize a "Police Reserve," renamed the "Security Force," which in 1954 developed to what is Japan's current "Defense Force."

Purges against former political and economic leaders were canceled. Instead, communists were purged from government offices and key industries. The return of capable persons experienced in planning and executing economic policies was good for the Japanese economy. Many restrictions on economic concentration were lifted. In addition, special procurements by the U.S. force for the Korean War was a shot in the arm, or as the Japanese proverb says, "It was a welcome rain during a dry season." A series of economic booms followed in succession in the 1950's, marking the beginning of Japan's miraculous growth over the next three decades.

Even with U.S. assistance, the road to prosperity was long and hard. According to the "Chronicle of Prices" edited by the *Asahi Shinbun Sha* (newspaper) in 1988, the first basic salary paid by Japanese banks to new university graduates in 1950 was 3000 yen per month, which at the then prevailing exchange rate was only US $8.33. In 1960 it increased to 15,000 yen, or US $41.67 per month; in 1970, US

$108.33, and in 1980, US $572.22. In 1990 it was about US $1380. During this period, the U.S. dollar has been devalued from 360 to 130 yen. In the 1950's, a U.S. army sergeant's housing allowance was US $150 per month (54,000 yen). In 1968, my basic salary as an international sales manager was the equivalent of US $ 266.40 per month. Even with my additional allowances and bonuses added in, my annual income was US $5600. Remember, Japan was merely a small and poor country in the Far East.

To Japanese companies the world market appeared to be limitless. Under the precept of a family company, Japanese management was convinced that by supplying good products at low prices to the world market the company could grow exponentially. This primitive, optimistic presupposition was typical of Japanese Style Management from the outset, and continued into the 1990's.

"Permanent employment" and a "seniority system" are considered special features of Japanese Style Management. Both are related to a company's growth and the concept of a family company within a family country. But the intrinsic benefit of permanent employment and a seniority system depend on reality, rather than optimistic assumptions of limitless economic growth.

Permanent Employment: If an employee in a Japanese company has not personally failed by reasons attributable to himself, he is guaranteed lifetime employment. Japanese schools finish on the last day of March and graduates begin work in the company that has hired them April 1. Most university graduates are 22 years old and will work for the company till age 60-65. High school graduates work four more years. After some 40 years of work, most people will be offered another job at subsidiaries or related companies to work several more years.

The president of a family company is the father and does not kick out his children (employees) heartlessly even if the company has financial problems. In return, employees are expected to dedicate their lives to the company, in a variation of the *okami* idea. The *okami*, be he emperor, shogun, government, or administrator, protects his subjects, who in turn render homage.

The Japanese constitutional monarchy has positioned its symbolic emperor as great father of the nation, above the cabinet and Diet. Among his children are corporate managers and employees, political leaders and government officials who share the great father's love, and protect their own "children" for him. This is the concept of "Japan, Incorporated." Ministers and presidents have resigned because their mistakes damaged the integrity of the *okami*.

The idea of "Japan, Inc." was powerful in the fight against communism, successfully removing communists from production lines and offices. Japan, Inc. was also a great help to the government which had been suffering from severe financial deficits, allowing them to shift a substantial unemployment allowance budget burden to private business and industry, in return for which the government formulated protections and assistances.

The basic salary of Japanese employees is held down, while allowances and subsidies helped augment costs. Commutation is fully paid by the company; there are family, job qualification and housing allowances, executive perks, meal subsidies, etc. The job qualification allowance is paid for the rank indicating the level at which an employee performs. The sales allowance is paid to salesmen who need more apparel yet are not entitled to overtime. A special allowance is often applied to the re-employed to adjust differences.

Overtime and holiday pay amounting to a substantial part of income are provided. In many cases overtime pay has been firmly built into one's living plan as fixed income. As one is promoted to managerial position he is no longer entitled to the allowance, but still has to work late at night or on holidays voluntarily. This offers an excellent opportunity to show loyalty to superiors and okami. Allowances help employees, while giving flexibility to the company. In difficult times they may be cut back or abolished. Japanese companies can reduce personnel expenses significantly by cutting back bonuses.

If a company pays a bonus equal to six months' salary, it is paying bonuses equal to three months salaries twice, in June and December. In many Japanese companies 1/2 of one month salary out of a bonus equal to three months' salary is paid in accordance with employee achievement evaluation.

In Japan most companies do not offer a 100% sales commission. Salesmen are paid fixed salaries plus a bonus, the same as other employees. Some are offered incentives, but the major portion of the bonus is paid as deferred salary, so that part of the bonus is paid irrespective of company results. It is hard to understand why a company holds a portion of the employee's salary for six months. If management as father of the family company is saving an amount from his children's salary each month for safekeeping so that the employee will not waste the money, what contribution could management expect from such childish employees who cannot control themselves?

The economic depression forced companies to severely cut bonuses, unduly harming employees' lives. Employees should not be forced to sacrifice deferred payment because of a company's poor results, for the company's implied commitment is not to lay off or dismiss.

Japanese companies can benefit from keeping employees' basic salaries low. Normally severance pay was calculated based on the number of years the employee served the company. Now many large companies have converted the severance pay system to a pension system, because it is more beneficial to the company.

Japanese management takes much fatherly pride in its social responsibility to permanently employ the members of its family company, but to keep a permanent employment system, company growth is essential. To keep growing, the company must keep developing good products, mass producing in high quality and supplying to the world markets at competitive prices. It is like a jihad fought by management and employees together, with everyone giving his best effort as in a holy war.

As Japan is a vertical society, so the Japanese company is also a vertical society. Titles such as *shacho* (president), *senmu* (senior managing director), *bucho* (departmental manager), *kacho* (section chief) etc., are given to indicate status in the vertical society. For a man of independence, this society can be hard to live with; however, once resigned to the lack of independence, the obedient employee can adjust.

Seniority System: Japanese management bases pay increases, job promotions and bonuses on the amount of time an employee has served the company. Time is an important standard to measure employee loyalty. A longtime employee is trustworthy. Since the job of each employee is not precisely defined in Japanese companies, check systems often do not work well; therefore employee reliability is very important.

Management, as father of a family company, is supposed to love and trust every employee as a child of that family in *tatemae* (official statement), but in reality, this is true only for long-time employees. In Japanese companies it will take about ten years to become a *kacho* (section chief). Companies are reluctant to employ workers from other companies, preferring fresh graduates. Suppose a company was founded 50 years ago. It would be organized as follows; management in their 60's, who have served the company for over 40 years; *bucho*, 40's-50's; *kacho*, 35-45. All executives are time-proven to be fully reliable; younger employees are managed very closely. Management wants to run a company with the *tatemae* of trust in this way, rather than by a strict check system.

This system does not apply to Americans. The president of a U.S.-based Japanese subsidiary cannot wait 10-20 years until a pyramid of time-proven, trustworthy employees who work voluntarily and systematically in concert with him is built up. The first most critical problem is how to find an American president for the subsidiary. Suppose a capable, trustworthy American president is found, how do he and the Japanese understand each other? There is a language barrier. Of course many Japanese speak English; however, when Japanese say "man," the meaning of "man" is entirely different from the American; it is the difference between a vertical and a democratic society; it is nearly impossible to understand each other exactly. There is no way the top man sitting in Japan can understand Americans and the American way of business, even though many Japanese subsidiaries in the U.S. are doing well with their American staffs.

In the vertical society there are traditional precepts one must abide by. As one's stature rises, one is required to reach perfection in precepts, step by step. For example, it is questioned what a true *kacho* should be. This is *tatemae*. But there is always a gap in reality. A real *kacho* is not what a true *kacho* should be. This is *honne*. So the Japanese conceal *honne* for fear of retribution. This fear travels vertically to the top, and anything that may spoil *tatemae* will be concealed.

No matter how adept or proficient an employee may be, he is of no use to the company unless he is loyal. When one employee's achievement is rewarded with extraordinarily rapid promotion or an exorbitant pay increase, it disrupts and harms *wa* (order and harmony) among other employees. This disruption will do much more harm to the company than any benefits the employee seems to provide with his ability or achievement. The Japanese company is a pyramid of employees in a seniority system, with everybody merely an assistant to his superior. The whole is always more important than any of its components. Japanese management believes the "seniority system" is best to maintain the *wa* of the whole. (This *wa* is not to be confused with Wa, the country of Japanese history, which, though phonetically the same, has a completely different Chinese character and meaning).

In Japan, new graduates are divided into two groups, technical and business, in accordance with their education. It is up to the company to decide specific job assignments, though they are not as clear as in American companies. Typically, an employee with a technical education might be assigned to Research and Development, while another with a business education would be assigned to accounting or sales. During an employees' first three years with a company his abilities will be tested to see if he is properly suited for his job assignment. During this period the new graduate is considered an apprentice to become fully competent in his assignment. First and foremost, he will learn and understand how *wa* is maintained and how he can contribute to the group. Management will treat all new employees equally with the same salary increase for that group.

Big Japanese companies have a model for an employee's life. All employees are classified into several ranks according to qualifications, starting from apprentice to executive level. Managerial positions are given to employees according to rank. For example, managers of sales divisions will be selected from rank "X" and up. Twice a year a board will evaluate an employee's achievement during the past six months. Means of evaluation to determine salary increases and bonuses vary. In one case, ability may be more important, while in another, achievement takes precedence. Evaluation results are displayed by numerical points. If an evaluation shows an average score, an employee will be promoted to the next highest rank within the standard period.

A special examination is given to those seeking executive level positions. Even if an employee stays within the same rank, his salary will continue to increase each year. But an upgrade to a higher rank will significantly increase his salary. The model provided by the company exemplifies the standard expected from initial hiring to retirement. From this model, an employee knows immediately if he is above or below the average. This model is a guideline for lifetime competition by all employees, but it is controlled on the basis of loyalty and *wa*. There is no quick success in a Japanese company. Every salary increase and promotion require time, and accumulated years of service always count.

When Japanese entrepreneurs started their ventures in the 1950's and 60's most of the top management knew nothing about foreign markets. Most did not speak English or any other foreign language. Ironically, export to Western countries has become the major part of their business. For them it was impossible to adopt a "performance pay" system for sales staff, because they could not determine reasonable targets in foreign markets.

Japanese management is not eager to study marketing in the same way that Japanese military headquarters was not eager to rely on reconnaissance in battle. Both deny figures that indicate infeasibility of their plans.

To establish sales targets, the market size must be known; product marketability and sales channels must be counted; competitors and competition must be considered. To the pioneer Japanese entrepreneurs, the size of foreign markets appeared limitlessly huge, and the market situation was unclear. Even within their own domestic market they used no scientific method to estimate its potential. Rather than wasting time by setting goals determined by modern marketing techniques, they based their business plan on management's needs for expansion only, which would enable the company to produce profit after rapidly increasing expenses were paid.

Employees push and push markets with all their power, working day and night. At the end of the year, they arrive at a result. It could be 150% or 85% of the target, but it does not matter, if management knows everyone has done his best. In this loyalty oriented society, an employee who might otherwise be demoted for failure to reach the desired goal in a performance pay system, is instead evaluated with higher points if the record shows he selflessly devoted himself to do his best, even though he fell short of the target.

Most Japanese companies provide many employee benefit programs, such as company housing, financing for buying a home, subsidies to events, excursions, club activities, athletic meets, etc. Some large companies have their own hotels in resort areas for employees. All Japanese companies have health insurance programs that cover 50% of monthly premiums. All the benefits a company provides are feasible if the company continues to grow indefinitely. Otherwise, it is impossible for management to bear so many expenses and still show a reasonable shareholder profit.

Shareholders are the most ignored in the Japanese business structure, even though they own the company. Dividend is negligible compared with investment. In the Japanese stock market, the profit earning ratio (P/E = the ratio between the share price and the earnings per share) is abnormally high, often 60 times profit per share. For example, if the profit earned per share is 30 yen and the share market price is 1800 yen, the P/E ratio is 60. Normally Japanese dividends are about 10% or 5 yen for a face value of 50 yen per share. Suppose we have a good share, dividend of which is 25% or 12.50 yen per share, the return on investment (ROI) calculated as interest is merely 0.7% per annum, based on the market price of 1800 yen per share.

This means investors in Japan do not buy stocks for dividends, but for growth. If you invested US $100 in Sony Corporation in its early days, its market value would be about US $400,000 today, 4000 times initial investment. This growth happened over three decades. As the company keeps growing it must increase its capital. Today this is done by equity financing, issuing convertible bonds to the public. Normally, after this financing, the current shareholders will receive a stipulated number of free shares (called a stock dividend in the U.S. and taxed as capital gains income) to offset their disadvantages from that financing, i.e., profit per share goes down. When this free share is given to current shareholders, shares' market price will go down. While Japan's extraordinary economic growth continued, stock prices always rose. A current market drop in share prices can be offset by future rising prices, yielding shareholders good profits in the long run.

Every time a company increases its capitalization, the amount of shares in the hands of shareholders automatically increases. Multiplied by the market price per share which continues to rise, shareholders' assets increase tremendously.

This method is much more profitable to investors, particularly to individuals. According to the latest Japanese tax laws, you are required to pay a tax equal to 1% of stock sales proceeds; you are not required to pay any additional income tax. The profit you have gained from the sale of stock, after the payment of the 1% separate tax, does not have to be declared in consolidated tax declarations, regardless of amount. Under this system, investment is advantageous, even if dividends are low. Quarterly profits are of little concern if sufficient growth is promised over the next few years.

The Japanese system of capital growth allows management to make long-range plans, while U.S. management is compelled to be short-sighted to show quarterly profits that will yield investors high year-end profits. The Japanese method of investment has a significant influence on company policy because management can operate the company on less profit as long as the company continues to grow on a sound basis. The result is more aggressive pricing in the market, more investment for Research and Development, and more human resources with permanent employment under the seniority system. If Japanese board members and executives were exposed to the risk of dismissal for failing to yield sufficient short-term profits in one or two quarters of the year, they would have been unable to perform the so-called Japanese Style Management.

Japanese Style Management has been feasible under exceptionally favorable conditions: there have been limitless open markets; fundamental innovations occurred at the same time Japanese companies started their growth; technical revolutions have advanced Japanese innovations in electronics, i.e, from transistors and diodes to small scale, middle and large scale integration. Japan was a poor, small country which was allowed to protect and assist its industries and businesses against foreign invasion. Above all the new emperor system helped tremendously to overcome communism and to establish a loyal, obedient work force.

The expansion of Japanese businesses, however, is now hitting finite limits. It is unrealistic to assume that Japanese businesses can continue to grow at the same rate they have enjoyed for three decades. Japanese companies will soon learn that there is no more room for growth despite efforts of selfless employees. Japanese Style Management will face serious difficulties. The young generation will be more like Westerners and the Japanese will have to learn Western management to cope with a declining economy. Pride goeth before a fall.

I first wrote about this subject several years ago. My concerns regarding Japanese Style Management have since materialized. Many Japanese companies are practically dismissing employees and changing the pay system to a form of "performance pay." But society will not change so quickly. I am afraid the *okami* will not take effective measures such as deregulation to improve the economy, but will pass damage to the people, as usual. Similarly, management will not take responsibility, but will settle problems at the sacrifice of employees, as usual.

Chapter Thirty Eight

Stifled Creativity

Wa is a value peculiar to Japanese culture, not only in business management, but in all phases of society, that often puts Japanese and Western cultures at odds. For the Japanese, order and harmony can only be maintained by loyalty within a vertical society where individualism has little importance. In Western society, individuals who stand out and excel are heroes rewarded with fame, honor and big salaries. Not so in Japan, where individual excellence could disrupt the harmony of the team, the group, the company, the industry, even the nation.

Hero worship of excellent performers and achievers is typified in U.S. culture by professional sports. The big bonuses and multi-million dollar contracts awarded to baseball players, for example, conflict with Japanese culture, where such emphasis would destroy the *wa* of a sport, which epitomizes team play, the very essence of harmony.

In his 1989 book published by Macmillan, *You Gotta Have Wa*, Robert Whiting illustrates this basic difference between Western and Japanese cultures when they play baseball together. Whiting portrays Americans as egotists who laud individual performance, such as home run championships and league-leading batting titles. American superstars in sports flaunt their achievements and expect special treatment. Japanese ballplayers, just as Japanese employees in any other business, never talk back. Americans often resent Japanese humility; but a Japanese manager, whether on a baseball diamond or overseeing a production line, would punish any outspoken player or worker by benching him or holding back promotion, especially if such behavior were demonstrated in front of the team.

According to Whiting, a Japanese manager believes the most important ingredient of a winning team is *wa* and the best way to knock a team's *wa* away is to hire an American. A familiar complaint by many American sports fans who have cheered for their favorite team made up of "individual" stars with great statistics and astronomical contracts is that these great "individuals" often will not make up a championship team. Each individual player tries to outdo the other in earnings and extended contracts, all well-publicized in the media. This kind of one-upmanship does not exist in the Japanese vertical society, where a man above men comes first: the manager under the director under the president under the emperor.

The most popular Japanese professional baseball team is the Giants, sponsored by the *Yomiuri Shinbun*, the largest national newspaper in circulation. The Giants' management issued a list of ten rules for American players to observe which the Japanese press called: "The Gaijin (foreigners') Ten Commandments:"

1. Obey all orders issued by the manager.
2. Do not criticize the manager's strategy.
3. Take good care of your uniform.
4. Do not scream and yell in the dugout or destroy objects in the clubhouse.
5. Do not reveal team secrets to other foreign players.
6. Do not tease your teammates harshly.
7. In the event of injury, follow the treatment prescribed by the team.
8. Be on time.
9. Do not return home during season.
10. Do not disturb the *wa* of the team.

The idea of *wa* derives from the oldest known constitution as set forth by Shotoku Taishi (Prince Shotoku) in 604 A.D., according to the chronicles of *Nihon Shoki*. The constitution stressed three specific values; respect *wa*; practice Buddhism; and obey the emperor. The first of seventeen articles begins with this famous sentence which is often quoted as proof that the Japanese are essentially a peace-loving people: "Do respect *wa* (order and harmony) most preciously and make it a principle not to defy." The articles continues: "People belong to each clique and only a few are wise. For this reason, some do not follow the lord and father and some quarrel with their neighbors. But if superiors are gentle and subordinates are peaceful in discussing a problem, there will naturally be a reasonable conclusion. By respecting *wa*, anything can be accomplished without a fight."

The prince was Buddhist, but Yagiri doubts that Prince Shotoku existed. Rather, Yagiri believes the prince was created as the ideal figure of a ruler to win over the Japanese aborigines, who made up 90% of the population. The description of the prince in *Nihon Shoki*, Yagiri advises, is mere fiction, and the precepts were edited in 720 A.D. by the T'ang Chinese in power to win over the aborigines.

Although it was called a "constitution," it was rather a precept for the governing lords. For example, it says not to levy heavy taxes or be despotic. One article demanded: "Government officials must come to the office early in the morning and leave late in the evening." This may be the root of the Japanese people's hardworking tradition.

No doubt there was an ulterior motive, in that this first constitution was merely a demand for the people to obey the ruling despotic powers. Since the period in which the "constitution" was written was several decades before the T'ang Chinese occupation, the rulers were Koreans, probably Paekche. These Korean nobles were greedy and despotic, and the precepts were probably written in fear that people would revolt without the flowery words of the prince to fall back on.

Wa is a convenient tool for a ruler to suppress trouble: once the ruler says, "Here is the way the matter is to be settled," the parties concerned may still have differences in opinion but must agree with the ruler. *Wa* must be accepted as the wise judgment of a loving father. The Japanese tradition of making half way compromises without making clear which party's claim is more reasonable probably derived from the concept of *wa*.

How comfortable for the ruler who has set these precepts, knowing his people will not quarrel, that harmony will reign as the status quo. Accepting the law of the land, people will not band together to make changes, or insist on improvements in their lives. For this reason, *wa* cannot be considered an ultimate value; rather, self-awareness is essential to realize what needs to be done. With voluntary cooperation, people can achieve common goals.

The contradiction in this supposed harmony comes when the Japanese baseball manager, though still faithfully believing in *wa*, demands to be the boss who rules over his team. His hierarchy rules beyond his position as an organ of the team. He rules, the same as the emperor, as "a man above men". No wonder Robert Whiting sees little chance of success in the cooperation of these two cultures when Japanese management would try to control American employees by the hard-set rules proclaimed in "The Gaigin Ten Commandments".

Why are Japanese employees afraid to speak out? It is inherent in their history as an enslaved people. When the American forces occupied Japan in 1945, a rumor spread that all Japanese men were to be castrated. This actually occurred during the T'ang Chinese occupation in the 7th century A.D., so the possibility may not have seemed so far-fetched to the Japanese.

The T'ang Chinese dealt severely with their Japanese slaves. If they were not obedient, they were killed. The only chance for a slave to leave descendants came from his obedience, which could be rewarded. For the race to survive, the ancestors of the current Japanese people had to suffer under conditions of severe discipline, surrendering themselves totally to their foreign rulers. The mark of a thousand years of slavery is on today's Japanese society and reflected in Japanese management which, as Robert Whiting claims in his book, "tends to treat its charges like the inmates on a Georgia chain gang." The American player on Whiting's Japanese-managed team criticizes his Japanese teammates who "never speak up...run in the hallway to cough...and are afraid to say anything."

Yes, Japanese players and workers are afraid to speak up, especially to say in *honne* what they really think. Instead, out of fear of losing their positions, Japanese are compelled to say what they are expected to say in *tatemae*, to please their managers.

Notorious as a despotic business owner in Japan is Yoshiaki Tsutsumi, owner of the Seibu Group, which controls railroads, department stores, hotels, supermarkets and real estate. Tsutsumi was ranked by Forbes in 1987 as the richest man in the world. Among his assets is the professional baseball team the Seibu Lions. A famous Tsutsumi quote is: "If you want Sundays off, don't be a manager in my company." His workers are terrified of him, referring to him as being "like the emperor."

Tsutsumi can fill a stadium with Seibu employees, who are expected to buy tickets and appear at as many games as possible as an expression of company loyalty. Seibu's *oendan* (cheering group) chiefs are known to take attendance before each game to see who is attending from which group. Department managers are encouraged to boost attendance. It is a familiar sound before a game begins to hear a sub-*oendan* group leader call out, "Group A, all present and accounted for!" It is much like the military where a no-show will cost an employee demerits towards a drop in company standing.

If you ask Seibu employees how they feel about going to Seibu Lions' games after 5 p.m. or on weekends and holidays, their *tatemae* reply will be that they enjoy supporting their team and they love the Seibu Lions. But if they could speak up and tell you what they really thought by giving you their *honne* answer, it would be: "I have no choice. I love my family and can't afford to let my company standing suffer by not showing up."

These well-educated Japanese employees have learned about the French Revolution, read Shakespeare and studied Keynesian Economics at the university. Although they are sophisticated enough to realize this kind of manipulation is a cheap trick, they accept the ideology. They fully realize the system they live by makes them like children who are told stories with picture cards, yet they would not speak up for fear of jeopardizing their lifetime employment and seniority. They realize they were not born merely to make the shareholders rich, yet they work in silence.

The Japanese employee has built up his standing over many years. His mortgage is held by the company he works for. A move to another company will make him a new face in a strange environment where he must start from scratch again. Rationalizing his silence is easy. He has many advantages, especially the security that his children will be well-educated and the company will not foreclose on his home. The emperor wants the system to work this way, so why not? This is the way of the world.

In a Japanese manufacturing company, product research, development and marketing are the most important measures of future growth, which is essential to Japanese Style Management working. But Japanese management does not put enough emphasis on marketing. They invest a lot of money in R and D to put out innovative products of greater quality than the competitors'. Though they spend a lot on advertising and promotion, they are less eager to allocate budgets towards research to learn about consumer needs and wants. This attitude resembles that of the imperial forces of the Empire of Japan during World War II, which never attached due importance to reconnaissance in battle.

Japanese success can be attributed to the devotion of engineers, material procurement buyers, subcontractor controllers and production line workers whose hard work and cooperative efforts enabled the companies to put new products on the market every three months at competitive prices. Success came from manpower rather than innovative ideas or calculated plans.

There is a direct parallel between Japanese success in world markets and the imperial forces' early victories in initial battles of World War II. The imperial forces won by sacrificing human lives rather than by means of a well-prepared strategy or tactics based on reconnaissance. Had they invested more resources in marketing, they would not have been exposed to so much trial and error and could have saved much manpower. Like imperial headquarters in the war, Japanese management does not like any data or information that might cast a shadow of doubt on success.

In developing new products, the imagination of the engineer can sometimes replace marketing, if he has insights and intuition about market needs. But without a marketing strategy, it is impossible to lay out a sound annual sales plan with realistic quotas. Marketing is essential in a "performance pay" system, applied in European management. Japanese Style Management is based on loyalty, with a self-serving "try and find" system based on management's needs, by which an annual plan is devised to show figures better than the previous year.

In a business plan for the coming year, sales 15-20% higher than the previous year will be settled on in order to cover significant increases in expenses, yet leave sufficient profit. The sales plan is given to the sales manager as sales quotas. He will mark up the quota by another 10% before allocating quotas to his sales department, feeling that higher quotas assure 100% achievement of the plan. Since sales quotas are so high, few salesmen can attain them, unless, by good fortune, the potential in the allocated area exceeds the quota or the salesman illegally sells outside his assigned territory. Incentive schemes do not help. But even if most salesmen fall short of their quotas, achievements will differ, so that evaluation for promotion and bonuses can be done on those differences. This system is based on the premise that everyone has done his best.

You might call this a "cow in the dark" system, because Japanese management, like cows in the dark, cannot see how far they can go, yet when whipped from the rear, they blindly and desperately stumble forward. They do not stop until they hit a wall and can go no further no matter how hard they try. Management accepts the end result as the best they could squeeze out. The most important issue for management is that the salesman has worked with all his heart and soul. For this reason, long work days and nights, weekends and holidays are musts in Japan.

Even in professional sports, grueling practice sessions exhaust players before a game. But this is the means by which a player can demonstrate to the manager that he has done his best. Irrespective of a game's outcome, win or lose, this demonstration of loyalty in an all-out effort in practice is essential to Japanese management.

While Japanese employees are afraid to speak up, they are even more afraid of making mistakes. Unlike samurais of yore, they no longer face *hara-kiri* or *seppuku*, committing suicide by cutting open their bellies with a knife. But in the modern business world, it is not so easy to remove the memory of mistakes from a supervisor. Over-optimistic sales forecasts can result in excess inventory and big losses for a company. Overselling into untried territory with extended credit to unproven accounts could potentially lead to bankruptcy. Negative outlooks frighten employees from taking risks, yet if a gamble turns out well, one suddenly hears the voices of those who want to take the credit. Japanese management depends on growth to function, yet applies no-risk strategies which are self-defeating to that very growth.

In R and D, Machiavellian tactics are sometimes used by a group of veteran engineers. They will purposely ruin the good idea of a younger staff, or steal credit for some innovation. They might throw cold water on a younger man's hot new idea, then wait some duration after it has been initially rejected by management, to resubmit it with group support as their own idea. In this way, competition and cut-throat tactics are applied to defend a group's position as the development engineering group.

It may be little known by Westerners that when Japanese are employed by a company, they are requested to submit a guarantee signed by a parent and independent guarantor, that the employer will be compensated for any damages or losses the company may incur by crimes the employee may commit. In an actual case, a company employee embezzled funds, and his father was obliged to liquidate his assets to appease the company. It may be easy for new graduates to find a guarantor, but I was quite embarrassed at the request to submit the guarantee when I was employed by the duplicator company at the age of 56. Parents? My father died when I was 13. It made no sense to ask my mother. Friends? I could find no one. The company finally withdrew the request.

This system, which originated from the Edo period (1603-1867) just before the Meiji era, is rooted in feudalism, whereby relatives are held accountable for a person's putative crimes. This policy may not apply to the majority of Japanese companies anymore today, but for those companies still using it, they are not employing personnel under their own judgment and responsibility.

Essential differences directly reflected in business management exist between Japanese and American culture which cannot change. Japanese Style Management is loyalty-oriented whereby employees must do whatever job is assigned to them. Sometimes job specifications in Japanese companies are vague or even nonexistent. Since a new employee's responsibilities and authority are left unclear, he tends to ask for the manager's approval on anything. This dependence on superiors ultimately conforms to the vertical line of loyalty.

Executive titles in Japanese companies are often misleading because they may sound more authoritative than they really are. A "department manager" might be an assistant to a higher executive and his authority may be very limited compared to his American counterpart. Transfer of authority in Japanese companies is rare, because responsibility filters up rather than down. Every manager is personally responsible for his subordinates in work and in their personal lives. When some flagrant mishap occurs in American companies, management will take responsibility by improving the company system or seeking a scapegoat at the lower level to protect the upper echelon from dismissal. In Japanese management, blame is sought at the top because of the vertical society. For this reason, the resignation of Japanese company presidents is more prevalent than in the U.S. But first they try to hide the mistake.

Japanese management restrains from delegating authority to lower-level executives to keep a firm control on responsibilities that could come back to haunt them if mishandled by subordinates. Japanese management gives lip service to transferring authority to lower levels, but in reality it is a rarity. Managers keep most of their power as an unwritten law whereby they are more than just an organ of the business, but rather the "man above" who governs subordinates. Managers assign some of their powers by implied agreement, but only among subordinates who have been trustworthy over many years of service. This implied practice is called *aun-no-kokyu*, and is more convenient to management than specific subordinate job descriptions, because it lets a manager interpret his underlings' responsibilities at his own discretion.

In Japan a *Torishimari Yaku* is a board director who is elected at a general shareholders' meeting. In many companies, the title is mistaken for an honorary executive title. The director is supposed to make decisions on business policies and future plans at board meetings, and direct the company executives to execute them. But in Japan the function of board directors and executives are not clearly separate. Most directors are insiders who hold executive posts concurrently. It is not unusual that executives without capabilities are nominated directors at the general shareholders assembly by recommen- dation of the chairman of the board as a reward for many years of loyal service to him. In actuality, this is nothing but an honorary title to make them feel better and serve more faithfully to the boss. In many cases they merely remain assistants to the boss.

American companies might have some problems similar to Japanese, but to a lesser degree, because they pay employees for a job or for performance. The differences in the Japanese and American systems make it impossible to accommodate Americans to Japanese companies. Japanese culture puts a wall between the two, and American employees are alienated by Japanese loyalty-oriented management.

The Japanese will say, "Okay, they are Americans, so they can go home at 5:00 p.m. They take four weeks vacation because they are

Americans. We Japanese must work till 9:00 p.m. and on weekends, too. We never take extended vacations. This is a cultural difference that we cannot change, so let Americans be Americans and Japanese remain Japanese." But with that attitude, nothing can be improved in the relationship.

What can be done to break down this wall between Japanese and Americans? It is clear Japanese must take the initiative through communication. If Japanese think Americans should work longer hours, they should say so openly and discuss it to seek a mutual understanding. In my experience with Western colleagues, all were hard workers, willing to work overtime whenever necessary on a voluntary basis. We had a clear understanding. They thought important what I thought important.

If a Japanese company has a cross-cultural problem with its U.S. market, why not have an American director on the board? Half of the board members of a multinational company should be foreigners from the countries in which the company has subsidiaries. In kind, the prime minister of Japan should be someone who can communicate directly with the U.S. president. Learning English is obligatory in Japanese junior high school and is continued up to the university, but time and money are wasted, since no one can really communicate with Westerners. Yet the Japanese government does not review this wasteful education, which needs to be reformed, so that Japanese can learn to really speak and communicate in English.

The structure of Japanese society is the same as that of a company, with the relationship between boss and subordinates extended to the parent company and the *keiretsu* companies (companies under the reign of the parent company), or to the government office and the businesses under its supervision. The parent company demands the same loyalty from its subsidiaries and related companies as a single company demands from its employees. The government office controls businesses with the power to issue licenses protecting the profitability of the business. Laws and orders are written; however, the government office can interpret them either strictly or generously, which makes its power stronger.

Gyosei shido, government control beyond the power of law, is notorious for keeping businesses within government control through fear rather than by law. Businesses are afraid of the government just as baseball players are afraid of the manager. All are like sheep who follow and do not speak out. The idea of this kind of government hold on private enterprise must be unimaginable to Americans. Businesses fear government retribution if they should refuse to acquiesce to *gyosei shi-*

do. In the tradition of *aun-no-kokyu*, Japanese businesses surrender to this government power by implied agreement, which is incomprehensible to Western socio-political thinking. Voluntarily, Japanese companies respectfully accept *amakudari*, high-ranking retired officials, as directors on the boards who will maintain a "good relationship" with the government office, one hand washing the other.

Even in the university, students do not revolt against their professors. As "good boys" and "teacher's pets" they will be awarded nice posts in government subsidiaries in the long run if they remain loyal to their boss and predecessors throughout their careers. For example, seeking the truth as an historian could be detrimental to a student's career if his theory is contrary to his teacher's. He would spoil his chances for more money, honor and position if he asserted himself. Under such a system, how can there by any creativity in Japan?

Japan was fortunate to have been able to take advantage of many technological innovations made during World War II and to develop and improve on them in an economic environment that gave Japanese companies support to avoid communism. But in the next twenty years, when another wave of innovation burgeons, how can the Japanese compete without creativity and a willingness by management to take risks? Without a friendly and cooperative arrangement with the U.S. and other Western countries, how can Japan expect to be granted licenses by foreign innovators to participate in the opportunities of new technology? And if the extraordinary growth of Japanese companies should come to a stop, will the Japanese understand the true meaning of "Free Trade"?

In a "Free Trade" market, the government will no longer intercede, even if a company like Hitachi, Sony or Fujitsu approaches bankruptcy and has to lay off tens of thousands of employees. The political consequence will be the unwillingness of Japanese people to elect politicians who advocate this necessary "Free Trade". They will seek the countermeasures of government intervention to protect the big Japanese companies and have them refrain from laying off their "permanently employed" loyal workers. It will be a major crisis for the Japanese economic system as it has existed since the end of the war. The Japanese are not farsighted in this matter. I have admired the American people for having the courage and principles to elect politicians who believe in the long-range benefits of "Free Trade," despite the temptation to seek a quick but unlasting remedy with a policy of foreign restrictions.

The story of the divine and benevolent emperor must seem like a fairy tale to sophisticated Westerners. Can the Japanese accept an economic system based on myth as they face the 21st century? Like children, they have been content to silently listen to a narrative and accept their history as a colorful sequence of glossy picture cards which delight the eye but taint the truth. We Japanese must seek and discover our true history. Our miserable story of slavery will teach us the importance of freedom and give us an appreciation of its worth as a value to defend at all cost. This is the only way other nations can understand and accept us, so that we may proudly contribute to the peace and development of the world.

Chapter Thirty Nine

Resolution

The origin of democracy is love for mankind, including self-love. Although it is hard to live selflessly, one is obliged to give equal importance to others' egos and to respect their equal rights. We should not do things we do not want others to do to us. This "Golden Rule" sets a moral to control individual behavior, with democracy providing checks and balances to give each individual equal opportunity.

Regrettably, we find no democratic liberalism in Japanese history, except imported Western thought during the Meiji era, which was soon stifled by ultra-nationalism. Why? No doubt the reason is the slavery that was established in the 7th and 8th centuries, when Chinese *ryo* masters conquered aboriginal *sen* slaves. Thereafter Japanese society developed vertically downwards, and kept making *sen* below *sen*, in a world where the shogun held all political, economic and military power. Thus, samurai assumed first place in the *sen* caste system. Buddhism, the religion of *ryo*, was used to control registered people, below whom were the subhuman (*hinin*), including the *Sanka*. Even though after the Meiji Restoration all these were legitimatized as new commoners, the inescapable sense of discrimination remained.

Dame Margaret Thatcher, Ex-Prime Minister of the U.K., was right when she said Britain has nothing to apologize for, in its past history. Britain had no benevolent emperor of eminent virtue, it had kings and queens with human nobility as well as weaknesses. The British made efforts toward self-improvement: in British history, one does not find invasions of other countries as the Japanese did in World War II, in which Japan killed nearly 20 million people in an unprecedented disaster to the world.

Have we Japanese shed enough tears for the victims, including American sailors in Pearl Harbor and countless innocent civilians? We demand America apologize for the victims of two atomic bombs, but have we mourned enough for the skeletons of soldiers abandoned in the mountains, fields and seas, or those who died of starvation and sickness or in suicide banzai charges? We need a "balance sheet of the spirit."

In 1987, a book titled *Shinano! The Sinking of Japan's Secret Supership* was published by St. Martin's Press, New York. It was written by Captain Joseph F. Enright, United States Navy, captain of the submarine Archer-Fish, which sank my father's ship the Shinano.

The afternoon of July 19, 1990, a colleague was driving me down to Carmel Valley, California for an appointment with Captain Joseph F. Enright. I was nervous. I did not know how I would react meeting him. I might shed tears from sheer excitement. I knocked on the door.

Captain Enright appeared momentarily. He was a stout, courteous old man. He kindly led his troubled visitor into the living room. He offered me Californian white wine, spoke about his book, and showed me his collection of photos. His warmth relaxed me. He said he had no personal feelings against my father; he had merely done his duty. He expressed sincere condolences to my mother. I was deeply moved.

The historic moment was over. As I left the house, I smelled the Pacific and the bright summer sunshine. I felt at peace. I felt my father would be glad that I had met Captain Enright.

The war had ended in my mind at last.

AFTERWORD

Reviewing the last 50 years after World War II, we find a great victory of American democracy. The U.S. completely knocked down Japan, the brutal enemy. Then with its economic and technical aid, raised her to her feet. The U.S. has also provided its military protection without proportional compensation for the role. As a result, Japan has become the world's number two economic power. Even considering a few negatives, I do not know such a generous victor in the history of the world.

Usually losers in a war are plundered and raped by the victors; this pattern is in fact recurring in various areas of the world today. The customary scenario is that territory is divided and heavy reparations imposed, with military protection by another nation provided at high cost—look how much satellite nations had to pay the Soviet Union.

I wonder what Japan would have done to the U.S. if we had won the war. We might have taken Hawaii and California on top of enormous reparations. A Hirohito shrine might have been built in front of the White House and Americans forced to worship the Emperor. Even Americans names would probably have been changed to Japanese ones. No doubt Americans would have been placed at the bottom of Japan's vertical society below the Japanese *hi-nin* (subhuman) class—the Japanese did all these things in Korea, China, and other South Asian nations.

But nothing like that happened when the U.S. occupied Japan as victor. Whereas the Soviet Union fully exercised its victor's power over Japanese soldiers and civilians in Manchuria, the U.S. provided us with food, medicine, financial and technical assistance for our quick recovery. Above all, the U.S. gave us the structure for democracy.

Voices accuse the U.S. of the atomic bombings of Hiroshima and Nagasaki; but Japanese resentment should first be directed at Hirohito and his ministers, who made the reckless decision to open fire at the

U.S. without any provocation or consideration for the disaster that would ensue. We should consider the national system that allowed such a decision, and the fanatical idea that drove Japan to war in the first place.

Furthermore, we should not overlook that an undue delay in surrender caused the atomic disasters. It was already clear that Japan was going to lose the war. The reason for delay was merely to make sure the emperor institution would be maintained. If we had had atomic bombs prior to the U.S., what would we have done with them? Would we have hesitated to use them against the U.S.?

One reality overshadowing the victory of American democracy in Japan is that all political, administrative and economic systems in Japan move on the feudalistic idea of *okami*. This makes even democratic systems work undemocratically, thanks to the poison of feudalistic values firmly established in the Japanese vertical society, over which the emperor reigns.

President Clinton visited Japan in April 1996. The figure of Emperor Akihito in ceremonies welcoming the President, widely televised throughout nation, gave us a strong image that Akihito and his imperial family remain masters of this nation, despite the provisions of our Constitution. In photos, Japan's Prime Minister, true head of Japan, elected by the people, was clearly positioned merely as a faithful subject serving the Emperor. To me he looked as though the head of slaves.

During meetings with Japan's Prime Minister, President Clinton urged Japan's military cooperation and contribution to peace and security in the Far East. The Japanese Government is again trying to make a broader interpretation of the Constitution to enable Self Defense Forces to take part in military actions in support of U.S. military operations. Leader of the opposition party, Ichiro Ozawa, claims the text of the Constitution encourages Japan's military participation in multinational self-defense operations, if authorized by the United Nations.

One can agree to such an argument only if it is made clear that Japanese soldiers will die solely for the principles of democracy and freedom when necessary—but never for a man called *Tenno* (the emperor). To assure this, Japan should become a republic. It is time to think of radically changing the entire Japanese Constitution, not merely Article 9

The Japanese Government must widely publicize to the nation that U.S. protection and nuclear arms, as well as America's sacrifice of its soldiers, are chief factors that have helped us Japanese live so well. Efforts to reduce the burden of Okinawans in rendering bases to U.S. forces must be increased significantly. On the other hand, it must be brought to the attention of the Japanese people that military cooperation with U.S. forces to secure peace and order in the Far East is our obligation and pride.

There is no doubt that the principles of democracy and freedom will have to rule Japan's diplomacy or that human rights should be respected. A similar position must be taken with China. However, Japan's compensation to China for the past invasion and wrongdoings in World War II should be continued, clearly separated from other diplomatic relations. The Japanese people must be informed how much aid has been given up to the present, and how much more remains to be paid in the future until a complete settlement of this matter is rendered. The same policy should be effected in other cases as well, such as the sexual enslavement of Korean girls and ill-treatment of British soldiers. There is no reason to refuse or delay these compensations.

In long, difficult trade negotiations between the U.S. and Japan, American attacks were focused on the *okami* system that stifles free market economy, with economists insisting that only government deregulation can save Japan's economy. Policies to protect corporations against foreign competition must be abolished and markets left to their own moves.

All indications show the *okami* system to be the cause of recent troubles. The word *okami* means emperor, shogun, feudalistic lord, governor, government official, central or local government, or sometimes employer. To the people they are all rulers. The *okami* system is very simple. In feudalistic Japan, *okami* protected vassals and clans in ex- change for their pledges to submit themselves to the *okami*. This relationship still remains alive in Japan today; for example, the Ministry of Finance has complete control of banks' profits and decisions, overriding the shareholders.

* * *

As of early 1998, Japan was in a serious crisis which might eventually cause the breakdown of the country's entire financial order. The crisis was caused by bankruptcies of a series of banks and securities firms, each with huge debts, all within one month of each other. Once Japan's credibility is gone, not only Japan but also the rest of the world could also be led to financial panic. Yet Japan's Hashimoto administration has found no solution; it has taken few measures. The market has been disappointed and the Nikkei Index average has sunk below 16,000 yen. (The last peak was 22,000 yen in June, 1996). The yen has lost credibility in international markets and has been devalued to a record low of 130 yen to the dollar over the past several years. It still remains soft. The nation feels helpless with the perception of the coming depression and unemployment.

At the end of October, 1997, Hong Kong's Hang Seng Index crashed, a shock which extended to Japan, causing the Nikkei averages to drop sharply. Financial stocks in particular were heavily sold, for the reason that they might have far more unrecoverable credits than officially announced. To the surprise of market observers, the next day, the Hokkaido Development, one of Japan's leading banks, fell on November 17, 1997, the Nikkei averages were up sharply by 1200 yen, due to rumors that the government had decided to bring in enough national funds to help the banks and other monetary institutions in crises, the precise solution the market had been demanding of the current administration. But the Prime Minister, absorbed in administrative reforms, went about his usual tasks, paying no serious attention to the incident.

The following week brought the failure of Yamaichi, one of Japan's leading securities firms. The stock market experienced volatility, but still Hashimoto did not realize the imminent danger to the financial system until he was questioned by a foreign journalist after an APEC meeting in Vancouver and asked: "When will Japan ask for IMF help?"

In the spring of 1997, a serious financial crisis began in Thailand. Stock prices and real estate dropped sharply. Many Thai banks and financial institutions went belly up, as did developers and construction firms. The Thai government asked for IMF help; the same aid was extended to the Philippines, Indonesia, and Malaysia during the summer. Then the second wave hit Singapore, Taiwan, Hong Kong and South Korea in the fall (The situation in South Korea remains critical as of this writing). The IMF decided on ten billion dollars in loans to Korea, but additional aid is necessary in order to stabilize the situation, and Japan will play the role. Only Hong Kong dollars have not been devalued so far, with the Chinese government allowing the markets to drop freely. Japanese banks have been financing these nations quite heavily, and fear newly added huge unrecoverable loans from their failures.

When I started to write this book in 1990, Japan's economic power was at its peak, and no American publisher was interested in a work that insisted Japan Inc. would fall. What the publishers wanted me to write was an insider's view about Japan's ambition to conquer the world with her superior economic power. In less than a decade what I predicted in this book has all come true. Japan Inc.'s dire dilemma has become quite clear by now. Many Japanese predict Japan's second defeat in the near future.

Japan surrendered fifty years ago, in a war in which the military played the main role. This time bureaucracy is the leader. Both are *okamis* and observe the same principles: they never admit their mistakes and their ultimate objective is to survive by any means and at any cost. At the beginning of 1945, there was absolutely no hope of winning the war. The decision to hoist the white flag was supported merely to make sure of the continuation of the imperial institution. Should the war have ended two weeks earlier, hundreds of thousands of people in Hiroshima and Nagasaki would not have had to die in the flames of atomic bombs. At the sacrifice of people, the military successfully saved Hirohito and the tradition of the imperial system. Now the military is called the "Self Defense Force." Whether it belongs to the people is yet to be seen.

Bureaucracy works on the same principles as military ones, Japan's current economic situation can be compared with the Battle of Guadalcanal in World War II. Just as the Japanese Navy was bitterly beaten by the U.S. navy in the battle of Midway, Japan Inc. incurred heavy losses and damage from the crash in the stock and real estate markets at the beginning of the 1990's. Japan Inc. did not take drastic measures to clean up the damage and losses without delay, but chose to make them bit by bit, just as Japan committed military forces to the island bit by bit in the battle of Midway.

What will happen? I am somewhat pessimistic. The bureaucracy may never admit their mistakes in policy. They may not assume any radical measures to correct the situation. They will simply pass all the bills from their failures to the people. Japan's economic power will go down gradually year by year, in spite of tremendous efforts by the people. In the end, Japan can go bankrupt. But before that happens, social unrest will cause both right and left wing movements to rise rapidly. Also, religion will become a greater influence on the people. A coup d'etat can happen. There can be serious efforts by the people to make Japan a truly democratic nation.

To achieve the revolution, democracy and freedom should be regarded as more important than the life of the individual in Japanese society. The revolution requires dedication. Unless the people are prepared to stake their lives, a revolution will be impossible. The Japanese achieved a revolution in Meiji, making the emperor the master of modern Japan, now the Japanese must make themselves masters of a democratic Japan.

In 1997, many arguments occurred over the U.S. situation in Okinawa. All of these concentrated on the dark side of the problem. No one mentioned appreciation for the dedication of young Americans maintaining peace in the Far East, or the pride of Okinawans to support American efforts. When Japan becomes a true democratic nation this will have to change.

You may not believe it, but the Japanese have never appreciated their own soldiers. The Japanese Socialist Party, which used to take an anti-American and pro-Communist stance, once insulted the Self Defense Force as tax thieves. Just a few years ago, the party admitted its mistakes in order to make an alliance with the Liberal Democratic Party and join in the cabinet. T. Murayama became Prime Minister due to a compromise made by the LDP. This shameless alliance is still going on. I will not forgive the Japanese Socialist Party and its successor for misleading the constituency; I will not forgive Murayama, who betrayed the constituency by changing the Party's policy 180 degrees to become Prime Minister. I will not forgive LDP members for continuing the alliance. Ichiro Ozawa could be a good leader. But he should sever his hands from Soka Gakkai, a religious institution. Currently 50% of the Japanese people do not vote, finding no political party to support.

I really hope the Japanese people will read my book as well as Yagiri's works—particularly the 50% of the people mentioned above. No one will help these people but they themselves. I hope Westerners will understand our people and maintain their sympathy and friendship.

I wish the best.

BIBLIOGRAPHY

The Life of Shinano	Jo Toyoda	Shueisha	1980
Shinano	Capt. Joseph F. Enright	St.Martin's Press	1987
Isoroku Yamamoto	Hiroyuki Agawa	Shinchosha	1973
A Study of Emperor Showa	Shichihei Yamamoto	Shodensha	1990
Yagiri's Reverse History	Tomeo Yagiri	Nihon Shell Shuppan	1974
A Surprising History of New Heike	Tomeo Yagiri	Bancho Shobo	1971
A Surprising History of Japan	Tomeo Yagiri	Bancho Shobo	1972
A Primer of Japan's Ancient History	Tomeo Yagiri	Nihon Shell Shuppan	1983
A Study of "Ama" Dynasty in Japan's Ancient History	Tomeo Yagiri	Nihon Shell Shuppan	1982
A Study of Discrimination against "Burakumin"	Tomeo Yagiri	Nihon Shell Shuppan	1984
Trail of Japan, Supplement to Yagiri Historic View	Tomeo Yagiri	Nihon Shell Shuppan	1983
A History of "Sanka"	Tomeo Yagiri	Nihon Shell Shuppan	1985
Story of "Sanka" Life	Tomeo Yagiri	Nihon Shell Shuppan	1985
Argument about "Hara-kiri"	Tomeo Yagiri	Nihon Shell Shuppan	1970
Blood of Japanese	Tomeo Yagiri	Nihon Shell Shuppan	1983
Comprehensive New History of Japan	Prof. S. Masuda, S. Yamaoto & M. Inoue	Buneido	1991
A Study of Japan's History	Kuzuo Kasahara	Yamakawa Shuppanasha	1990
A History of Japan	Saburo Iyenaga & Kiyotaka Kuroha	Sanseido	1992
Chronical of Japan's History	Academy of History	Iwanami Shoten	1987
Debunking Prince Shotoku	Yasuko Kobayashi	Bungei Shunju	1990
Revival of Himka	Takehiko Furuta	Shinshindo	1987

Title	Author	Publisher	Year
Doubt about Acient History	Takehiko Furuta	Shinshindo	1985
From the Ancient Mist	Takehiko Furuta	Tokuma Shoten	1985
A New History of Ancient Japan	Takehiko Furuta	Shinshindo	1991
Begining "Tenno(Emperor)-logy"	Takehiko Furuta	Ronsousha	1990
Truth of a Dynasty in North Eastern Japan	Takehiko Furuta	Shinshindo	1990
The Constitution of Japan	Masayasu Hasegawa	Iwanami Shoten	1991
The Constitution and Imperial system	Kouichi Yokota	Iwanami Shoten	1990
The Constitution of Japan	Edited by Shueisha	Shueisha	1992
The Japanese came from "Mu" Continent	Hitoshi Takeeuchi	Tokuma Shoten	1980
The Japanese came from "Mu" Continent (Again)	Hitoshi Takeeuchi	Tokuma Shoten	1980
Nomonhan	Junpei Gomikawa	Bungei Shunju	1980
Post	Weekly Magazine	Shougakukan	
The Japanese Style Management on Trial	Ken Ohtani	Soushisha	1992
The Price of a Constitution, The origin of Japan's Postwar Politics	Tetsuya Kataoka	Crane Russak Taylor & Francis, Inc.	1991
News Archaeology	Naoki Inose	KK Bungeishuju	1992
Christian's View of Life	Hidenobu Kuwata	KK Kodansha	1990
Gozen Kaigii	Gomikawa Junpei	Bungei Shunju	1981
Oxford Illustrated British Monarchy	John Cannon & Ralph Griffiths	Oxford University Press	1988
The Chronical of Price	Edited by Shukan Asahi	Asahi	1989
You Gotta have Wa	Robert Whiting	Macmillan	1989
Midway	Mitsuo Fuchida Masatake Okumiya	KK Asahi	1979
Record of Midway Battle Bushido	Hiroshi Kamei	KK Koujinsha	1985
Bushido	Inazo Nitobe	Charles E.	1991
Bushido	Inazo Nitobe	Mikasa Shobo	1993
Hagakure	Tsunetomo Yamamoto by William Scoot Wilson	Kodansha	1989
Hagakure	Tsunetomo Yamamoto	Shin Jinbutsu	1975
Modern translation	by Miyoshi Osumi	Ohraisha Shobo	1992
Banzai, You Bastards! Translated by	Jack Edwards Shinji Nagino & Megumi Kawashima	Komichi Shobo	1992

Title	Author	Publisher	Year
Current British Affairs	Kiyoharu Nagai	Yomiuri Shimbunsha	1986
Guadalcanal	Junpei Gomikawa	Bungeishunju	1980
Guadalcanal	Hiroshi Kamei	Koujinsha	1980
Paradoxical History of Japan	Motohiko Izawa	Shogakukan	1993
Japan's Modern Myths Ideology in the Late Meiji Period	Carol Gluck	Princeton University Press	1985

GLOSSARY

Amakudari. High ranking retired government officials who sit on the boards of Japanese companies and who maintain helpful relationships with the current government.

Article 9 of the Japanese Constitution. Japan becomes the first nation of the world to renounce all forms of warfare.

Banzai. The Japanese battle cry meaning, "May his Imperial Majesty reign eternally."

Bucho. A department manager of a Japanese company.

Bunkajin. Those in the academic and artistic professions, many of whom the author claims have never thanked the United States for its military protection and who are somewhat antagonistic towards the US.

Burakumin. Descendents of the Japanese aboriginal races, some of whom still suffer from discrimination in modern Japan.

Bushido. Samurai ethics. "The Way of the Warrior." In battle, a samurai losing has only two options—be killed in battle or commit suicide.

Daimyo. A feudal lord. A president of a company

Dango. The winner of a bid for government funding is pre-determined in a private meeting. Although illegal, it is a widespread business practice throughout Japan.

Diet. The Japanese Parliament.

Do. The way of living. E.g., *gado*...the way a painter should live; *shonin do*...the way a businessman should live.

Enright, Joseph F. Captain of the US submarine *Archer-Fish* which sunk Japan's largest carrier ship, the *Shinano*, on November 29, 1944, on its maiden voyage. The author's father, Toshio Abe, was captain of the ship and went down with it.

Gaijin. Foreigners in Japan.

Gaijin Ten Commandments. Issued for foreigners who play on Japan's most popular professional baseball team, the *Giants*, the management asks foreigners, among other things, to obey all orders issued by the manager, do not criticize the manager's strategy, do not scream or yell in the dugout or destroy objects in the clubhouse, do not tease your teammates harshly, and do not disturb the harmony (*wa*) of the team.

Gaistsu. Outside pressure on Japan, especially from the United States.

GHQ. General Douglas MacArthur and his staff at general headquarters.

Gyosei shido. Government control of businesses beyond the law, whereby fear is used rather than law to keep businesses in line.

Hagakure. A book written by Yamamoto in the 17th century from which the Japanese military took the phrase, "the Way of the samurai is found in death," and used it manipulatively in World War II to drive young men to their deaths. *Hagakure* means "hidden by leaves," a phrase applied to those who hide themselves under leaves in battle.

Han. A fief or province ruled by feudal lords (*daimyos*).

Hara-kiri. Ritual suicide by disembowelment.

Honne. The true motive. The true face.

IC. Integrated circuits.

International Military Tribunal for the Far East. This body revealed that the Japanese army was involved in the massacre of six million civilians during WW II, approximately the same number of Jewish people executed by the Nazis.

Japan Inc. The notion that Japanese industry is beholden to the emperor as father of the nation, where the corporate managers, political leaders and employees are part of a family. As such, employees are protected even when the company has financial problems. Only when ministers or company presidents damage the integrity of the emperor do they resign. In return for their submissiveness, people are protected and employees receive many advantages, such as paid commutation, housing allowances, meal subsidies, and executive perks.

Japanese Plutocracy. The triangular relationship in post-war Japan among politicians, government officials, and businessmen.

Japanese Style Management. Based upon a vertical society, there is little room for independent though and initiative. Although it offers many protections for employees, argues the author, it has greatly contributed to Japan's recent economic problems.

Jitsuryokusha. In Japanese management, the ultimate decision maker, who generally makes his decision before a meeting ever takes place.

Joman man. Considered to be the direct ancestor of today's Japanese population. The Joman Age was from 12,000 B.C. to 3rd or 2nd Century B.C.)

Kacho. A section chief of a company.

Kamakura. A famous resort town south of Tokyo where the author was born and raised.

Kami. Belief by Japan's aborigines in the immortality of the soul. (Also *jin* or *shin*.)

Kobuns. In management, followers of the key decision maker (*jitsuryokusha*) who are informed of a decision before a meeting starts and who steer the meeting to produce the predetermined result. The term is also used among the "Japanese Mafia."

LDP. Japan's Liberal Democratic Party.

Meiji Ideology. A system of myths developed from 1868-1912 to foster Japan's emperor institution. These myths are based upon feudalistic ideas. The Meiji Constitution of 1889 defined the Emperor as divine and inviolable and who rules the Great Empire of Japan.

MITI. The Japanese Ministry of International Trade & Industry.

Nihon Shoki. The *Chronicle of Japanese History*, which the author and others claim to be flawed, first written in 720 A.D.

OEM. Original Equipment Manufacturer.

Okami. The Emperor, or rulers such as shoguns, feudal lords, governments, or employers.

Ryo. Ruling class or nobles

Samurai. Warriors with fighting spirit, willing to fight for their lord without fear of death. Master of martial arts, especially the sword (kendo), karate, judo. A man of loyalty, honor, self-control & pride—a shogun, daimyo, and ninja. Also, a respectable man of his word, with justice, integrity, courtesy & scholarship.

Sen. Those who are ruled; the humble slaves.

Senmu. A senior managing director.

Shacho. President of a company.

Shiko-no-Mitate. In the Japanese military, a shield of men

Shinano. A secret Japanese supership which was to be the world's largest carrier, with 72,000 displacement tons. It was destroyed by an American submarine, the *Archer-Fish*. The author's father, Toshio Abe, was the ship's captain and sunk with it.

Shinyo. Suicide speedboats made of plywood and used during WW II.

"Shogun in the Dark." The name given to former Japanese prime minister Kakuei Tanaka who, having resigned because of a scandal, still exercised great political and economic control until the mid-1980s.

Shomin. Illegitimate people. Japanese of mixed racial origins, never legitimatized by their T'ang Chinese and Korean masters.

Sodanyaku. A consultant or advisor to a company board who may actually have more power than the president or chairman of the company.

T'ang Chinese. Foreign conquerors who Yagiri believes enslaved the Japanese for 1,000 years since the 7th Century, along with the Korean Paekche.

Tatemae. Principle. Belief System. The official view. The official excuse. The outward face.

Toraijin. Immigrants, including political refugees & protected immigrants with specific skills.

Treaty of Security. The treaty between the US and Japan, where American soldiers are prepared to risk their lives to defend Japan from possible attack.

Vertical Society. In Japan, a vertical chain of submission begins with the emperor and then moves downward to the president and members of the Liberal Democratic Party; the prime minister & cabinet; presidents, directors, executive officers, and managers of companies; and finally the workers.

VLSI. Very large scale integrated circuits.

Wa. Order & harmony. (Also: a geographic location and dynasty.)

Wakon Yousai. The Japanese mind with Western technological knowledge.

Ya. One of the indigenous aboriginal races of the Japanese archipelago, who were enslaved by the T'ang Chinese and Korean Paekche. They make up about 45% of Japan's current population.

Yagiri, Tomeo. The author of books on Japanese history that greatly influenced Mr Abe. Instead of the popular notion that the Japanese are a pure race, Yagiri showed how Japan evolved from many different warring races. Some of his writings are quite controversial.

Yakuza. Japanese gangsters.

"Yellow Cabs." Young Japanese women who travel to the United States for dissolute experiences and return home to marry Japanese men. Called "Yellow Cabs," because they let anybody ride.

Yottsu. One of the indigenous aboriginal races of the Japanese archipelago, who were enslaved by the T'ang Chinese and Korean Paekche. Considered sub-human by the Koreans because they ate meat.

Zoshiki. The oldest of the indigenous aboriginal races of the Japanese archipelago, who were enslaved by the T'ang Chinese and Korean Paekche.

INDEX

I

J

K

ABOUT THE AUTHOR

Toshihiko Abe was born in Kamakura, Japan in 1931. He is the only surviving son of Captain Toshio Abe, commander of Japan's secret supership, Shinano, of the Imperial Navy during World War II.

Mr. Abe joined Casio Computer Co., Ltd. in 1966 as the Manager of Foreign Trade. In 1970, he became Director of Casio, Inc. U.S.A. and Director of Casio Computer Co., Ltd., Tokyo, in 1972. He was assigned as Resident Director in London for U.K. and Europe in 1975. He held the position of Managing Director of Casio in U.K. and Europe, then later in Tokyo. In 1982, Mr. Abe became General Manager of Foreign Trade at Casio's Head Office in Tokyo. In 1986, he resigned his managerial position in Systems Products at Casio to establish the business consulting firm, Integrated Marketing Japan, Inc. As President of IMJ, Mr. Abe contracted a Consultancy Agreement with Riso Kagaku Corporation in 1986, then was hired by them and promoted to the position of Senior Managing Director. He resigned from Riso Kagaku in 1991 to resume his independence as an international project integrator and executive consultant for IMJ.